DATE DUE			
Nov1 '82			

The Princes of India In the Twilight of Empire

The Princes of India In the Twilight of Empire

Dissolution of a Patron-Client System, 1914–1939

Barbara N. Ramusack

Published for the University of Cincinnati
By the Ohio State University Press : Columbus

Library of Congress Cataloguing in Publication Data

Ramusack, Barbara N
The Princes of India in the Twilight of Empire
Bibliography: p.
Includes index.
1. India—Politics and government—20th century.
2. India—Kings and rulers. I. Title.
DS480.45.R294 320.9'54'035 78-18161
ISBN 0-8142-0272-1

For Joseph and Nelle Ramusack

Contents

Illustrations

Acknowledgments

First books seem to appear very quickly or very slowly, and this one definitely belongs in the second category. When I went to India in late 1964 to do research for a doctoral dissertation on the princes, there was little serious analysis of these displaced autocrats and their erstwhile states. During the past twelve years, many substantial studies of individual princes or states have emerged as dissertations and more recently as monographs. Even so there have been few efforts to survey the princes or the states from an all-Indian perspective. Thus I have attempted a broad synthesis by focusing on a selected group of ambitious princes who wanted to become imperial politicians in the arena of Indian politics. Their accomplishments fell short of their goals, but knowledge of their activities adds another dimension to our understanding of the breakdown of an imperial system and the diverse styles and types of Indian leadership. Although this book might not achieve that objective, it hopefully will stimulate further research and discussion of the Indian princes, their subjects, and their states.

Although a scholar bears primary responsibility for the ultimate quality of his or her scholarship, he or she survives and produces only with the generous support and encouragement of others. It has taken me an excessive amount of time to publish this book, and consequently those whose help I want to acknowledge are particularly numerous. Among institutions I first must thank Alverno College and two of my history professors there, S. Joel Read and and S. Martine Hundelt. They demonstrated not only the desirability but also the possibility for a woman to choose history as a profession. The University of Michigan with its superb Graduate Library provided my initial encounter with the published records of the Chamber of Princes and with stimulating professors and fellow graduate students. My major research in India and in England from September 1964 to June 1966 was funded by a Fulbright-Hays NDEA-related Fellowship. Upon returning to Ann Arbor, I received a Rackham Dissertation Fellowship and a subsequent summer grant and office space from the Center for South and Southeast Asian Studies that supplied the room and subsistence conducive to writing. The University of Cincinnati has assisted the completion of this book in several ways including a Summer Faculty Fellowship in 1969 for additional research in London and a Taft Faculty Grant in 1971 for a summer devoted exclusively to revision of the manuscript. A grant from the American Council of Learned Societies for another project enabled me to survey recently opened collections at the India Office Library and Records in 1973.

I would like to thank collectively the archivists and staff members at the National Archives of India, the National Library of India, the Punjab State Archives, the *Tribune* newspaper office, and the India Office Library and Records for permission to consult their collections and for their wideranging assistance. Transcripts of Crown-copyright records in the India Office Records appear by permission of the Controller of Her Majesty's Stationery Office. In New Delhi V. C. Joshi first directed my steps to key archives around India, and then Sourin Roy helped me to utilize fully the extensive resources of the National Archives; in Patiala, Harigopal Verma introduced me to the wealth of Patiala state records; and in London, Richard Bingle extended extraordinary help with, and advice on, the available European manuscripts.

I owe special appreciation that will never be adequately

acknowledged by words to my teachers and colleagues who read my manuscript at various stages and offered their penetrating and often extensive comments: John Broomfield, Richard Park, N. Gerald Barrier, Paul Wallace, Robert Crane, William Richter, and Craig Baxter. They prodded me to raise my sights from the trees to the forest and to articulate more explicitly my arguments and conclusions. At the University of Cincinnati, W. D. Aeschbacher, Zane Miller and Henry Shapiro especially encouraged and supported this study, though their own research is far removed from South Asia. Patricia Mooney-Melvin and Mary Lindemann liberally gave their time and intelligence during the last bout of typing and proofreading. Finally I want to thank my husband, Larry Goodman, for helping me to cope with the large frustrations and small triumphs that occurred during the long process of preparing this manuscript for publication. He and my parents, to whom this book is dedicated, probably thought that it would never be finished, but they still sustained me.

Introduction

At the beginning of the twentieth century, men as diverse as Romesh Chunder Dutt, the Bengali who popularized the theory that the British drained India economically, and Lord Curzon, the most paternalistic of viceroys, extolled the Indian princes as "natural" leaders who represented significant elements of the traditional Indian polity. Three quarters of a century later these rulers and their descendants seem to be on the shadowy periphery of Indian political culture and of twentieth-century historiography. They are generally characterized as losers in the battle for power between the British Empire and Indian nationalist leaders, which came to a dramatic resolution in 1947 with the creation of India and Pakistan. Still many members of former princely families continue to be active in Indian and Pakistani politics, and events since 1971 indicate that the political configuration of South Asia was not set in cement in 1947. Traditional political structures and allegiances now appear to be reemerging, or else we now perceive them more clearly despite their modern idiom. Thus it is timely to reexamine the princes who embodied certain traditional values such as the attraction to personal rule in order to understand how these rulers attempted to adapt to changing circumstances, why they chose and followed the strategies they did, and what they gained in political assets.

The princes are not an entirely unknown aspect of Indian society. The extravagant life style of some and the unusual sexual habits of others provided material for political exposé, journalistic accounts, and romantic novels.[1] Rajas of both the good and treacherous varieties are stock characters in American-made movies on India, and their palaces with marble floors, heavy hangings, and ornate furnishings are frequently depicted Indian locales in such films.[2] At the other extreme of accessibility, much scholarly research in the past concentrated on British efforts to incorporate the Indian princes and their territories into their expanding empire through a framework of subsidiary alliances.[3] A few decades ago attention turned toward the seemingly dramatic integration of these autocratically ruled units into India and Pakistan.[4] During the past few years some historians and political scientists have begun pioneering investigations into the multiple relationships between a ruler and various groups of his subjects or of political, social, and economic change within individual states.[5] Few have attempted to analyze the Indian princes as political actors on the all-Indian stage, and those who have, have generally surveyed constitutional developments.[6] In that sphere the princes might be considered losers with the Princely Derecognition Act of 1971 in India and almost simultaneous executive action in Pakistan being the final blow to their formal existence. Nevertheless, in order to survive in public life as they have, the princes must have acquired political skills and explored political roles that could be utilized and performed in independent nation-states. This study will analyze those rulers who became active in all-Indian politics during the period between 1914 and 1939. It will seek to discover what options were open to them when the balance of power was changing in an imperial system and to understand what political baggage they carried from the collapsing structure.

In the early 1800s about forty Indian princes had signed treaties with the British East India Company that promised them protection from external and internal threats in return for military support and political loyalty to the British. The foreigner had initially sought the indigenous ruler as a military ally. Throughout the nineteenth century the sources of power available to each side altered substantially, and the British were able to contain challenges that ranged from the melodramatic revolt of 1857 to proliferating memorials from Indian political associations. During this same period the British had evolved the doctrine of paramountcy, which was not defined in any treaty. Paramountcy was used to legitimatize whatever action the British, as the paramount power, deemed necessary or desirable to secure the objectives outlined in the treaties.

The relationship between the British and the princes had come to resemble one of patronage. They interacted in an asymmetric series of personal transactions that were based on reciprocity.[7] Although the British were dominant, each participant thought that he had achieved certain benefits in return for concessions that were tolerable even if not fully acceptable. As long as each party was convinced that there was a balance between their mutual interests, the relationship remained in a state of equilibrium.

The late nineteenth century was a heyday of imperial power and imperial concern for their Indian collaborators. Viceroys such as Lord Lytton consciously formulated policies such as the Press Act of 1878 partially to protect the princes from blackmail. Still the princes had become restive by 1900. They resented the growing centralization of control by the British over their persons and territories as well as the British Indian provinces through communication and transportation networks, fiscal and economic policies, and structural reorganization. Thus they rejected or attenuated many measures such as railways that would have helped modernize their states in order to resist imperial encroachment on their authority. Since the British strictly controlled the princely possession of firepower, the battleground between the two shifted to the ritual occasions when they met, and their weapons were the procedures that governed these events. The princes considered any British-initated change in them as a further diminution of their autonomy and prestige.

During these same decades the princes hardly noticed the rising demands by Indian nationalist leaders for a greater share in formulating and executing governmental policies in

British India. The agitation over the partition of Bengal in 1905, on the one hand, revealed the extent of the gradually accumulated political sophistication of these men and of their ability to mobilize various groups to support their programs. The repartition of Bengal in 1911, on the other hand, should have served as a warning to the princes as to the willingness of the British to sacrifice the interests of collaborators—in this episode, the Bengali Muslims—in response to pressure from more vigorous competitors.

As they became vaguely aware in the first two decades of the 1900s that political alignments on the South Asian subcontinent were changing, certain princes, such as Maharaja Ganga Singh of Bikaner, Maharaja Bhupinder Singh of Patiala, Maharaja Scindia Madho Rao of Gwalior, Nawab Hamidullah of Bhopal, Maharaja Ranjit Sinhji of Nawanagar, and Maharaja Jey Singh of Alwar, entered the all-India political arena to buttress their own position and hopefully that of their British overlord. As debates between the British and Indian leaders over constitutional reform came to the forefront, the princes began to seek constitutional guarantees of their authority and position. Simultaneously they also attempted to extend their contacts with British Indian politicians and to participate in imperial conferences and indigenous associations. Here they would be particularly prominent in diplomatic affairs and communal politics. That the British generally allowed, and in some instances encouraged, them in these activities was a reflection of their understanding that they needed new forms of political support from their longtime clients. Indian politicians at first accepted these overtures and even promoted some themselves, since they hoped that the princes might provide financial patronage and active members to their organizations. Both British officials and Indian politicians also wanted to enhance the legitimacy of their positions by embellishing them with the historical prestige that they thought the Indian princes possessed.

The outbreak of World War I accelerated the pace at which the balance of power between British authority and Indian leadership shifted. It also allowed the princes to reaffirm their value in their traditional capacity as military allies during an imperial crisis. More importantly it sounded the death knell to the longstanding British policy of isolating the princes from each other and from the outside world. Thus 1914 forms the starting point for this study, since it was then that both the British and the princes became publicly conscious of the need for new policies to guide their relationship and that Indian nationalist leaders began programs that impinged more directly on the future of the princes and their states.

Along with most Indian groups the princes had high expectations as to the scope of concessions that they would receive from their imperial patron in the postwar settlement. Confronted by burgeoning opposition from wide segments of Indian society, the British, however, responded halfheartedly to proposals from a client group that might express displeasure but would not openly seek the extinction of British authority. Thus the British confined their efforts largely to the establishment of a deliberative assembly, the Chamber of Princes, in 1921. Possessing limited powers and an active membership of about forty, the Chamber served to raise new points of contention between the princes and the British and among the princes themselves and to demonstrate the lack of administrative and legislative skills among the princes. The British attempted an interim solution by the appointment of an Indian States Committee in 1928, but it was equally timid in its approach to the princely predicament and caused further discontent by its ambivalent report.

In the political sphere the princes continued to demonstrate their usefulness as imperial clients in order to win bargaining points in future constitutional negotiations. Their persistent support for British policies during the 1920s and the second noncooperation movement in the 1930s coupled with their resistance to constitutional and political changes within their own states alienated increasing numbers of Indian political leaders both within and outside their states. Their allies within the all-India arena were narrowing to groups within their own religious communities and conservatives who felt threatened by any political, economic, or social change.

An opportunity for constitutional survival appeared when Sir Tej Bahadur Sapru, an Indian Liberal leader from Allahabad, called for the creation of a federation between British India and the princely states at the First Round Table Conference in 1930. The princes' initial response was affirmative because they saw federation as a means by which they might escape from the scrutiny of their British overlord as well as a mechanism by which they might achieve a more-defined status protected by legal provisions. Once again during the early 1930s many groups courted the princes for their allegiance. Their egos were inflated as moderate Indian politicians, British political officers, and conservative British politicians in England sought their support for or against federation. It was an era of mirages.

Once the possibility of federation evaporated because of princely intransigence, British ambivalence, Congress opposition, and the advent of World War II, the princes would never again be key parties in later constitutional deliberations. The activities of Muhammad Ali Jinnah and the Muslim League as well as the Congress government that controlled eight Indian provinces from 1937 to 1939 meant that the British, the Indian National Congress, and the Muslim League would be the protagonists in the devolution of imperial power. Thus 1939 marks the end of this study, since what comes after is the denouement following the protracted climax of the debate over federation.

A secondary theme that permeates this analysis in which the princes are the focal point is what happens within the hierarchy of imperial power and officialdom as it approaches its demise. Much recent scholarship has eroded the monolithic facade that the British so carefully nurtured in their days of glory. This account, which is confined to the British and one important client group, reinforces and adds detail to this newer view. In the prime relationship between the secretary of state for India and the viceroy, there were politicians who had to respond to an elected body but enjoyed distance from the immediate challenges and the men on the spot who operated within a more autocratic structure but had to contend with the brushfires of opposition. Here we see differences of opinion erupting over the Chamber of Princes but more momentously in the discussions over federation. Then there is the process by which policy decided at the center is enforced and how implementation can modify or even determine policy. This issue is explored through an analysis of the dependency of the viceroy and his political secretary on the members of the Political Department, who are their agents in princely India. Again the federation proposals reveal that opinions and actions within the British ranks can differ. On the allied question of the propriety of allowing the princes to intrude into the politics of British India, there was a similar range of variance.

A related issue is how the imperial power can prepare their clients to cope with the political situation after their departure. Here the key question is whether the British should have pushed the princes to institute constitutional, political, and social reforms within their states. That they did not is apparent, and we will seek to discover whether it was ever a realistic alternative.

When mentioning the Indian princes, most people first indicate that they numbered about 565 and controlled over two-fifths of the South Asian subcontinent and then declare that these rulers are too varied to describe as a group. This study, however, will maintain an all-India perspective but will focus primarily on those princes who ventured beyond the confines of their states to the broader orbit of all-Indian politics. They remained a persistent core of six or seven that expanded at times to include a wider circle of about fifteen individuals. They reflected the diversity of Indian culture, since Bikaner was a Rathor Rajput, Alwar a Naruka Rajput, and Nawanagar a Jadeja Rajput; Patiala was a Jat Sikh; Gwalior was a Maratha; Bhopal was an Afghan Muslim; and they came respectively from the deserts of Rajasthan, the coastal area of Kathiawar, the plains of the fertile Punjab, and the jagged ravines of central India. They were theoretically members of a common social order but often were personal rivals whose families or ethnic groups had heritages of enmity toward each other. Within their own territories they were autocrats whom few would openly question or defy. Their chief source of opposition usually arose from palace intrigues, since British power protected them from the threats of overt internal challengers such as ambitious relatives or powerful military supporters.

Now they would enter a sphere where they would need the skills, if not the goals, of middle-level politicians if they were to retain their status and authority. That the knowledge they acquired was limited in quality and quantity is evident from their failure to achieve the desired constitutional safeguards, but that it was not unimportant is apparent from their continued participation in political affairs after 1947.

The Princes of India In the Twilight of Empire

chapter one

The Princes in India in 1914

One Maharaja and His State

Tall, dashingly masculine with his full black beard, Maharaja Bhupinder Singh was the ruler of Patiala, an Indian state of 5,412 square miles of territory in the eastern half of Punjab.[1] He had succeeded to his *gadi*, or throne, in 1900 at the age of nine upon the death of his young father, Maharaja Rajindar Singh. While a Council of Regency ruled during his minority, Bhupinder was educated first by an English tutor and then from 1904 to 1908 in Lahore at Aitchison College, which was modeled after an English public school. He returned to Patiala for a brief period of administrative training and further cultivation of the manly leisure pursuits of birdshooting, poker, cricket, and wrestling. In October 1909 he took over the administration of his state, and on 3 November 1910 Lord Minto, the viceroy of India, formally invested him with full ruling powers. On this and other ceremonial occasions, Bhupinder Singh fulfilled a popular fantasy of the Asian potentate in his aigrette-decorated turban and gem-encrusted brocade court dress. Shortly after his investiture he made a grand tour to Europe, traveling on the same steamer with an older Rajput prince, Maharaja Ganga Singh of Bikaner. Patiala returned to

India in time to participate in the Imperial Coronation Durbar in Delhi in December 1911, when King-Emperor George V appointed him as a knight grand commander of the Order of the Indian Empire.

Bhupinder Singh was a Sidhu Jat Sikh who claimed descent remotely from Jesal (d. 1214), a Bhatti Rajput, and more immediately from Phul (d. 1652), a local revenue official in the cis-Sutlej area of Punjab under the Mughal Emperor Shah Jahan. Ala Singh (1691–1765), a grandson of Phul, was the actual founder of Patiala State and the first of his family to signify his allegiance to Sikhism by taking the name of Singh. Even so he was willing to accept a court dress and the title of raja in 1762 from Ahmad Shah Durrani, the Muslim Afghan invader, and as a result many have questioned the depth of his commitment to Sikhism.[2] The rulers of Patiala, nevertheless, remained Sikhs, though Bhupinder Singh shared his religious affiliation with only a minority of his subjects. According to the 1911 census Hindus constituted a slight plurality of the Patiala population, with Sikhs almost equal in numbers and Muslims as a significant minority.[3]

Bhupinder's ancestor Raja Sahib Singh had entered treaty relations with the British East India Company in 1809 in order to obtain protection from the advancing grasp of Ranjit Singh, the fabled, one-eyed Sikh who had consolidated the territories of several Sikh rivals and other Punjabi chieftains into a powerful kingdom centered at Lahore. In return for British protection from external attack and any internal uprisings, Sahib Singh agreed to recognize the British Company as his paramount overlord in foreign affairs and defense. Although the British would allow him freedom of action in all internal matters, they were to be his sole channel of communication with other Indian and non-Indian states.[4] In 1914 Bhupinder Singh maintained his relations with the successor to the company, the British crown, through Lieutenant Colonel B. E. M. Gurdon, the political agent for the Phulkian states. Gurdon, an officer of the Political Department of the Government of India, was responsible to the Punjab government at Lahore, and the Punjab government in turn answered to the Political Department of the Imperial Government at New Delhi. Ultimately the viceroy himself was responsible for the conduct of relations between the crown and the Indian princes, though he was assisted by a political secretary who served as the administrative head of the Political Department. It was an extended channel of communication.

As the paramount power pledged to support its allied princes against any internal revolt, the British Government of India was theoretically responsible for the maintenance of good government in Patiala. Although the British had established no direct, institutional checks on the authority and policies of the Patiala rulers, they did attempt to promote good administration through personal counsel. The British Government of India gave solicited and unsolicited advice on internal state affairs through its political officer responsible for the conduct of relations with Patiala state. It also offered, and sometimes forced Patiala rulers to accept, its candidates for official posts in areas of the state government that it deemed in need of reform. In 1913 Bhupinder Singh expressed his displeasure with a ministerial form of administration and proposed a reorganized arrangement in which the various governmental departments would communicate directly with him through six secretaries.[5] Punjab and Political Department officials tentatively approved the new scheme but disliked Patiala's choice of Sardar Gurnam Singh, the father of his senior maharani, to be his chief secretary. Claiming that such an appointment would lead to intensified intrigue and factionalism, the British offered to loan a competent officer from the Indian Civil Service (ICS).[6] Eventually a compromise was effected, with Gurnam Singh being designated confidential secretary but no ICS officer entering the Patiala administration.[7] The others appointed were Sardar Bhagwan Singh as foreign secretary, Khalifa Hamid Hussain as financial secretary, Lala Chaman Lal as judicial secretary, Sardar Bakhshish Singh as military secretary, and Major K. M. Mistri as the maharaja's secretary.[8] Although they had some power because of their capacity to decide what should be presented to His Highness, the secretaries functioned mainly as advisers and administrators and not as formulators of policy. All authority and responsibility was now concentrated in the person of the youthful maharaja.

There was no legislature or representative assembly in Patiala, and the laws were a conglomeration of enactments based on British Indian models and personal decrees of the maharaja issued as firmans or *hidayats*. Any British Indian law or personal decree once enacted could be arbitrarily modified or withdrawn at the discretion of the maharaja. This heterogeneous complex of laws was interpreted by a judicial system capped by a Chief Court of three puisne judges who heard all appeals from the lower courts. The judicial secretary had the right of revision of the court's collective decision, but Bhupinder Singh reserved for himself the prerogatives of confirmation of sentences of life imprisonment and of death and of the right of mercy. In this polyglot state the language of the judicial system was Punjabi in the Gurmukhi script.[9]

These laws were enforced by armed police who numbered about 1,600 and who had been reorganized by a British police officer, J. O. Warburton, during the minority of the maharaja. Although the British government carefully restricted the number of state police and the type and number of weapons they possessed, it imposed few restraints on the discretionary use of this force to distribute summary justice.[10] British intervention in Patiala internal affairs occurred only if there was strong evidence of flagrant misuse of this force or of general maladministration.

Besides his armed police, Bhupinder Singh maintained a small state army of 1,204 infantry, 452 cavalry, and 212 artillery.[11] Since he and his predecessors were forbidden by their treaty with the British from declaring war on any state, these local military forces were used as a bodyguard for the maharaja, for ceremonial duties, and as a supplementary force for the preservation of law and order. Although their discipline and efficiency were poor, these forces always remained in the background as a potent threat to the opponents of the maharaja.

To fulfill his obligations as a military ally of the British crown, His Highness maintained several contingents of Imperial Service Troops that totaled 1,212 infantry and 605 cavalry.[12]

Under the Imperial Service scheme that had been inaugurated in 1885, these units were trained, equipped, and partly officered by the British and utilized only for the defense of British imperial interests, but they were paid for by the Patiala state government. They were by far the most efficient force in the state, but could not be employed by their honorary commander, the maharaja, for services within the state.[13]

During the Hindu Vikrama Samvat year of 1970, which ended on 12 April 1914 according to the Christian calendar, the revenues of Patiala state totaled almost ninety lakhs of rupees.[14] Bhupinder Singh allotted this income at his own discretion and did not designate any definite percentage as his privy purse. Accountable to no one for his expenditures, he only spent what he personally considered necessary for administration and public services.[15]

About a quarter of the state's income came from land revenue.[16] The assessment of the land revenue was based on a land revenue settlement completed in 1908 by Major F. Popham Young, an ICS officer lent by the Punjab government to the Patiala government. Located in an area of fertile land, the value of Patiala holdings was further increased because of the availability of irrigation waters from the Sirhind Canal, the Sirsa Branch of the Western Jumna Canal, and the Bannur and Inundation Canals. During 1913–14 these canals irrigated 457,469 acres in Patiala state and contributed almost twenty lakhs of revenue.[17]

The Patiala government did provide some basic social services, but they were confined mainly to education and medical services of limited quality and quantity. In the area of medical services there were 3,722 new inpatients and 387,486 outpatients treated at forty state hospitals and dispensaries during 1913–14 (only ten state hospitals had facilities to admit inpatients). A smallpox inoculation program had been begun; but malaria and plague were common afflictions, as they were throughout most of India.[18]

Education was free in all state schools, but there were only 262 schools of all types, including one for higher education, Mohindra College, founded in 1875 in Patiala City. In 1914 attendance at these institutions totaled 14,586 pupils,[19] but according to the 1911 census there were 648,241 inhabitants of Patiala under twenty years of age. It is hardly surprising that the census also records that only 51,427 citizens of Patiala were literate in any language, with 3,818 literate in English.[20] Few students in Patiala had the preparation or inclination to seek further education in British Indian institutions, and so the development of any professional or intellectual elite in Patiala was greatly retarded. Some major consequences of this void were the need to recruit administrators from outside the state, the lack of leaders to spearhead movements for social or political reform, and the lack of any support for an independent press.

In the area of communications and transportation, Bhupinder Singh shared control over the development of these facilities with the British government. Basing their right to intervene on their obligations to defend the states, the British had run telegraph and railway lines through Patiala as it suited their imperial purposes. In order to ensure the security of these vital channels, they had by a variety of methods induced earlier Patiala rulers to relinquish sovereignty over the railway rights of way, with the result that British police had jurisdiction along these lines. The main British railway line from Delhi to Lahore passed through the eastern part of the state, and Patiala City itself was not on a major railway trunk line.

Within his state Bhupinder Singh had nearly full control over the internal network of railway, telegraph, and telephone lines and roads. During the late nineteenth century the Patiala administration had financed the construction of a railway connecting Rajpura, a town in the east on the main line between Delhi and Lahore, with Bhatinda in the western end of the state. This line also passed through Patiala City and thus joined the capital to the major trunk line in eastern Punjab. Although operated by the British Indian Northwestern Railway, the Rajpura-Bhatinda line was owned by the state and yielded an annual income of approximately nine lakhs of rupees. Besides this east-west line Patiala State was crossed by two north-south feeder lines: the Ludhiana-Dhuri-Jakhal line bisecting the state and the Rajputana Malwa line running through Bhatinda in the west. In 1914 Bhupinder Singh was planning the construction of additional feeder lines, but he first had to seek British approval.[21]

This pen portrait of Patiala raises several crucial questions about the Indian princes and their states on the eve of World War I. The British supposedly prided themselves on their administrative efficiency and lack of concern for sentiment in policy formation, so it seems incongruous, superficially at least, that they would continue to tolerate these picturesque rulers and semi-autonomous entities. Yet they retained, sometimes actively promoted, and occasionally glorified, them. British policies toward the princes, therefore, must indicate something about imperial strategies for the retention, and eventually the devolution, of power. If the princes provided little or no support, they would have been encouraged to expire long ago. Some effort will be made to assess their contributions to the maintenance of British rule in India. Then there is the proposition that Bhupinder Singh is more similar than he is dissimilar to other princes. His likenesses to, and differences from, them reveal the extent of the diversity among the princely order and one source for the varying responses among princes to changes in Indian society and British imperial goals. Finally, this portrait is in a temporal vacuum and must be placed, as must all Indian princes, into the broader perspective of Indian history. The princes were neighbors to British Indian provinces where political, social, and economic changes were occurring that were to impinge on them and on their governments and subjects. An examination of these issues will provide an introduction to an extended survey of how changing conditions within the British Indian Empire were shaping the leadership opportunities available to the Indian princes.

Reasons for the British Retention of Indian Princes

The subsidiary alliance system had been a major factor in the extension of British dominance in India during the early nineteenth century. Lacking the finance and manpower necessary to conquer and, more importantly, to administer the entire subcontinent, the empire-builders had sought to limit their direct rule to economically and politically strategic areas and to control other regions indirectly through a system of alliances with indigenous rulers. In its drive to subdue more formidable opponents, the East India Company concluded its first alliances with Indian political units such as Hyderabad, Oudh, and certain Maratha states, as well as with Patiala. These states were usually surrounded by British-controlled territory and cut off from the sea, so they were in a difficult geographical position from which to challenge British power.

The second major category of Indian states accepted as British allies were those who would have been troublesome to conquer, even if unlimited resources were available, because of their remoteness or hostile terrain. These physically secluded areas included the vast desert tracts of Rajputana; the hills of central India, riven by deep defiles; the lush highlands of Orissa, clogged by dense jungle growth; and the remote recesses of Kathiawar. Moreover, these regions usually contained little arable land capable of yielding taxable crops, so the income from land revenue would scarcely justify the expense involved in conquest or administration.

As one of the major terms of the treaties, the British Company promised to shield the contracting ruler and his descendants from any internal or external enemies. In return for this guarantee, extended during a period of political flux, the client-princes provided their patron with varied services. First, they pledged their own loyalty and that of their subjects to the Company and maintained the administration of their states under British suzerainty, all at negligible expense to the Company. Second, they gave military support when it was requested, either in the form of contingents of troops paid for out of state revenues or of annual cash tribute payments. Third, though of diverse origins they seemed to the British to possess a certain legitimacy that the latter lacked. Anxious, sometimes consciously but frequently unconsciously, to justify their position as usurpers of political power, the British tried by a variety of means to acquire a veneer of legality and a moral basis for their rule.[22] Two alternatives were to act in the name of formerly powerful Indian rulers (the Mughal emperor being the prime example) or to work through Indian agents such as the allied states.[23]

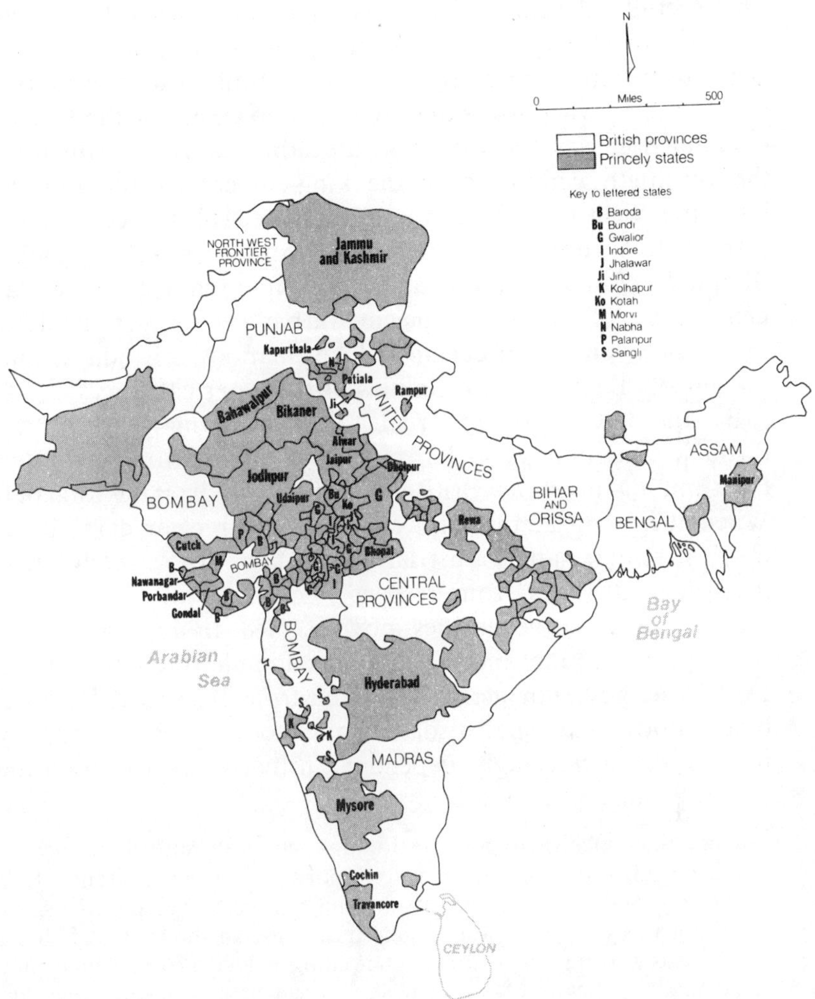

Fig. 1. Some Princely States and British Indian Provinces, 1914

This desire for legitimacy was a prime reason why the British carefully developed symbols that emphasized the paramountcy of their position over the princes while allowing the latter to retain extravagant ceremonial trappings of authority within their own possessions. A choice example of the former phenomenon was the British salute table for India, which by the twentieth century gave the king-emperor a 101-gun salute, the viceroy a 31-gun salute, some 113 princes salutes from 21 to 9 guns, and the remaining princes no salute at all.[24] Bhupinder Singh of Patiala, for example, enjoyed a permanent salute of 17 guns. Ancient durbar ceremonies, held by the princes on the occasions of coronations, birthdays, and religious holidays, were examples of the latter category.

By the late 1840s the zeal to improve man's condition through Christianity, social reform, and education permeated the thinking of many British officials in India and England. When these considerations were linked with clear demonstrations of military and industrial power, there was a modulation in British attitudes from respect to disdain for the princely states. These native entities now seemed to represent cesspools of corruption and social and economic stagnation. Lord Dalhousie, governor general of India from 1848 to 1856, combined both zeal and disdain and modified British policy toward the increasingly dependent princely clients. Ignoring earlier promises, he wrote:

> I cannot conceive it possible for anyone to dispute the policy of taking advantage of every just opportunity which presents itself for consolidating the territories which already belong to us, by taking possession of states that, may lapse in the midst of them; for thus getting rid of these intervening principalities, which may be made a means of annoyance, but which can never, I venture to think, be a source of strength, for adding to the resources of the public treasury, and for extending the uniform application of our system of government to those whose best interests, we sincerely believe, will be promoted thereby.[25]

Throughout his term of office Dalhousie energetically pursued a policy of consolidating British territorial possessions in India. He annexed the Punjab kingdom ruled from Lahore; Satara and Nagpur, two Maratha states in treaty relations with the Company; Jhansi in central India; parts of Burma; and the faithful kingdom of Oudh, an ally since 1801.[26] The fear and suspicion aroused by these annexations among other princes were part of the discontent that fired the revolt of 1857.[27]

Most princes, probably astutely realizing that the British would be the eventual victors, remained outstandingly loyal to the threatened British government during the 1857 disturbances. While Hyderabad and Mysore in the south secured the southern flank of the British, Narindar Singh of Patiala and other Punjab princes guarded British ties between Delhi and Lahore, the capital of the recently annexed Punjab. Once the revolt was successfully contained and suppressed, British officials found their awareness of the value of the states as military, administrative, and political allies dramatically revived by princely aid during the recent hostilities. They were quick to reward loyal princes with land, money, and honors and to affirm the British guarantee of their continued existence.[28] Upon the assumption of the governmental functions of the dissolved Company by the British crown, Queen Victoria solemnly assured the princes that

> all Treaties and Engagements made with them by or under the authority of the Honourable East India Company are by Us accepted and will be scrupulously observed. . . . We desire no extension of Our present Territorial Possessions. . . . We shall respect the rights, dignity, and honour of Native Princes as Our own.[29]

Her promises became known as the Magna Carta of the Indian princes.

Differences among the States

Most accounts of the Indian states emphasize their diversity, and the basis of many of the differences, even as late as 1914, can be traced to the political situation that prevailed when the British subsidiary alliance system came into existence on the initiative of Lord Wellesley in the 1790s and was consolidated by Lord Hastings in the 1810s. At that time most of the Indian states were not stable, well-defined territorial units but rather remnants of the Mughal Empire, haphazard conquests of newly formed groups within the subcontinent or strongholds of local magnates. Their rulers usually had achieved their position through their ability to dominate rival power factions and not by any firmly established pattern of succession. The subsidiary alliance system solidified many transitional political and territorial boundaries and ordained the reality of primogeniture succession within the family of the contracting prince. It also arrested the trend to the amalgamation of the weaker units into stronger ones and definitely outlined states, such as Patiala, with widely scattered territorial holdings and without natural boundaries. Thus there were ludicrous variations in physical size between Hyderabad, which had an area of 82,698 square miles, and, for instance, the minor states of Bundelkhand such as Banka Pahari, which had an area of 5 square miles.[30]

A source of later conflict between the British Government of India and the Indian states and among the states themselves was the relationship that existed between the two parties at the time that they entered treaty relations. On one side there was the nizam of Hyderabad, who had signed his treaty in 1798 ostensibly as an ally of the Company in the war against Mysore. On the opposite side there were those such as the Maratha chiefs Holkar and Bhonsle, who accepted treaties only after military defeat by the Company's forces. Then there were others such as the cis-Sutlej princes, including Patiala, and the Rajput princes, who sought treaties as protection against covetous neighbors. Finally there were hundreds of miniscule units, located mainly in Saurashtra, that had been estates of locally dominant landholders who had no formal treaty with the Company. They simply accepted British suzerainty as a *fait accompli.* Therefore, there could be no uniform treaty; and the obligations imposed, the rights allowed, and the privileges granted to each state and its ruler varied greatly. These differences in treatment by the British overlord were a festering source of discontent among the princes, who were already divided by resentments based on pre-British rivalries between their ancestors.

The Rajputs and Marathas are a prime example of long-term adversaries. The Rajputs had been the most glorified Hindu opponents of the extension of Mughal rule into Hindustan in the sixteenth century, and the Marathas, under their leader Shivaji, had been the most persistent Hindu enemies of Mughal incursion into the Deccan in the next century. During the eighteenth century the Maratha Confederacy expanded into four military units of Baroda, Gwalior, Indore, and Nagpur under the titular leadership of Shivaji's descendants, who were dominated by the Peshwas, their Chitpavan Brahmin prime ministers. Once the Mughal authority began to decline, the Marathas struck against the Rajputs, who, though fellow Hindus, were also *mansabdars*, or nobles, in the Mughal system, contemptuous of Maratha military skills and tactics, and possible contenders for the imperial mantle.[31]

Although Maratha and Rajput princes could no longer fight one another on the battlefield, they as well as other princes now attempted to best each other in the world of symbols, and here the prime arena was the salute table established by the paramount power. Originally, the British had assigned salutes to the princes on the basis of the historical importance and the friendliness of their dynasty to the Company rather than on criteria of territory controlled, subject population, or revenue collected. Sometimes the two sets of factors would coincide, as in the case of Hyderabad; but frequently they did not, and the result was an admittedly incoherent table of precedence. Although a ceremonial salute may appear to be of little consequence in the world of mid-twentieth-century politics, for the princes this symbol of authority and prestige had assumed inordinate importance by 1914. The anachronisms it maintained would constitute a major roadblock in any movement toward a rationalization of existing political relations between the princes and the British as well as a source of dissension among the princes themselves.[32] The end of the physical isolation of the princes was a major factor in intensifying the conflict among them over their salutes. A British official pointed out in 1915:

> As the Chiefs now come together much more frequently than in former times both at Court functions in England and also at various official or semi-official gatherings in India when salutes are fired, the unduly inferior position of the Punjab Chiefs as regards salutes is daily becoming more marked.[33]

The rulers confirmed in the possession of their vaguely defined territories by treaties with the British shared varying degrees of consanguinity with their subjects. Some of the princes, such as the nizam of Hyderabad, who had first come to the Deccan as a provincial governor of the Mughal Empire, had created their states by acting increasingly independently of a declining political overlord. A Muslim representative of a Muslim empire, the nizam ruled a Hindu majority area where Muslims numbered only about fifteen percent of the total population. Although his territory contained a predominance of speakers of Telugu, a Dravidian language, and a sizable minority of speakers of Marathi, an Indo-European language, the erstwhile Mughal noble used Persian and later Urdu as the languages of his court. Despite these religious and linguistic disparities, the first nizam and his immediate successors were able to weld a variety of groups and institutions into a viable political system operating under the symbolic suzerainty of the Mughal Empire.[34]

An instructive contrast to Hyderabad in origin, source of legitimacy, and ties between ruler and subjects was the princely state of Jammu and Kashmir. Although this extensive, mountainous border area had also once been a province of the Mughal Empire, it had changed hands until, by the 1840s, the Sikh kingdom at Lahore controlled Kashmir directly and Jammu indirectly through a Hindu Dogra ally named Gulab Singh. After forcibly establishing its overlordship of the Lahore kingdom by the First Sikh War in 1846, the British, for strategic reasons, bartered away control over Kashmir for seventy-five lakhs of rupees to Gulab Singh, who was also confirmed as the ruler of Jammu in his own right. By this agreement, embodied in the Treaty of Amritsar of 1846, the Hindu Rajput ruler had sought some legitimacy for his position from the dominant power in India.[35] Motivated by considerations based on power relationships, neither party was concerned that Kashmir contained a Muslim majority of over ninety percent, and Jammu had a Muslim majority of about sixty percent.[36] This disparity was exacerbated when, confronted by a lack of qualified indigenous personnel and by the desire to ensure the loyalty of subordinates, Gulab Singh and his successors utilized Hindus from outside the state in their administration. They never developed a political system that integrated local and outside groups as did the nizams in Hyderabad. As ideas of nationalism became more prominent, it was, therefore, to be expected that this anomalous political entity would be increasingly attacked as a prime example of imperialistic divide-and-rule policy.

Another group of princes who entered the subsidiary alliance system were those who had first emerged as upstart challengers of the Mughal Empire, such as the Maratha chiefs in central India and the Sikh leaders in Punjab. Generally emanating from a local stronghold into nearby Mughal territory, they extended their base by conquest, which was haphazardly confirmed by Mughal treaties or acquiescence. Their legitimacy was tenuous, and their states usually included large minorities of conquered inhabitants who viewed their rulers as little more than successful raiders. Religion and language were not always similar between ruler and subjects, though not as dissimilar as in Hyderabad or Kashmir.

Still other princes such as those in Rajputana and the tribal areas of Orissa and Assam had been rulers of their states for several centuries prior to their contact with the British. Since they usually governed sparse populations in remote areas, the Mughal imperialists as well as the British were content to exercise a nominal suzerainty over them. This group enjoyed a legitimacy that was widely acknowledged, and they generally shared the most extensive common ties of history, religion, language, and culture with their subjects.

Similarities among the Princes

As pointed out earlier, all states had acknowledged the British Company and later its successor, the British crown, as their suzerain for almost a hundred years prior to 1914. They had come to be staunch collaborators with British rule, and usually their support was in the form of military aid. At first this military aid was given in defense of the British imperial interests when they were threatened on the subcontinent, such as during the revolt of 1857 or the various frontier campaigns in the 1880s and 1890s; but gradually it was extended whenever British interests required it, whether during the Boxer Uprising in China or the holocaust of World War I.

A major provision of all treaties was that the states and their rulers could have no relations with any foreign power or with any other Indian state except through British official channels. A related stipulation provided that a prince could employ no European or American without the explicit permission of the British government. Originally designed to prevent the Indian princes from forming a menacing combination against the British, this policy of isolation remained in force throughout the nineteenth century. Many princes resented the petty regulations developed under this policy such as the restrictions on their travel outside their states, but were not overly concerned about the possible ill-effects of being cut off from the wider world and from each other.

The British conducted relations with the princes through political officers who resided near, and visited regularly, their capitals. This practice was a reversal of the indigenous one, in which a client kept an agent, or *vakil*, at the court of his suzerain. The political officers were members of the Foreign Department of the Government of India or the Bombay Political Department. In the early nineteenth century this Foreign Department handled treaty negotiations and subsequent relations with native rulers, including those on the frontiers of the subcontinent. Its members included such prominent Company servants as Mountstuart Elphinstone in Bombay, John Malcolm in central India, and James Tod in Rajputana. In 1914 this department was separated into two distinct sections: the Foreign, which governed frontier areas in the northwest and northeast and handled relations with the Persian Gulf states, and the Political, which maintained contacts with the Indian states.[37] A strong sense of continuity was preserved on the political side by various means, including assigning the writings of earlier members such as Malcolm and Tod as the texts for entrance examinations into the department.

In 1914 many states followed the Patiala pattern and had a political officer who was responsible to a nearby provincial government as their initial contact with the viceroy at the top of the hierarchy. One of two alternatives to this arrangement occurred in the large, strategically significant states of Hyderabad, Mysore, Baroda, and Kashmir, which had government residents stationed in their capitals. The other was followed in Rajputana and central India, where myriads of states were under the over-all supervision of agents to the governor general (AGGs), who maintained contact with individual states through subordinate officers. Both the residents and the AGG's could communicate directly with the political secretary of the government. Thus in all states except for those with residents, communications between client and patron passed through three levels: local agent, intermediate authority (either provincial governor or AGG), and political secretary before reaching the viceroy.

The responsibilities of a political officer were twofold. General departmental instructions stated that

> the first duty of a Political Officer is to cultivate direct, friendly, personal relations with the Ruling Princes and Chiefs with whom he works. This has been the practice of all great Political Officers from Sir John Malcolm to Sir David Barr. A Political Officer as the representative has a dual function; he is the mouthpiece of the Government and the custodian of Imperial policy; but he is also the interpreter of the sentiments and aspirations of the Durbar.[38]

As custodian of imperial policy, he recognized successions as valid, handled communications between prince and British hierarchy, and watched over the internal administration of the state. Although he was advised to follow a policy of noninterference in the last sphere, just how dominant a role he played in internal affairs depended on several factors: his own personality; the policy of the viceroy in office; whether the state was under minority rule; and the personality and attitudes of the prince concerned.[39]

Within their own boundaries most princes viewed themselves, as did Bhupinder Singh of Patiala, as the final source of all authority, and were not burdened by many internal restraints upon their arbitrary rule. Most had no legislature; their laws were a jigsaw puzzle of personal decrees, British Indian acts, and local customs; the judicial procedure was rarely defined; the independence of their judicial systems was more myth than fact; and they permitted no appeals to an authority higher than themselves. In some states the princes shared power with *jagirdars*, who controlled varying areas of land and its resources because they were relatives or military supporters of the rulers, or both. Although they enjoyed differing degrees of authority, these feudatory nobles usually collected and retained the land revenue and held limited police and magisterial powers within their estates.[40] British control was exerted, as in Patiala, informally through the advice of political officers and the influence of ICS officers lent to, or imposed upon, state administrations.

The very few maharajas, such as those in Baroda, Mysore, Travancore, and Cochin, who fostered the development of constitutional governments were widely cited as exceptions to the prevailing pattern in 1914. Attempting to rule as constitutional monarchs, those in this latter group instituted legislative assemblies and tried to upgrade their judicial systems. Even so, at this period, these constitutional checks were only as strong as the rulers desired them to be. For example, the effectiveness of the legislative assemblies was frequently undermined by large nominated majorities, by brief sessions called at long intervals, and by the fact that the ruler retained the power to determine what was to be discussed and to veto any resolutions passed.

Although the number of princes who were entitled to maintain local armies or Imperial Service units was limited to less than a hundred, all princes could maintain armed police for the preservation of law and order in their domains. The British government closely regulated the number of police, but the ruler was free to utilize them in an arbitrary manner to enforce the laws of his state. British intervention came only if there was a flagrant misuse of force on a major scale, such as firing on a large crowd or the murder of a particularly prominent official or state noble who had connections in British India.

Although there were many princes who ruled smaller states or more barren lands than did Patiala, and consequently had smaller revenues, most princes looked upon the revenues of their states as incomes to be spent at their personal discretion. A handful of them did set aside a definite percentage of state revenues as a privy purse, but even these could circumvent such a restriction by describing palace expenditures as public works and tours abroad by minor sons as educational improvements.[41]

In most states social services were at the same minimal level as prevailed in Patiala in 1914.[42] Medical service was primitive to the extreme, and education was practically nonexistent. Once again, outstanding exceptions to this generalization occurred in the more southern states of Baroda, Mysore, Travancore, and Cochin. Here the increased expenditure of state revenues on education coupled with missionary activity in education was reflected in a higher rate of literacy, a larger number of printing presses and English and vernacular newspapers, and the greater numbers of state subjects in British Indian educational institutions.

All states had to share control with the British government over the development of modern communication and transportation networks. Basing their claim to intervene on their right and obligation to defend the subcontinent, the British were particularly active in the construction of railway and telegraph lines. The railway increased the physical unity of the subcontinent and stimulated trade, but it also enabled the British to utilize more effectively their limited resources in the governance of their domains. The concurrent development of a telegraph system by the government further tied the districts to urban centers and allowed decisions made at a few points to be more quickly and more thoroughly transmitted up and down the administrative hierarchy.

When these new lines of communication cut across state territory, the princes had not only to give up possession of, but also sovereignty over, the right of way. The negotiations over compensation and sovereignty appeared to the princes as encroachments upon their rights and privileges, and they left a residue of rankling grievances among them. The rulers had to obtain British permission to develop feeder lines within their states. When consent was refused because British interests were thought likely to be affected adversely by the new lines, princely tempers were further exacerbated.

In the development of roads and postal facilities, the princes remained the primary agents, and here progress was slow. Expenditures, particularly in the more remote or mountainous areas, would be heavy to build these facilities, and revenues were limited. Some rajas, moreover, preferred their physical isolation. It had two advantages: first, it hindered the British from greater surveillance and intervention in state affairs, and second, it prevented potentially disruptive outside influences from upsetting the established social and political structure of the state. Where state territories were scattered throughout British possessions, as was the case of Patiala, or were located on the main paths of British communication, as Hyderabad and Mysore were, it was impossible to maintain this condition of geographical isolation, and these states became more integrated physically with British India.

Transportation and communications present excellent illustrations of how British policies interacted and produced a wide range of contradictory and sometimes unforeseen results. The imperial desire for efficient transportation and communication not only enabled Indian nationalist leaders to meet more easily and stimulated certain forms of Indian entrepreneurial activity but also created problems in the Indian states. It introduced new sources for complaint for both parties, since the princes resisted any formal diminution of their authority either to develop or not to develop their own railway policies and the British officials were indignant over princely opposition to British interests cloaked in the garb of progress. For those princes who opposed the web of railways, roads, telegraph lines, and postal stations, their territories became cut off from the possibility of large-scale economic development. The majority of princes who permitted their states to be crisscrossed by those connections would increasingly have to confront new groups of external challengers armed not with rifle and spear but with memorials, petitions, and threats of boycott. Thus imperial policy decisions made because of one set of considerations had created consequences for which neither the British nor the princes were prepared.

Princes, the British, and Other Indian Groups

During the 1860s and 1870s the British thought that they had evolved an administrative structure in India capable of perpetuating their rule until they chose to withdraw. This period has been aptly characterized as one when the illusion of permanence dominated British thoughts about India.[43] It was during this era that the British tightened their bonds with groups whom they viewed as the natural leaders of Indian society, such as the princes and the *talukdars*, or landlords, in the United Provinces of Agra and Oudh.[44] They dramatically reversed their earlier policies, which had aimed at the gradual extinction of such elements. Now the British sought to associate such groups more closely with the governance and benefits of the empire.

When enlarging his Legislative Council in 1861, Lord Canning, the viceroy who had characterized the princes as conservative breakwaters in a sea of revolution, appointed Maharaja Narindar Singh of Patiala and Raja Dinkar Rao, a minister from Gwalior State, to it. Upon his arrival in Calcutta the Sikh prince refused to sit on any council that included a mere official from another state. As soon as the viceroy threatened to withhold the symbolic favor of an official visit, Patiala relented and appeared at the council session.[45] Even though it was quickly resolved, this incident foreshadows some of the difficulties involved when client autocrats tried to become imperial politicians. Influenced by their concern for status and respect, the princes would not be effective in the give-and-take of political debate and in establishing close personal contacts with other Indian politicians. Such sentiments also precluded younger sons of princely families from gaining administrative experience from such schemes as the Statutory Civil Service, to which Indians from aristocratic families gained admission by nomination.

Lord Lytton, the Conservative viceroy from 1876 to 1880, who had inaugurated the Statutory Civil Service to deflect Indian demands for changes in the entry regulations for the ICS, concentrated much of his domestic policy around those classes he deemed vital to British rule; and here the princes were a key element.[46] He astutely recognized their attachment to symbols of power when he argued that the proclamation of Victoria as Kaiser-i-Hind would help to rally them around her as their feudal head. Consequently, the princes and chiefs of India were accorded a particularly prominent place in the lavish pageantry of the Delhi Durbar of January 1877 when the venerable queen was proclaimed empress of India.[47] Lytton simultaneously had also attempted to launch a major reexamination of British policy toward the Indian states. Favoring a carrot-and-stick approach, he had hoped to extract revision of the treaties to provide the basis for a uniform policy and greater military and monetary contributions in return for some concession toward more internal autonomy and membership in a privy council.[48] Facing opposition from members of his Executive Council on the question of a reconsideration and from the India Office on the formation of a privy council, Lytton retreated and made the futile gesture of appointing certain princes as imperial councilors.[49]

The problem of defining the most effective role for clients such as the princes would become more acute as developments occurring within Indian society increasingly affected British control over the resources of their Indian Empire. British rule was possible only with the active collaboration of some Indians like the princes, with the acquiescence of most like the peasants, and with the active hostility of few. By the 1880s various associational groups with diverse goals ranging from political boons to economic concessions, to social reform, to the provision of educational facilities for their members, were shifting along the spectrum from collaboration to hostility. Their initial assaults were usually limited to certain segments of Indian society and to particular geographical areas. Still they were sources of concern, especially when these opponents sought links with active supporters of British rule such as the princes.

Many political leaders in British India saw the princes as exemplars of the ability of Indians to rule themselves and as sources of legitimization as well as future allies. Two Bengalis, who both were employed by Baroda State, illustrate the range of views held. Romesh Chunder Dutt, a former member of the ICS, when referring to Mysore and Baroda proclaimed that "no part of India is better governed today than these States, ruled by their own Princes."[50] Arguing for self-government but not necessarily democracy, he thought that the princes as well as local *zamindars* and spokesmen for native associations such as the Poona Sarvajanik Sabha and the Indian National Congress should help represent and govern India.[51] Aurobindo Ghose, who had lived in England for thirteen years while being educated, returned to India in 1892 to accept a teaching position in Baroda, which he used as a base for immersing himself in Indian culture and for expanding his network of political contacts. While there, he evolved political theories that were much more radical than those propagated by Dutt, since Ghose advocated defensive resistance and even violent insurrection as means to achieve self-government.[52]

Besides epitomizing divergent political philosophies for followers in British India, these two men and their presence in Baroda point out that the princely states were not so insular as their stereotypes portray them to be, even though Baroda did have a reputation for being progressive. Administrators from British India were found in many states ranging from the graduates of the Muhammadan Anglo-Oriental College at Aligarh in Hyderabad to the graduates of the colleges of Lahore in Patiala.[53] The isolation of the states was also not so great as to prevent the movement of men like Mohandas Karamchand Gandhi from Porbandar in western India and Muhammad Ali from Rampur into the vortex of British Indian politics.

British Indian political figures had not only courted employment and prestige from Indian princes but also financial patronage. Early on, associational groups had to face the critical problem of how to obtain funds to pay full-time organizers and publicists and to acquire the resources, such as newspapers, necessary to mobilize new groups into the political arena. Mahadev Govind Ranade, a judge and venerable Indian nationalist from Maharashtra, received financial support from princes for the Poona Sarvajanik Sabha, an association with goals ranging from social reform, to the epousal of the views of nonvocal elements of Maratha society, to agitation against proposed revisions of land revenue assessments. The princes also provided him with a useful link between his modern-style political organization and traditional authority.[54] On the national level both the Indian National Congress and the Indian Patriotic Association of Sir Sayyid Ahmad Khan, the modernist Muslim leader who founded the MAO College at Aligarh, appealed to princes for assistance.[55] When some, such as Maharaja Chamrajendra Wadiyar of Mysore and Nizam Mir Mahbub Ali Khan of Hyderabad, did respond to initial appeals with monetary aid, the British became concerned.[56] Eventually the viceroy and the resident expressed their disapproval and thereby discouraged further financial contributions.[57] Even so, contacts were established in some cases that would ensure favorable consideration in less overt ways by the princes of solicitations from British Indian leaders.

With the advent of Lord Curzon as viceroy in 1899, there was a peak of disdain for the potential threat from groups such as the Congress and a renewed scrutiny of relationships with the princes. The proconsul proclaimed that

> the Native Chief has become, by our policy, an integral factor in the imperial organization of India. He is concerned not less than the Viceroy or the Lieutenant Governor in the administration of the country. I claim him as a colleague and partner. He cannot remain *vis-à-vis* of the Empire, a loyal subject of her Majesty the Queen-Empress, and *vis-à-vis* of his own people, a frivolous or irresponsible despot. . . . His real work, his princely duty, lies among his own people. By this standard shall I, at any rate, judge him. By this test will he, in the long run, as a political institution, perish or survive.[58]

Inspired by this vision, Curzon pursued an activist policy of interference and regulation in order to increase administrative efficiency in the states and the exploitation of the princes as symbols of legitimacy. As in the case of Lytton, he was more successful in securing the participation of the princes in sumptuous spectacles such as the Coronation Durbar of 1903 rather than in any governmental bodies.

Although Curzon's viceroyalty probably represents the apogee of British imperial power in India, the agitation mounted against his decision to partition Bengal was a significant sign of its potential vulnerability. As the events of 1857 had changed attitudes toward the princes, so, on a lesser scale, the partition agitation led to reconsiderations. Once again, a policy of active interference in princely affairs was supervened by one of non-interference in order to refurbish ties with known allies. In a famous speech at Udaipur, the premier and perhaps most conservative state in Rajputana, Lord Minto, Curzon's successor as viceroy, reaffirmed Victoria's promises and declared that

> the foundation-stone of the whole system is the recognition of identity of interests between the Imperial Government and the

> Durbars and the minimum of interference with the latter in their own affairs. I have always been opposed to anything like pressure on Durbars with a view to introducing British methods of administration. I have preferred that reforms should emanate from Durbars themselves and grow up in harmony with the traditions of the State. It is easy to overestimate the value of administrative efficiency.[59]

His words quickly became a favorite text of Indian princes as well as a *bête noire* to subsequent generations of political officers and viceroys.[60] Minto also attempted to implement the idea of an advisory or privy council of princes that could possibly serve as a counterpoise to Congress appeals.[61] Receiving strong support from the prince of Wales, this proposal was debated between London and Calcutta for over two years. Opposed by some princes for reasons of prestige and by the India Office on questions of effectiveness, Minto, in late 1908, agreed to drop further promotion of this project.[62]

Although half a century had elapsed since Victoria had outlined the general orientation of British policy toward the princes, the imperial government had yet to devise an effective mechanism for bringing these clients into their constitutional structure. All their efforts had been stillborn because of a lack of agreement among the various levels of the official hierarchy, both in India and in England, on the best means of implementing broad policy pronouncements. The British, moreover, had never been able to formulate a positive, well-defined statement of the rights and responsibilities of both themselves and the princes. Even though such a document might have been highly desirable, it probably was an impossible goal. Still in any relationship, such as this one, based on the delicate balance of mutual interests, tension heightened as each side came to feel that it was not receiving an adequate share of the benefits. This stress would swell as both the British and the Indian rulers would come under new pressures from within Indian society.

During the crucial period from 1914 to 1939 the patron-client relationship between the British Government of India and the Indian princes proved to be inadequate for the needs of its participants. Both sides tried to adapt, and we will examine some specific issues in order to understand and evaluate their efforts. The princes expanded the type and extent of their supportive activities as the British faced the challenges of World War I and the first non-cooperation movement. The imperial overlord then attempted to find suitable rewards for princely assistance that would not cost them too dearly. Here they were bound to be relatively unsuccessful.

As constitutional reform began to yield some devolution of power, the princes desired a more protected position within the constitutional structure as well as some long-coveted concessions. Once again the British disappointed the princes. The princes gradually found themselves in a quandary as they tried to protest against British policies and actions that they deemed infringements upon their authority while they were more strongly identified as supporters of British policies on an all-India scale. Frustrated by growing British indifference and accumulating hostility from Indian nationalist leaders and their own subjects, some princes would renew their efforts to form alliances and to explore new roles that hopefully would enable them to contain opposition to their continuance and ultimately to survive the extinction of their states.

chapter two

Broadening of Political Horizons: The Impact of World War I

In early December of 1916, in order to reward and to stimulate anew Indian contributions to the flagging war effort, Lord Chelmsford announced that two representatives from India, one Englishman and one Indian, would be sent to the Imperial War Conference to be held in London in March 1917.[1] It was not immediately divulged that there was the possibility of a third delegate coming from India. Austin Chamberlain, the secretary of state for India, had telegraphed privately to Delhi to solicit opinions on the feasibility of inviting an Indian prince to the conference and on the suitability of Maharaja Ganga Singh of Bikaner, a highly visible Rajput prince, for the position.[2] Chamberlain's proposal was politically apt, for a few weeks later the Jam Saheb Ranjit Sinhji of Nawanagar independently broached the same suggestion and candidate in a letter to the viceroy.[3] On the very next day, which was 31 December, Maharaja Bhupinder Singh of Patiala, further articulating the princely desire for representation at the conference, declared:

> I am not aware as to what will form the necessary qualifications for selection for such an important deputation but considering

> that questions of supreme importance connected with and affecting the entire British Dominion will be discussed at this Conference, it would be to my mind advisable if the Indian States which comprise practically 1/3rd of the country and which have in this Crisis given practical proof of their loyalty to and unity with the Imperial interests should also be represented.[4]

Apparently hoping to be chosen for this honor himself, he did not nominate anyone, as Nawanagar had done. In British official circles Patiala's aspirations were promoted by Leslie Crump, the political agent in charge of the Phulkian states, who cited the following reasons in support of Patiala's candidacy:

> The Punjab has done more than any other province and he is the leading Punjab Chief.
>
> The Sikh community have taken a larger share in the war than any other Indian Community and he is the leading Sikh Chief.
>
> The State may fairly claim to have given more direct military aid to Government than any other State.[5]

It is noteworthy that Crump considered that the selection of Bhupinder Singh would be compensation for the Punjab province and the Sikh community as well as for the maharaja and his state for their miscellaneous contributions in support of British interests.

Bikaner was the choice of the Government of India as well as of the India Office for this new honor. In a reply to Crump, John Maffey, private secretary to Chelmsford, emphasized that "the present occasion demanded the selection of a man who, though chosen from the Chiefs, should represent India. You will understand the importance of this, and I think you will agree that the right man has been chosen."[6] The maharaja of Patiala was overtly enthusiastic and covertly annoyed at the selection of Bikaner, but some voices in British India openly questioned the qualifications of the Rajput prince to fulfill his mandate to represent all of India. In its editorial comments of 23 January 1917 the *Tribune* asked:

> But as regards the Maharaja of Bikaner, who is one of us, though a prince, the question arises, whom does he represent? We are of the opinion that no Indian prince, however advanced his views, is competent to voice the opinion of British India, edu-

> cated or uneducated; and the Congress and Muslim League will alike promptly repudiate the title and capacity of any of that class to represent and safeguard our interest.[7]

Although the *Tribune* was probably the most influential of the nationalist newspapers in Punjab, the *Khalsa Advocate*, an English-language weekly devoted to Sikh interests, declared that the *Tribune* was not representative of Punjab sentiment and gave high praise to Bikaner's qualifications.[8] On the whole, moreover, the appointment of Bikaner was warmly received by the princes and almost all the moderate Indian politicians.

Princes had previously gone to London to attend imperial functions, but these had been ceremonial occasions such as Victoria's Diamond Jubilee Celebration or Edward VII's coronation. The appointment of the cosmopolitan, articulate Ganga Singh as a representative to the Imperial War Conference marked the first time that an Indian prince sat with other imperial leaders at a policy-making meeting. This appointment reveals both a new kind of involvement in imperial politics by the princes and some of the problems created by this new activity. The British policy of attempting to isolate the Indian princes physically and politically, a constant principle throughout the nineteenth century, had outlived its usefulness by the beginning of the twentieth century. By emphasizing the irrelevance of this policy to current political conditions, World War I delivered a death blow to this anachronism as it had done to other policies and institutions appropriate only in a vanished era of world politics. Princely support of the British war effort demanded suitable recognition and compensation by the imperial recipient. The fact that an invitation to such an august gathering had been suggested by a Conservative secretary of state was one sign of a major shift in British policy toward this group of Indian allies.

Although both London and Delhi agreed that the princes should be given an expanded role in imperial political affairs, any implementation of this policy objective was likely to create new difficulties. In the episode of the first princely appointment to the war conference, the question of whom to select discloses many significant points. Among all the Indian princes, Nizam Mir Osman Ali Khan of Hyderabad, the premier prince of India and a staunch supporter of the war effort, would have seemed to be the most prominent candidate. The British acknowledged his claim but rejected it because of his reputed lack of political sophistication.[9] They chose instead Ganga Singh of Bikaner, an equally faithful ally, because of his political poise, his well-known oratorical skills, and his artful combination of Indian and British social manners, which more completely fulfilled the official stereotype of an Indian prince. Many princes were most enthusiastic about the explicit recognition of their prominence within the British Empire offered by attendance at the war conference. As seen above, Nawanagar and Patiala had actively supported such a proposal even before it had been made public. After Bikaner's appointment was announced in early 1917, several princes expressed their gratitude in a joint statement drawn up by Bhupinder Singh of Patiala. From the beginning, however, this imperial boon would create antagonism, for many of the princes regarded themselves as the most qualified candidate for any future appointment. They prized any symbols that reinforced their self-image of superiority, such as honors from the British king-emperor. Any new British favor, consequently, provoked an eruption of personal rivalries and jealousies among the princes. They furthermore were not prepared for participation in activities in which they would have to recognize any Indians, whether princes or commoners, as equals. Their paternalistic and autocratic methods within their states did not encourage the formation of political relationships on the basis of equality.

When Bikaner declined an invitation to the Second War Conference in 1918, Chelmsford turned to Maharaja Scindia Madho Rao of Gwalior. Ruler of the largest Maratha state, and one of four princes entitled to a twenty-one-gun salute, Scindia was known more for his interest in mechanical devices, especially trains, than for his intellectual sophistication.[10] His banquet table was adorned by a sterling silver toy train that dispensed after-dinner mints, nuts, and cigarettes. Lacking the polished rhetoric of Bikaner in any standard language, he was lauded for his dedication to administrative tasks and for his ostentatious and practical displays of loyalty to the British *raj*, going so far as to name his two children George and Mary.[11] Chelmsford's successor, Lord Reading, aptly described why the British favored Gwalior:

> Indians understand the staging and the performance of ceremonies, and the Maharaja of Gwalior, who is in himself an unceremonious person, is most punctilious about these occasions. . . . I have a great liking for him; he is a great Prince, rules over nearly four million people, the most powerful among the Mahratta Princes. . . . Perhaps because his importance is so well established, he never—thus differing from some Princes, particularly Alwar—is on the look-out for either some fancied slight to his status and dignity or for some opportunity of pressing for some further outward recognition of himself as a Ruler. Again, unlike some of the Princes, he is never trying to speak of His Majesty as his ally, but says quite plainly, in the presence of his ministers and feudal chiefs, that the King is his Master, and the Viceroy, as the King's representative is therefore his Master in India.[12]

After Gwalior declined for family reasons, the viceroy once again resisted Bikaner's nomination of Nawanagar and decided on Bhupinder Singh of Patiala, who eagerly accepted the coveted appointment.[13] Although this choice was warmly applauded as a deserved reward for the Sikh contributions to the war effort,[14] it annoyed both Edwin Montagu, the successor to Chamberlain at the India Office, and Ganga Singh of Bikaner. Angry because Delhi had rejected his advice, which was unfavorable to Patiala, the outspoken secretary of state for India threatened to take away from the Government of India the power to nominate representatives to future conferences and to retain it solely at the India Office.[15] Ganga Singh shared Montagu's sense of being the possessor of superior wisdom and of disgust that his advice had also been ignored by Delhi. Resentful of the growing prominence of his ambitious junior peer, Bikaner showed his dislike of the appointment by not attending the public banquet given to Patiala by his fellow rulers prior to his departure for London in May 1918. Fully cognizant of the subtleties of princely protocol, the Sikh prince was appropriately angered by this rebuff.[16] In the end, however, his Rajput competitor would have the greater honor since he would be selected as the princely delegate to the Peace Conference at Versailles, which would try to rearrange the world "to make it safe for democracy."

The preference for Bikaner and aversion to Patiala is indicative of priorities at the India Office in their employment of the princes. Their twin objectives were to parade a convincing example of Indianization before English and imperial political leaders and to stimulate the war effort. Although they shared these goals with the British hierarchy in Delhi, the London officials placed more emphasis on the first one. The secretary of state sharply criticized Chelmsford's choice of Patiala because of his disdain for that prince's intellectual abilities and political skills.[17] Montagu was more concerned about having an attractive personality in London than the impact in India of this political tactic. The viceroy later defended his selection by reasoning that no prince was the equal of the giants attending such a conference and by citing the educative value of such an experience for the young maharaja. Attendance at, if not active participation in, policy discussions might stimulate him to take a more serious interest in improving the internal administration of his state as well as in imperial affairs.[18] Upon his return from abroad in October 1918, Patiala did, in fact, introduce an elective system in the makeup of municipal and district boards, but it is doubtful that his conference experience had the long-range constructive influence hoped for by Chelmsford.[19]

The appointment of a ruling prince to an imperial function with emphasis on his position as a representative of all-India was a red flag, however, to certain emerging groups of politically conscious Indians in British India. There were Indian politicians still willing to concede the right and ability of a prince to represent Indian India, meaning that part of the Indian subcontinent ruled by princes; but frustrated by the lack of outlets to utilize their talents and training, they were not prepared to allow the British official to be replaced by the Indian prince as the representative of all-India. For this role they considered themselves to be the only qualified candidates. The opposition from British Indian aspirants to political power would be a limiting factor on princely experimentation with roles in British Indian and imperial politics.

The remainder of this chapter will focus on the efforts of the princes to expand their activities beyond their borders during World War I. The stage for greater princely involvement in affairs outside their states had been prepared when the long-standing policy of isolation had been breached from several directions in the decades prior to 1914. The Great War, consequently, did not mark a decisive break with the past but rather speeded up and initiated further changes in imperial attitudes and policies and in Indian society that provided new opportunities for the princes to demonstrate their value as allies to both British and Indian leaders. After tracing the gradual decline in whatever isolation did surround the princes, the following sections will examine the princely responses to incursions from British India, the new and enhanced forms of their assistance to the British, the areas of British Indian politics in which the princes seemed to be interested, and the characteristics of those princes who were most active.

Encroachments on the Political Isolation of the Princes

The strategy of isolating the princes that Lord Wellesley had instituted at the beginning of the nineteenth century to prevent alliances among menacing Indian princes or between princes and foreign powers such as Napoleonic France had long lost its relevance to prevailing political conditions. The Revolt of 1857 had demonstrated that the princes were incapable of forming among themselves or with other powers a military alliance able to evict the British from India. Development of a political infrastructure in British India of associational groups, networks of experienced politicians, and modern means of communications had produced conditions and individuals who would provide the prime challenges to the existence of the British Indian Empire in the twentieth century. As they grew in scope and strength, certain political movements in British India also began to spill over from British Indian provinces into adjacent Indian states. Two early instances of this phenomenon, which in later decades was to recur with unexpected rapidity throughout the subcontinent, may be cited from north India.

By May 1907 Maharaja Pratap Singh of Kashmir and his

subjects had become aroused by political occurrences in the neighboring British Indian province of Punjab. Governmental measures to change the terms of contracts in the canal colonies and to prosecute coincidentally a popular nationalist newspaper, the *Punjabee*, had sparked unrest and rioting.[20] In an area such as Punjab, where religious communities existed in an uneasy balance, antigovernment agitation intensified communal tensions, since major participants included organizations such as the Arya Samaj, a dogmatic Hindu revival group that sought the purification of Hinduism by returning to the Vedas, a Muslim League organized by Fazl-i-Husain to protect Muslim political rights, and the Hindu Mahasabha, formed to safeguard Hindu political rights.

The British resident in Kashmir, Francis Younghusband, reported that the Muslim majority was fearful of increased Hindu dominance in Kashmir through the aid of their coreligionists from Punjab, and the Hindu minority indulged in wild speculation about new increments of glory and power.[21] Apprehensive over any possible threat to his position, the Dogra Rajput ruler issued a notification condemning these "disloyal agitations" in the Punjab and warning his subjects how he would treat all who succumbed to this "poisonous contagion."

> . . . Persons found to have any dealings, directly or indirectly, with any disloyal or seditious movements, or to have even taken interest in, or expressed sympathy with persons connected or associated with such movements will be subject to the severest punishment that the Durbar can, under the Political law, inflict.
>
> Persons making any speech, either in public or private, or even holding private meetings to cause any kind of disaffection or public demonstration of individual feelings of discontent, will be equally severely dealt with.[22]

The local British representative supported this sweeping prohibition, but the foreign secretary at the imperial capital thought that the action, though somewhat excessive, was helpful, since the maharaja was a pillar of orthodox Hinduism.[23]

A more dramatic incident involving some of the same participants was the Patiala Sedition Case of 1909–10. In mid-

1909 Maharaja Bhupinder Singh of Patiala, then a minor, became apprehensive that Arya Samaj members in his state were indulging in disloyal activities directed against both his government and that of British India. On his behalf, John Thompson, the officiating chief secretary of the Punjab government, warned the Council of Regency then administering Patiala state to take prompt measures to deal with this menace.[24] When the maharaja assumed full administrative powers, on 1 October 1909, he soon issued orders to his Police Department to arrest eighty-four persons who had some connection with the Arya Samaj. In December 1909 seventy-six of these accused were brought to trial on charges of sedition. In his opening speech at the special trial, Arthur Grey, the chief prosecution counsel for Patiala, emphasized that the accused were particularly dangerous because they represented a group effort to spread disaffection rather than an individual expression of discontent. Although he did not condemn the Arya Samaj outright, Grey argued that membership in the Samaj must be questioned if the charges against the accused Arya Samajists were proved true.[25]

On 19 January 1910 the accused Arya Samajists presented a full apology, a statement of loyalty, and a petition for their release to the maharaja of Patiala, but no immediate action was taken.[26] At the end of January Sir Louis Dane, then the lieutenant governor of Punjab, saw Patiala, at the latter's request, to discuss this case, and Dane's advice was to prosecute further only a few men against whom there was substantial evidence.[27] Soon after this interview Patiala reexamined the papers relating to the case and dropped all charges against the accused, but banished them from the state. By spreading the net too wide, the young prince had failed to convict anyone and only inspired the Arya Samajists to greater zeal in the face of persecution. His ineptness had aroused the ire of British officials in the Punjab Government and the Government of India, since the British thought that there was adequate evidence of "simmering sedition" and wished that it had been more adroitly handled.[28]

About the same time that Patiala had first expressed concern about the Arya Samajists, Lord Minto had written to his representatives in the Indian states and voiced the need for mutual cooperation against the common danger of sedition. To prevent the eruption of this dread political disease within the states, the viceroy requested that the princes be polled on what preventive measures they were taking and on what kinds of assistance the Government of India might render.[29] The princely replies emphasized the strengthening of police and intelligence activities, the prevention of the circulation of literature considered seditious, and severe punishment of seditionists as a warning as the safeguards undertaken internally. They desired external cooperation in matters such as the exchange of intelligence information, censorship, and stronger restrictions on the religious aspects of seditious agitations.[30]

In the episodes involving Patiala and Kashmir and in the responses to Minto's survey, patterns began to appear that would be repeated in future encounters between the princes and British Indian groups. Unaccustomed to opposition from beyond palace or British circles, the princes tended to overreact and to employ an elephant gun to kill the fleas of popular opposition. Local British officials were usually more sympathetic to such methods, but those at the capital who had broader policy objectives to consider questioned them. The one aspect that both levels were willing to exploit was the position held by various princes within their religious communities. On their side the princes seemed aware of the potency of religious appeals and anxious to seek stronger controls over them. The political isolation of the princes was slowly being eroded.

Princely Response to World War I

Upon the outbreak of hostilities many princes quickly volunteered their personal services and those of their troops and the resources of their states. The precedent for princes and Imperial Service troops serving abroad had already been set in 1900 when the maharaja of Bikaner, the maharaja scindia of Gwalior, and the maharaja of Idar, Sir Pertab Singh, accompanied Imperial Service units to China.[31] During World War I Bikaner and Pertab Singh again left India and served at the front for several months. But this time many other princes, such as the jam saheb of Nawanagar, the raja of Akalkot, the nawab of Sachin, and the nawab of Loharu, also proceeded to active duty on the various western fronts and in the Near East.[32] Of even greater consequence for the war effort and for future political developments in British and princely India were the extended tours of duty made by several units of Imperial Service troops. One among many notable examples was the two infantry regiments and one cavalry regiment supplied by Patiala State that left India in late 1914 and did not return until 1919. Generous service, moreover, was rendered not just from the important traditional supporters of British rule such as Hyderabad, Mysore, Kashmir, Bikaner, and Patiala, but was also volunteered from remote areas such as Manipur in northeastern India. The isolated, orthodox Hindu ruler of Manipur, Raja Chura Chand Singh, overcoming his religious scruples of crossing the seas, spontaneously offered to lead a contingent of his subjects wherever needed.[33]

Furthermore, the princes' support was not limited to grants of troops and personal services. Many of them made substantial money donations for various war expenses and relief funds. Most spectacular was the largesse of the nizam of Hyderabad, who donated over thirty-five lakhs of rupees to the war effort.[34] Another popular form of war aid, probably because of its novelty, was the donation of an airplane. Among others, the Rajputana princes contributed to a collective fund that was utilized to purchase airplanes for the war effort.[35] An instructive sidelight to this incident is that Maharaja Madho Singh of Jaipur refused to join this effort because it had been started by Maharao Umed Singh of Kotah and Maharaja Madan Singh of Kishengarh, who were of inferior status to him in the hierarchy of Rajput clans.[36] Jaipur was extremely generous in his donations, but he had to give in his own way.

Princes further rendered valuable support when they permitted British officers to recruit troops for the British Indian army from their states. In many instances the princes themselves frequently addressed recruiting durbars. Because of a strong British preference for military personnel from Punjab, Bhupinder Singh became one of the most active recruiters.

Although he usually appealed to his subjects on the basis of duty,[37] he once admonished them that it was far better to die a manly death on the battlefield than to stay at home and meet the Angel of Death through the unmanly diseases of cholera and plague.[38]

What was unique about the princes' assistance rendered to the British Empire during World War I was its extended scope and unusual intensity. Prior to World War I troops from princely states had fought in support of British interests, but most of these campaigns, such as the Mutiny, the Tirah, and the Chinese action, had only lasted for a year or so. As British home reserves of essential war material and manpower dwindled, greater reliance had to be placed on contributions from member countries of the empire. Consequently, the princes were called upon to maintain their support over an extended period of four years, and their subjects served abroad for long periods either in Imperial Service units or in units of the British Indian army. These troops could not remain unaffected by their new experiences obtained in strange surroundings under great tension. Moreover, this war effort also affected the princes, who came in contact with different types of people and new ideas during their tours of duty on the battlefields or in their activities on the home front.

Increased Imperial Status of the Princes

As we have observed, attendance at the Imperial War Conferences was one new arena of activity opened to the princes by their war efforts. In June 1917 William Meyer, the president of the Central Recruiting Board in India, suggested that the princes be brought into this scheme and proposed the appointment of the maharaja of Bikaner to the board.[39] This arrangement, he hoped, would facilitate a request to the princes to supply a definite quota of recruits, as was being asked of the British Indian provinces. In a subsequent note John Wood, the political secretary of the Government of India, agreed with this general suggestion but added that Bikaner should not be the sole princely member of the board, since such a situation would increase jealousy and raise political complications among the princes. Remembering, perhaps, earlier disputes, Wood recommended that some other princes should be appointed and proposed the names of the maharaja scindia of Gwalior and the maharaja of Patiala because of their war contributions and their experience in troop matters.[40] His suggestion was accepted, and Gwalior was appointed as a full member along with Bikaner, and Patiala was later co-opted as a member by the board itself.

At the end of World War I, the Central Recruiting Board was reconstituted into an Indian Soldiers Board. This new body was to advise on questions affecting the interests of the serving, discharged, and deceased Indian soldiers and noncombatants and their dependents. It was decided to have a prince on this board, and in March 1919 Sir George Lowndes, the president of the Indian Soldiers Board, asked Sir Michael O'Dwyer, the lieutenant governor of Punjab, for his views on the qualifications of Patiala. The latter gave the Sikh prince a strong recommendation, stressing that he had to deal with many of the same problems that confronted the Board. Subsequently Patiala was offered the appointment, and he accepted.[41]

Shortly after the Germans had launched their spring offensive of 1918, Chelmsford decided to convene a conference to secure the cooperation of all Indians

> firstly, in sinking domestic dissensions and bringing about cessation of political propaganda during the great crisis; secondly, in securing active support of all classes in measures necessary for prosecution of war with special reference to man-power and development of India's resources; and, thirdly, in cheerfully bearing the sacrifices which may be necessary to achieve victory.[42]

The viceroy invited princes as well as British Indian politicians to attend.[43] Although princes had been mustered to Delhi to glorify all-India gatherings, such as the Imperial durbars in 1877 and 1911, the Delhi War Conference was the first time that several of them were asked to participate in a political meeting concerned with problems on an all-India and all-empire scale. Still largely onlookers, the princes were moving from the realm of pageantry to that of political negotiation.

Previously, individual princes had met and maintained some contacts with individual Indian politicians, but this occasion provided evidence of the growing strength and expanding goals of a wide variety of leaders in British India. Although militant leaders such as Annie Besant, Bal Gangadhar Tilak, and Shaukat and Muhammad Ali were excluded from the deliberations, Home Rule Leaguers led by Ganesh Shridhar Kharparde tried to pass a resolution calling for a Parliamentary bill to grant responsible government to India within a reasonable time in return for further wartime mobilization of Indian manpower and resources. Mahatma Gandhi, who also attended the conference, opposed the resolution because it made help conditional on concessions.[44] Such debate must have been alarming to the princes, who viewed the British as an all-powerful protector.

A few weeks after the Delhi conference, Michael O'Dwyer wrote to the viceroy to give his version of the impact of the conference on Patiala and the latter's views on the current political situation in India:

> He [Patiala] says, however, that he sees the possibility of trouble in India, his experience of some of the advanced politicians at the Delhi Conference were not reassuring, and I think he thought the eagerness to carry them with us was carried too far and created an impression that we were not too sure of our ground or of our hold on the country.
>
> He spoke quite frankly of the British way—sporting but not oversafe—of tackling a tiger with weapons only suitable for a jackal, and in view of the menace from the North-West dwelt strongly on the need of increasing our armed strength in India, that too would prevent any internal disturbance and enable us to repress any that might arise. I fancy at Delhi he and many others got talking about the possibility of India being denuded of troops and the consequent danger of trouble from without or within, and magnified the dangers of the situation.[45]

Patiala's response may have been overstated by the Punjab governor, but the dislike of open negotiation and the readiness to rely upon force or show of force as a solution to political problems is typical of Patiala's handling of his political opponents.

As mentioned earlier, Patiala and his brother princes rarely recognized the legitimacy of popular opposition. After exercising direct personal rule under British protection for an extended period, they were mentally unprepared for, and frequently intellectually incapable of, bargaining with leaders of such opposition. Constantly declared to be the natural leaders of their people by their British overlord after 1857, they acted as if it was impossible to challenge their position. Still, as the balance of power on the Indian subcontinent began to shift from their imperial patron to groups within Indian society, the princes, both individually and collectively, would be forced into situations that required an acute understanding of, and skill in, the techniques of negotiations. In any attempt to act jointly, their political judgment would be further clouded by other aspects of their political orientation and style.

Because of their origins, they maintained divisive regional jealousies that came to be petrified during years of isolation. This latter factor also helped sustain personal vanities and rivalries that led to a lack of commitment to little except the preservation of their own status and privileges. Their inflated ideas of self-importance reinforced a seemingly inherent dislike for the mundane work necessary for successful political organization. Although their internal political authority differed from that enjoyed by the princes, another British client group, the *talukdars* of the United Provinces, shared many similar characteristics that would also reduce their ability to respond effectively to challenges to their position.[46]

Princes and British Indian Politics During World War I

Prior to World War I the princes usually had acted only in response to British Indian political movements. Although anxious to suppress any possible hostility to their own or British authority raised within their territories, they were content to let their imperial patron handle such disaffection beyond their borders. After 1914 some princes began to act on their own initiative or on the slightest promptings from their patron in the arena of British Indian politics. Hoping to capitalize on their image as natural leaders of Indian society, they sought to provide an indigenous counterbalance to native groups and leaders deemed potential or actual threats to their own or British power.

In 1914–15 the Punjab princes, and particularly Maharaja Bhupinder Singh of Patiala, aided the Punjab and Central governments in their efforts to control the disturbances arising from the Ghadr movement. Although the Ghadr party is perhaps most known for its organization and activities outside India, it is also associated with the *Komagata Maru* incident of 1914. The *Komagata Maru* was the name of a Japanese steamer that some Sikh emigrants had chartered in Hong Kong to take them to Canada. When the ship reached Canada, the passengers, some of whom were Ghadr members or had Ghadr sympathies, were not allowed to land and were forced to return to India. After a trying return voyage and tactless handling by the police when they landed at Budge Budge near Calcutta, some passengers formed a core of vocal, revolutionarily inclined opponents of the British rule that had rebuffed them in Canada and now in India.[47] Consequently, the Government of India was anxious to prevent these returned Sikhs from spreading disaffection with the government and disrupting the war effort in India. As a typical example of how the Punjab princes cooperated in this matter, the Patiala durbar restricted most of the emigrants of Patiala origin to their ancestral villages and placed the majority of them on security. The local officials, usually *zaildars* or *lambardars*, were made responsible for the conduct of these Sikhs, who were forbidden to leave their villages without prior permission. At times the system was not effective, but on the whole it forced most of the *Komagata Maru* people and similarly returned Sikhs to settle down to the normal routine of village life.[48] On several occasions Michael O'Dwyer, as lieutenant governor of Punjab, acknowledged the helpfulness and effectiveness of such princely support.[49]

Moreover, the Punjab princes did not act only in response to British requests for support. In late 1916 the maharaja of Patiala spontaneously volunteered to send a mission of orthodox Sikhs to British Columbia and the western United States to combat the Ghadr propaganda at its source. Patiala proposed that this mission should include a Sikh religious leader, a good lecturer acquainted with the Sikh services in the war, Sikhs noted for their charitable work, and some musicians. This Sikh road show was to inculcate a sense of duty to religion and government among the emigrant Sikhs, to examine their local grievances, and to assure them of the contentment of their countrymen in India.[50] When Chelmsford asked Chamberlain for his opinion and that of the Colonial Office on the proposed mission, both London authorities stated that the project was inopportune. The main reasons for their decision were the lack of appeal of orthodoxy to the emigrant Sikhs, the possible disquieting effect of the trip on the members of the mission, and the difficulties that would arise in an effort to reconcile local Sikh grievances.[51] No further action was taken, but this incident is notable, for it reveals Patiala, on his own initiative, suggesting a program to help combat a political problem that had its origin outside his territory.

The momentous debate on the dimensions of political reform to be granted to British India was another area of princely concern. Here the leading figure was the maharaja of Bikaner, Ganga Singh. At the farewell banquet for him at Bombay in February 1917 prior to his departure for England to attend the Imperial War Conference, Bikaner pleaded for an adequate measure of reform in British India:

> We may, therefore, confidently assume that Great Britain and the British nation, who have so bravely made, and are still making, such tremendous sacrifices to uphold the cause of justice and humanity, will not forget the just claims and aspirations of India to enable her to work out her destiny under Britain's guiding hand and protection.[52]

This moderately worded statement attracted attention on all sides. Radical Indian nationalists regarded such a temperate statement as a mere platitude, but British officials considered it to be undesirable propaganda. Soon after the banquet Chelmsford privately wrote to Chamberlain suggesting that Chamberlain should warn Bikaner that he should not hold out any encouragement to political extremists.[53]

When he was in England, Bikaner made another plea for greater reforms in British India in a speech before the members of the Empire Parliamentary Association. On 4 November 1917, in a later speech to his brother princes, Bikaner explained that he felt it incumbent upon him as their representative to express concern that their fellow countrymen progress and receive their just reward. In this manner he wanted to refute the statements made in England that the princes were alarmed by, and resentful of, any movement toward political advance made in British India.[54] Bikaner followed up his speech before the Empire Parliamentary Association with a note outlining basic reforms that should be granted in British India. In this note, which he presented to Chamberlain in April 1917, he went much further in his plea for political reforms in British India than he had gone in his public speeches. His basic recommendations were:

> (1) the extreme importance of a formal and authoritative declaration by the British Government that self-government within the British Empire is the object and goal of British rule in India;
> (2) the advisability of liberal political reforms in British India in the constitution and functions of Provincial Legislative Councils and the Imperial Legislative Council of India;
> (3) the desirability of greater autonomy being granted to the Government as well as to the Provincial Government and a lesser degree of interference with both in regard to matters which are not of great Imperial concern; and
> (4) the vital importance to the Indian States, their Rulers and their subjects of establishing, at an early date, on constitutional lines, a Council of Princes to deal with matters which concern the British Government on the one side and the States, their Rulers and their people on the other.[55]

At the beginning of May 1917, the secretary of state had a long interview with Bikaner and cautioned him to be more judicious in his statements on British Indian politics for two reasons. In the first place, the princes did not invite, and greatly disliked, any interference by the Government of India in the internal affairs of their states. If they wanted a minimum of British interference, then they should avoid becoming active in British Indian affairs. In the second place, Chamberlain prophesied that if the reforms advocated by Bikaner were implemented, the Government of India would become more interfering as it became more popular.[56]

Although not as publicly as Bikaner, the maharaja scindia

of Gwalior also gave advice on political reform. Contained in a series of notes submitted to the Government of India during the first half of 1918, his suggestions were vague and moderate. For instance, he advocated associating three or four leading Indian "gentlemen" with each member of the viceroy's and provincial governors' Executive Councils to guide them so that governmental policies might be more popular with the governed.[57] Although Bikaner's speeches and Gwalior's notes indicated a growing princely awareness and concern about political events in British India, they also illustrate the princely dilemma with regard to the reform movement. The Government of India was unwilling for the princes to forge any alliances with British Indian groups that might threaten British power. At the same time they were reluctant to bring the princes into the decision-making process within the imperial structure and to evaluate seriously princely suggestions on political reform in British India. The imperial patron seemed unwilling to accept the consequences arising from the breakup of their earlier relationship with their princely clients.

A final instance of princely penetration into British Indian politics during the war years is the settlement of the dispute over the installation of irrigation canal controls on the Ganges River near Hardwar. When the government decided in 1914 to install some regulatory equipment, they held a conference of Hindu leaders and obtained their general approval of the project. Maharaja Madho Singh of Jaipur had participated because of his reputation as a devout Hindu who almost annually went on pilgrimage to this sacred site. In the following years, however, misunderstandings had arisen, and Pandit Madan Mohan Malaviya, a leading spokesman for orthodox Hindus of the United Provinces and the Hindu Mahasabha as well as a Congressman, spearheaded a protest against this scheme of control works.[58] Subsequently, Malaviya enlisted some Hindu princes to support this opposition during his tours of Indian states to raise funds for the new Hindu University at Benares. The complaint was that the holy water of the Ganges, which washed the bathing *ghats*, or steps, at Hardwar, should not be regulated in any manner by man.

In order to settle this dispute, Sir James Meston, who had recently became lieutenant governor of the United Provinces, convoked a second conference of Hindu representatives in December 1916 at the site in Hardwar. Along with the officials of the all-India Hindu Sabha who had raised the original protest, Meston had invited moderate Hindu leaders, Hindu landlords, and the following princes: Jaipur, Gwalior, Bikaner, Patiala, Alwar, and Benares. Although not invited, Malaviya also showed up. There followed two days of hard negotiating by Meston and his engineering staff. In a letter to Chelmsford, Meston gave an informative description of the attitudes of the princes. Jaipur had become agreeable to a solution shortly after the conference began. Gwalior treated the proceedings as a joke and pleaded occasionally with the Pandits "not to make asses of themselves." Bikaner supported the United Provinces government in every way and argued skillfully against the Malaviya group. Alwar sided with Malaviya and kept quoting long passages of Sanskrit law that Benares said had nothing to do with the situation. Meston claimed that Bikaner was very bitter about Alwar's conduct and that those two almost came to blows. Patiala had originally inclined toward Alwar but became annoyed at the whole affair and by the second day told everyone that the "whole business was d----d rot." After much haggling an agreement was finally reached on a compromise basis that necessitated greater expenditure but allowed for a control channel as well as a channel of uncontrolled water that would flow past the *ghats*.[59]

This incident at Hardwar illustrates well three factors associated with princely involvement in British Indian politics. First, the government utilized the princes as Indian representatives so it could be assured of sympathy if not outright support from one quarter in its disputes with Indian political, social, and religious leaders. Such aid was particularly helpful in the difficult arena of communal affairs.[60] The government also wished to prevent the princes from lending their support and prestige to Indian politicians. Second, princely rivalry and antipathies often surfaced at critical points and could influence political judgment and allegiances. Alwar may not have been convinced of the validity of Malaviya's opposition, but he was willing to oppose his rival Bikaner, who was acting as chief advocate for the British. Third, the princes were conspicuous representatives of their respective religious communities. As mentioned earlier, they realized the importance of promoting common ties with their subjects that would strengthen the personal loyalty of the latter. Religion was a dominant influence in much of Indian life, and many princes assiduously cultivated their positions as religious leaders.

Princely Involvement in Religious Revivalism

As revivalism gathered momentum in most Indian religions during the nineteenth century and religious symbols and concepts were gradually employed by Indian politicians during the twentieth century to draw new groups into politics, the princes acquired new potential, which some were quick to exploit, in their acknowledged position as religious leaders. Religion transcended political boundaries and represented a unique area of opportunity for the princes to develop as all-India leaders as well as to fortify their position within their own states. In religious matters neither the British officials nor the Indian politicians could rightfully criticize the princes for unwarranted interference in activities outside their competency or their legitimate concern. Because they had no ritual status in any of the major religions of the Indian subcontinent, the British were anxious to utilize the princes in their capacity as religious figures whenever it suited their purposes to do so. For their part many Indian politicians who were active in communal politics were eager to secure support from any possible source to advance the interests of their religious community and so actively solicited princely participation.[61]

In particular they sought princely largesse for institutions of higher education that were dedicated to developing a Western-educated elite within a particular religious tradition. All located in British India, they included the Hindu University at Benares, the Deccan Educational Society at Bombay (its most prominent institution was Fergusson College in Poona), the Muhammadan Anglo-Oriental College at Aligarh, and the Sikh Khalsa College at Amritsar. Some of the major princely contributors to Benares were Patiala, who gave five lakhs of rupees, and Alwar, Jodhpur, Kashmir, and Mysore, who gave one lakh as initial offerings and smaller sums as annual grants.[62] The princes of western India channeled their support to the Deccan Educational Society and accounted for over half of its contributions between 1884 and 1910.[63] Bhopal and Hyderabad were prominent sustainers of Aligarh, and all Sikh states, but especially Patiala and Nabha, contributed heavily to Khalsa College.[64] Since some princes such as Patiala and Nabha were ecumenical in their patronage (the former even becoming a patron of Aligarh), their contributions might superficially appear to be demonstrations of noblesse oblige.

From the beginning, however, such donations constituted entry into British Indian communal politics. Besides creating a modernist element within the community, these institutions hoped to provide their graduates with the educational qualifications necessary to compete successfully for governmental jobs. Support for these colleges meant support for a communal effort to obtain more leverage within the British administrative structure. Then too, as students were mobilized into political activity from the partition of Bengal agitation onward, these schools became battlegrounds for British Indian politicians and British officials canvassing the loyalty of their pupils. As early as 1908, Tikka Sahib Ripudaman Singh, the heir to the Nabha *gadi*, expressed concern about the radical influences on the students who had unyoked the horses from and pulled the carriage of G. K. Gokhale during his visit to the college.[65] By the 1920s the students were inclined to much more drastic political action, and the princes would become helpful allies of the British in controlling these institutions.

The three major religious groups in twentieth-century Indian politics are the Hindus, the Muslims, and the Sikhs. Hinduism is spread throughout India in many variant sects and manifestations. Perhaps as a reflection of the amorphous nature, the regional orientation, and the majority position of Hinduism, no single Hindu ruler in the twentieth century emerged as the leading Hindu prince. In the Hardwar dispute the maharaja of Jaipur was considered the prime Hindu ruler whose objections needed to be adequately satisfied. Jaipur, however, could not claim first place among the rulers of Rajputana, let alone all the Hindu princes of India. Within the hierarchy of Rajput clans, the ruling house of Udaipur as the head of the Sisodia clan was recognized as preeminent. Although the Udaipur dynasty was proud of its tradition of stout resistance to the Muslims, boasting that it had never given a female in marriage to the Mughals, it never regained prominence as a defender of Hinduism after the Marathas had ravaged the state in the early decades of the nineteenth century. Another Rajput prince who did try to project an all-India image was Maharaja Jey Singh of Alwar. Claiming descent from the Hindu sun god, Jey Singh displayed his ritual purity by refusing to sit on leather chairs in the offices of British officials and by wearing cotton gloves to prevent even accidental contact with impure objects.[66] Quick to parade his learning in Sanskrit philosophy and literature, he overloaded his public speeches with long and not necessarily relevant references to Vedas and Puranas, embellishing them with elaborate philosophical conceits.[67] Although he maintained close contact with Hindu communal leaders such as Pandit Madan Mohan Malaviya and participated in Hindu communal affairs, he never attracted a mass or enthusiastic following. Bikaner, the most prominent Rajput prince politically, never cultivated his position as a Hindu *per se*.

In western India some Hindu princes were active in promoting Maratha identity and the ritual acceptance of non-Brahmin Marathas by the Marathi-speaking Brahmin priests and politicians. During the nineteenth century the rulers of Baroda and Gwalior had continued to hold public celebrations in honor of Ganesh, the elephant-headed god, who was the titular deity of the Peshwas and popular with the Marathas. In the 1890s B. G. Tilak, the Chitpavan Brahmin rival of G. K. Gokhale, developed festivals in honor first of Ganesh and then of Shivaji in order to mobilize greater numbers, especially of non-Brahmins, into his political campaigns. Initially, Maharaja Shahu Chhatrapati of Kolhapur, a Kshatriya whose house claimed descent from Shivaji's younger son, agreed to serve as president of the Shivaji Fund Committee. The original objectives of the Shivaji Festival had been to boost the non-Brahmin founder of Maratha political power as a militant activist who bridged the social categories of Brahmin and non-Brahmin. After the upheaval of a famine and the display of British insensitivity to orthodox Hindu feelings during the plague epidemic of 1896, the festival became a rallying point for violent speeches and actions. Kolhapur dropped his support and suppressed the Shivaji Club in his state.[68] He, however, became increasingly active on his own initiative as a ritual and political leader of non-Brahmin Marathas. Though he might argue on ritual matters, his goals were secular, since he wanted to end Brahmin dominance in his administration and to raise political capital with the British, who were also hostile to the Brahmin politicians of Bombay and Poona.[69] Although Kolhapur's appeal extended beyond his state and throughout the Maratha area, it was necessarily limited to a particular segment of the Hindu community even though it was one gaining political significance.

Among south Indian Hindu princes, the maharajas of Mysore, Travancore, and Cochin supported Hindu institutions and had prominent ritual positions, but mainly within their respective states. The most extraordinary example was in Travancore. Raja Marthanda Varma, who consolidated the territories of modern Travancore in the first half of the eighteenth century, dedicated the state to Sri Padmanabhaswami, and he and his successors ruled as servants of this deity.[70]

Among the Muslims of India, Nizam Mir Osman Ali Khan of Hyderabad held the most prominent position, since he was the most important prince of India in terms of revenue and population and the last remnant of Mughal power and glory. The nizam, however, was in an ambiguous position, since he ruled a Hindu majority area that included vestiges of Arab Muslim retainers as well as a local Indian Muslim minority. Thus he had to exercise leadership in the Indian Muslim community with discretion, and the vigor of his ventures varied according to the situation and his own personal inclination.

With the outbreak of World War I the British government

obviously wished to enlist the sympathy and assistance of this prestigious ruler. In this undertaking they were successful beyond their expectations. As related earlier, the nizam had been generous in his contributions of troops, money, and material. But even more important was the firman he issued upon the entrance of the Ottoman Empire into the war in November 1914. In a *kharita*, or official letter, Lord Hardinge wrote:

> I accordingly call upon Your Highness to stand forth as the spokesman and leader of Mahomedans in India and to declare that England's cause is both right and just. I would suggest to Your Highness to issue a proclamation which, after reiterating Your Highness' well-known loyalty to the British Throne, shall proceed to describe the situation in detail as in the statement which I am making public and shall explain the reason why the Khalif's appeal should be disregarded by all law-abiding Indian Mahomedans.[71]

The nizam responded to this overture with a manifesto that the Ottoman Empire entered the war for political reasons; therefore this was not a *jihad*, or an Islamic holy war of conquest. Thus Indian Muslims would not violate their consciences if they fought on the British side. This quasi-official statement on policy was particularly helpful, since most Indian units fought on the Western Asian front against troops of the Ottoman Empire.

A few years later the nizam expanded his purview as the spokesman and leader of Muslims in India. In July 1918 he sent a memorandum to Lord Chelmsford calling for the release of the interned Muslim *ulama*, or religious teachers, at Deoband, a center of orthodox Muslim learning. He argued that their internment had caused great unrest among the Muslim community and that their release would quieten this unrest. Furthermore, the nizam offered to use his influence with the *ulama* so that they would conduct themselves in the future in such a way that no suspicion of sedition would surround them. In his memorandum on this subject the nizam offered this unwelcome advice as the "Faithful Ally of the British Empire" and the leader and spokesman of the Muslim community.[72] Ironically, both titles had been conferred upon him by the British government. John Wood, the political secretary, advised the nizam to leave alone the matter of the Deoband internees, but Lord Chelmsford more tactfully wrote to the nizam that he would take the nizam's advice under further consideration.[73] Here again, the British government had opened a Pandora's box when it called upon the nizam in 1914 to make a statement in support of the war as the spokesman for the Muslim community. At that time the British wanted a Muslim figure who could effectively counter the sherif of Mecca's call for *jihad* among the Muslims against the Allies. Later the British would want the nizam as a counterpoise to Muslim activists such as Muhammad and Shaukat Ali. To their dismay, they soon discovered that the nizam would attempt to play a more independent role as a Muslim leader than suited the British purposes.

Two other princely clients active in Muslim politics were the rulers of Bhopal and Rampur. The principal Muslim state in central India, Bhopal had been established in the early decades of the eighteenth century by an Afghan, Dost Muhammad, on the basis of leases and offices granted by the Mughal emperors at Delhi. After suffering from the raids of Pindaris and Marathas, Bhopal entered formal treaty relations with the British in 1818.[74] As allowed by Muslim law, Bhopal had been ruled since 1844 by a succession of capable women. The third one, Nawab Sultan Jahan Begum, succeeded to the throne in 1901. Although she maintained purdah restrictions and spoke broken English learned from a private secretary, she was known for an efficient but autocratic internal administration, a sharp tongue, and a strong interest in all-India Muslim politics.

Begum Sultan Jahan and her state were staunch supporters of the Muhammadan Anglo-Oriental College at Aligarh, even though she publicly criticized the institution for its lack of attention to practical details and to female education.[75] These ties were reinforced by the close contact between the Ali brothers, both graduates of the MAO College and the begum. Muhammad Ali had been tutor to her youngest son, Nawabzada Hamidullah Khan, and the latter also attended and graduated from Aligarh.[76] In 1914 Hamidullah was rumored to have contributed two thousand rupees himself and to have helped in the solicitation conducted by Shaukat Ali for the security of the *Comrade,* a newspaper founded by

Muhammad Ali to provide a vehicle for his views and those of other politically active, Western-educated Muslims.[77] The *Comrade* had to provide financial security because of an article sympathetic to the Turks written by Muhammad Ali. The begum justified continued association with these opponents of British policies because of her hope to convert them to more desirable lines of thought.[78] Later it became known that Dr. Mukhtar Ahmad Ansari, organizer of a medical mission to aid the Muslim Turks in 1913, visited Bhopal to care for the begum's personal and family medical problems and probably to keep her *au courant* on Muslim politics.[79] Although the British Government deprecated these activities of the begum and her youngest son, they were quick to seek her advice and support on issues affecting the Muslims of India.

Another vestige of Afghan power in northern India was Rampur State, a small enclave encompassed by the United Provinces of Agra and Oudh. Although its limited area and population were an inadequate reflection of the eighteenth-century power of its Rohilla founders,[80] Rampur was famed for its Arabic College, the Madrasa-i-Alia, and its Oriental Library, which contained many rare manuscripts. Unlike the rulers of Hyderabad and Bhopal, who were orthodox Sunni Muslims, Nawab Muhammad Hamid of Rampur was a Shia Muslim.[81] Despite this sectarian difference he became known for his monetary donations to, and participation in, Muslim groups and for his strong advocacy of maintaining cordial relations between the Muslim community and the British government.[82]

A final and perhaps most significant example of princely involvement in religious affairs is the role of Maharaja Bhupinder Singh within the Sikh community. Although they constitute only about one per cent of the total Indian population, the Sikhs have occupied a prominent place in modern Indian history because of their valor as soldiers, their industriousness as farmers, their control of a border province, and their efforts to strengthen their cohesiveness as a community. Toward the close of the nineteenth century the atmosphere of religious revivalism current in India had led certain Sikhs to promote the unity of the Sikh community and to emphasize its distinctness from the Hindu community, which threatened to absorb Sikhism within its amorphous totality. To highlight the uniqueness and greatness of Sikhism, Sikh revivalists were anxious to utilize any available symbols of the Sikh heritage, such as the Punjabi language written in the Gurmukhi script, which had been evolved by the Sikh gurus, or holy men.

Although the British had long before annexed the greatest symbol of Sikh political power, the Punjab Kingdom of Ranjit Singh, the cis-Sutlej Sikh states remained as tokens of Sikh political domination. The three Phulkian states of Patiala, Nabha, and Jind were the most important of them. Although challenged by Maharaja Ripudaman Singh of Nabha, Bhupinder Singh's Patiala was generally recognized as the premier Sikh state both by members of the Sikh community and by the British government.[83] It was a logical policy for various Sikh leaders to seek the support of the maharaja of Patiala, who served as a potent symbol of past Sikh glory and might serve as a helpful intermediary with the British Government.

Little specific information is available about the relationship between the Patiala dynasty and the Sikh community during the nineteenth century. In any case, by the opening decades of the twentieth century the position of Patiala as the major Sikh ruler and a prominent member of the Sikh community was acknowledged in many ways. When Khalsa College, the main Sikh institution of higher education, was reorganized in 1908 and its constitution was revised, the maharaja of Patiala was given two places on the Managing Committee.[84] He personally continued as the patron of the college. This educational tie cut across political boundaries, since Khalsa College was located in Amritsar, the holy city of the Sikhs, which was in the British province of Punjab. Another such bond was the Sikh Education Conference founded in 1908 to promote and encourage education among the *Panth*, or Sikh community. Receiving support from the Sikh states as well as Sikhs throughout India, the conference asked Bhupinder Singh to preside over its fifth session at Sialkot. Although the Patiala prince declined ostensibly for reasons of health, there is evidence that the British were against such participation by a prince in a conference held in British India.[85]

A second example of Patiala's prominence and close ties to Sikhs in British India occurred in 1910. In late December the maharaja of Patiala went to Ferozepore in British Punjab for some alligator-shooting, and while there he received an address from the Sikhs of that district. The address traced the rise of the Phulkian house and its association with Guru Govind Singh, who had laid the foundation for the Sikhs as a political organization in contradistinction to a purely religious order. The address interpreted the growth and continued existence of the Phulkian house as a sign of the special blessings of the guru. It further postulated that the guru blessed the English nation to save India from misrule and tyranny and thus justified the close ties between the guru's own house, *i.e.*, the Phulkian house, and the British nation. The heart of the address was a petition that the Sikh citizens of Patiala should be given greater educational opportunities and greater representation in the public services of Patiala State.[86] Although this petition is similar to memorials being circulated by Hindus and Muslims at the same time, it is particularly pregnant since it acknowledged the role of Patiala as a Sikh ruler and propounded many arguments later utilized by Patiala to enhance his position within the Sikh community.

During the war years Patiala seized the opportunities available to advance his position as a leading figure in the Sikh community. The Sikhs represented a major element in the British Indian Army as well as Imperial Service units, so Patiala attempted to become, and was recognized as, an important figure among a minority who had contributed with great generosity to the war effort. It has already been pointed out how Crump considered that Patiala had some claim to being the princely representative to the Imperial War Conference because of his position as the premier Sikh ruler of India and the support this suggestion received from the Punjab press.

On his own behalf Patiala actively promoted this image as a Sikh ruler by various means. In 1916 he commemorated the anniversary of the declaration of war with a great celebration at Patiala to which he invited Sikhs from Punjab, Delhi, and Sind, as well as the principal *sardars* of his state. The main attraction was a speech delivered by Patiala at the *gurdwara* of Sir Guru Singh Sabhain. Most of the speech was devoted to a plea for continued support of the war effort, in which the British were represented as the forces of righteousness and the Central Powers as the forces of darkness. Patiala also alluded to the close association between Guru Govind Singh, the Phulkian house, and the English. Here his reasoning followed closely that previously enunciated by the Sikh leaders in Ferozepore. Furthermore, Patiala used the words of the guru to justify his action toward the returned Sikhs who were pro–Ghadr party. Patiala declared:

> One of the sublime teachings of our Guru Father is unflinching loyalty to the ruler and implicit obedience to his orders. The Sikhs cannot forget the words:
>
> "He who is impertinent to his master, is put to great shame" and
>
> "None should bear arms against his rulers."
>
> It was due to the teachings like these that when some misguided emigrants divorced from Sikh teachings and traditions and under the influence of the wicked enemies of our faith, returned to India with an evil purpose, they were openly disclaimed by the Sikhs and handed up even by their own relatives to receive punishment which they deserved. I am well pleased to see how my co-religionists stood against these fools.[87]

Not only his coreligionists but also Bhupinder Singh himself took action against these misguided brothers.

After Patiala's speech Sardar Gajjan Singh, the leader of the Ludhiana Bar, the vice-president of the Municipal Committee there, and member of the Punjab Legislative Council, spoke in laudatory terms of the rulers of Patiala and how the Sikhs in British India would be proud to follow Patiala's lead in any effort to further relations between the Sikhs and the government.[88] Then Sardar Sunder Singh Majithia, a large landowner, supporter of Sikh educational institutions, and then a member of the Imperial Legislative Council, read the messages of loyalty being sent from Patiala to the lieutenant governor of Punjab, the viceroy, and the king-emperor.[89] Finally the proceedings were closed with Sikh prayers and religious hymns.

On the following day, 5 August, the maharaja of Patiala had a garden party for his guests, who constituted the political, educational, and religious elite of the Sikh community. These guests included Sardar Sunder Singh Majithia and Sardar Gajjan Singh, mentioned earlier; Sardar Gurbakhsh Singh Gyani, secretary of the Khalsa College Managing Committee; Sardar Arur Singh, the manager of the Golden Temple; and Bhai Arjan Singh of Bagarian, who was the spiritual guardian of the Phulkian states.[90]

Patiala concluded these war anniversary celebrations not by yet another contribution to the war effort but by donations to Sikh educational institutions both in British India and Patiala State. He donated ten thousand rupees to the Khalsa High School in Ludhiana and five thousand rupees to the Sikh Kanya Mahavidyala in Ferozepore, the leading Sikh educational institution for girls, and assumed the burdens attached to the operation of the Khalsa High School at Moga in Patiala State.[91] Later that same year, in October 1916, Patiala reinforced his position as a patron of Sikh learning by his support of historical writing on Sikh history: he sponsored the publication by his State Press of the historical writings of Panth Ratan Gyani Gyan Singh. Gyan Singh was ninety-five years old, and had recorded the events of Sikh history that he had witnessed plus a compilation of a history of the ten gurus of Sikhism and the twelve *misls*, or confederacies, of the Sikh community.[92]

Although the leadership role assumed by Maharaja Bhupinder Singh in Sikh communal activities was an extraordinary one, it was a graphic indication of the changing position of the Indian princes. When British imperial power was at its zenith at the beginning of the twentieth century, the Indian princes seemed dependent partners whom Curzon could lecture as a schoolmaster. A few short years later World War I strongly reinforced and extended the challenge to British imperial rule that was gathering strength in the opening decade of the twentieth century. After 1914 the princely clients forcefully demonstrated their value as military allies. Then, and more importantly, some of them began to utilize new opportunities for participation in all-India politics opened to them by changes occurring within Indian society. In this sphere Patiala was just one of a cluster who acted both to establish their position as all-India figures and to accumulate assets as political allies.

Others equally prominent were the urbane Ganga Singh of Bikaner, the equivocal Jey Singh of Alwar, the plainspoken Madho Rao of Gwalior, and the cricket-playing Ranjit Sinhji of Nawanagar. Although they had diverse religious and regional backgrounds and varied personalities, members of this circle as well as future inductees shared some common characteristics. All had some exposure to Western education either through attendance at college, such as Patiala at Aitchison and Alwar at Mayo, or through a private British tutor, such as Bikaner and Gwalior. Each had close personal relations with highly placed British officials, especially viceroys, whom they entertained both formally and informally within their states with spectacles such as the imperial sand grouse shoot held by Bikaner every Christmas and the tiger hunts at Alwar and Gwalior. These close relations were furthered by the physical proximity of their states to New Delhi, the imperial capital since 1912. None was much over a twenty-four-hour train trip from New Delhi, and ease of travel was a prime consideration on both sides. All these princes also had traveled abroad and had attended various imperial extravagances such as Edward VII's Coronation. These experiences broadened their political vision and made them aware of the far-flung extent of the British empire. Unfortunately they also opened seemingly interminable disputes over precedence and new avenues for lavish expenditure. Finally all seemed to possess ambitions of such proportions that they were not satisfied by the routines connected with the internal administration of their respective states. Although mutual friendship seemed to exist among them, it oscillated greatly because of the personal vanities of such arrogant men. No one figure was acknowledged as leader, though the British tended to look upon Gwalior and Bikaner as special confidants. By 1910 Patiala was a zealous rival despite his lack of comparable years and experience.

chapter three

Maneuvers for Constitutional Boons 1917–1921

In February 1917 the maharaja of Bikaner wrote to Lord Chelmsford requesting that the princes be given land grants, in India or in conquered areas abroad such as German East Africa, as rewards for their war services as had been done in appreciation for princely support during the Revolt of 1857. The comparison of their assistance during the Great War with that given sixty years earlier would become a constant refrain in princely speeches and memoranda for the next thirty years. When he forwarded Bikaner's letter to the secretary of state for India, Austen Chamberlain, the viceroy made the revealing comment:

> The position today may be as important as that at the close of the mutiny, but it differs *in toto*, inasmuch as while at that time we had land to give away, today we have none. The truth is we are in a great quandary so far as the chiefs are concerned.[1]

In that last sentence he unknowingly but prophetically characterized the future state of British policy toward the princes during the turbulent interwar period. Once their original policy principles had been finally discarded, the British official hierarchy seemed unable, or unwilling, to formulate any set of consistent principles to guide their relations with the princes. The British are freely criticized for a lack of bold initiative in dealing with the postwar demands of Indian nationalists, but they displayed even less audacity and imagination in their efforts to integrate the princes into the changing constitutional structure of their Indian Empire.

It must be emphasized that the situation was complex and that the three interested parties—the British, the princes, and the Indian nationalists—varied as groups and within their own ranks in their assessment of the princely position and in their programs for the constitutional adjustment of their status in the postwar era. Within the British structure the secretary of state for India, the viceroy, and the political secretary of the Government of India were the parties most involved in policy formulation. There were two subsidiary influences in London. One was the permanent undersecretary of state, who frequently corresponded privately with the viceroy about the general atmosphere and progress of cases at the India Office. The other was the crown, who viewed the princes as fellow rulers but was ambivalent to princely overtures and complaints.[2] Even within this restricted circle, unanimity was difficult to achieve, and once reached could be modified by the attitudes of British officials more closely in contact with the princes, such as the residents, the agents to the governor general, and the political agents. These last three classes of officials served as the principal and frequently exclusive channel of communication between Delhi and the more than five hundred princes of India.[3]

Among the princes there was the clique headed by the maharajas of Bikaner and Patiala who were aware that changes were taking place and were anxious to confirm and strengthen their positions within the British Indian Empire. There was a second category, again limited in number, who realized the import of postwar changes but preferred to concentrate their attention on the internal affairs of their states. Prominent examples here were Maharaja Krishnaraja Wadiyar of Mysore and Gaekwar Sayaji Rao of Baroda. Both of these rulers had acquired the label of nationalists for their programs of social reform in such areas as reduction of caste restrictions and spread of education and political advances such as legislative assemblies.[4] The overwhelming numerical majority, however, comprised a third grouping who were barely cognizant of the surrounding atmosphere of flux and so made little or no effort to adjust in either their external relations with the British or in their internal control of their states.[5]

In the immediate postwar years the Indian politicians were most concerned with obtaining additional leverage within the British Indian governmental structure and refining the techniques and impact of the Indian nationalist movement. When they considered the matter of the Indian states, their main proposals centered on the introduction of more representative and responsible government and firmer measures by the British to prevent misrule and maladministration. Characterizing the princes as more helpless and enslaved than their own subjects, Shaukat Ali, himself a subject of Rampur, voiced sentiments typical of this position in 1921. He implored the princes to

> support the movement for improving the national life in their own territories and help the leaders of the country in the religious struggle. . . . [and begged] the Almighty God that he may give them courage to cooperate with us that they may lead us and that we may all follow them.[6]

His concluding remark was representative of those Indian politicians who still viewed the Indian princes as potential sources of political leadership or support. Few British Indian politicians considered it possible or even desirable to abolish the states, and the Indian National Congress expressly declared political reform within the states to be beyond its proper concern.

Proceeding from this general outline of differing attitudes, we will examine British policy-making efforts in the area of constitutional reform, the princely program of reform largely framed by the Bikaner-Patiala group, and the scattered comments and suggestions made by Indian nationalists.

Early Efforts at Constitutional Integration

In the spring of 1913 Lord Hardinge, Minto's successor as viceroy, made a limited but concrete beginning toward bringing the princes into closer contact with the government on matters of common concern. No attempt was made to utilize the princes as counterweights to rising political elites in British India; but rather, selected princes were invited to Delhi, the new capital, to discuss a topic of concern and controversy only among the princes and British political officers, namely, the education of princely sons, especially the heirs apparent. Arguing that training under competent native guidance would thoroughly instill the customs and traditions of the state and its people, one faction in this controversy contended that a prince should be educated at the court of his state. Since many Indian rulers looked upon the personal loyalty of their subjects as the strongest support of their rule, the establishment of cultural rapport between a prince and his people would be of great importance. The main defect of this scheme was that princely courts were frequently permeated with intrigue and personal faction fighting. Consequently, the minor prince was often regarded as a prize to be won by flattery and indulgence rather than a maturing individual to be educated in local traditions and the principles of good government.

The opposing faction asserted that a prince should be educated among his fellow princes at a boarding school modeled after English public schools. In 1877 Lord Lytton laid the foundation stone for Mayo College at Ajmer, an institution for the education of princes and members of the British Indian aristocracy that had been first proposed by Lord Mayo. Later similar institutions were organized in other areas: Aitchison College in Lahore, Daly College in Indore, and Rajkumar College in Rajkot. Supporters of these colleges claimed that they provided an environment where a young prince could acquire a broad education that would enable him to cope more effectively with the complex tasks related to the administration of his state. The defect in this type of education was that it divorced the prince from his native surroundings and frequently conveyed the superficialities of an English public school education, such as an inclination toward cricket and horse racing rather than the substance of a classical education.[7]

At the 1913 conference, discussion centered on a proposal to establish a Higher Chiefs' College[8] that would further educate the princes to be more effective administrators in the modern world. Although nothing definite was decided at this conference, it did serve Lord Hardinge's objective of drawing "the Chiefs nearer to the Viceroy by inaugurating an annual informal conference between them" and it "answered so well that it was followed up each year."[9]

At the second conference of princes, held in Delhi in March 1914, the princes renewed their discussion on the scheme of a Higher Chiefs' College and decided that such an institution should be located in the new imperial capital at Delhi. The proponents of this scheme contended that further education in an all-India atmosphere was necessary to broaden the outlook of the princes who had received their earlier education at the regional-oriented Chiefs' Colleges in Ajmer, Indore, Lahore, and Rajkot. This group also proposed to invite selected aristocratic families from British India to participate in this project in order to secure for it adequate financial support. In return for their generous financial assistance, these aristocratic families would be permitted to send their sons and other dependents to this institution. Obviously, the proponents of a purely native education opposed this Western-type institution in varying degrees.

The importance of these two conferences under Hardinge is not to be sought in the ultimate success of the Higher Chiefs' College, since it never came into existence. This educational scheme foundered on the princes' dislike for a central institution, which would dilute local and regional ties, their dispute over the entrance of British Indian families, and their financial exhaustion during and after World War I.[10] Rather, the significance of the conferences was that they stimulated a princely demand for a greater voice in imperial affairs, particularly in matters of interest to the princes and their states. In January 1914 the maharaja of Bikaner forwarded a long note expressing this request for greater princely participation:

> . . . The time would certainly seem to have come when something must be done to show that the Ruling Chiefs, who, on the whole, command a not inconsiderable amount of respect in British India also, should, as the representatives and leaders of their States, have some formal part in the government of the Empire. They have a right, in view of their partnership and of their con-

> tributions towards the defence of the Empire, to be heard in regard to the great matters of Imperial interest, and they also desire to have an opportunity for mutual consultation and for the discussion of matters affecting their own Order.[11]

Bikaner elaborated this demand at the conference in March 1914 when he asked that similar conferences on other topics of concern to the princes be convened in the future.

In response to Bikaner's note, Sir John Wood, who became political secretary of the Government of India in 1914 when the Foreign Department was divided into Foreign and Political branches, investigated the issue of an organization for consultation with the princes. In the conclusion to a lengthy note he argued that

> discussion with the Chiefs in Council or with representative Chiefs in Committee ensures that the Chiefs' views are adequately put forward in matters affecting themselves and save Government from the errors resulting from a misconception of their attitude. These Conferences act moreover as a safety valve through which minor grievances find a harmless vent, and tend to prevent subterranean communications behind the backs of Political Officers which are a source of danger to our administration. The old practice of what Lee Warner calls 'subordinate isolation,' still favoured by some unenlightened reactionaries, is now, owing to the greater facilities of communication and the spread of education, impossible to maintain, and it is recognized on all hands that the collective goodwill and support of the Ruling Chiefs is an Imperial Asset of incalculable value. If the growing demand for collective discussion is disregarded, we run the risk of alienating the sympathies of those whose support is most worth having.[12]

Lord Chelmsford, who had succeeded Hardinge as viceroy in April 1916, solicited additional views from his Executive Council and a few selected political officers. He soon decided to follow the advice of his political secretary and of Bikaner and to invite some princes to Delhi for discussions of broader topics than the education of young princes.

The Political Department of the Government of India was to organize the conference and to determine which princes were to be invited, what were suitable topics for the agenda, and assorted procedural items. In the last category the Political Department designated English as the language of the conference and ruled out any public proceedings. The first decision meant that Western-educated and English-speaking princes would play the dominant roles even though an aide might read an English translation of the remarks of some participant, such as Maharaja Pratap Singh of Kashmir, who could not speak English. The second ruling would shelter the princes from any direct public criticism but simultaneously would allow the circulation of wild rumors as to the intent and proceedings of such closed sessions.

As matters of concern requiring discussion, Chelmsford advanced the following items for the agenda: the ceremonies observed at installation and investiture durbars in the states, reorganization of Imperial Service units, amendment of an insolvency act to enable the realization of assets in the states, plans for a Higher Chiefs' College in Delhi, armorial bearings for princes, granting of indigenous titles by princes, and questions related to minority administrations.[13] Although he welcomed the idea of such a conference as long as it remained modest in scope and goals, Chamberlain was apprehensive about the possible difficulties that might arise as a consequence of such meetings. He discouraged any discussion on Imperial Service units, which was a delicate topic during wartime; on armorial bearings, which he considered a money-consuming folly; and on indigenous titles because they might diminish the prestige attached to imperial titles.[14] On its own initiative the Political Department dropped the items to which Chamberlain had objected, thereby achieving accord between London and Delhi on the proposed conference and its agenda.[15]

Several princes enthusiastically accepted the invitations to confer in Delhi, foremost of whom were the maharajas of Bikaner, Patiala, Alwar, and Gwalior. Possibly learning from the operations of associations in British India, Ganga Singh of Bikaner now sought to organize the princes through a series of informal meetings held prior to the formal conference sessions.[16] At these caucuses, which became a regular feature of succeeding conferences, the princes discussed the agenda items, formulated resolutions, designated supporting speakers, chose someone to deliver their reply to the viceroy's opening speech, and appointed a committee to draft this speech.[17] Resolutions other than those accepted at these gatherings could be presented at the conference, but their passage was doubtful.

When the Conference of Ruling Princes and Chiefs formally opened on 30 October 1916, it was first addressed by the viceroy. After the courtesies associated with such a ceremonially minded group, he stated the dual purposes of the conference to be to serve the interests of the princes and to assist the Government of India in the solution of administrative problems related to the states.[18] In order to lessen the apprehension of some princes and to disarm possible Indian nationalist critics of the conference, Chelmsford declared:

> You are jealous, and rightly jealous, of your position as Ruling Chiefs and Princes owing allegiance to His Majesty the King-Emperor, and there is, I hope, no need for me to assure you that I have no desire to impinge on that position or to interfere in your domestic concerns; conversely Your Highnesses will, I am sure, not be desirous of intervening in the domestic affairs of British India.
>
> With this agreement in essentials between Your Highnesses and the Government of India, we may, I think, leave the future to decide for itself the question of constitutional development as it arises.[19]

In contrast to this wait-and-see attitude toward the future of the conference, the gaekwar of Baroda, who delivered the princely reply to the viceroy's opening remarks, urged:

> For with the march of the times—and no man can put back the hand of the clock—it is in our opinion of the utmost importance to ourselves, our States and our people that we should have a regularly assigned and definite place in the Constitution of the Empire; and indeed that there should at an early date come into existence an institution, which we have consistently advocated, such as a Council or Assembly of Princes formed on proper lines, where important questions concerning ourselves can be discussed and settled.[20]

The disparity between these two statements was a bad omen for the constitutional aspirations of the Indian princes. Unsure of what institutional forms would yield the desired benefits of mutual discussion and legal safeguards, the princes had sought a regular assembly as a first step. Although their thinking was nebulous, it was decidedly more audacious than that of the viceroy or the secretary of state. Further complications would arise as conservative rulers raised formidable opposition to any formal assembly and tended to reinforce the go-slow thinking of the British.

When the assembled princes began to discuss the agenda items, controversies erupted over seemingly innocuous matters. The first one occurred during the debate over the form of minority administrations. Here the princes opposed British participation but were reluctant to define any standardized form for minority administrations that would ignore local customs. Eventually a committee of princes formulated a resolution declaring that the wishes of the late ruler should be observed and that a council of state officials headed by an Indian regent was the preferred form.[21] Sir John Wood, who was presiding after Chelmsford's opening speech, offered an amendment that the local political officer should be consulted in important matters so that the British government could discharge its responsibilities as guardians of the interests of the state. When the princes displayed their reluctance to accept his amendment, Wood warned them not to propose anything which would not be acceptable to the Government of India.[22] His admonishment clearly indicated that the conference resolutions would have value only as they concurred with government thinking.

The major surprise of the conference occurred during the discussion over the ceremonies appropriate at an installation durbar when a prince, regardless of age, is installed on the *gadi* and at the investiture durbar when a prince upon coming of age is invested with full ruling powers. When they had suggested this item for the agenda, the Political Department had hoped to define the vague grievances of the princes on these matters and then to attempt to remove the sources of irritation so far as they considered possible. Princely tempers quickly reached a boiling point because of introductory statements contained in the memorandum on this topic prepared by the Political Department for the guidance of the princes. The offending passages declared:

1. Every succession *requires the approval and sanction of Government.*
2. It is essential that such approval and sanction should be announced in a formal installation *durbar* by a representative of the British Government.[23]

From the princely viewpoint this statement denied the right of non-adopted sons of a prince to succeed to the throne. The content and outcome of the conference debate on this issue reveals the intense princely fear of British encroachment on their sovereignty and status.[24] Their obsession with such trespassing had deep roots that were traceable back to the treaty demands of Wellesley and Hastings and the annexationist policy of Dalhousie. The participants at the 1916 conference were anxious to prevent any future arrangements that would, in reality or even in appearance, concede any prerogative or symbol of sovereignty and to revise, wherever possible, existing practices considered to be infringements on their position as rulers. This pervading concern with their relationship with the British government gradually would obfuscate the political vision of the princes and would lead them to misjudge the relative present and future strength of the British and the Indian nationalist challenges to their position.

The princely concern with ceremony was often reinforced by the outlook and actions of British officials from the viceroy down to the local political agent. Examples of this concern are numerous, but two from the top and the bottom of the official hierarchy will suffice. During the Imperial Durbar of 1911, Lord Hardinge judged the gaekwar of Baroda to have committed a grievous insult by the latter's performance of a perfunctory bow before the king-emperor and then not walking away backward for the required number of steps.[25] At the opposite end of the scale, E. M. Forster has recounted how a local political officer showed his disapproval of Forster's position in Dewas Junior as tutor to the minor prince. During the course of an official visit to the state, the political officer refused to offer the ceremonial gifts of *pan* and *attar* to Forster, though they were given to other state officials.[26] Isolated from the new political realities of British India and surrounded by such British representatives, the princes naturally came to place undue emphasis on ceremonial aspects of their status.

Through the medium of the conference, Delhi had hoped to mend their relations with a loyal ally and to increase the usefulness of such an ally in a period of political tension. Labeling the conference "a weird assembly ranging in ideas from the 20th to the 16th century,"[27] Chelmsford considered it successful because it certainly had elicited princely opinions, even if they were offensive to the government.[28] Wood elaborated on this favorable judgment, arguing that the attitudes expressed could serve as guidelines in formulating policies. He also stressed the educative value, since the princes were learning to express their views clearly and to defend them.[29] Once again Delhi showed more concern than London about the need to widen the political horizons and skills of the princes.

The secretary of state was less positive in his assessment of the conference and more concerned about the problems it created. After consulting with his staff, Chamberlain sent a highly critical letter to Chelmsford. He began by questioning whether the viceroy had been aware of the views of Morley about the difficulties associated with a Council of Princes and by hinting that the Political Department was derelict in its duty to keep him informed on such matters. He also thought that the Political Department could have avoided problems by being more careful in the selection of topics for discussion and in the phrasing of the government's position on them. He addressed a further rebuke to Sir John Wood when he argued that the views of the Government of India could be presented more effectively by someone other than the presiding officer.[30]

Moving with unusual dispatch, Chelmsford defended his government and its officers against Chamberlain's complaints. Chelmsford declared that he had been aware of Morley's views but that the Conference of Princes convened in 1916 was vastly different from the Council of Princes proposed in 1908.[31] Next the viceroy defended Wood's handling of the conference. He pointed out that the conference was a unique gathering of leaders who had little or no familiarity with the rules of procedure governing such meetings and were unaccustomed to having their opinions questioned. Therefore one had to expect certain irregularities and procedural difficulties. Finally, Chelmsford deemed himself fortunate that only one serious problem had arisen and declared that he was not afraid of the consequences of a decided answer to the problem. He further argued that perhaps the British policy in the past had suffered from too much fluidity of opinion and utterance and that now might be the time for some definite policy statements.[32]

Meanwhile, Ganga Singh of Bikaner, in London for the

Imperial War Conference during the spring of 1917, lobbied with the chary secretary of state. The Rajput prince first explained that he and his peers were disturbed by British encroachment on their sovereignty and prestige and had chosen the issue of succession and its accompanying ceremonies as the one on which to fight. He also pressed for the continuation of the Conference of Princes. Either his reputed charm or the persistence of Delhi persuaded Chamberlain to concede privately to Chelmsford that the Government of India might have to accede to the demand for annual conferences. He remained concerned about the princely "tendency to meddle with the affairs of British India and, when collected at Simla, to become tools of the opposition to . . . Government,"[33] and cautioned the viceroy to restrict the scope of princely gatherings by rigorous control over the topics chosen for discussion.

Prospects for the 1917 Conference

Although Delhi and London had yet to resolve all the problems raised by the 1916 conference and were uncertain as to their precise objectives for future conferences, Chelmsford proposed another princely assemblage for late 1917. Chamberlain extended a grudging approval of the project but requested a copy of the agenda as soon as possible. Apparently the secretary of state thought that his staff would be more successful in eliminating agenda items that might serve as sources of controversy than the viceroy's staff had been in arranging the 1916 conference. There was no basis for Chamberlain's anxiety, for though the princes had suggested several items for consideration at the conference, the Government of India refused to admit any of them and chose such inoffensive questions as the quality of horsebreeding in the states, the need to collect accurate agricultural statistics, and the licenses of motor cars belonging to the princes.[34] Maharaja Jey Singh of Alwar later commented to Chamberlain's successor as secretary of state, Edwin Montagu, that "someone may have tested the Conference idea with a bad agenda deliberately to see whether any chiefs turned up."[35]

The unexpected, dramatic change at the India Office in the summer of 1917 had breathed a new atmosphere of anticipation among Indians, princes and nationalists alike, about future British policy toward India. When the report of the Mesopotamian Commission, critical of the Indian administration for some of its policies concerning units involved in that campaign, was issued in 1917, Chamberlain resigned to maintain parliamentary tradition even though there was no evidence of any error of judgment on his part. Montagu was a very different individual from his predecessor, quick to judge and to act but satisfied by his own opinions, sympathetic to a wide variety of individuals but antagonistic toward those he deemed pompous or overbearing. Previously undersecretary of state for India from 1910 to 1914, Montagu had first toured India in the cold weather of 1912–13 and had established informal contacts with a wide variety of Indians, including many of the more prominent Indian princes, whom he visited in their respective states.

While preparations were continuing for the 1917 conference, Montagu, in August 1917, made his often-quoted statement on self-government as the goal of Indian constitutional development. At the same time he announced that he would go to India to assess personally the situation and then recommend appropriate constitutional reforms jointly with the viceroy. Unfortunately for the princes, their 1917 conference was scheduled to conclude just before Montagu's arrival in Delhi. Logistical problems rendered it impossible to change the dates of Montagu's arrival or of the conference. Chelmsford, nonetheless, assured the princes that there would be an opportunity for the princes to meet with him and Montagu.[36]

Although the Government of India was perfunctory in its preparations for the conference, the maharaja of Bikaner was more active than ever in his efforts to generate princely enthusiasm and sent an exhortatory letter urging the princes to attend both the informal sessions beforehand and the conference. To reinforce his plea, Bikaner pressed other regionally prominent princes such as the maharaja of Patiala to contact princes in their respective areas and to urge them to respond to Bikaner's circular.[37] In a subsequent letter to Patiala, Ganga Singh promoted the discussion at the preliminary meetings of an item not on the formal agenda by advocating

> the desirability of our discussing the all important question as regards the position of the Indian States in the constitution of the British Empire as a whole and the Indian Empire in particular. Your Highness is aware that one of the most important things in this connection is the question of the Council of Princes which, I think, will very substantially improve our position in a great many ways and contribute largely in assigning to us a definite and substantial place constitutionally. . . . My idea, if you approve it, is that we should thoroughly discuss this question when we meet at Delhi before the Conference actually opens.[38]

Besides prompting other Punjab princes to channel their views through Bikaner, Bhupinder Singh also addressed himself to the matter of the princely position in the Indian Empire. In a subsequent letter to Bikaner, he proposed the establishment of a multilevel organization to increase the scope and depth of the annual conferences. This organization would include provincial groupings of princes, a general subcommittee of princes, and a central office with a paid full-time secretary. Besides providing continuity between conferences and aggregating regional support, Patiala reasoned that the central office could keep the princes informed of events in British India, thereby enabling them to consider measures necessitated by developments in British India to maintain their prestige and to secure their interests.[39]

An episode in this correspondence between Bikaner and Patiala reveals that even these two astute autocrats were plagued by an unwillingness to sacrifice their own personal convenience for the general good of their order. Bikaner had requested the loan of the services of Daya Kishan Kaul, Patiala's *diwan*, or prime minister, to assist in the drafting of the princely resolutions to be presented at the 1917 conference, but the Punjab prince replied that Kaul could not be spared because he was engaged in urgent state business. After a second appeal from the insistent Rajput, Patiala revealed that the pressing affairs were his birthday celebration and the Dussehra durbar.[40]

Disappointment at the 1917 Conference

At their informal meetings on 3-4 November 1917, the princes expressed great concern over the issue of precedence at social functions and ranking of princes by salutes. Under the old policy of isolation, questions of precedence were dormant, since each prince was without peers within his own territories and he rarely had occasion to meet anyone of higher rank except for the formal viceregal visits and great imperial durbars. As they began to meet more frequently with each other and with British officials, many princes became apprehensive of their prestige as they were placed below some brother ruler or British official in a receiving line or at a dining table. After much deliberation the consensus reached was that the issue of social precedence could not be settled until there had been a general rationalization of the salutes and hereditary titles of all princes.[41] Because its haphazard growth had created many anomalous relationships, the salute table was considered unsuitable as a basis for determining social precedence.

Although many princes pushing for a revision of the salute table were from the middle ranks and stood to gain from such changes, their request for reform presented an excellent opportunity to clarify a confused arrangement. In their dilatory manner the Political Department of the Government of India postponed any consideration of revision until after the termination of the Great War. In 1919, harassed by the rising nationalists, involved with demobilization, and burdened with financial problems, the Government of India was still not willing to make any major alterations and distributed salute increases as war rewards in random fashion. The salute table, consequently, remained a source of irritation to, and bickering among, the princes when they might have been concentrating on more pressing matters. By 1922 the viceroy, Lord Reading, argued that

> the question of precedence between Princes in so far as it is at present unsolved must remain insoluble, unless we are prepared to come to, and act upon, our own conclusions, for the Princes will never agree. . . . I cannot but think that we shall bring a hornet's nest about ourselves if we attempt to do that which hitherto has proved impossible, and that, unsatisfactory as it is, it is better to leave this matter where it is.[42]

Despite the dull agenda, princes—forty-six as compared with forty-one in 1916—attended the 1917 conference. Chelmsford quickly set a tone of stifling caution in his opening address on 5 November. With regard to minority administrations, Chelmsford declared that due regard would be given to a prince's wishes, but that the government was free to accept, reject, or modify such proposals after careful consideration. The wide powers enjoyed by the political officer in his capacity as guardian of the interests of the state were also emphasized. On the matter of succession Chelmsford reiterated that recognition by the king-emperor was necessary for a valid succession. To soften this pronouncement, the viceroy conceded that the phraseology describing this power in the 1916 memorandum had been inept and agreed that installation and investiture durbars should be held in the name of the prince.[43] On such occasions the British representative would be seated at the right hand of the presiding prince as the chief honored guest.

The tiresome disagreement between the princes and the British over these two questions of minority administrations and succession procedures were not disputes over substance. These skirmishes had significance as illustrations of the swelling concern of the princes over symbols of sovereignty as they sensed their internal autonomy being steadily eroded. Modern communications and transportation networks, an increasingly centralized British administrative structure, and the demands of some Indian political leaders were the main princely antagonists, but they were also more inaccessible targets for princely attacks. For their part the British tried to keep concessions to the minimum necessary to retain princely good will and confined them largely to ceremonial gestures that had meaning for the British as well as the princes. Meanwhile, the British would continue to tender advice and oversee minority administrations and to regulate successions much as they had done beforehand, and the princes would seek other channels for the alleviation of their grievances.

Immediately after the closing speeches of the 1917 conference, the princes present in Delhi held an informal session on 10 November. Here they elected a Committee of Four—Bikaner, Alwar, Patiala, and Nawanagar—to draft a scheme of proposals to be presented to Montagu during his Indian tour. The committee was authorized to consult past and present ministers from the states and anyone else they considered likely to be helpful. Once a tentative statement was framed, it was to be submitted by correspondence to all princes for their comments and criticism. After collating the replies, the committee was to hammer out a final version that would be fully representative of princely sentiments. Then a delegation of princes would present their program to Montagu and Chelmsford in a major interview.[44] Now, for the first time, the princes were joining the ranks of interest groups who sought to further the position of their respective membership when concessions were to be granted by the imperial patron. Although the 1917 conference had failed to provide a vital channel of communication between the government and its princely clients, it did provide opportunities for the gathered princes to consider privately critical matters.

Montagu and the Princes

On the next day, 11 November, Montagu arrived at Bombay and proceeded directly to Delhi. Shortly afterward he wrote in his diary:

> I have only been here two days; all the Indian Chiefs have called on me and talked to me as a friend, and I have got far more out of them than the Viceroy got in ten days of Conference. They asked for interviews; interviews were granted them of ten minutes each because it was not considered that anything but formal interviews were necessary. They have all come back unofficially, and we have an hour and a half or three-quarters of an hour together at odd times, and they talk to me as they never dare to talk to anyone else.[45]

These unofficial conversations and interviews continued as Montagu stopped in princely states for respites from the never ending schedule of official interviews and receptions that greeted him throughout his tour of the British provinces. Although he met about forty princes at least once in Delhi and on tour, Montagu cultivated repeated contacts with less than a dozen of the six hundred princes of India. Most prominent in this select circle were Alwar, Gwalior, Bikaner, Patiala, Cutch, Kolhapur, Dholpur, Bhopal, and Kashmir. Many of these princes had already entertained Montagu in their states during his earlier tour of India and were active participants in the recent princely conferences. Although he characterized all of them in complimentary tones in his diary, the activist secretary of state considered Jey Singh of Alwar to be far and away the cleverest of the princes and a real statesman who saw all difficulties in all problems. Conceding that Alwar's talk and ideas were not always of value, Montagu was strongly attracted by the range of Alwar's conversation and his charm as a tennis and hunting companion.[46] In sharp contrast to this affinity was Montagu's association with Nizam Mir Osman Ali Khan of Hyderabad. Although acknowledging that this arrogant ruler was "enormously important" to the British because of his efforts to keep the Muslims of India loyal, he paused in Hyderabad, while on his southern tour, only long enough to have lunch with the resident, Stewart Fraser, and some state officials and later met the nizam personally for a ten-minute formal interview in Delhi.[47] His own haughtiness and the antipathy of key British officials served to cut off the nizam from effective participation in the debate over the future constitutional status of the Indian princes.

At the outset of his unprecedented tour of India, Montagu outlined his ideas on a possible policy toward the Indian states. His program included (1) a council of princes presided over by the viceroy to discuss general affairs of states, with the princes as well as the viceroy suggesting items for the agenda; (2) upon the invitation of the viceroy, this council could sit with the upper chamber of the Indian legislature to discuss imperial questions such as customs duties or the war effort; (3) an advisory council of four princes associated with the political secretary to advise the viceroy on matters dealing with the states; (4) two disinterested members of this council plus a judge and a political officer to sit as a tribunal to settle interstate disputes; (5) abolition of agents to the governor general and strict instruction to residents to prefer persuasion over blunt orders to avoid further estrangement of the princes from the government; (6) the separation of the Political Office from the Foreign Office.[48] Some of these items, namely the council of princes, the abolition of AGGs, and the separation of the Political Office, were carry-overs from Montagu's policy recommendations on the princes framed during his first tour of India.[49] When princes suggested the establishment of a council of princes or advisory councils, they encountered someone more imaginative and adventurous than Chelmsford or Wood and someone predisposed to many of their suggestions, since they frequently paralleled Montagu's own thinking on the subject.

While the secretary of state toured Bombay and Madras, the princely Committee of Four met twice and devised a series of constitutional proposals that they then circulated to 105 princes for their comments and criticisms. The main components were (1) the maintenance of the *izzat*, or honor, and treaty rights of the princes; (2) a council or chamber of princes; (3) an advisory board of princes; (4) a judicial tribunal to settle interstate and government-state disputes; (5) commissions of inquiry to investigate charges against any princes; (6) direct relations between the states and the Government of India; (7) separate representation of princely India at Imperial Cabinet meetings; and (8) some form of coordination with the British Indian legislature. Forty-nine princes forwarded their comments. Most of them were favorable to the basic elements, but many respondents suggested modifications in the composition or functions of the proposed bodies.[50]

In order to incorporate these criticisms and further refine their scheme, the princes scheduled a third meeting at Patiala for 4-10 January 1918. They now wanted advice from constitutional experts and reactions from men active in legislative circles. Significantly, they invited ten Indian politicians as well as eleven state ministers to attend these joint deliberations "to assist us [the princes] with your mature experience and wise counsel."[51] State ministers who were recruited both from British India and the states themselves had long been prominent as proponents of political, social, and economic reform within the states. Increasingly, they would be utilized as bridges between the princes and British Indian politicians as the princes were drawn into constitutional negotiations. British Indian politicians in person were a new addition to princely caucuses, as were the caucuses themselves.

The princely desire to seek a wide range of opinion was not welcomed in all quarters. As soon as he learned of the invitations extended to Indian politicians by Patiala, Sir Michael

O'Dwyer, the lieutenant governor of Punjab and an intermediary in relations between that prince and the viceroy, sent the following protest to Delhi:

> The Native States, taken singly, cannot give us serious trouble, but by encouraging them to form themselves into a sort of trade union, we are calling into existence a formidable power which will most certainly be used to bring pressure to bear on Government, and that just at a time when far-reaching changes are in contemplation which may affect the strength of the British administration of the country. The undesirability of allowing the Chiefs to entertain visions of interference in the internal affairs of British India is sufficiently obvious, but what is perhaps not quite so obvious is that it is bound to lead to intrigue between the Chiefs and the political leaders of British India. The association of Pandit Madan Mohan Malaviya with the Committee of Chiefs is, in His Honor's opinion, of evil omen for the future.[52]

O'Dwyer further argued that the cardinal principles of isolating the princes from each other and of noninterference by the princes in the affairs of British India had been violated. To prevent added problems, O'Dwyer proposed to the Government of India that they prevail upon the men associated with the government in various capacities, namely, Ali Iman, Sinha, and Malaviya, not to attend the Patiala conclave. Moreover, O'Dwyer requested a clear statement on what were the legitimate limits of the proposals to be discussed.[53]

Although Wood and Chelmsford were annoyed that they had not been informed by the princes of the invitations to the Indian politicians, they refused to censure the princes or pressure Executive and Legislative Council members not to attend. They reasoned that this joint deliberation between the princes and politicians hopefully would be conducive to the formulation of some method of cooperation between British India and princely India on matters of common interest. Furthermore, the isolating of the princes from each other was an obsolete policy. Political conditions had altered, and the conferences at Delhi were indicative of a new policy approach to the princes. Wood had been invited to attend the Patiala sessions so he would be able to counteract any efforts at collusion against the government.[54]

By 4 January 1918 a heterogeneous group of public figures of the Indian subcontinent had assembled at Patiala. Present were the four princely committee members, various state ministers, including Manubhai Mehta and Khasherao Jadhava from Baroda, M. Visvesvaraya from Mysore, and Daya Kishen Kaul from Patiala, and Indian politicians of the first rank: N. M. Samrath, Srinavasa Shastri, Sinha, Chintamani, and Malaviya. The maharaja of Patiala inaugurated the proceedings with a presentation of the princely proposals, which were the same as those agreed upon at Bikaner with the addition of a recommendation that one place on the Viceroy's Executive Council be allotted to the native states.[55]

On succeeding days there were general discussions and private committee meetings, and eventually the opinions of the politicians were solicited. Crump, the political agent for the Phulkian states, later reported:

> From certain politicians they did not receive an enthusiastic reception in what were regarded as their efforts to get their finger into the British India pie. Indeed Mr. Samrath told them plainly that one school of thought in British India considered the Indian States anomalies and anachronisms and ripe for abolition already.[56]

In a conversation with Montagu, Wood confirmed that the views expressed by the Indian politicians at Patiala had worried the princes about what to expect next.[57] The item that appeared to arouse the most opposition from the politicians was the allotment of a seat on the Viceroy's Executive Council to the states. All the politicians present, despite their differing political stances, opposed this measure because it might take away a seat from them, was inefficient in terms of selection, and militated against the principle of responsibility of ministers to the legislature. Others from the states, such as Khasherao Jadhava, argued against this measure because it violated the principle of noninterference in each other's affairs.[58]

Even so, most of the Indian politicians present were willing to support the princes in their other proposals concerning relations between the princes and the Government of India. They assented to the proposals on the Chamber of Princes and advisory councils and even argued in favor of separate representation for the princes at the Imperial Conferences.[59]

During the remaining weeks of January, the Committee of Four worked on a final draft of their scheme. Prior to their scheduled meeting in early February with Montagu and Chelmsford, they had to face criticism from within their order, the source of the disturbance being Maharaja Ripudaman Singh of Nabha. At odds with the Punjab and Central governments over issues ranging from the ceremonies at his installation durbar to the reform of Khalsa College and with his neighbor Patiala over their rivalry for leadership within the Sikh community and assorted disputes involving their subjects, Nabha launched an agitation against "the secret machination" of the Committee of Four and the Government of India.[60] He telegraphed various princes to ask them to protest that the Committee of Four was violating its mandate and to urge the committee to present its draft scheme to a general meeting of princes for further comment before its presentation to Montagu and Chelmsford. Apparently, he did not think that written consultation was adequate. In response to Nabha's appeal the rulers of Malerkotla, Dewas Junior, and Gwalior protested to Patiala, and so Patiala and Bikaner decided to petition Wood for permission to hold another meeting of the princes.[61] Their request was refused because of lack of accommodation in Delhi, but this excuse would not repair the damage done by Nabha's accusation that the Committee of Four was becoming unrepresentative of the princes in general. This situation was complicated by ominous signs in the other camp. On 30 January 1918 Montagu recorded in his diary:

> In the afternoon I had a long sitting with Chelmsford and Wood about the princes. It was not at all satisfactory. They want to leave everything in a very wooly condition, and I am not at all sure that it is not true that we shall have to be very indefinite in our recommendations. The great thing is to show the way. Wood is particularly of the school which wants to keep the princes in cold storage.[62]

On 4 February 1918 Chelmsford presided with Montagu over a historic meeting, noteworthy because, for the first time during the British *raj*, the princes were being consulted as a group about their problems when there was an assessment of the general situation in British India.[63] The two British officials spent two days in discussion with the princes and accepted the proposals on the Chamber of Princes, the advisory committee, and direct access to the Government of India, preferably through the agents to the governor general. They agreed to push the request for separate representation for the princes at Imperial Conferences and accepted, after redrafting, the proposal on commissions of inquiry and judicial tribunals. The last item considered was the plea for joint cooperation with British India. Chelmsford opened this discussion with the warning "Here we come on to very dangerous ground,"[64] after which inauspicious beginning the debate foundered and ended inconclusively. The most radical part of the scheme was on its way to a quick demise. Caution and the reluctance to tackle difficult constitutional issues were dominant in the British sphere.

Disagreement within the British Hierarchy over the Princes

After the meetings Wood prepared a memorandum on which proposals with regard to the princes should be included in the final report by Montagu and Chelmsford. Montagu was very critical of this memorandum, particularly of its hesitancy and vagueness. His first complaint was that it made the Chamber seem to be a creation of the viceroy. To remedy this defect, Montagu wanted greater initiative to be given to the princes in calling of the Chamber and the formulation of the agenda. Second, Montagu argued for more explicit statements on the method of joint cooperation and the composition and functions of the advisory committee, the judicial tribunals, and the commission of inquiry. Montagu claimed that Wood's memorandum gave far less than was promised at the February meetings with the princes and that the princes would not be satisfied with less. In his concluding paragraph of his letter of complaint to Chelmsford, Montagu made a revealing comment: "I need not remind you that, after all, we owe a greater,—or at any rate as great,—a debt to the Princes than to British India, and it is equally incumbent upon us to try and satisfy them."[65]

Yet less than three weeks after Montagu sent this letter to Chelmsford, Wood forwarded a draft agenda for the 1918 conference to Bikaner and advised him that the questions of direct relations with the Government of India and joint cooperation with British India were not included on the agenda because of their delicate nature.[66] Delhi, particularly the political secretary, resisted successfully the pressure from Montagu to respond positively to the expressed hope of the princes for some form of joint consultation. This episode along with future ones should have warned the princes that there was a widening gap between what might be promised and what would be delivered.

Princely Disunity

To add to the predicament of the princes who were seeking constitutional adjustments, there was acrimonious debate within their own ranks over the political wisdom of their goals and methods. Here rational disagreement was sharpened by personal vanities and rivalries. When the Committee of Four first started their work, Nizam Mir Osman Ali Khan of Hyderabad refused to be associated with their endeavors. His decision was in accord with his policy "to avoid assuming outside his own Dominions any public capacity or position which may involve him in communal politics or which may make him the centre of factional controversy; or which may lay on him responsibilities of a personal nature." He later explained that this policy enabled him "to maintain an aloofness or isolation which is as necessary to his prestige as it is in keeping with his high position."[67] Here is a striking example of the princely willingness to sacrifice unity to personal ambition and pride.

As their discussions proceeded, the Committee of Four was attacked from the outside and undermined from within. As earlier noted, Ripudaman Singh of Nabha, largely motivated by personal antipathy toward Patiala and the British, had launched his campaign to discredit the Committee of Four and had been moderately successful in acquiring princely supporters. After the committee sidestepped this challenge and presented their recommendations to Montagu and Chelmsford, Maharaja Ganga Singh of Bikaner was unable to obtain the approval of Alwar and Nawanagar on the reports of these February sessions. The former pleaded that he had to go on a shooting trip before he could consider the matter, and the latter never bothered to respond.[68] Eventually, a disgusted Bikaner issued the report over his own signature. Here the aversion of Alwar for his Rajput rival and the apathy of Nawanagar served to prevent the formation of even a facade of unity among a select group of princes at a critical juncture.

Implementation of Recommendations in Montagu-Chelmsford Report

Once Montagu returned to London and the Montagu-Chelmsford Report was issued in April 1918, the Government of India faced the complex tasks connected with the implementation of the recommendations of the report. Two areas of concern to the princes aroused intense controversy and made implementation a dilatory, difficult process. One controversy centered on the establishment of direct relations between the Government of India and all major states, and the other one arose over the question of eligibility for membership in the Chamber of Princes.

During the remainder of 1918 the Political Department of the Government of India corresponded with the local governments about the transfer of major states from provincial to central jurisdiction. Prior to this time only four states, Hyderabad, Mysore, Kashmir, and Baroda, conducted their relations with the Government of India directly through residents appointed to their capitals. All other states maintained contact through local political officers who reported either to a nearby provincial governor or to an AGG. In order to reduce the labyrinth of intermediaries that had arisen between the viceroy and most princes, the Montagu-Chelmsford Report proposed a change whereby princes would communicate with agents appointed by, and directly responsible to, the political secretary in Delhi.[69] It was further argued that such a measure was particularly appropriate because further devolution of responsibility to the local governments would render them unsuitable as agents of the Government of India in matters related to the states. There was the general feeling that an effort should be made to prevent any direct confrontations between the princes and the popularly elected officials, who would become increasingly prominent within the provincial governments under the dyarchy scheme.

Local governments, such as Assam, Bengal, and the United Provinces, who controlled few states were neutral in their responses. Those, however, who controlled large numbers of states, particularly the Punjab and Bombay governments, strongly remonstrated against the proposed transfer. Lord Willingdon, the governor of Bombay, refused even to discuss the matter, so Chelmsford postponed further talks with the Bombay government until George Lloyd succeeded Willingdon as governor in December 1918.[70] Unfortunately Lloyd proved to be almost as hostile to such a step as Willingdon had been. His opposition was based on the complexity of the state situation in Bombay, which made it difficult to separate the states into categories, and the loss of political ballast to the Bombay government that would result from such a decrease in firmly dominated territory.[71] Shortly before his departure from India, Chelmsford agreed to a brief postponement of the transfer because of the complexities involved.[72] His successor, Lord Reading, was left to discuss the issue *ad nauseam* with Lloyd until the first step was taken in late 1923.[73]

Sir Michael O'Dwyer was the second tenacious opponent of the transfer of states from provincial to central control. In repeated letters and interviews he argued that such a transfer of Punjab states would disrupt administrative affairs such as the operation of the canal system, the excise collection, and the maintenance of roads, cause the disintegration of the Sikh nation, reduce the political value of the states at critical periods, and result in a loss of political prestige for the Punjab government. He further reasoned that the interlocking territories of the Punjab states and Punjab province would make the implementation of administrative changes related to the transfer most complicated.[74] J. P. Thompson, chief secretary to the Punjab government, added that O'Dwyer's previous extensive political experience as resident in Hyderabad and agent to the governor general in central India lent further weight to the lieutenant governor's objections.[75]

In spite of O'Dwyer's numerous objections and his persistence in reiterating them, the Government of India repeated its request for a tentative scheme from the Punjab government for the transfer of the Punjab states.[76] On 12 October 1918 Thompson forwarded a scheme which advised that all states having salutes and maintaining Imperial Service troops should be transferred. Their single intermediary would be an AGG, who would have his headquarters in Lahore. As irrepressible as his superior, Thompson concluded this letter with the query, Why should the existing system be changed when it had worked so well?[77] Despite this remonstrance the Political Department in Delhi decided to push ahead with the proposed transfers but with greater caution. Later, some of Chelmsford's own council became apprehensive about this policy because of the additional load that would be placed on the already overburdened Political Department.[78]

The task of the Political Department was further complicated by the vacillation of the princes. At the February 1918 meeting in Delhi, the princes had generally supported the demand for direct relations with the Government of India;[79] but once they returned to their own capitals, they began to waver in their support of this proposal. Some claimed that their local political agents exerted a restraining influence, and others questioned the benefits of the proposed change.

The maharaja of Patiala, unexpectedly, was a prime example of this ambivalence. In January 1919 Chelmsford prodded him to meet with other Punjab princes and the Punjab government in order to rally support for direct relations. The Sikh prince did nothing for almost eleven months, and only in November did he meet with his cabinet and later with his neighboring peers on the issue.[80] Finally, on 19 December 1919, the Punjab princes assembled with Sir Edward Maclagan, O'Dwyer's successor as lieutenant governor of Punjab, and lobbied for the establishment of direct relations. The princes countered the earlier arguments of the Punjab government by declaring that a Sikh remained a Sikh regardless of political boundaries, that the canal system and excise collection operated under well-defined regulations and would continue to do so, that the princes would remain loyal to the government regardless of their administrative ties, and that changes must be made now to keep pace with the changes in the Indian constitution.[81] Attacked on two fronts and now led by a man desirous of conciliation, the Punjab government modified its tactics and advocated direct relations with the lieutenant governor acting as an AGG.[82] The Government of India, however, was not in a bargaining mood, and established in 1921 an independent agent to the governor general who would be responsible for the conduct of its relations with all the Punjab states that were eligible for entry to the Chamber of Princes.

This episode over direct relations highlights the internal divisions within the governmental structure that caused the British Government of India to expend so much time and energy in internal negotiations in order to project a facade of unity. It also illustrates the difficulties encountered in effecting changes within a complex imperial bureaucracy. Improved communications and transportation tightened central control, but individuals still implemented policy. Montagu and Chelmsford might evolve a plan, but Willingdon, Lloyd, and O'Dwyer could influence its impact by their delaying tactics. Such men as O'Dwyer who led British official opposition to provisions for British Indian provinces in the Montagu-Chelmsford Report could also reduce the extent of change in the final legislation. Lastly this incident reveals that both local and central governments thought that the princes were useful enough as allies to quarrel over them. The princes still brought value in the coin of stability and prestige.

The second major debate with regard to the Montagu-Chelmsford proposals on the princes arose over the composition of the proposed Chamber of Princes.[83] Various aspects of this controversy reveal much about relationships among the members of the princely order.

Since there were over six hundred princes in India, it was evident that not all could be conveniently included in the proposed assembly. At first Chelmsford and Montagu had suggested that all princes who possessed "full powers of internal sovereignty" would be eligible for membership. After several unsuccessful efforts to define and to apply this phrase to concrete cases, Chelmsford decided that a more precise criterion would be the salute table and so declared that all princes with a permanent salute of eleven guns or higher would be eligible for membership.[84] This norm proved hardly less troublesome because of the anomalies in the salute table. Many nine-gun princes complained that they had greater resources and fuller powers than eleven-gun princes. Chelmsford, therefore, promised some revisions in the salute table, but in spite of these revisions some of the more articulate smaller princes were apprehensive about their future status. The Bombay area princes met to organize their demands for adequate safeguards,[85] and other smaller chiefs appealed to the leading figures in the Chamber movement like Bikaner and Patiala to protect their interests. Because he wanted to strengthen the representative character of the Chamber, Bikaner played the role of the tireless champion of the smaller rulers. He argued that the Chamber must include these people because they would not be eligible for the safeguards granted, for example, to the large landholders of British India. Excluded from the Chamber, they would be relegated to a constitutional limbo.[86] After much deliberation between Political Department officers and various princes, a compromise was effected whereby 127 smaller princes elected twelve from among their ranks to represent their particular interests in the Chamber.

Princely Opposition to the Chamber

For other reasons the most important princes remained aloof from the proposed assembly and thereby further undermined its claims to be a representative institution. The most prominent recluse was the nizam of Hyderabad, who refused to attend any of the conferences in Delhi and rejected all overtures from the Bikaner-Patiala group. Montagu alleged that the nizam was conscious of his own incompetence and therefore preferred written communications expressing his views, since they could be prepared by his minister or even the resident.[87] The nizam advanced quite different reasons for his attitude, declaring that his position as the premier prince of India, which had been recently reconfirmed by the title of "Exalted Highness and Faithful Ally" from the king-emperor, precluded an association with lesser princes that would tarnish his status. Moreover, as Sir Ali Imam, the prime minister of Hyderabad, confided to the resident, the nizam feared that his brother princes might fail to pay him proper respect.[88] Hyderabad was not alone in his anxiety that his prestige would be diminished by meeting with his brother autocrats. The maharana of Udaipur, the premier Rajput prince, did not attend the Chamber because of the question of precedence,[89] and central Indian states such as Gwalior and some Bombay states who had feudatory states subordinate to them wanted definite assurances that this feudatory relationship would not be prejudiced if they participated with their feudatory states in the same assembly.[9] Even among those princes who had attended the conferences, Chelmsford had noted that they carefully scrutinized the location of their chairs in relation to those of other princes so that they would not lower their prestige by sitting next to a prince of inferior status.[91]

The hostile attitude of many princes toward the Chamber was reinforced and in some instances possibly initiated by the counsels of certain members of the Political Department. In March 1919 Montague wrote to Chelmsford:

> I wish I could think that we have a fair field with the five chiefs who held aloof from the Conference but all the information that reaches me gives me more reason to suspect that it is mainly their Political Agents who, for reasons of their own, have set themselves to oppose what we desire to do, and to use their influence with their Chiefs against their co-operation with their brother Chiefs.[92]

In reply to an earlier letter making the same accusation, Chelmsford advised Montagu that such actions had been confined to central India, where the presence of princes with feudatory states had made the situation exceedingly complex. Some princes, particularly in central India, had sought the advice of their political agents, who gave them frank opinions that were not necessarily favorable to the Chamber.[93] At a later date Wood conceded in a telegram to Charles Russell, the resident at Hyderabad, that Delhi thought the nizam's intransigent attitude toward the Chamber might be partly due to the advice of Russell's predecessor.[94]

Besides the issue of prestige there was a fear among many of the larger princes that their proposals would be swamped in an assembly that operated on the principle of one man, one vote. The maharaja of Kolhapur even suggested that princes such as Hyderabad and Mysore should be given multiple votes to attract them to the Chamber,[95] but the Government of India was unreceptive to this scheme and as a matter of policy decided not to press the princes to attend the Chamber if they were disinclined to do so.[96] Since most of the nineteen- and twenty-one-gun princes, such as Hyderabad, Mysore, Indore, and Baroda, chose to stay away from the Chamber, it remained vulnerable to the criticism that it was unrepresentative.[97]

Although less disruptive than the conflict between the larger and smaller states, another rivalry based on regional and religious differences hindered the formation of a united, representative Chamber. It appears that the Maratha and the Muslim states were apprehensive of domination by Rajput princes, who were in a definite numerical majority and enjoyed strong leadership from Bikaner and Alwar. It was further alleged that the Sikh states were willing to join such a Chamber because of their ancient tributary status under the British government.[98] Although there is evidence that Rajput and Sikh princes did tend to dominate debates during the conferences and later in the Chamber, there existed sharp rivalries between Rajputs such as Bikaner and Alwar and between Sikhs such as Patiala and Nabha that rendered their majority position more vulnerable than might have appeared from the outside.

Establishment of the Chamber of Princes

The next regular session of the Conference of Princes was held in Delhi in November 1919. For the first time Chelmsford's opening speech touched on items of immediate concern and possible controversy. Although he carefully qualified his remarks, Chelmsford called for progress in the states to meet the difficulties arising after the war. Chelmsford counseled the assembled princes:

> As to the lines on which progress is to take place, Your Highnesses must decide for themselves with due regard to local circumstances and sentiment. . . . I would counsel you in the first place to determine that whatever measures of reform may be introduced shall be substantial. . . .
>
> In the second place I advise you in planning additions, to maintain the fabric of your society and preserve its substructure and its solid walls, pillars and towers.[99]

Chelmsford also announced the formation of a Committee on Codification of Political Practice that would seek to identify sources of princely grievance and then to define political practices that would handle the problem in such a manner as to eliminate the source of irritation.[100] Composed of both princes and officials, this committee represented a distinct break with past policy and a positive effort to eliminate petty obstacles to friendlier relations between the princes and the government.[101] Once the Chamber of Princes was established, its Standing Committee would take over the functions of the Codification Committee.

There was no general conference of princes held in 1920 because the Government of India was occupied with attempting to contain Gandhi's noncooperation movement and to channel political activity into the expanded Legislative Councils. The abridgment of the recommendations of the Montagu-Chelmsford Report into the provisions of the Indian Councils Act of 1919, the firing at Amritsar followed by the callousness and racial bias of the Hunter Report on this incident, the harsh peace terms imposed on Turkey, all aggravated the disillusionment of Indian nationalists with British institutions and promises. To counter the radicalization of the Indian nationalist movement, the Government of India moved to launch the promised constitutional reforms with appropriate displays of pomp and power. The prince of Wales was originally scheduled to preside at the inauguration of the Imperial Legislative Assembly and the Chamber of Princes. When his visit to India had to be delayed for reasons of health, his uncle, the duke of Connaught, initiated the two assemblies in February 1921.

As the self-proclaimed successor to the Mughal Empire, the Government of India thought it fitting to hold the inauguration of the Chamber of Princes within the walls of Shah Jahan's Red Fort in Delhi. Chelmsford later recounted to Montagu that

> the ceremony of the Inauguration of the Chamber of Princes was exceedingly effective. The setting of the old fort and palace gave a wonderful background to the proceedings. . . . His Royal Highness (the Duke of Connaught) and I took our places on a platform built out from the edge of the Diwan-i-Am and faced the great throng. Fortunately the acoustic qualities of the shamiana were quite excellent, and I understand that His Highness's speech was heard by everyone. It was admirably delivered and contained the personal touch which he has so skillfully embodied in all the speeches that he has made during his visit.[102]

The formal proceedings of this opening session of the Chamber of Princes followed the familiar pattern established at the earlier conferences. On the one hand, the duke of Connaught delivered the royal message inaugurating the Chamber and thanked the princes for their generous support during the Great War. Next Chelmsford traced the evolution of the Chamber and assured the princes from larger states that participation in it would not lower their position or prestige. The princes then discussed the report of their committee on the representation of smaller states, debated whether and how minority administrations should be heard in the Chamber, and elected a chancellor and a Standing Committee. It was not a surprise that Ganga Singh of Bikaner became the first chancellor and that the Standing Committee was composed of rulers from north of the Narbada River—Gwalior from central India, Patiala from Punjab, Cutch, Nawanagar, and Palanpur from western India, and Jhalawar from Rajputana. If social origins are considered, the Rajput element was dominant, since four out of seven were acknowledged as Rajputs.[103]

The Chamber of Princes was an innovation in British policy toward their autocratic collaborators and formally ended the earlier practice of isolation. This body would be a vehicle by which some princes could weave alliances among their peers, lobby with British officials, acquire some deliberative experience, and maintain a group status in future constitutional negotiations. It was, however, a timid solution to a complex problem that required bolder initiatives.[104] Moreover, Delhi had carefully limited its structure and functions, and princely rivalries and concern for *izzat* had reduced its representativeness and potential effectiveness.

For the princes the Chamber was only a partial response to their quest for constitutional boons. In several areas the British had backed away from princely proposals, especially the one for joint consulation with British India. The princes had stated this particular plea in nebulous terms, had underestimated the difficulty in restricting such meetings to topics that they deemed appropriate, and had been overly optimistic about the likely results. Still, if the British had seized this opening, they might have provided the opportunity for common deliberative experiences that would have created some basis for a future federation. Such contacts would have intensified princely exposure to political developments in British India and possibly provided more leverage to those, both British and Indian, who wanted to promote political reform within the states.

Meanwhile, some of the princes who were most involved in the Chamber began to look beyond constitutional safeguards to secure their positions. They were alarmed by the shift in leadership among the Indian nationalists, the radicalization of demands being voiced in British India, and the growing attention that nationalists and their own subjects focused on their administrations. In the turmoil of postwar India, they would be quick to emphasize their value as political allies and to ask for political safeguards for their persons and administrations from the British and from their allies in British Indian politics.

chapter four

Political Allies and Communal Leaders 1918–1922

> Amritsar shops opened yesterday, all quiet Lahore. Martial law proclaimed. City quiet still occupied by troops. Gujranwala aeroplane paid two visits and used bombs. . . . Patiala, Jind, Nabha, Kapurthala, Bahawalpur all rendering valuable assistance. Please make this known and also contradict rumours of damage having been done to Golden Temple. . . .[1]

Thus, on 16 April 1919, the British government at Lahore informed Delhi of the aid rendered by the Punjab princes in the tense days following the Jallianwala Bagh incident. This tragic episode occurred as one consequence of Mahatma Gandhi's effort to launch a moral protest against a government policy that he considered immoral, the Rowlatt Bills, which were to continue wartime restrictions on certain civil liberties after the end of hostilities. Contrary to Gandhi's plans and aspirations, violence erupted in Punjab during a *hartal* and provoked the British to impose marital law. On 13 April a protest meeting was held in Amritsar within the confines of a walled garden known as Jallianwala Bagh. When the assembled crowd was unable to disperse upon being advised that they were in violation of martial law regulation, General Reginald Dyer ordered his men to fire. The casualties totaled about 380 dead and 1,200 wounded.[2] In the aftermath of this confrontation, which shattered the trust and respect of many nationalists in the British government,[3] the princes revealed clearly their willingness to serve as political allies of the paramount power and as intermediaries with their religious brethren.

As the premier Sikh and most ambitious Punjab prince, the maharaja of Patiala was the dominant, but also a typical, figure among his Punjab brothers. In a broad sense, he and the others acted to support the British *raj* in three ways. First, they deployed their Imperial Service troops to guard the main railway and telegraph lines wherever they crossed state territory. This action was especially helpful in a region in which state territories did not form compact groupings but rather were scattered throughout the British Indian province of Punjab. In order to coordinate his efforts more closely with British tactics, Patiala personally maintained contact with the British general officer commanding at Ambala, a key military and communications center in Punjab. Second, Patiala, Nabha, and Jind, all Sikh rulers, distributed Urdu and Gurmukhi propaganda to combat the rumor that the Golden Temple, a major center of the Sikh religion at Amritsar, had been bombed. Third, the princes arrested political suspects sought by the British and extradited them with a minimum of legal formality.[4]

The viceroy directly requested another form of assistance. On 17 April Lord Chelmsford wrote privately to the maharajas of Patiala, Nabha, Jind, Baroda, and the nawab of Malerkotla requesting their aid in the suppression of any disturbances in British districts contiguous to their states as well as in the preservation of tranquility within their own domains. Once again it should be noted that all these princes ruled over territories widely dispersed in the British Indian provinces of Punjab and Bombay. As a consequence, any aid they would give in controlling agitations along their borders would cover a much more extensive area than if they were ruling compact geographical entities. All those petitioned agreed to apply themselves and the resources of their administrations to the maintenance of law and order, though the gaekwar of Baroda was less zealous in his offer of support than were the Punjab princes.[5] Chelmsford even received an unsolicited expression of sympathy and offer of assistance from Maharao Raja Raghubir Singh of Bundi, a physically isolated and politically conservative but historically important Rajput ruler.[6]

The above occurrences during April 1919 mark a new phase in the evolution of the princes as imperial politicians. During World War I, when the British Empire in India was threatened by external dangers in an unprecedented manner, many princes had been quick to respond in their well-established role as military allies of their imperial patron. A few princes—most notably, Alwar, Bikaner, Gwalior, Nawanagar, and Patiala—had begun to attend assorted imperial conferences and organizations related to the war effort. This small group also had started to enter all-India politics on an *ad hoc* basis usually as political allies of the British *raj* but sometimes as spokesmen for their respective religious communities. Now during the crucial postwar era when changes within British Indian society and politics were creating an even more potent challenge to the continuation of British rule in India, certain princes became increasingly active in an effort to render political support to their hard-pressed overlord.

By 1919 in the sphere of British Indian politics, an older generation of nationalist leaders such as Pherozeshah Mehta, G. K. Gokhale, and B. G. Tilak was being superseded by a younger, more activist cadre including such luminaries as C. R. Das, Motilal and Jawaharlal Nehru, and M. K. Gandhi. More impatient and more self-confident than their predecessors, this latter group sought to transform postwar political, social, and economic discontent among varied groups of Indians into potent instruments of organized opposition to British rule. Their dissatisfaction with the long-awaited postwar constitutional reforms and their resentment toward British policies as exhibited in the Rowlatt Acts and the Amritsar firing led them to articulate more specific economic and social grievances within a demand for full responsible government as a minimum and independence as a maximum. Mahatma Gandhi organized the first noncooperation movement as a protest against the injustice of British policies, and through his unique personality and strategy, he was able to secure men like the Nehrus, Rajendra Prasad from Bihar, and Vallabhbhai

Patel from Gujarat and the Indian National Congress as his collaborators. In this process he extended the political nation to include groups and regions beyond the Western-educated elites of the three presidencies of Bengal, Bombay, and Madras.[7] Although Gandhi ultimately was unable to control the new forces he mobilized, the noncooperation movement presented the most extensive challenge yet seen to the British Indian Empire. Perceiving their future as closely tied to that of the British *raj* in India, a self-selected band of princes widened their activities as allies of the British. They still responded most dramatically in times of danger from external threats, but more frequently they were acting in more subdued roles as instruments of control and intermediaries in communal politics.

During this same period the tensions within and among religious communities intensified. The Muslims felt betrayed and frustrated over the peace terms imposed on the Turkish sultan, whom they recognized as their caliph, or nominal political-cum-religious head; Sikhs were concerned over the unorthodox practices within, and control over, their *gurdwaras*; and Hindus sought unity and political strength through associations such as the Hindu Mahasabha.[8] Proliferating clashes between religious communities near temples and mosques and during festivals reflected heightened hostilities. Each community and factions within them now searched for allies and expanded their institutional network. Some princes were quick to exploit the opportunities this situation created. Their motives and impact were mixed, but communal leadership could buy concessions from both British and Indian leaders. It could also provide access to new sources of prestige and political power.

The rulers who acted as political allies of the British and as communal leaders were frequently those princes who had gained experience and prominence in imperial and all-India political circles during the early decades of the twentieth century. Although many princely excursions into politics beyond their borders were in response to specific requests for support from British officials, they were almost as frequently the result of princely initiative. These men and one woman were eager to reaffirm their usefulness as allies. During the nineteenth century military support had earned protection from raiding neighbors and ambitious relatives. Now these rulers offered new forms of fidelity in return for protection from attack by petitions, newspaper editorials, boycotts, and economic measures such as nonpayment of land revenue.

Princely Response to External Threats to British Stability in India

No sooner had the British thought that they had stamped out the flames of anarchy in the Punjab than they sighted a flash fire on the northwest frontier in the form of troop movements by Amir Ammanullah Khan of Afghanistan. Accordingly, war was declared on Afghanistan, and on 9 May 1919 Lord Chelmsford sent to all ruling princes a private letter that stated the British justification for war and appealed for support in two areas. He asked the princes to guide and encourage their Muslim subjects to right thinking on the war and then solicited assistance in the prevention and suppression of any internal disturbances occurring during the war.[9] His requests reflect a definite shift in British priorities from military to political control. Even though the viceroy did not formally request military aid, many princes volunteered their personal services plus those of their Imperial Service troops.[10]

On the internal scene the princes responded with equal enthusiasm. Although his message was vaguely worded, the nizam of Hyderabad once again exhorted his subjects to follow the lead of their ruler, who was a "Faithful Ally" of the British government.[11] Next the nawab of Rampur, himself a descendent of the Afghan Rohillas, termed the Afghan opponents mere marauders of India, volunteered the services of his troops, and called for continuing Muslim loyalty to the British. Harcourt Butler, the lieutenant governor of the United Provinces, thought Rampur's statement would carry considerable weight among the Muslims of Rohilkhand.[12] A third Muslim voice urging loyalty came from the begum of Bhopal, the ruler of the largest extant Afghan state within the British subsidiary alliance system. Fortunately for the British, the Afghan menace subsided as quickly as it had erupted, and a month later peace negotiations were begun. British appreciation of princely support during the Afghan war and the Punjab crisis was extended both individually and collectively to the princes, most notably at the November 1919 Conference of Princes.

Another external threat, this time from the general direction of Russia, led the Government of India to seek renewed political assistance from the princes. In the years immediately following the 1917 Russian Revolution, the British in India were obsessed with the fear of Bolshevist infiltration. British officials speculated that the Bolshevist strategy would be to utilize existing sources of discontent to advance their philosophy and its solutions as an alternative to the existing situation. For various reasons the British considered that the Muslim disaffection over the impending partition of the Turkish Empire would provide fertile ground for Bolshevist activity. To combat this peril from the north, the Government of India formulated the following three-point policy: to collect more accurate information on the Bolshevists; to prohibit the entry into India of all known or suspected Bolshevists; and to prohibit the circulation of Bolshevist literature and Russian ruble notes. In December 1919 the political secretary wrote to all residents and local governments requesting them to secure the cooperation of the princes with this policy.[13]

Most princes replied with the customary pledges of support. Certain princes, however, exploited this opportunity to enact measures that conveniently could be applied to Indian-inspired as well as Bolshevist threats to the internal stability of their states and the strength of their positions. Three notable examples in this category were the maharajas of Dholpur, Bikaner, and Alwar. Udaibhan Singh of Dholpur claimed that he was certain of the fidelity of his subjects but that he regarded the Arya Samaj as a possible agency for Bolshevist activity. An Arya Samaj newspaper had published articles favorable to some Bolshevist leaders and doctrines, and some Arya Samajists were known to approve of Bolshevist doctrines.[14] Although Dholpur's connection of the Arya Samaj with Bolshevism might appear strained, it is instructive to note that Dholpur was entangled during this period with the Arya Samaj over the alleged desecration and destruction of an Arya Samaj temple at his orders.[15] Whatever the purpose, Dholpur considered it essential to strengthen his CID staff to fight Bolshevism.[16]

As part of an effort not to provide any suitable grounds for Bolshevist activity, Maharaja Ganga Singh of Bikaner thought it would be helpful for the princes to be kept informed of the comments, criticisms, and attacks that appeared in the Indian press about the princes and their governments. Not all local governments were willing to cooperate in such a project, but the Government of India agreed to supply such material from their records to Rajputana princes who requested it. By his initiative Bikaner had provided for his fellow rulers access to a most comprehensive press survey service.[17]

Maharaja Jey Singh of Alwar proposed and actually promulgated the most drastic political control measures ostensibly designed to close all avenues of activity to the Bolshevists. As a beginning, he prohibited all political publications and meetings in his state unless his prior permission had been obtained. To make this measure effective, he advocated the use of force, if necessary, to implement it and asked simply that there be no interference from outside agencies such as the Political Department of the Government of India. Next he sought the cooperation of the Imperial Post Office in the confiscation of undesirable publications mailed to state subjects. (What was undesirable was to be determined solely by Alwar.) Then he asked that the British government take stern measures to prevent the holding of meetings in British India to which state subjects were invited and at which there was "violent speechmaking."[18] Although the British government did not accede to the last request, Jey Singh still was able to regulate arbitrarily all political activity within his state and to isolate his subjects to a considerable degree from knowledge of, and participation in, politics outside. Although the Bolshevists were too occupied consolidating their own revolution to constitute a major threat to the British Empire, assorted princes had proven adept at utilizing available opportunities to secure political concessions from their imperial overlord.

Princes and Communal Issues

When functioning as communal leaders, the princes acted in

diverse ways for various objectives. Sometimes they protested against British policies viewed as discriminatory, as in the Katarpur case. Other times they worked as political allies to secure the loyalty of their coreligionists to British policies, as in the episodes surrounding the Khilafat movement and Aligarh. Frequently they participated in order to enhance their own prestige within their communities and with their British overlord, as in Patiala's maneuvers among the Sikhs. In most cases, moreover, these roles and motives were all present in differing proportions.

In 1918 during Bakr 'Id a communal riot occurred at Katarpur near Hardwar in the United Provinces. Hindus attacked Muslims in a dispute over cow sacrifice, and thirty Muslims were killed, over sixty Muslims injured, and all Muslim homes burned down.[19] A Special Tribunal had been appointed to investigate and to try the Hindu culprits. Many death sentences and sentences of transportation for life were given, and there arose much discontent among Hindus throughout northern India. Maharaja Ganga Singh of Bikaner spearheaded the princely effort to obtain mercy for the Hindu prisoners.

During October 1919 Bikaner wrote privately to Sir William Vincent, the Home member of the Viceroy's Executive Council, requesting a reduction of the sentences meted out to the Katarpur prisoners. He pleaded that many innocent persons had been unjustly convicted and that the guilty had been unduly punished.[20] Apparently obtaining no satisfaction from Vincent, Bikaner later wrote directly to Chelmsford petitioning for clemency.[21] Meanwhile, the maharaja of Patiala approached Chelmsford personally during the meetings of the November 1919 Conference of Princes in Delhi and later wrote a reminder letter to him on the subject.[22] Finally, the maharaja scindia of Gwalior added his voice in a curious manner. Without comment, he forwarded a letter that he had received from Madan Mohan Malaviya, the Hindu Mahasabha leader, in which Malaviya asked Gwalior to use his influence with the viceroy to obtain redress for the Katarpur prisoners.[23] All these petitions emphasized that any modification of the sentences would have positive political influence as well as religious importance.

Although some of the sentences were eventually reduced, it is not certain what degree of influence, if any, the princely appeals had on the final decision. Rather, this incident is noteworthy in that it reveals some of the new types of favors desired of the imperial patron by its princely clients; an effort by the princes to strengthen and exploit their status as religious leaders; and finally, that certain Indian nationalist leaders still thought that the princes had some influence with the British government that might prove beneficial for them.

The princes' involvement in communal politics, this time as supporters of British policy, was even more in evidence during the Khilafat agitation. This movement, largely organized by the Ali brothers, Muhammad and Shaukat, protested against the proposed dismemberment of the Turkish Empire and demanded a strong territorial base for the caliph, the nominal political-religious leader of the Islamic community, who was also the sultan of the vanished Ottoman Empire. Apprehension among Indian Muslims over the Great Powers' treatment of the Turkish Empire during the peace treaty negotiations had been growing slowly during 1919 but became pronounced only at the end of that year. Their anger was directed toward the British government, whom they held responsible for the future of the Khilafat. In November 1919 Gandhi had presided over an All-India Khilafat Conference in Delhi, where he urged the use of noncooperation to bring the government to work for the desired policy on the Khilafat issue as well as to protest over the Punjab wrong that had primarily hit the Hindu community. At the end of December 1919 the Ali brothers were released from prison and thenceforth began to work aggressively to promote the Khilafat issue. When the terms of the Treaty of Sèvres were announced in May 1920, and it became known that the future Turkish state would be deprived of parts of Anatolia, the Ali brothers quickly organized their Khilafat Committee, which began to pursue a policy of *hartal* and noncooperation in an attempt to effect a change in British policy.[24]

Throughout the war but especially in the immediate postwar period, the British had been careful to cultivate the support of Indian Muslim rulers for its position on the Khilafat issue. Although the nizam of Hyderabad and the begum of Bhopal felt that Turkey must accept its punishment, they both counseled the viceroy that the British must honor the pledge extended during the war to preserve the Khilafat, that temporal power was always viewed as a necessary qualification for an effective Khilafat, and that the Khilafat needed Istanbul for its *izzat*.[25] The nizam went so far as to advise Chelmsford to take the most prominent Indian Muslims into his confidence and to inform them of his efforts to fulfill the earlier British promises.[26] In the margin of the letter containing this suggestion, the viceroy sadly noted that the Government of India had repeatedly warned London of the dangers associated with a drastic dismemberment of the Turkish Empire but that it was impossible to make public the differences between the Government of India in New Delhi and His Majesty's Government in London.[27] Edwin Montagu later would not be so discreet and as a consequence of publishing the Government of India's protest to the Treaty of Sèvres would be forced to resign as secretary of state for India.

Although concerned about the injustice of a severe peace treaty, most princes moved to contain and suppress the activities of the Khilafat Committee whenever possible. In the home state of the Ali brothers, the nawab of Rampur jailed four men, including two nephews of the Alis, for their attempt to organize a *hartal* in support of the Khilafat agitation.[28] Despite continuing, though reduced, contacts with the Alis and Dr. Ansari, both the begum of Bhopal and Nawabzada Hamidullah Khan remained staunchly loyal to the British.[29] Such non-Muslim rulers as the maharajas of Kashmir and Patiala also acted to prevent any Khilafat meetings among their considerable Muslim populations.[30] Others such as the maharao raja of Bundi, who had a negligible number of Muslim subjects, expressed their indignation over the Khilafat campaign and offered their services whenever needed.[31]

Most important was the continuing support of the nizam of Hyderabad, who acted firmly in opposition to the Khilafat movement. Prohibiting by firman all Khilafat meetings within his dominions, he issued another firman attacking the Khilafat movement as disloyal and unjustified by historical circumstances.[32] These actions were highly appreciated by the government, but they infuriated the nationalist, particularly the vernacular, press. Both the nawab of Rampur and the nizam of Hyderabad were characterized as traitors of Islam.[33] The nizam, however, was the prime target, and the papers ascribed various motives and different degrees of responsibility to his action. One section placed full guilt upon the British for coercing the nizam; another party attributed the major share of responsibility to the counsels of Sir Ali Imam, the Bihari Muslim lawyer who had recently resigned from the Viceroy's Executive Council and was then serving as an adviser in Hyderabad; a third faction placed full responsibility on the nizam and usually claimed that he hoped to regain control of the Berar territory and the title of "His Majesty" as a reward for his support.[34]

All the above factors probably were operative in determining the nizam's response to the Khilafat challenge. Circumspectly avoiding any overt pressure, the British resident in Hyderabad assiduously set forth the government position in private interviews and warmly praised action supporting that stand. In an interview in September 1921 with John Wood, the political secretary, Ali Imam asked for renewed protection for the princes from attacks in the press, the title of "His Majesty the King of Hyderabad and Its Dominions" for his patron, and the restoration of Berar to Hyderabad.[35] The nizam, however, gave different motives for his support when he wrote to Chelmsford in July 1920 asking for a political favor.

> I am glad . . . to learn from Your Excellency that my policy with reference to the Khilafat agitation has proved beneficial throughout British India. My decision to act in the way I have was influenced by considerations of guarding true Islamic interests no less than of rendering such service to the British Government as is expected from a Friend and Ally. The more I reflect on the situation that has arisen over this agitation the more convinced I am that if it did not subside it would bring in its train untold miseries to the Mahomedans themselves. This is obvious enough to all sober-minded men, but the agitators in their mad desire to create disaffection against British rule stop at nothing. The virulence of the Urdu Press has broken all bounds, and I feel sure Your Excellency's attention has been invited to the scurrilous attacks that are incessantly directed against you and me.[36]

Although the nizam did not specify what measures should be

taken to control the Urdu press, he warned that it would become increasingly difficult for him to give the right lead to Indian Muslims if the attacks continued.[37] Once again, the British were being told that payment was expected for princely support whether given on the battleground or in the political arena.

In 1878 Lord Lytton could guard the princes from blackmail and general criticism in the newspapers through the Vernacular Press Act. Since this viceroy considered the Western-educated Indians and their political associations as groups to be controlled through repression, he had no qualms about enacting highly restrictive legislation.[38] Forty years later and much too slowly, the Government of India wished to avoid alienating the Indian moderate politicians who were the lineal descendants of those earlier disdained men. Since the British wished to channel political activity into the elections for the newly enlarged Legislative Assembly, they now moved cautiously in the area of press censorship and confiscation. At the center they had to weigh carefully the consequences of satisfying one band of collaborators at the expense of another one. On the provincial level most officials seemed to think that control measures had the opposite effect desired and usually provided only further publicity to attacks on the princes.[39]

Unfortunately for the *amour propre* of His Most Exalted Highness, his critics multiplied. The *Hindu*, the leading English-language nationalist newspaper of south India published at Madras, soon launched a running assailment on his policies. At one point the *Hindu* labeled him "the tiny Czar of Hyderabad acting probably under orders descending from the clouds at Simla."[40] Then, when Shaukat Ali alleged that the nizam would have taken the field in a mad rush with his artillery and would have sacrificed his state for Islam but for his relations with the British, the nizam renewed his pleas for protection from such attacks.[41] After much debate within the British administrative system, Reading finally told the nizam some of the hard truths of the changing political scene in India. First, in the existing state of law, the British government was powerless to stop such attacks. Second,

> that Your Exalted Highness and all of us who bear authority in

> India including myself and my officers must make up our minds to ignore a great deal that is said about us in the press. In British India we have for many years past been exposed to the full blast of press criticism, but the experience is more or less new to the Princes, and it must, I realise, come to them as a shock. I sympathise deeply with Your Exalted Highness and the pain that the attacks on Your Exalted Highness have caused me is deepened by the knowledge that it is your attachment to His Majesty the Emperor which has in some cases been the inspiring cause, but let me assure you that to my mind such attacks merely serve as another proof of your steadfast loyalty and add lustre to your devotion to the British Crown.[42]

In the nizam's estimation these sweet words did not sugarcoat the bitter pill he was being asked to swallow.[43] The former British policy of isolation had ill-prepared him for being pilloried by assorted British Indian politicians and newspapers. As a consequence, the British refusal to grant political favors for loyalty seemed particularly unjust to the beleaguered remnant of the Mughal Empire. His sense of grievance against both the major participants in the battle for political dominance in India was one increasingly shared by other princes.

A few months after the announcement of the Turkish peace terms, the British patron again called upon its Muslim princely clients for political aid in a matter involving the Muslim community. As part of his campaign to gather support for noncooperation, Gandhi had requested the trustees of the Muhammadan Anglo-Oriental College at Aligarh to relinquish their government grant and to disaffiliate themselves from Allahabad University, a government institution. The Board of Trustees of the college were to meet at the end of October 1920 to consider his request. To stiffen the trustees against Gandhi's appeal, the political secretary asked local political officers to contact princes who were patrons of the college for their support. The princes, Hyderabad, Bhopal, Bahawalpur, and Patiala, were to be requested to withdraw their students temporarily from the college and to threaten to terminate their annual grants to the college if the trustees voted favorably on Gandhi's proposals.[44]

As was hoped, the begum of Bhopal threatened to withdraw her grant and sent her youngest son, Hamidullah, himself a graduate of Aligarh, to report on the meeting of the trustees.[45] The nizam, however, who was the prime patron of the college, was not so cooperative. Hyderabad stated that he and his father had always pursued a policy of strict noninterference in affairs outside of their dominions and consequently he was unable to comply with the wishes of the government. This policy had evidently been held in abeyance during World War I and the Khilafat agitation. In his telegram transmitting the nizam's reply, Charles L. Russell, the resident at Hyderabad, related that the nizam was particularly sensitive to criticism since the anti-Khilafat firman incident and was anxious to avoid further abuse.[46] Although this incident was of secondary importance, it should be viewed as one weakening link in the chain of friendly relations between the nizam and the Government of India. The crisis point in this relationship was reached in 1926 over the nizam's demand for the retrocession of the Berars. It may be noted that even without the direct support of the nizam, the college trustees rejected Gandhi's pleas and adopted a motion of censure against Shaukat Ali.[47]

The Muslim princes were not alone in their attempts to influence their coreligionists in favor of their imperial overlord. Hindu and Sikh princes were also active as British allies when their respective communities were shaken by conflicts between loyalist, generally older leaders and younger, activist insurgents. Two prominent figures in such endeavors were Maharaja Scindia Madho Rao of Gwalior among the Marathas and Maharaja Bhupinder Singh of Patiala among the Sikhs.

Although his central Indian state was physically removed from the Deccan, the heartland of the Maratha patrimony, and contained only a small Maratha minority, scindia of Gwalior was widely recognized as a leading figure within the Maratha community. The historical significance of his state in the development of the Maratha empire, his close ties to the Maratha business community in Bombay, and his known friendly relations with the British all contributed to scindia's importance. During the tense days of 1921 he became the leader of twin projects designed to enhance the self-esteem of the Maratha community. They provided for memorials in Poona to honor the Maratha war dead and Shivaji, the seventeenth-century founder of the Maratha nation and empire.[48]

In order to associate these undertakings with the British *raj*, Gwalior led a delegation of Maratha princes and public men to petition George Lloyd to secure the presence of the prince of Wales at the dedication of the two memorials. The Bombay governor strongly supported this request for both military and political reasons. In the former case, the recognition given by this act of the Maratha contribution to the war effort would serve as a powerful stimulus to their recently regained martial spirit and to increased recruitment. Even more important, however, was the political aspect. Lloyd argued that

> the non-Brahmin communities during the passage of the Reforms and the late political upheavals have given unstinted support to Government; they are just beginning to realise their political strength, and their various national movements are gaining a weight which will soon be preponderant all over Maharastra. It is of the utmost importance that we should direct this growing strength and win its support against the extremists, and the tribute of a personal attention from His Royal Highness would have exactly the required effect.[49]

Not content with this approach on the provincial level, Gwalior also wrote directly to Lord Reading. His plea was seconded by Maharaja Shahu Chhatrapatri of Kolhapur, who had been the first president of the Shivaji Fund Committee in 1895.[50] When the Government of India procrastinated, Gwalior wrote a second time to the viceroy stressing the all-India character of the effort and the need for a definite decision in order to complete arrangements.[51] After bureaucratic juggling of schedules, the prince of Wales eventually laid the foundation stone of the Shivaji memorial on 19 November 1921 in a picturesque ceremony during which both the maharajas of Gwalior and Kolhapur were conspicuous participants.[52]

The sequel to this display of Maratha prestige was less happy as bickerings led to Gwalior's resignation of the presidency[53] and a drying up of funds until late 1925 when the maharaja holkar of Indore, another Maratha prince, gave five lakhs. The latter's motives were probably mixed, since he was then in the midst of a scandal over the murder of the lover of his former mistress in Bombay.[54] The memorial was completed in 1928 under the direction of Shahu's son Maharaja Rajaram, who had succeeded to the Kolhapur *gadi* in May 1922 upon the death of his father. By this time, however, the Shivaji cult, despite the intentions of Gwalior and the British, had once again become an influential factor in the rising tensions between Hindus and Muslims. The British no longer considered it of political value to be associated too closely with the project, and the viceroy, Lord Irwin, thought it best not to attend the unveiling and instead to send a cautiously worded eulogy on the Maratha people rather than Shivaji himself.[55] Although the involvement of the Maratha princes in this affair had helped to increase their status, it also revealed the ever-present princely vanities that thwarted united action as well as the potential danger to Indian political stability of any effort to glorify a particular community.

As might be anticipated, Maharaja Bhupinder Singh of Patiala continued to enhance his image as a Sikh leader in both ritual and political matters during the postwar era. When a controversy arose in 1917 over whether the Rag Mala, the Sikh Apocrypha, should be separated from the Guru Granth, the sacred scripture of the Sikhs, the *Khalsa Advocate* was a persistent voice appealing to Patiala for a decision against the expunction.[56] After the Executive Committee of the Chief Khalsa Diwan, an association formed in 1902 to promote education and reform among the Sikhs and generally considered to be pro-British, had voted against the removal,[57] Bhupinder Singh eventually seconded that judgment. Although his ruling did not immediately silence the debate in the Sikh press,[58] his action reinforced his position in religious matters. At the same time Bhupinder Singh sustained his generous support of Sikh institutions such as the Khalsa College and projects such as the building of flood protection works around Kartarpur Gurdwara, the first Sikh temple established by Guru Nanak, the founder of Sikhism.[59]

Because of his status within the Sikh community as well as his close relations with high British officials, Patiala occupied a strategic position in 1920 when antigovernment sentiment among Sikhs swelled again. In the early decades of the twentieth century Sikhs had agitated in opposition to policies that affected them adversely, like the Punjab Land Alienation

Act, which prevented Sikh Khatris and Aroras from acquiring more agricultural land; the destruction of a boundary wall at Rikab Ganj, the site of the cremation of the ninth Sikh guru, Tegh Bahadur, in Delhi; and the immigration restrictions, dramatized in the *Komagata Maru* incident. Except for those involved in the last episode, most Sikhs had remained outstandingly loyal during World War I. By late 1920, however, Sikhs had launched sharp protests against the official control of the management of Khalsa College and the Golden Temple in Amritsar, the modern centers of Sikhism. The first issue was quickly resolved when the Managing Committee of the college acted to revise the college rules to exclude all government elements. The second one led to a movement whose legacy is still a major force in Punjab politics.

In October 1920 Edward Maclagan, the lieutenant governor of Punjab, met with Bhupinder Singh of Patiala to obtain his suggestions on the appointment of a committee to formulate procedures for the return of the Golden Temple to Sikh control and to manage the temple and its extensive income in the interim.[60] When the government announced the composition of such a committee, it was soon rejected as unrepresentative by a subsequent meeting of Sikhs called to discuss the reform of all *gurdwaras*. This meeting, then, proceeded to elect a committee of 175 members on the basis of territorial representation to consider the broader question of *gurdwara* reform and a smaller committee of 72 members to manage the Golden Temple. Half of the members of the smaller committee were chosen in consultation with Patiala, but the larger committee, which came to be known as the Shiromani Gurdwara Parbandhak Committee (SGPC), was quickly dominated by ultra or radical Sikhs. By early 1921 the SGPC launched a campaign of forcible seizure of *gurdwaras* from managers they considered corrupt or unfaithful to Sikh tenets, and this action brought them into conflict with the British government. The British continued to hope that Patiala would direct the *gurdwara* reform movement into channels more in conformity with governmental policies, but they became increasingly apprehensive about the implications of intervention by a princely client as mediator between themselves and their subjects in British India.[61] Still the agitation over the *gurdwaras* gave the Sikh ruler a prominence that the British continued to exploit even while they disparaged it.[62]

As in the episodes involving the Muslim rulers, Hyderabad and Bhopal, and the Marathas, Gwalior and Kolhapur, Patiala's activity among his coreligionists had a variety of motives and implications. In each case the individual prince sought to enhance his personal prestige within his religious community as well as lend political service to his patron. Each acted on an all-India scale with little regard for internal conditions within his state. Sharing their religious affiliations with only a minority of their subjects, none attempted to build an organizational base among these coreligionists. They tended, instead, to base their claim to leadership and status on historical precedence and recent generosity to communal causes. Although history did provide a certain aura of legitimacy, it would be a weak reed to support princely ambitions in the years ahead of political struggle between associational groups. The value of princely allies in communal struggles would fluctuate for a variety of reasons, but their ties to communal associations would be one major determinant of strength.

On the other side the British gradually came to view princely participation in communal issues with mixed emotions. Willing to utilize the status of these clients when threatened by confrontations with communal demands, the British found it difficult to keep princely involvement under control. Some British officials became suspicious that the princes might attempt to play both sides against each other in order to aggrandize their own prestige. Others were exasperated by princely requests for political and even personal favors that were clearly difficult to fulfill. Despite their continuing requests for princely assistance in communal disputes, the British overlord was apprehensive about the ultimate benefits achieved.

Princes and Noncooperation

As the noncooperation movement expanded in late 1920 and throughout 1921, the princes spoke and acted more openly against this many-headed monster that increasingly threatened the internal tranquility within their states. Their statements and actions varied considerably in scope and intensity.

Shortly after the Central Sikh League adopted a resolution supporting the noncooperation campaign in the fall of 1920, the maharaja of Patiala went to Lahore at the invitation of Edward Maclagan to plan a counter campaign among Sikhs.[63] In December 1920, when Maclagan visited the state of Nabha, the maharaja of Nabha stated in an official speech that "to say that nonco-operation does not end in violence is as incorrect as to say that fire does not produce smoke."[64] This evaluation is mild but surprising from a prince usually in opposition to the government. In central India the leader of princely opposition to noncooperation was scindia of Gwalior, who delivered a fighting speech against the movement at the Maratha Educational Conference held in his capital in April 1921.[65] Not content with verbal attacks, Gwalior also proscribed eight prominent Indian nationalist newspapers within the boundaries of his state.[66]

The most vocal princely opponent of noncooperation was Maharaja Shahu Chhatrapati of Kolhapur. As early as January 1920, Kolhapur was writing to Chelmsford that the viceroy should take strong measures to repress the wild abuse of liberty of speech at Congress meetings.[67] Kolhapur continued to offer unsolicited advice on handling the noncooperation movement and later accused the government of doing nothing to stop noncooperation. His suggested policy advocated greater use of police and military forces, subsidy of loyal and influential newspapers by the government and by princely states, more propaganda directed to agricultural workers, and the creation of a non-Brahmin party to fight the religious bureaucracy of the Brahmins.[68] As related earlier, Kolhapur had long been an active leader of the non-Brahmin movement in Maharashtra as well as within his own state.[69] He was particularly interested in evolving means to combat the Indian National Congress, since he viewed it as Brahmin-dominated in the Maharashtra area. To the intense embarrassment of Kolhapur and the British, the *Bombay Chronicle* and the *Kesri* obtained a copy of Kolhapur's correspondence with British officials and devoted several issues to a full publication of this damaging evidence.[70]

The princes proved to be especially helpful to the government with regard to the visit of the prince of Wales to India. This peregrination was originally scheduled for the cold weather of

1920, and early in that year Chelmsford asked the maharaja of Gwalior to use his influence with nationalist leaders to ensure a peaceful reception for the royal heir.[71] Gwalior later reported to the viceroy that in May and June 1920 he had met with several of his nationalist friends in Bombay and most did not support a boycott of the visit. Among those he cited as anti-boycott were Narayan Chandavarkar, Lallubhai Samaldas, Narottam Gokuldas, Jamnadas Dwarkadas, and Madan Mohan Malaviya. Gwalior also thought that Tej Bahadur Sapru and C. Y. Chintamani along with Malaviya could be counted upon to keep the United Provinces free from boycott. Although he also met with Gandhi, Gwalior could only report that the Mahatma refused to bind himself with an unconditional promise not to practice noncooperation against the royal visit.[72]

When a postponement to the cold weather of 1921 was decided upon, the government had to begin anew their efforts to secure a suitable reception for the prince. In April 1921 Montagu turned to Patiala for his opinion on the probable effect of a royal visit to India. Patiala thought that

> unless something further is done to conciliate public opinion and to impress on the people of India, through H.R.H. the Prince of Wales, the fact that the British Government sympathises with, and is very anxious to guide and help India towards the attainment of its legitimate aspirations, it is hardly advisable to put the Prince to the trouble of going to India empty-handed.[73]

To ensure that the royal visit would strengthen the loyalty of the princes and people of India to the British *raj*, Patiala suggested that the prince of Wales should announce suitable boons. A few days later Montagu wrote to Lord Reading, Chelmsford's successor as viceroy who arrived in India in March 1921, and asked him to consider Patiala's suggestions and to consult other princes about the royal visit.[74] Unfortunately we have as yet no evidence of whether Reading consulted other princes and if so what their views were. When the prince of Wales did arrive in India, he spent at least half of his tour in Indian states where the government could be assured that he would receive a colorful but peaceful welcome.[75] Of course, most of the princes were anxious to entertain the royal heir for reasons of personal prestige as well as political expediency.

Politics at the Chamber of Princes

In order not to give an entry to British Indian politicians interested in the internal affairs of princely states, British officials strictly excluded British Indian affairs from the purview of the Chamber of Princes. Even so, at the informal meetings that preceded and followed the formal sessions of the Chamber, the princes discussed political problems that seemed to menace their position both within and without their states. In February 1921, during the informal meetings held concurrently with the inauguration of the Chamber, two political items were considered at the request of the maharaja of Kolhapur. Kolhapur first called attention to a resolution passed at the December 1920 Nagpur session of the Congress that advocated the promotion of agitations against the princes and their administrations. To combat such intrusions, Kolhapur argued, the government should be called upon to prohibit demonstrations against princes held in British districts bordering state territories, and he cited instances in Bombay when district magistrates had issued such orders. After some discussion the princes referred this question to the newly constituted Standing Committee of the Chamber. Second, Kolhapur urged the princes to seek more adequate protection against vilification in the British Indian press. In his argument he claimed that libelous defamation as opposed to legitimate criticism had increased greatly during the past year. On this question the princes decided to have the chancellor address the political secretary. So that a forceful case on the need for protection could be presented to the government, individual members of the Chamber were asked to send concrete instances of such vilification to the chancellor and the Standing Committee.[76] Early in its career the Chamber would act as a pressure group in order to secure a major concession from the British Government in the form of special legislation dealing with press criticism of the princes and their administration.

Conclusion

As outlined above, a limited number of Indian princes followed several approaches to participation in all-India politics during the fateful years immediately following Montagu's historic declaration of August 1917. Just as they differed in their methods, these princes had a variety of motives. Some, such as the maharaja of Kolhapur, entered British Indian politics to gain ammunition against adversaries who menaced their ritual or political status. Others, such as the maharaja of Alwar, sought to satisfy a lust for prestige and prominence.[77] It is important to note that most princes active in constitutional, political, social, and religious activities beyond their borders came from middle-sized states. The explanation would appear to be that the administration of one of these middling states did not fully occupy or satisfy its ruler, and its resource base was sufficient to enable him to indulge in all-India affairs. To attend an imperial gathering in London in appropriate style or to entertain the prince of Wales with traditional lavishness was a drain even on the treasury of a prosperous state like Patiala. Few rulers of the hundreds of insignificant Indian states could afford to participate or seemed to care about what was happening beyond their borders.[78] Most rulers of the largest states seemed content to focus their attention and energies on internal affairs. Finally, many involved princes, such as the maharajas of Bikaner and Patiala, were anxious to highlight their position as staunch allies of their imperial patron. All these motives were usually present in varying proportions within each individual prince.

Despite the variety of motives and ways of participation, there were certain general advantages to be gained by astute involvement in all-India politics. It was basically less dangerous to fight against, and to attempt to suppress, political and social unrest in someone else's territory than within one's own borders. An optimist would hope for early control of such disturbances before they upset the balance of power within a state that was favorable to its ruler. A pessimist would hope that defeat outside one's own possessions might have less severe repercussions and might still permit a successful holding action against change within his state. Another beneficial factor was that any political support freely given might be employed as a lever to extract desired concessions from the imperial patron.

From the British viewpoint the princes had proved to be of some value during the deepening confrontation between the Indian nationalists and the British *raj*. When the nationalists threatened a boycott of the visit by the prince of Wales, a threat effectively carried out upon his arrival in Bombay, the timely and loyal hospitality of the Indian princes ensured that at least half of his tour would be conducted with appropriate displays of imperial splendor. Princely support in that widening sphere where politics and religion were closely related was particularly helpful. In this area the maharaja of Patiala as a Sikh leader and the nizam of Hyderabad and the begum of Bhopal as Muslim leaders were especially prominent.

Despite these definite advantages, princely clients acting as political allies were not a totally positive asset for the British. Without proper direction and some degree of control, their actions could be a political detriment, as in the case of the overzealous Kolhapur. In return for their services the princes began to demand certain political concessions that were increasingly difficult for the government to grant. As mentioned earlier, Kolhapur and Hyderabad pressed for protection from libelous press attacks. Alwar, Kolhapur, and later some Kathiawar states all pleaded for protection from criticism of princely administrations at meetings held in British districts and administered areas contiguous to states.[79] Still other embarrassing petitions included a demand to exercise some form of censorship over telegrams within princely states;[80] a plea by Rajputana princes for an effective method to prevent the transmission of seditious newspapers to their states;[81] and opposition to any increase in the percentage of Indians in the Political Department cadre of the Indian Civil Service.[82] These requests were politically awkward, since it was precisely in these areas that the Government of India was attempting to make meaningful concessions to Indian nationalists.

As a consequence of such difficulties, the British government seemed to prefer to mobilize the princes in their role as political allies only in times of great crisis and when the consequences of their involvement could be controlled. As the first noncooperation movement gradually came to an end, the British appeared to encourage ambitious princes to direct their energies to imperial conferences and League of Nations sessions, to participation in Chamber activities, and to the closer supervision of their own internal administrations. A detailed survey of princes as administrators within their own states is beyond the scope of this study, but the next chapter will focus on the princes and their involvement in imperial gatherings and at the Chamber of Princes.

chapter five

Autocrats Assembled: The Chamber of Princes, 1921–1929

When the Chamber of Princes was inaugurated in February 1921, Indian nationalists, British officials, and princes alike had mixed feelings about its future role and probable impact on their respective interests.

Indian nationalist comment as reflected in the press varied considerably. Extremist newspapers generally adopted one of two hostile positions. Some saw the Chamber as an effort to strengthen the princes as an opposition force to the rising nationalist movement.[1] Others viewed it as a British trap that would ensnare the princes in discussions over trivial matters and thereby prevent them from devoting their full attention to political and social reform within their individual states.[2] Both moderate and extremist newspapers assailed the veil of secrecy that surrounded the proceedings of the Chamber.[3] This lack of publicity allowed the more extremist newspapers to depict it as a cabal of princes and officials directed against the nationalist aspirations of the Indian people.[4] In this context it is ironic that the Government of India had early rejected a suggestion to involve the Chamber as an institution in British Indian politics. During the height of the first noncooperation movement, Maharaja Sir Rameshwara Singh of Darbhanga, the leading landlord of Bihar, had proposed that selected members of the Chamber meet with selected official and nonofficial legislators to analyze the causes of the current unrest and to recommend means by which law and order might be maintained.[5] The government speedily rejected his proposition as inappropriate in view of the constitution of the Chamber.[6]

Most British officials considered the Chamber a major concession and a step forward in the evolution of a new imperial policy toward the princes. Montagu, undoubtedly the most sympathetic advocate of their interests, envisioned several functions for this new institution. They included awakening its members to changing political conditions throughout the Indian subcontinent, attempting to alleviate princely grievances against British policies toward them, and hopefully integrating these allies more fully into the imperial structure. In India, Chelmsford and later Reading deemed the Chamber to be the most-advanced step possible in the political circumstances of the period. Their goals for the Chamber resembled those of Montagu but were interlaced with restrictions designed to maintain the Government of India in the dominant position at all times. There was a change in viceregal ambitions for the Chamber with the advent of Lord Irwin in 1926. Interested in formulating a clear-cut policy toward the princes, this Conservative viceroy encouraged greater princely participation in the Chamber and attempted to utilize it as a vehicle to promote basic political reforms within the states. He was even willing to undertake special measures beyond the Chamber to deal with princely grievances against their British overlord.

Among those princes, such as the maharajas of Bikaner, Patiala, Gwalior, Nawanagar, and Alwar, who had petitioned and lobbied for the establishment of a constitutional assembly of princes, there was general satisfaction that their primary goal had been achieved. These same leaders, however, were disappointed by the circumscribed character of the Chamber and the failure of the government to implement all their recommendations that had been incorporated in the Montagu-Chelmsford Report. Even so, this group was anxious to work through this new body to achieve a wide variety of objectives viewed as necessary to stabilize their position within the British Indian Empire.

Their goals may be divided into two broad categories. Most immediate was the issue of securing protection from attacks launched from British India on the princes and their administrations. Since they were nearly absolute autocrats within their own territories, the princes could effectively squash most internal opposition by arbitrary means. As the tempo of political activity across their borders quickened into the first noncooperation movement, these autocrats became the target of criticism from that quarter with annoying frequency. Although censure by British Indian nationalists assumed many forms, the princes became most concerned about the attacks appearing in the nationalist, particularly the vernacular, press. Press criticism was nothing new, and had been launched in the past for blackmail purposes as well as the promotion of long-overdue reforms. The recent press controversies involving the nizam of Hyderabad and the maharaja of Kolhapur revealed the growing potency of these attacks in a society becoming increasingly literate. The princely fear of these undesirable but often justified condemnations was heightened once it became known that the Press Act of 1910, which had operated to protect them, was to be modified. In this situation the Chamber would form a lobby to obtain some new measure of protection.

Aware that their requests for special protection would choke off only one source of assault, an inner core of the Chamber also sought to define their position within the Indian political system so that their continued existence would be assured despite the uncertain future. Their thinking, dominated by concepts of Indian politics as they were during the nineteenth century, viewed the British government as the prime force encroaching on their status and privileges. Although they recognized the rising position of Indian nationalist leaders, these men reasoned that they could neutralize that threat by improving and strengthening their ties with the British *raj*.

Initially this inner circle, which usually constituted the Standing Committee of the Chamber, sought to eliminate the source of numerous grievances against British policies and procedures by obtaining a legalistic definition of paramountcy and the rights and duties of the British acting as the paramount power. If paramountcy was defined and the paramount power, therefore, limited in its rights and prerogatives, the princes dreamed that governmental practices demeaning to their status and *izzat* would be ended. In addition they attempted to strengthen their position within the British Empire by predicating that their treaties, originally concluded with the British East India Company, were now binding upon the British crown, the successor to the rights and obligations of the company in India. Their objective in promoting a special relationship with the crown was to secure a sympathetic patron likely to remain unchallenged despite any possible changes within the internal relationships of the empire. Since the composition of the Government of India was slowly changing to include Indians and even some British officials hostile to the ambitions of the princes, the British crown seemed a safer refuge. Finally, these princes sought some form of joint consultation between themselves and British Indian legislators over matters of common concern such as custom duties and transportation development. A similar proposal had been included in the Montagu-Chelmsford Report but was not implemented.

This chapter delineates how a small group of princes pursued the various objectives outlined above through the medium of the Chamber. After relating their successes and failures, it analyzes the reasons for them, with emphasis on the inadequacies of the Chamber. Then it discusses how some members attempted to achieve their program by other means, particularly the Indian States Committee, appointed in 1928 and known as the Butler Committee after its chairman, Sir Harcourt Butler. Although the primary focus is on the princes, every effort is made to point out the varied reactions within the British official hierarchy and mixed responses of Indian nationalists to the political activities of the princes during this period.

Princes Lobby for Press Protection

As related in the last chapter, the maharaja of Kolhapur had been the first to bring the issue of protection from press attacks before his brethren assembled for the inauguration of the Chamber in February 1921. Shortly after raising this matter at an informal session, he was placed in a difficult position when the *Bombay Chronicle* published the complete texts of his correspondence with British officials on the noncooperation movement. By the second session of the Chamber, which was held in November 1921, it was general knowledge that the restrictive Press Act of 1910 would probably be repealed. The princes, consequently, wanted to secure some other instrument of protection, and Maharaja Jey Singh of Alwar moved a resolution during the November session requesting the viceroy, now Lord Reading, to provide adequate safeguards for the princes and their administrations to replace those to be lost by the rumored repeal of the 1910 Press Act.[7] This resolution was not the first time that the princes had entered the discussion about the repeal of the Press Act. Throughout the debate over this topic, the princes had been considered, but there were differences in the British hierarchy over what should and what had to be done to protect these clients.

As part of an effort to bring about a reconciliation between the government and the nationalists, Montagu, in late 1919, had urged Chelmsford to forgo the use of repressive legislation such as the 1910 Press Act.[8] By this Act the princes as well as the Government of India had been afforded protection from such press criticism as in the government's opinion was calculated to arouse hatred or disaffection. In the simplest case, the executive branch was empowered to demand a security from a suspect newspaper and later to confiscate the security if the newspaper published criticism leading to disaffection. Nationalists had loudly condemned this legislation because it allowed the executive to be both judge and party in a dispute and prevented recourse to the courts. This feature of executive control had particular appeal for the princes, who considered court actions beneath their dignity and status.

Although Montagu continued to plead with Chelmsford for a dispatch on the press law issue during 1920, the viceroy moved slowly and appeared more concerned about the attitudes of his provincial governors rather than those of his parliamentary superior in London or the politicians in India.[9] Eventually in December 1920 Chelmsford argued that he did not want to bind his unknown successor to a definite policy.[10] His final gesture was the appointment of a nine-man Press Act Committee with Tej Bahadur Sapru, the Law member of his Executive Council, as its chairman.[11]

John Wood, the political secretary, was responsible for

presenting the position of the princes before the committee, but Reading later asserted that their case had not been well handled.[12] In its report the committee unreservedly advocated total repeal of the Press Act. With regard to the Act's function in protecting the princes, the committee stated that it had been handicapped by the unwillingness of the princes to place their opinions before it. Although the committee took notice of the argument raised by Wood, about governmental obligations to the princes, it observed that other witnesses had argued that any protection given to the princes would stifle all legitimate criticism. Consequently, the committee concluded:

> . . . We do not, in the circumstances, think that we should be justified in recommending on general grounds any enactment in the Penal Code or elsewhere for the purpose of affording such protection [for the princes] in the absence of evidence to prove the practical necessity for such provision of the law.[13]

In August 1921 Montagu gave his general approval to the introduction of legislation to repeal the Press Act but asked for further attention to three points, the last of which was "to consider whether you could not afford the protection of your courts to Princes and Chiefs in some form which would not be rendered nugatory by their objection to appear in court."[14] The India Office was advised, subsequently, that the question of special protection for the princes was being deferred for further consideration and would be referred to the Chamber of Princes at their next meeting.[15] So in October 1921 Wood informed Bikaner that a resolution on press protection could be included on the Chamber agenda.[16]

During the discussion in the Chamber on this topic, there was only one dissenting voice. Bold and independent, the maharaja scindia of Gwalior reasoned that to ask for special protection would emphasize the weakness of the princely position. Suggesting that the Government of India should review the problem independently and decide what should be done, he argued that any protection given under those circumstances would place all responsibility for such action on the government.[17] All the other members present, however, were staunchly enthusiastic in their support of special protection. The maharaja of Kolhapur went so far as to propose that offenders in this matter should be extradited to the native state attacked for trial,[18] but Reading pointed out that it was against legal principles for extradition to be made for political offenses. In concluding the debate over this resolution, the viceroy assured the assembled members that his government would consider carefully their apprehensions.[19]

As might be anticipated, the reaction in most of India to the princely plea for press protection was negative and varied only in its intensity. Although in an embryonic stage of organization, associations of state subjects such as the Kathiawar Hitvardhak Sabha and the Praja Mandal of Rajkot forwarded resolutions of protest to the Government of India.[20] Representative of nationalist press comment, the *Tribune* of Lahore expressed regret that the government was still interested in the matter when they should be quietly dropping it.[21] Even the *Feudatory and Zemindari India*, a south Indian monthly journal devoted to the interests of the princes, suggested that they should not ask for special legislation. Instead, an editorial in this journal proposed the establishment of counter-propaganda measures such as a well-organized news service to disseminate news from the states to the British Indian press and the encouragement of newspapers within the states, which could then ventilate the grievances of their subjects and counter any misrepresentations about state affairs before molehills became mountains.[22]

It was evident that any measure to give special protection to the princes was likely to destroy whatever stock of political good will had been purchased by the government with the repeal of the Press Act. Even so, pressure from the India Office as well as the plea of the Chamber forced Reading to reopen governmental debate on this delicate issue. As Gandhi was launching his no-tax campaign in February 1922, the viceroy directed the Political Department to solicit local governments and political officers for their views on the advisability of special legislation.[23]

During March there were two personnel changes within the British hierarchy that were to prove beneficial to the princes. One vital shift occurred at the India Office. Because of his handling of the Government of India's protest against the treaty terms imposed by the Great Powers on Turkey, Montagu was forced to resign and was succeeded by Lord Peel, a

Conservative. Peel had little of his predecessor's Indian experience or personal contacts and was less sympathetic to the aspirations of the Indian nationalists. The other notable change was at the Political Department in Delhi. Exhausted by an extraordinarily long term as political secretary, the unimaginative Wood resigned and was succeeded by John P. Thompson. As chief secretary to the Punjab government during O'Dwyer's term, Thompson had been closely associated with the repressive policies of his superior during the 1919 troubles. In a conciliatory gesture directed toward nationalist sentiment, he had been moved to Delhi and temporarily made an additional political secretary and eventually Wood's successor.[24] Thompson, proud of his oratorical skills and aspiring to a place on the Punjab Governor's Executive Council, regarded his removal from Punjab more or less as the end of his career.[25] He believed that William Vincent, the Home member of the Viceroy's Executive Council, had been primarily responsible for his demise.[26] Their subsequent antipathy for each other would make Thompson more sympathetic to the princes and less appreciative of the problems that their requests might create for Vincent. Otherwise, neither Thompson nor Peel was especially concerned about the princes, but rather saw them as allies to be conciliated if it was possible to do so without making any essential concessions.

Shortly after these changes, the bill to repeal the Press Act passed the Legislative Assembly on 25 March 1922. On that very same day Lord Peel sent an urgent telegram to Delhi advising the Government of India that he would invoke Section 69 of the Government of India Act if adequate protection was not given to "those whose interests it is [the] responsibility of the Government of India and myself to safeguard."[27] Section 69 empowered the secretary of state to advise the king in council to disallow any legislation that he thought should not be implemented. Naturally enough, Reading and his council were furious at this unprecedented threat and strongly protested this lack of support from home at a critical juncture.[28]

After receiving the generally favorable views of local governments and political officers, the ever-efficient Thompson produced a lengthy note by 25 July that outlined the whole problem and advocated a new bill to extend protection. He argued that protection should be given because of British obligations to respect the rights, dignity, and honor of their princely clients.[29] His note was immediately circulated to the members of the Viceroy's Executive Council, and Vincent pounced on it. From his experience on the Press Act Committee, the Home member declared that special protection had been impossible when the original bill to repeal the Press Act was being debated but that he would now reluctantly agree to new legislation in the face of changed circumstances. He rejected any effort to base such a concession on treaty obligations but rather asserted that he was

> guided largely in [his] views as to the legislation by considerations of a practical nature, namely that it is not desirable to leave the Princes with a real grievance and secondly, that if we do not protect them, we shall ourselves suffer from the reaction and the Princes might, as indeed some have done in the past, encourage sedition and intrigues against the Government of India in their States.[30]

Neither man was as honest as C. W. Gwynne, the deputy secretary in the Home Department of the Government of India, who had noted on 17 June that the dispatch from Peel determined that protection should be given and that the only question was the form in which it was to be extended.[31]

Strong opposition came from Sapru, the Law member and chairman of the Press Act Committee, who bluntly stated that he remained unconvinced of the necessity or expediency of such legislation. Elaborating on his views, he argued that the subjects of the princes needed protection more than the princes did and that it was exceedingly difficult in systems of personal rule to differentiate between the ruler and his measures. He further predicted that any such legislation would create a storm of controversy and would require certification by the viceroy to become law. He was prepared to support legislation designed to penalize attempts made in British India to foment rebellion in the states but nothing more.[32] These comments are of special interest because Sapru had served frequently as legal adviser to many Indian princes before assuming his official position.[33] Even though a political moderate and sympathetic to the predicament of the princes, he was against any legislation that would restrict the freedom of the press and prevent honest criticism.

Though reluctant to introduce such an explosive piece of legislation, most members of Reading's council took Vincent's position and agreed to it as a matter of political expediency involving a choice between the lesser of two evils.[34] Thus on 23 September 1922, just six months after the repeal of the Press Act, Vincent asked leave in the Legislative Assembly for the introduction of a bill to prevent dissemination of news calculated to bring into contempt or excite disaffection against the princes and their governments. After a vigorous debate, the assembly rejected the motion by a vote of 45 to 41.[35]

On the following day, a Sunday, Reading met with his council and the decision was made to certify the bill as vital to the interests of British India, thereby allowing it to bypass the assembly. The certified bill was introduced into the Council of State on Tuesday, 26 September, and passed after the viceroy promised to utilize its provisions only in extreme cases. As was anticipated, the nationalist press was furious in its condemnation of the measure and Reading's action, but the battle was over.[36] On 3 October 1922 the secretary of state wrote to the viceroy that it was satisfactory that certification under the Indian Councils Act of 1919 had first occurred in a matter that was one between Indians and Indians.[37] Peel's attitude reflected the divide-and-rule approach to imperial control. It also worked to help the princes delay confronting the problems created by the movement toward responsible government across their borders. The Princes Protection Act was a boon but one whose ultimate consequences would be unfavorable for the princes.

Princely Grievances about British Policies

Although no state had been annexed by the British since 1856, most princes had accumulated a long list of complaints about British encroachment on their personal dignity and internal sovereignty. Lord Minto had attempted to allay these grievances with his policy of noninterference in the internal affairs of the states in order to secure renewed commitments of loyalty and support from the princes. Despite this real shift in British policy, princely dissatisfaction persisted. They had obtained a decline in interference but not a positive statement on their future position within the British Indian Empire. Because the British continued to act as the paramount power, there were perennial quarrels over procedures that the princes thought demeaning, as in the prolonged controversy between Ripudaman Singh of Nabha and the Punjab government, and over assertions of imperial authority, as in the abdication of Ripudaman. Furthermore, Minto and his successors could not abolish British-controlled railway, telegraph, postal, and coinage systems, which necessitated many measures that the princes viewed as unwarranted intrusions on their internal authority. Delhi also had little direct control over the daily routines and personal habits of their political officers, who sometimes were more active in inflating their own egos than in smoothing the ruffled feathers of their princely charges.

At their periodic meetings with members of the Political Department, the Standing Committee of the Chamber of Princes repeatedly elaborated on the broader perspective in which they viewed their grievances. Their concerns were not limited to such details as framing a standard procedure for licensing radio receivers but rather were directed toward the broad objective of securing a defined status for themselves within the Indian political system.

The attitudes of both sides were well illustrated at a meeting held in January 1924 between the Standing Committee and Thompson and G. D. Ogilvie, the deputy political secretary. Here discussion centered around the method to be followed when attempting to improve disputed governmental practices. The princes favored the so-called analytical approach, which was defined by Jey Singh of Alwar as establishing procedures based on the status accorded to the princes by their treaties with the East India Company.[38] Ganga Singh of Bikaner supported the position of his brother Rajput and explained why the Chamber was so anxious to have the status of the princes based on those agreements. As more Indians sympathetic to the Indian National Congress replaced British ICS officers in the Political Department, the princes feared increased governmental interference in their internal administrations. To prevent this situation, they wanted their position clearly and generously established so as to reduce the legitimate occasions of intervention. They sought to have their internal administrations placed beyond the purview of government officials, both British and Indian.[39] Bhupinder Singh of Patiala summed up the feelings of the others present when he stated

> that if the position of the States was strengthened in the manner proposed great benefit to the Empire might be expected. When the Government of India is surrendering its power into the hands of the people why should the Government not increase the powers of the Princes who have always been loyal and who do not desire to be handed over to the British Indian democracy.[40]

Speaking for the Political Department, John Thompson claimed that any effort to find solutions for future problems by extracting principles from agreements concluded a century earlier would raise innumerable difficulties. He argued further that the princes were in a stronger position than they had ever been and had much to lose by an exact interpretation of all the provisions and implications of their treaties and sanads.[41] The government approach, based on resolving differences according to the status of the princes as it had evolved up to the present, was labeled the synthetic method.

In the usual pattern of such discussions, nothing definite was decided, but the opinions expressed are indicative of the preoccupations of Chamber members. The Standing Committee contained the most articulate and politically aware members of the Chamber, and their arguments reveal the great reliance they placed on a strong constitutional definition of their position. They looked backward to treaties made under entirely different circumstances for principles to guide them in the area of constitutional reform, one reason that the princes seem, in retrospect, so isolated from political realities. For the next two decades these leaders would continue to expend much time, energy, and money on this project of minimal value.

The indecisive nature of their intermittent discussions with the Political Department was discouraging, and an incident occurred in early 1926 that caused deep alarm among Chamber members. This matter had its origins in the dispute between the nizam of Hyderabad and the British government over the possession of Berar. Located on the northern side of Hyderabad state, the Berar area had been taken over by Lord Dalhousie in 1853. Although they continued to acknowledge the nominal sovereignty of the nizam over the province, the British became responsible for the administration and the collection of revenues from this rich cotton-growing area in order to obtain an assured source of support for the Hyderabad Contingent, a subsidiary force maintained by the state for the use of its imperial patron. From thenceforth control over Berar was to be a source of constant friction between the nizam and the British. In 1902 Lord Curzon thought that he had ended the debate when he secured the agreement of Nizam Mir Mahbub Ali Khan to an arrangement whereby the British held Berar on a perpetual lease in return for an annual rent of two and a half million rupees.[42]

However, after World War I Nizam Mir Osman Ali Khan, who had succeeded his father in 1911, launched a vigorous campaign to terminate the lease and to have Berar returned to Hyderabadi administration. Despite intense newspaper propaganda, lobbying with British officials, and formal exchanges of letters,[43] the Government of India ultimately rejected the nizam's request.[44]

Probably as a last desperate measure, the nizam in a letter dated 20 September 1925 disavowed the idea that a negative decision by the Government of India on this question could be binding on him. He argued that both Hyderabad and British India were independent of one another with regard to their internal affairs, and, in his view, the administration of Berar was an internal matter. Accordingly, a negative decision by the British on this matter could not be binding on the government of Hyderabad. The nizam claimed that such a decision could only be made by a joint commission consisting of representatives from British India, Hyderabad, and Berar.[45]

Irritated that any prince, even one as important as Hyderabad, should advance claims of equality with the British, Reading and Birkenhead, the secretary of state for India, were prompt to squelch such pretensions.[46] In his reply to Mir Osman Ali Khan, issued on 27 March 1926, Reading categorically declared:

> The sovereignty of the British Crown is supreme in India, and therefore no Ruler of an Indian State can justifiably claim to negotiate with the British Government on an equal footing. Its supremacy is not based only upon treaties and engagements, but exists independently of them, and, quite apart from its prerogative in matter relating to foreign powers and policies, it is the right and duty of the British Government, while scrupulously respecting all treaties and engagements with the Indian States, to preserve peace and good order throughout India.[47]

This uncompromising pronouncement of the absolute supremacy of the British government coupled with British intervention in the internal affairs of other states such as Nabha, Udaipur, and Indore caused growing apprehension among the princes. Instead of being rewarded for services rendered with the desired recognition of their special status, the princes saw their status increasingly diminished by their imperial patron.

The governmental attitude toward complaints from state subjects against their rulers aggravated the princely discontent with British policies. Although the Indian National Congress formally had abstained from activity within state boundaries, some Congressmen, acting as individuals, were establishing political organizations of state subjects. Isolated and local in their orientation, such groups occasionally presented petitions and complaints against the administration of certain princes to the Government of India. At a meeting in May 1926 the Standing Committee criticized the government's willingness to consider and even investigate these allegations. Although the political secretary did not reply immediately, he later sent a note justifying governmental action.[48] Arguing that the government could not permit itself to become an indirect instrument of misrule and oppression, he claimed that it could not support any administration so deficient that it was likely to cause an uprising against its ruler. It could not acquiesce, furthermore, in financial mismanagement that would ruin the state or permit the decline of the feudal aristocracy in the state. The government considered itself bound to intervene in state affairs if there was any evidence of oppression, seething discontent, or financial mismanagement.[49] Coming so soon after Reading's statement to Hyderabad, these views seemed to extend further the possibilities of British intervention.

The Chamber members were disappointed by the refusal of the Government of India to implement a proposal in yet another area. This concerned the provision of joint consultation between themselves and British Indian legislators on matters of common concern. Although they had successfully obtained the incorporation of this demand in the Montagu-Chelmsford Report, the princes had not been able to prod the government to move on the matter. In January 1926 the Chamber finally voted to appoint a committee to meet with British Indian representatives and to report back on:

(1) the best means of safeguarding the interests of the Indian States on occasions when an enquiry is undertaken into matters of common interest to the States and to British India, and

(2) what machinery should be devised for giving effect to the proposal contained in Paragraph 311 of the Montagu-Chelmsford Report regarding joint deliberation.[50]

After five years of attempting to work through the Chamber, its members had become more apprehensive and irritated than reconciled in their relations with the British government. As we have seen, there were several factors of varying importance contributing to the feeling of frustration. Basically, the princes had failed to assess realistically the extent to which the balance of power within the Indian political system had shifted from the British to the Indian nationalist leaders. Woefully overestimating the staying strength of the British, the princes placed too much emphasis on improving relations with their imperial patron, and they overrated their own importance as imperial allies.[51] Even if one accepts their goals as legitimate, the Chamber must be seen as a pathetically defective institution for the achievement of positive ends.

Weaknesses of the Chamber of Princes

Among the principle defects of the Chamber was the dominance exercised over it by the viceroy and the Political Department. Despite Montagu's warnings about the ill effects of excessive British control, the viceroy retained the final authority in determining when sessions would be held and the content of the agenda, as well as serving as the presiding officer.

Sessions were held irregularly depending on when it was most convenient for the government to have the princes at Delhi. In some years there were two meetings, each lasting a week; in others there were no meetings at all. The usual reason given for not convening the Chamber more frequently was a lack of suitable agenda items.

Members could suggest items for the agenda, but their suggestions had to be filtered through the Political Department, which usually vetoed any topics it did not care to consider or thought might be provocative.[52] Most matters of greatest concern to the princes seemed to belong in one of these two categories. Agenda topics were normally confined to such apolitical areas as the granting of mining concessions in the states; the ownership by princes of nonresidential property in British India; and the compensation to be paid existing tramways when new railway lines were constructed.

If Chamber discussions on approved topics appeared to be moving in a direction unacceptable to the government, the viceroy, as presiding officer, could always give his opinion and thereby influence the voting. An outstanding example of such intervention occurred at the November 1924 session of the Chamber. The maharaja of Alwar moved a resolution, seconded and strongly supported by the maharaja of Patiala, that the public should be admitted to hear the discussion of any resolution when that was desired by the mover and seconder and a majority of the Chamber members.[53] The main purpose of this change of procedure was to counter nationalist allegations that the princes were plotting against political reform in British India. Although there was mixed support among the members, Lord Reading authoritatively cautioned them to weigh the implications of a positive vote. He argued that it would be difficult to give publicity to some resolutions and not to others, and that the content of the viceroy's opening speech would be affected if it was to be made public.[54] Faced by divided ranks among fellow members and viceregal opposition, Alwar withdrew his resolution. This question of publicity was referred to the Standing Committee, where it became entangled in repetitive discussions for over five years. In 1929 the Chamber finally accepted a resolution on limited publicity similar to that first proposed in 1924.[55] Their action was ten years too late to win any political good will from the moderate or the extremist sections of the Indian nationalist press.

Even when the Chamber passed a resolution, this did not necessarily produce any immediate effect. Chamber resolutions were not binding even on those who had voted in favor of them. Once carried, a resolution was referred to the Political Department of the Government of India for comment. After consultation with any other relevant departments of the Government of India and local governments, the political secretary would prepare a composite statement of the government's position. Since this opinion rarely agreed with the Chamber's resolution in its entirety, the matter would be referred to the Standing Committee. At this juncture, which usually occurred two or three years after the Standing Committee had first considered the issue, it would seek to reconcile the conflicting recommendations. Here the entire cycle began again, and it was sometimes repeated indefinitely.[56] This bureaucratic labyrinth effectively reduced the possibility that the Chamber would achieve any amelioration in relations between its members and the government. It ensured, furthermore, that petty grievances would slowly fester into major disputes, and it dissipated the time and energies of the Standing Committee.

All these factors—governmental domination, an unattractive agenda, cumbersome procedures, uncertain scheduling—plus princely indifference and inertia contributed to low attendance at Chamber sessions. Although the inaugural session attracted 70 out of 127 members, at succeeding sessions the average attendance was between 30 and 45, and normally was closer to the lower figure. Even the Standing Committee suffered from the problem of poor attendance. In 1923 Ganga Singh of Bikaner moved that the quorum of the Standing Committee be reduced to 3, and Jey Singh of Alwar moved that the quorum of the Chamber be lowered to 25.

Although the latter resolution was defeated, the former was passed.[57] This change meant that any two princes could form a majority on the Standing Committee and could present their personal sentiments as representative of the entire Chamber. This possibility, along with the election of the same members to the Standing Committee year after year and poor attendance at the general sessions, made the Chamber vulnerable to charges that it was unrepresentative and the mouthpiece of a pretentious few.

Even the most enthusiastic members of the Chamber were aware of its deficiencies. As early as May 1922, Bikaner, as chancellor, had proposed to Lord Reading that an informal round table conference of princes be called so as "to enable the Viceroy to understand at first hand the difficulties, the hopes and aspirations of the princes and the remedies they suggest."[58] In his negative reply the viceroy emphasized that any such informal gathering would lower the prestige of the Chamber, which was the established constitutional means for the ventilation of grievances.[59] Reading could conveniently ignore the inadequacies in the organization and operation of the Chamber, but its members became increasingly discouraged by its record and lack of potential for further development. Reading's letter to Hyderabad in March 1926, unequivocally declaring the absolute authority of the paramount power and the total dependence of the Indian states, registered concretely the failure of the Chamber.

Major Changes in Key Positions

Reading's letter, however, was one of the last acts of his viceroyalty, and the Chamber princes looked for greater sympathy from his Conservative successor, Lord Irwin.[60] An aristocrat with empathy for fellow aristocrats, the new viceroy was eager to win the confidence as well as the respect of all segments of Indian society. Although he refused to accept the gifts traditionally bestowed upon the viceroy when he visited princely states and although he was quick to push for internal reforms, Irwin took advantage of his visits to various states to establish close personal ties with their rulers.[61]

About the time of the arrival of the new viceroy, some major changes occurred in the personnel of the inner core of the Chamber. Wearied by long years of activity outside his state, Ganga Singh of Bikaner declined to seek reelection as chancellor at the January 1926 session.[62] Reading privately favored his decision and argued that it was desirable for other princes to become more involved in the work of the Chamber. Although he expressed approval of the election of Bhupinder Singh of Patiala, Reading characterized the new chancellor as "not disposed to overwork himself and . . . not capable of framing the resolutions and generally of supervising the business of the Chamber without expert assistance."[63] The retiring viceroy, consequently, was pleased to note that a new appointment in Patiala, L. F. Rushbrook Williams as foreign minister, would ensure the smooth running of the Chamber.[64] A former professor of modern Indian history at Allahabad University and director of the Central Bureau of Information of the Government of India, Rushbrook Williams possessed a facile pen and quick intelligence that he would place at the service of a variety of princes in the forthcoming decade. His employment by Patiala was a portent of a growing princely reliance on ministers to perform the burdensome tasks associated with the operation of the Chamber and with the creation of public opinion favorable to their continued existence.

Succession changes during 1925 and 1926 also took away old faces from the Standing Committee and added new ones. Two first-rank, twenty-one-gun salute princes, Maharaja Madho Rao Scindia of Gwalior and Maharaja Pratap Singh of Kashmir, died during 1925. A Maratha and an active investor in business enterprises, Madho Rao had numerous contacts among nationalist leaders in the Bombay area and was always ready to utilize them to counteract the growing political unrest in British India. Strong-willed, insolent, but thoroughly loyal to the British, he was the only prince of his rank to participate consistently and prominently in Chamber activities.[65] Upon his death in Paris at the age of forty-nine, his nine-year-old son succeeded him, and Gwalior State entered a long period of minority administration. Under a policy determined by the Chamber, a state remained unrepresented in it when under minority administration.[66] Although Gwalior State would not be represented by its ruler until 1936, it frequently contributed the services of an able minister, Kailas Haksar, to the behind-the-scenes work of the Chamber.

Maharaja Pratap Singh of Kashmir had attended a few Chamber sessions, but his advanced age (he was seventy-five at his death) precluded his playing a part commensurate with the status of his state. He was succeeded by his thirty-year-old nephew and designated heir, Hari Singh. Characterized as fat and good-natured, the new maharaja of Kashmir projected an image that contrasted sharply with the one maintained by his uncle, who was most celebrated for his adherence to the prescriptions of orthodox Hinduism. Pratap Singh never left India in obedience to caste restrictions about the crossing of the deep seas, but his nephew was a frequent visitor to the centers of European society. Although his attraction to this glitter led to an unpleasant episode of blackmail known as the "Mr. A. Affair," Hari Singh's charming combination of stereotyped oriental splendor and Western manners paved the way for his quick entry into the inner circle of the Chamber.[67] Attributing his past escapades and suspicions to poor advice and handling, Irwin claimed that, given the opportunity to develop his good intentions, the new Kashmir ruler would be a "valuable reinforcement to the more progressive party among the Princes."[68]

In 1926 a significant change also occurred in Bhopal. After waging a shrewd campaign to obtain British approval of her desire to have succession pass to her youngest son instead of the grandsons of her deceased first and second sons, the begum of Bhopal abdicated in favor of Hamidullah Khan.[69] There was some apprehension in official circles about the future value of the new incumbent because of his earlier contacts with the Ali brothers and his desire to play polo in England, but Irwin personally liked him and was anxious to avoid raising any feelings of antagonism in him.[70] Experienced in administrative affairs and Chamber routines because of his work as chief secretary to his mother, Hamidullah soon joined the inner circle of the Chamber.

Irwin and the Princes

Eager to enhance his personal reputation, the maharaja

of Patiala worked energetically to improve the quality of the lackluster Chamber sessions. In a circular letter to all members dated 23 July 1926, the new chancellor spoke in glowing terms of the personal concern evinced by Lord Irwin toward them. He emphasized the importance of full attendance at Chamber meetings and the need for more substantial resolutions.[71] Making a special effort to obtain representation from Hyderabad and Mysore, he was rewarded when the maharaja of Mysore deputed Mirza Ismail, his diwan, to attend the forthcoming meeting.[72] On the whole, however, the response to his plea was disheartening, though not entirely unexpected.[73] Only twenty-two princes had replied, and only nine of those bothered to suggest resolutions, most of which pertained to petty issues.

Irwin, nevertheless, was concerned about the princes and attempted on his own initiative to breathe new life into the moribund Chamber. Shortly after his arrival in India, he held conversations with most members of the Standing Committee of the Chamber and became convinced of the necessity of dealing with a topic his predecessors conveniently ignored, namely, the future of the princes. He argued with Birkenhead that "it must be faced sooner or later and failure to do so will inevitably breed uneasiness in the minds of the general body of Princes."[74] After receiving reluctant permission from London, the new viceroy announced in his first speech before the Chamber, in November 1926, that he was willing to hold informal discussions with the princes on their future relations with the Government of India.[75] During subsequent debate the Chamber unanimously passed a resolution authorizing its Standing Committee to meet informally with the viceroy.[76] Although Irwin had succeeded in persuading some of the younger members to give maiden speeches at this session,[77] the Chamber elected the familiar faces of Alwar, Bhopal, Bikaner, Cutch, Kashmir, and Nawanagar to the Standing Committee. Even more ominously, the contest for the chancellorship witnessed a determined attack by supporters of Alwar against the reelection of Patiala, but Patiala was able to overcome it.[78] As recipient of the second-highest number of votes, Alwar became the prochancellor of the Chamber, but this position did little to heal wounded feelings on either side.

It will be remembered that in January 1926 the Chamber had appointed a committee to meet with representatives of the government to discuss possible forms of joint cooperation on matters of common interest. This committee had met in Bikaner City during August 1926 and was scheduled to reconvene in Patiala City in February 1927. Once the Chamber agreed to hold informal talks with the viceroy, this group also assumed responsibility for formulating position papers to aid the members of the Standing Committee. Although the newly elected members of that committee were all invited to attend, the only princes present at the February gathering were Alwar, Bikaner, Dholpur, and Patiala. They were aided in their deliberations by two prominent moderate politicians from British India, Lord Sinha (the former Sir S. P. Sinha, who was created the first Indian baron in 1919) and Sir Tej Bahadur Sapru, as well as ministers from various princely states.[79]

The range of topics discussed at Patiala was extremely broad, but as usual no definite conclusions were reached. Sinha and Sapru, who both had served as Law members in the Government of India, had been asked for their opinions on the legal position of the states once the Government of India became more responsive to the Indian population and possibly dominated by Indian politicians. Dissatisfied with their counsel, the maharaja of Patiala, acting on behalf of the other committee members, deputed Rushbrook Williams and Haksar to obtain other opinions from eminent English counsel, such as Sir John Simon and later Sir Leslie Scott.[80] What the Standing Committee sought were legal arguments to support their contention that their treaties originally concluded with the British East India Company were now binding upon the British crown, the successor to the rights and obligations of the company after 1857. If this principle was accepted, they reasoned that the crown would be responsible for the continued existence of the Indian states regardless of any changes in the structure or personnel of the Government of India and the India Office.

In a circular letter dated 25 February 1927, sent to most members of the Chamber, Patiala summarized the recent discussions held at his capital and outlined the topics to be raised with the viceroy during the May meetings. Besides the recurrent subject of the need to improve relations with the British government, the chancellor broached the issue of internal reform. Arguing that all tended to be judged by the weakest members of their order, he asked all princes to consider implementing some measures of reform. As a minimum he proposed that everyone who did not already have them establish an independent judiciary and a privy purse confined to ten percent of the state revenues. These steps would increase administrative efficiency within the states and enhance the external image of the princes as enlightened autocrats.[81] The initial proposal for the designation of privy purses seems to have come from Irwin, who in October 1926 had suggested to Patiala that he or a few other princes might raise the issue in the Chamber so as to strengthen the position of the princes against some recent attacks that were not without foundation.[82] Neither Irwin nor Patiala were aware of the depth of princely feeling on the crucial matter of internal reforms.

Compared with the response generated by Patiala's earlier circular letters, this one of 25 February brought down an avalanche of comment. By his own count the chancellor was buried under replies from 68 out of 95 princes contacted.[83] Although most of the letters were favorable, a strident opposition criticized the proposals of Patiala and his associates as unrepresentative, unauthorized, and dangerous. Leading this opposition was Maharaja Gulab Singh of Rewa, who countered with his own circular letter to Chamber members. In it this premier prince of Baghelkhand questioned the credentials of the Patiala meeting, advocated a stronger statement of the duty of the crown to protect the princes, and opposed any public commitment to reforms on the basis that it would reduce the freedom of the prince in his internal administration.[84]

Bhupinder Singh quickly sent a conciliatory letter to Rewa reminding him of the authorization from the Chamber in 1926 for their discussions, emphasizing the tentative character of their conclusions, and the voluntary nature of their forthcoming conference with the viceroy.[85] Concurrently, Patiala worked to break up the group of central Indian princes, including the nawab of Bhopal, whom Rewa had gathered as his supporters on the plea for regional unity. The maharao of Cutch, a member of the Standing Committee, served as an intermediary between that group and Rewa. As a unifying measure Cutch suggested to Rewa that he request to be co-opted to the Standing Committee for the discussions with Irwin.[86] The chancellor and the Standing Committee were amenable, for, as Patiala pointed out, if Rewa "agrees to join us such slight measure of dissatisfaction as had been expressed by certain Princes following his lead will only be naturally offset."[87] When the princes finally arrived in Simla in May 1927 to meet with Irwin,[88] Rewa abruptly returned home on the plea that his grandmother was sick. Although he had been neutralized as a possible menace, Rewa's activities reveal the fragile unity within the Chamber and the difficulties that its leaders encountered in trying to promote any program of positive action among its members. His reaction and that of his supporters also highlight the undercurrent of resistance among many princes to political reforms and the argument that such reforms were necessary to preserve some elements of authority.

The discussions with Irwin focused on governmental practices in administrative, economic, and fiscal spheres that the princes considered had led to unjustified intervention in the internal affairs of their states and on the necessity of defining the position of the princes toward a Government of India that was increasingly responsible to an Indian electorate. With regard to the first topic, Irwin acknowledged the disadvantages of the "sledge-hammer" intervention policy of the government and called for an effective substitute.[89] In response Bikaner proposed a resolution on internal reform for the next Chamber session. Correction from within, he argued, would render intervention from without unnecessary.[90] The viceroy heartily approved of this suggestion and a few weeks later wrote an informal note setting forth the basic elements of good government for the guidance of any prince who requested the note.[91]

The princes further appealed for a special inquiry to examine their present and future relationship with the Government of India and the India Office.[92] Although Irwin felt that their suggestions for common consultation on administrative matters of mutual concern and for greater protection or isolation from political control by a responsible Government of India were contradictory, he did think that a special inquiry would be of value if it was limited to consideration of the present situation and avoided questions about the "hypothetical future."[93] Although the secretary of state, Lord Birkenhead, thought that the princes probably had made a mistake in asking for an inquiry, he acquiesced in Irwin's recommendation as a matter of expediency so as to demonstrate imperial awareness of princely anxieties.[94] At long last the princes had succeeded in reopening the discussion on their situation, which they deemed had been adversely affected by the implementation of the Montagu-Chelmsford Report.

The Princes and the Indian States Committee

Now the princely expectations of the possible benefits to be derived from the long-awaited inquiry began to swell. A change of political secretary from the unyielding Thompson to the more amenable Charles Watson seemed to augur well.[95] At the first meeting of the Standing Committee with Watson in December 1927, however, there were already signs of disappointment ahead if the princes cared to read them. In the discussion on the forthcoming inquiry, the new political secretary stressed that the committee would consider "the existing constitutional position, but it is not proposed that they should go into the much wider and difficult question of future relations."[96] A second term of reference was the improvement of financial and economic relations between the government and the states. This meant that any changes would be made only in the economic sphere and not in the constitutional sphere, which was the primary concern of the princes.

In London the secretary of state deemed that the dread day of responsible government was remote and that any effort to strengthen the constitutional position of the princes would only serve to entrench them against their British overlord.[97] For his own reasons the viceroy shared his superior's views on the proper task for the Indian States Committee, and shortly after the committee arrived in India in early January

1928, he personally warned Sir Harcourt Butler, its chairman, that his assignment was to report on the existing constitutional situation and not to propose any new arrangements.[98] He also suggested that Butler should discreetly but firmly hint to Sir Leslie Scott, the chief counsel for the Chamber's Special Organization, that the committee would not accept any scheme for constitutional revision.[99] Once again the British patron refused to think seriously about the dilemmas posed by the continued existence of autocratic, dependent states within a changing imperial structure. The sympathetic Irwin hoped that a renewed emphasis on internal reform might help prepare the states to face the future, though many of his political officers bluntly stated that the princes gave little evidence of seizing the initiative and that the policy of noninterference launched by Minto was a definite handicap to their efforts to prompt the princes in this area.[100] Even Curzon's program launched in 1901 to push for the establishment of privy purses in all states within twenty-five years was strikingly unproductive.[101] Since their client states had long ceased to be the prime threat to imperial stability, British officials were ready to ignore princely pleas for a more defined constitutional status until it would benefit imperial interests to do so.

Even in the matters of personnel and timing, the Butler Committee was a disappointment to the princes. Despite their appeals for a broadly representative group, the committee was limited to three members: Butler, who had been foreign secretary under Minto and later had served as lieutenant governor in the United Provinces and in Burma; Sidney Peel, a financier with experience in the City and in Parliament; and Professor W. S. Holdsworth, a jurist.[102] Since the committee arrived in India more quickly than had been anticipated, mainly because they wanted to be able to leave before the hot weather began, the Chamber complained that they had not had sufficient time to formulate a comprehensive statement of their case. Both Irwin and Birkenhead were reluctant to extend the duration of the inquiry, the latter being particularly concerned that if the inquiry was continued in London, a few princes who would come to testify could arrogate to themselves the position of plenipotentiaries for all other princes.[103] In the end the inquiry had to be continued in London, and Birkenhead's fears were more or less realized.

Meanwhile the committee spent most of its time in India, touring individual states and holding informal discussions with princes and state officials. It visited fifteen states, including all those whose rulers served on the Standing Committee and the largest ones who remained out of the Chamber.[104] Besides this personal contact, the committee sent a questionnaire on the topics of the inquiry to all Chamber members and all local governments.

One of the committee's first visits was to Patiala State, where the maharaja sharply delineated the anxieties and expectations of most of his brethren. According to his view, as the Government of India became more complex and more centralized, it increasingly initiated policies affecting the entire subcontinent without considering whether they might have bad effects on the states. The princes, who were scattered, isolated units, found their position inexorably weakened vis-à-vis the government as it became more centralized. Their situation was rendered acute by the growing movement of the "educated classes" of British India into this powerful governmental structure. The chancellor pleaded

> for a fundamental consideration of the problem as to whether there is any justification for the British India of the future to exercise control over the Indian States; and as to whether there be not room within the wide confines of this country for two sister polities, albeit dissimilar in size and in organisation, in one of which the democratic, and in the other the monarchic, principle is embodied. In my judgment they can co-exist and work together for the common good of India.[105]

Unfortunately for the princes, the British were concerned with accommodating precisely those "educated classes" who so frightened the princes. The princes were whiny clients who were annoying, but far less dangerous than the "educated classes" and their new leaders such as Jawaharlal Nehru.

Shortly after Patiala had entertained the Butler Committee, the Chamber of Princes met in Delhi 20–25 February 1928. The assembled princes devoted most of their attention to planning their strategy to enhance the presentation of their views before the Butler Committee. During the formal sessions the maharaja of Bikaner moved the promised resolution advocating the establishment of an independent judiciary to administer a definite code of law and a clear-cut division of state revenues between a privy purse and public expenditures in all states.[106] Although no speaker dared oppose such a simple demand, many emphasized that such reforms could only be implemented in accord with the customs and traditions of each individual state. This plea of special conditions could be utilized to dilute the impact of even these basic political reforms.[107] Bikaner's resolution was passed unanimously, but it accomplished little, since it bound no one in the Chamber to any action. It was window-dressing to satisfy the viceroy.

At their informal meetings held concurrently with the Chamber sessions, the princes confirmed the actions of the Standing Committee taken with regard to the Butler Committee. Haksar and Rushbrook Williams were appointed director and joint director of a Special Office of the Chamber charged with the preparation of a joint statement for presentation to the committee. All present were urged to send any relevant material about their grievances against the government to this Special Office, which would collate the material and attempt to include all major points in the joint statement. Sir Leslie Scott was authorized to continue as counsel to the Special Office and the Standing Committee. Once Scott and that office had prepared a preliminary draft of the statement, it would be submitted to the princes at a meeting for their comments and criticisms.[108]

This Bombay assembly to consider the joint statement was held on 18–19 April 1928. In his circular letters preparatory to the meeting, Patiala emphasized the tentative, nonobligatory nature of any conclusions reached. This was an effort to obtain the widest possible support and representation, but even so only thirty-four princes and eighty-eight ministers from various states bothered to come to Bombay.[109] The first topic of discussion was the need for the reconciliation of larger and smaller princes so that the broadest support possible for the Chamber statement could be obtained. On the one hand, several larger states such as Hyderabad, Mysore, Baroda, Travancore, and Cochin, generally critical of the Scott scheme as impracticable and of Scott's fee as excessive, refused to be associated with Scott and planned to offer separate opinions to the Butler Committee.[110] On the other hand, many smaller states felt that the Scott statement did not make adequate provision for their future. Scott himself warned the assembly:

> . . . In order that you [the princes] may be able to maintain your rights intact in the future, you being the smaller part of India, you want to have as much support as possible from all the various individuals of the States. That is merely a statement of self-interest, but it is a statement of self-interest which applies to the bigger States just as much as to the smaller State.[111]

Such pleas for unity from either an outsider like Scott or from princes themselves such as Bikaner and Patiala had little effect on a group of men blinded by long traditions of personal rivalry. This virus of personal vanity and resultant infection of mistrust existed even within the Standing Committee, as is illustrated by the following incident. A few months after the Bombay meeting, Patiala was to go to England to assist in the presentation of the princes' position before the English public as well as the Butler Committee. According to the constitution of the Chamber, the office of chancellor, while Patiala was out of India, would be filled by Alwar, who had received the second-highest number of votes in the last election for this post. Bhupinder Singh was reluctant to hand over his office, claiming that Alwar might thwart the activities of the Standing Committee in London for reasons of personal jealousy.[112] The Punjab prince was not alone in his suspicions of, and dislike for, the Rajput prince, who had desired to succeed a fellow Rajput, Bikaner, as chancellor of the Chamber. After meeting with the Standing Committee of the Chamber in May 1927, Irwin had confided to Birkenhead "that the only point on which, with one exception, they [the princes] were all unanimous in private conversations . . . was their cordial dislike of Alwar."[113] This antipathy was mutual, and would intensify as Alwar was repeatedly rebuffed in his efforts to be elected chancellor of the Chamber.

At Bombay, Scott presented for the first time his triple-tiered arrangement for handling relations between the states and the British government. First, there was to be the Viceroy in Indian States Council, composed of the viceroy, the political secretary, and assorted British and princely representatives. This body would deal with all questions relating to the respective treaty rights and obligations of the crown and the princes. Second, there was to be the Governor-General in Indian States Council, composed of representatives from British India and the states, which would treat all matters of common concern such as commerce, irrigation, and agriculture. Third, there was to be the Union Court, composed of a judge and two English jurists, which would arbitrate disputes between the states and the paramount power, between individual states, or between the first two bodies mentioned above.[114] Scott argued that if these proposed arrangements replaced the haphazard existing system, many of the grievances of the princes would be eliminated or quickly alleviated. Since Butler apparently made it clear sometime after this Bombay meeting that his committee would not accept such programs concerning future relations, Scott's scheme was quietly dispatched to the Chamber archives. Still, this program illustrates what many princes had come to think would secure the redress of their grievances and the amelioration of their relations with British India. Their faith in legalistic, constitutional measures appeared to be as boundless as it was unrealistic.

In May 1928 the Butler Committee returned to England and shortly thereafter they were followed by members of the Standing Committee. Ostensibly these princes were to assist Sir Leslie Scott in his presentation of the Chamber's statement before the Butler Committee. In reality they were more actively engaged in a propaganda campaign among politically conscious sections of the English public in order to build up public support and pressure on the government for their views. Handsome, regal-looking Bhupinder Singh, who had long been an advocate of the benefits to be derived from effective propaganda, was the most prominent figure in this endeavor.

The opening shot in the campaign was a major address delivered by Patiala before the East India Association, carefully timed to come two days before the opening session of the inquiry in London. Patiala made three basic points that he would reiterate in most of his public statements during his stay in England. After a historical introduction on the close relationship between the Indian states and the British government, he complained that the present system was totally inadequate and that he and his colleagues desired some type of federation at the top that would allow for joint cooperation on matters of common concern between British India and Indian India. Next he earnestly declared that the princes bore no ill will toward the nationalist movement in British India, and simply desired the maintenance of close ties with Britain. Finally he lamented that they were generally misunderstood figures and that they were monarchs with rights and obligations according to the Indian ideal of kingship. Indian princes wanted progress but only as fast as local conditions allowed.[115] In his efforts to promote a good public image of the princes, Patiala was later to elaborate these points in articles contributed to journals and newspapers and in other speeches.[116] His efforts were reinforced by those of L. F. Rushbrook Williams, who, as head of the Publicity Bureau of the Special Office of the Chamber in London, made numerous speeches and wrote several articles stressing the princes' contributions to the maintenance of the British Empire.

There was another group actively propagandizing in Britain during the sessions of the Butler Committee. This one represented the states' subjects' movement that had been slowly organizing in the 1920s.[117] When the Butler Committee had been in India, spokesmen for this movement had attempted to present their grievances against the princes. The committee, however, refused to accept their testimony, since it considered such complaints outside its terms of reference.[118] On 11 July 1928 the executive committee of the Indian States' People's Conference decided to send a deputation to England in order to awaken public sympathy there for the oppressed peoples of the Indian states. Members selected to go were Diwan Bahadur Ramchandra Rao, the president, Professor G. R. Abhyankar, the general secretary, and Amritlal D. Sheth; they in turn co-opted Popotlal

L. Chudgar, who was willing to pay his own expenses.[119] In London the Butler Committee agreed to accept only a written statement from the deputation, so the recently arrived quartet turned to a variety of other forums where they elaborated their demand for a formal inquiry into the political conditions prevailing in each state. Although their principal targets were Labour party groups and parliamentary members, they also spoke to many of the same political associations, newspaper editors, and India Office officials cultivated by the Chamber princes and their publicity director.[120] Although the actual influence of their, as well as princely, propaganda on English public opinion is difficult to assess, the deputation thought that their talks and writings had countered the distortions spread by the princes and had stimulated interest in the internal conditions prevailing within the states and in the future relationship between the states and the rest of India.[121]

After an initial meeting on 25 July 1928, when they received Sir Leslie Scott's extensive statement of the Chamber's case, the Butler Committee did not reconvene until 15 October. Then in private hearings Scott took six weeks to present evidence and to elucidate further the claims of his clients.[122] The committee adjourned at the end of November to write its report, which was presented on 14 February 1929 to Lord Peel, who had succeeded Birkenhead as secretary of state for India in October 1928. As might have been anticipated, the report pleased no one except perhaps the British government.[123]

On the one hand, the princes were dismayed that the committee had refused to define paramountcy and thereby set limits on the actions of the paramount power. The report declared: "Paramountcy must remain paramount; it must fulfill its obligations, defining or adapting itself according to the shifting necessities of the time and the progressive development of the states."[124] In an effort at consolation it warned the princes: "On paramountcy and paramountcy alone can the states rely for their preservation through the generation that is to come. Through paramountcy is pushed aside the danger of destruction or annexation."[125] The vanity of this pledge would be painfully apparent in 1947.

The disillusioned princes were alarmed further by what Patiala termed "novel and unwarranted formulas of intervention." He cited three. Most frightening was the claim that the paramount power could suggest measures for change in the form of the government of a state should a widespread popular demand for change arise. To the princes this prerogative seemed like an open invitation to their political opponents to launch agitations for change. It was also asserted that if a state was unable to carry out the necessary functions of government properly because of its small size, the paramount power was obligated to intervene in order to provide adequate government. This claim could lead to the amalgamation of hundreds of petty states, particularly those too small even to warrant representation in the Chamber. The report also declared that intervention by the paramount power was justifiable on the grounds that it would be for the economic good of India as a whole.[126] It now seemed to the princes that the inquiry conducted by the Butler Committee had been a Pandora's box instead of a solution to longstanding problems. It seemed to render them more vulnerable than ever before to interference by the government and opened new fronts for attack by the emerging states' subjects' groups.

On the other hand, the states' subjects' groups were enraged by the very sections of the report that most enheartened the princes. The item causing the greatest controversy was the committee's opinion

> that, in view of the historical nature of the relationship between the Paramount Power and the Princes, the latter should not be transferred without their own agreement to a relationship with a new government in British India responsible to an Indian legislature.[127]

It is significant to note that this decision was a reversal of the earlier opinion espoused by Lord Irwin that "we should ourselves be disposed to hold, as a matter of political theory, that the Government of India must be regarded as the Agent for the Crown and Parliament in the conduct of the relations with the States, and that the Crown and Parliament must be deemed competent to appoint a Dominion Government in India to the same Agency."[128] Although it is uncertain whether the princes realized that the Butler Committee was responsible for this about-face, this incident once again reveals the wide range of opinion within the British hierarchy over the future of their princely clients. By disowning nationalists and states' subjects' groups as legitimate heirs to paramountcy and its rights, the Butler Committee Report served to prod these groups to evolve, outside of the British constitutional structure, a new relationship with the states. Although this rejection by the Butler Committee was only one factor among many, it did serve as a major stimulus to greater activity by these groups to achieve a bargaining position.

Conclusion

By 1929 the princes had become thoroughly disenchanted with British constitutional processes. For those who had been active in the Chamber, their labors seemed to have been futile. Despite repeated efforts to achieve their goals through petitions, resolutions, viceregal conferences, and governmental inquiries, their position seemed more insecure than it had been a decade earlier. Their apparent triumph over the issue of press protection had proved to be a hollow one, since the law was very difficult to apply in concrete circumstances. Paramountcy had been not limited but expanded by Reading's letter on Berar and the Report of the Indian States Committee. That paramountcy would not be delegated to a third party was a concession, but one of small consolation. Finally, the princes appeared further away than ever from some means of joint cooperation with British Indian legislators.

At the viceregal pinnacle there seemed to be a stalemate on the princes. Chelmsford had pushed vigorously for measures such as the Chamber that the princes desired and had generally continued the policy of noninterference. Reading had been less sympathetic to princely pleas for further consideration of their grievances and had pursued a more severe policy toward princes who abused their positions or challenged British authority. Irwin had tried to be more conciliatory, but also more active in promoting internal reform both through political officers and the princes themselves. The Butler Report irritated the princes, and the resolutions on internal reform within the Chamber raised more apprehensions among the princes about this body. At his meeting in July 1927 with political officers, Irwin encountered arguments about the difficulties of furthering political reform because of Minto's promise. This response indicates a lack of initiative and interest among political officers. If they had been more receptive to the new lead provided by Irwin, they could have used it as justification for a shift in activity and policy. Instead they ignored it until developments in British India consumed most of the viceregal time, energy, and thought.[129]

Within British India the late 1920s also proved to be an era of growing resentment and even incipient rebellion against the use of constitutional methods to achieve political reform. Although there had been a respite from major political agitations since the end of the first noncooperation movement in 1922, British India was in political turmoil by 1930. The 1919 Indian Councils Act had provided that an inquiry be held ten years after its passage to investigate the working of, and to suggest needed changes, if any, in, its provisions. Because of their desire to dominate such an undertaking, the Conservative Government appointed this Indian Statutory Commission, more popularly known as the Simon Commission after its chairman, in the autumn of 1927 when it appeared likely that they would be voted out of office. Since the commission was responsible to Parliament, the government in London, fully supported by Lord Irwin in Delhi, appointed only British members of Parliament to the commission. Both London and Delhi further argued that a commission composed of impartial Britishers would make fairer recommendations than one with Indians because of the deepening communal divisions throughout India. The composition of the Simon Commission not only alienated those Indians already discontented with the slow pace of constitutional methods but even those moderates dedicated to legal processes such as Motilal Nehru and Tej Bahadur Sapru. During its two tours of India the commission was the object of political and social boycott by a wide range of Indian groups.[130] Gradually realizing the potentially explosive forces building up within the nationalist opposition, Lord Irwin saw the need for some striking gesture that would win the support of moderate leaders and at least partially relieve the prevailing political tensions.

When the viceroy sailed for Britain in May 1929 on his mid-term leave, he carried drafts of a correspondence to be carried on between Sir John Simon and Ramsay MacDonald, the prime minister, in which the former initiated a proposal to hold a Round Table Conference with representatives from Britain, British India, and the Indian states to discuss the next installment of constitutional reform.[131] After laborious consultations with major party leaders in Britain and wearisome revisions to satisfy various objections, the correspondence was issued in October 1929.[132] Upon his arrival back in India, Irwin then announced on 31 October that full dominion status was the goal of constitutional development in India and that in accordance with Simon's recent letter, His Majesty's Government was to call a conference in London to discuss the forthcoming Simon Report and other constitutional issues raised by the delegates.

Most political groups in British India welcomed the viceroy's announcement. The Indian National Congress did not. After some initial uncertainty, it declined to participate in the deliberations when the government refused to concede that the Round Table Conference would plan the immediate inauguration of dominion status. In a stormy session at Lahore, the Congress passed a resolution calling for complete independence and proclaimed 26 January 1930 as Independence Day. Gandhi was also given the authority to launch a civil disobedience movement in whatever circumstances he deemed suitable. Their political isolation by now a golden memory, the Indian princes were to be increasingly enmeshed in the political turbulence surrounding the second civil disobedience movement of the early 1930s.

chapter six

Limited Opportunities as All-Indian Politicians

Princely involvement in political events on an all-Indian scale had begun in a haphazard manner during the early decades of the twentieth century when British Indian politicians first seriously challenged the political control of the British *raj.* The princes then acted as political allies in order to reduce political opposition to their British overlord. Within their own territories the princes had reasonably firm control through their activities as concerned paternalists and their employment of autocratic methods against sources of opposition. When they entered the political arena of British India, the princes carried not only their prestige as indigenous rulers who shared cultural bonds with their subjects and other Indians but also attitudes shaped by the methods they utilized and the deference they enjoyed within their states. They therefore possessed both assets and liabilities for dealing with Indian politicians who earnestly looked for treatment as equals and had goals of responsible government and some popular political participation.

In this wider sphere the princes, both at the request of their imperial overlord and on their own initiative, acted as Indian spokesmen for order and as mediators between the foreign British and Indian social and religious groups. They could perform such functions, since many Indian leaders had previously acknowledged the princes as symbols of Indian political authority and autonomy and had courted them as sources of legitimation and financial patronage. M. G. Ranade and B. G. Tilak both solicited princely endorsements for ventures such as the Poona Sarvajanik Sabha and the Shivaji Festival. As the states and British India became more differentiated in the extent of political participation allowed and legal safeguards for individual civil rights, the princes became less attractive as allies to Indian leaders. At the same time as the British were more seriously menaced by popular political movements, they became less concerned about the future of their collaborators.

After Gandhi had dramatically terminated the first civil disobedience movement in February 1922, the princes were less prominent in British Indian politics. Those formerly most aggressive, such as Alwar, Bikaner, Gwalior, and Patiala, constituted the inner core of the Chamber of Princes and now concentrated their attention on Chamber sessions and related activities such as attendance at imperial conferences and at meetings of the Assembly of the League of Nations.[1] The government, moreover, no longer felt an acute need for their political support, and was attempting to pursue a policy of business as usual. The mid-1920s appeared to be a period of calm as Congressmen debated entry into the legislative assemblies established by the 1919 Indian Councils Act, Gandhi spun khadi in jail, and Muslims nursed their wounds from the Khilafat debacle.

The absence of any major political campaigns was deceptive, and by the late 1920s the political situation in India had changed dramatically. The second civil disobedience movement launched an era of violent, and in some ways revolutionary, confrontation between Indian nationalists and the Government of India. The goal of the Indian National Congress was now independence; younger leaders such as Jawaharlal Nehru and Subhas Chandra Bose were advocating radical social programs and were organizing new groups; and terrorists were again active. The growth of Indian states' people's groups within and around the states presented an unprecedented challenge to the prince's ability to maintain internal order. The gradual change in Congress policy from noninterference to more active intervention in Indian state politics provided an additional focus for new and existing opposition to princely authority. Finally, the extension of communal disturbances, communal organizations, and communal electorates during the 1920s raised the apprehensions of communal leaders and impinged more directly on the internal political relationships between subjects and princes.

British officials, moderate politicians, communal leaders, and Indian princes all felt threatened by these changes. Each sought to utilize the other as allies, but each had objectives that did not necessarily coincide with those of whomever happened to be their allies. The British wanted to maintain control, the moderates fought to retain dominance in the constitutional process, the communal leaders pursued security and advantages for their followers, and the princes tried to retain power within their states and their semi-autonomous status within the British Indian Empire. The princes had a particularly difficult position as they juggled their goals as territorial rulers and imperial politicians. Action in one sphere undertaken for one purpose might produce undesirable or ambivalent results in the other. Here a prime example is communal activity. Because of his role as an all-Indian Sikh leader, Bhupinder Singh of Patiala could blunt opposition led by Sikhs within his state with pleas for Sikh unity at times of crisis for the Sikh community. Later, however, his non-Sikh subjects might protest any preferential treatment for Sikhs in the state service or regulations. The consequences of all-Indian communal leadership would be even more mixed for princes who shared their religious affiliations with a much smaller segment of their population, such as the Muslim rulers of Hyderabad and Bhopal.

Thus the structure of opportunities available to the princes was a restricted one because of the conflicting interests of the groups who sought them as allies and the dual position that the princes occupied. Frequently the princes were caught in the middle between contending factions in the all-India arena, and each group wanted the princes to proceed only insofar as such activity would benefit their own self-interests.

As a consequence, the princely space to maneuver on this external stage was being constricted just as they faced new pressures within their states on their political options. Their future was a difficult one.

Communal Tensions during the 1920s

Despite the superficial placidity of political life during the years after 1922,[2] the mounting incidents of communal violence in Bengal, the United Provinces, and Punjab were ominous portents of the holocaust that occurred two decades later. Earlier it had been freely alleged by British officials such as Sir Michael O'Dwyer that communal tension was virtually unknown in the Indian states. O'Dwyer contended that the princes, who did not have to pursue a policy of religious neutrality, could maintain a tight control over the religious practices of their subjects and thereby prevent an occasion arising for clashes between religious communities.[3] These British officials and those Indian nationalists who claimed that communal conflicts were exclusively the outcome of an imperial policy of divide and rule were rudely awakened by the sacking of a Hindu temple in Gulbarga, Hyderabad, in 1924 by a Muslim mob.[4] This single instance was the forerunner of communal agitations that would soon erupt throughout princely India, and with particular intensity in areas where the ruler did not share the religion of the majority of his subjects as in Hyderabad, Kashmir, and Bhopal.

In this atmosphere of tense communal relations, two princes seemed to acquire growing prominence as spokesmen within and for their respective communities.

Since his capital was close to Delhi and British Punjab, which both had explosive communal situations, Maharaja Jey Singh of Alwar was conveniently located for excursions into Hindu communal politics. His principal guru in this area of activity was Pandit Madan Mohan Malaviya.[5] A prime solicitor of funds from the princes for the establishment of the Hindu University at Benares, Malaviya was also conspicuously active in the Hindu Mahasabha, an organization founded in 1906 to protect Hindu interests from the machinations of the Muslim League. A major patron of the University, Jey Singh was not active within the formal structure of the

Mahasabha but rather participated in various regional or subsidiary groups loosely associated with it. One of his typical forays into Hindu communal politics occurred in January 1927, when he presided over the Fourth Provincial Sanatan Dharm Conference at Multan and made a donation of forty thousand rupees to its treasury.[6]

Concerned about being labeled a divisive influence, Alwar was careful to alternate his potentially disruptive exhortations with pleas for communal harmony. While chairing a session of the Kshatriya Mahasabha in Delhi during November 1924, he pleaded for religious tolerance of other groups. At the same time, however, he reminded the assembled Kshatriyas, who included the maharajas of Bikaner, Kashmir, Patiala, and Sitamau, of their religious duties to protect the weak and to preserve the Hindu tradition.[7] If pushed to the extreme, the latter injunction would preclude the possibility of communal peace during the tense atmosphere of the 1920s. Malaviya shared the platform with Alwar and made a nonpartisan speech stressing the need for more educational facilities and opportunities in the states.[8]

Even more significant on the all-India scene was Alwar's attendance as a Hindu leader at the Unity Conference held at Simla in September 1927. This venture had been initiated by Shaukat Ali of the Central Khilafat Committee when he invited B. S. Moonje, the president of the Hindu Mahasabha, to join in a search for remedies to heal the prevailing communal infection.[9] In his speech before the conference, Jey Singh emphasized that the states were ready to cooperate in bringing about communal accord and declared "that this communal strife is only the outcome of political thought—I can sum it up in one word, 'franchise,' in other words the safeguarding of minorities."[10] Alwar was firmly on the side of Indian nationalists, who saw separate electorates as a divisive plot by the British; but at the same time he revealed his antipathy for popular government. His final warning that communal conflicts only meant that Mother India was fighting herself failed, as did this and subsequent Unity Conferences, to lessen communal dissensions. The self-styled Hindu philosopher continued to be active in these sessions and in 1932 even agreed to serve as president of the Allahabad Unity Conference. His participation raised the indignation of the Aga Khan and his Muslim colleagues as well as the secretary of state, Samuel Hoare, who found it objectionable that princes should be interfering in British Indian politics in this manner.[11]

Maharaja Bhupinder Singh of Patiala was another ruler diligent in the fulfillment of his duties as a religious leader. Throughout the 1920s he continued his patronage of Sikh religious and educational institutions and his sponsorship of elaborate celebrations of Sikh festivals. One still-remembered episode occurred in June 1923 during a *kar sewa*, a periodic cleaning of the tank at the Golden Temple in Amritsar, a major pilgrimage center for Sikhs. Clad only in his undershirt and short drawers, the physically massive, heavily bearded Bhupinder Singh waded into the slimy water and picked up a shovelful of accumulated sediment, accompanied by the droning chants of Sikh priests.[12]

In the years immediately following the passage of the Gurdwara Act of 1925, which vested control of most gurdwaras in the SGPC, Patiala remained a significant force in Sikh politics despite the fact that he was accorded only four seats out of the total of 175.[13] Undaunted and resourceful, he maintained informal contacts with Sikh leaders of varying political persuasions. During 1926 and 1927 delegations from the SGPC, which even included Master Tara Singh at times, made several visits to Patiala to plead for further funding of SGPC projects as well as for the release of certain comrades held in state jails.[14] A lack of affirmative response to the latter request led to a growing alienation between Bhupinder Singh and the Akali members of the SGPC. In January 1929 Kharak Singh, Mangal Singh, and Master Tara Singh led the Akalis in a vehement harassment of Patiala to force the release of fellow Akalis, most notably Sewa Singh of Thikriwala.[15] A skillful counter campaign by Patiala and protests from other Sikh factions produced an abrupt termination of this agitation by late February.[16] Despite the deepening antipathy between the Sikh prince and radical Akali leaders, the former retained a certain stature within the total Sikh community that continued to be exploited by the British patron as well as moderate Sikhs.

In 1924 Bhupinder Singh agreed to host the Sikh Educational Conference, which still advocated the advance of Sikhs through improvement of their educational qualifications rather than obstructionist agitations.[17] A few years later, in 1927, moderate Sikhs such as Sundar Singh Majithia, a prominent leader of the Chief Khalsa Diwan, secured the election of Patiala as the chancellor of Khalsa College in Amritsar.[18] These relationships were based on the desire of all parties to reaffirm their position within the Sikh community in the face of the increasingly successful challenge for dominance by the leaders associated with the SGPC. In some ways Patiala's growing alienation from radical Sikhs and his expanding affiliation with moderate Sikhs was a reflection in communal politics of the changing patterns of relationships between politically active princes and British Indian politicians in the all-India debate on constitutional questions.

Growth of the States' People's Movement

A second major development during the 1920s that would drastically affect the future of the Indian princes was the rise of pressure groups advocating political and social reform in princely India. The general attitude of most British Indian political organizations, including the Indian National Congress, toward the Indian states had been one of noninterference in their internal affairs tied to a call to the populace of the states to agitate constitutionally for representative and responsible government and various social reforms.[19] During the years after World War I some British Indian politicians abandoned this passive attitude because they thought that British India could never achieve effective self-government or dominion status unless the states shared in democratic political advances. Joined by a small but militant number of state subjects, these British Indian activists began to organize local groups. Since most princes proscribed all forms of political opposition to their administrations and policies, these newly formed associations were usually forced to meet on British Indian territory, preferably near state boundaries. They contained a sizable number of British Indians and state subjects living in British India. Reflecting the clustered arrangement of states in the Deccan, Kathiawar, Rajputana, and Punjab, the first groups were regionally oriented, and only gradually did they develop interregional ties. In 1927 an All

India States' People's Conference was founded with headquarters in Bombay.[20]

The programs of the early, dispersed states' people's groups were moderate in tone, petitioning for representative institutions as preparation for responsible government under a monarch supported by the loyalty of his people.[21] Some of their manifestoes even contained expressions of sympathy and support for the princes in their efforts to maintain their rights and status vis-à-vis the paramount power.[22] During the 1920s the platforms became more radical but still temperate by comparison with the programs of many British Indian political groups. The first national meeting of the All India States' People's Conference in December 1927 called for a federal arrangement between the two parts of India, an amalgamation of smaller states into politically and economically viable units, political reforms such as an independent judiciary and responsible ministers within the states' governments, and various social and educational reforms.[23]

The usual princely response to this type of political activity was suppression within their own territories and requests to the British government to choke off such opposition on its side of the border. Instead of making a bold effort to seek an accommodation with these reasonable demands, the princes charged that the states' people's leaders were unrepresentative of the loyal masses within princely India and their programs unrelated to local customs and conditions. These accusations were reminiscent of earlier British allegations about the unrepresentative character of the leadership of the nationalist movement. Willingly deluded by their own rhetorical counterattacks, the princes were pitiably slow to recognize the growing adherence of their formerly obedient flocks to the states' people's leaders. Their political shortsightedness meant that they would have to cope with increasingly belligerent demands just when their bargaining power was declining.

Renewed Princely Participation in British Indian Politics

When the all-British composition of the Indian Statutory Commission was announced in the autumn of 1927, political activity on the Indian subcontinent remarkably quickened, and the princes were drawn once again into the vortex of British Indian politics. These autocrats were responding to pressures from such diverse sources as the All-Parties Conference, the British government, moderate Indian politicians, and communal organizations, as well as acting on their own initiative. During the second civil disobedience movement of the early 1930s, their involvement may be classified under two broad categories: taking part in political and politically oriented religious affairs outside their possessions and confronting British Indian leaders and organizations who sought to penetrate princely India.

British Efforts to Mobilize the Princes

During the first phase of the civil disobedience movement, from April 1930 to March 1931, the British seemed primarily concerned with securing the cooperation of the princes at the forthcoming Round Table Conference in London. Even so, they tried to use appropriate princes to reduce Muslim participation in Gandhi's current campaign. In May 1930 Lord Irwin arranged for the nizam of Hyderabad to issue a "manifesto exhorting all Muslims to stand firmly aloof from [the] civil disobedience movement."[24] In a more minor matter, Irwin asked the nizam and the nawab of Bhopal to exert their influence on the conservative Muslim theological school at Deoband to restrain their Sadr Mudarris, Husain Ahmad Madani, from continuing his vocal support of the civil disobedience movement.[25] After these two major patrons threatened to withdraw their annual grants, the faculty persuaded their director to undertake a pilgrimage to Mecca.[26] Apparently the British strategy was to avoid a repetition of the Hindu-Muslim coalition of 1921, achieved when Gandhi adroitly linked the Amritsar firing and the Khilafat question.

Except for these and a few other isolated incidents, the British made few requests of their princely clients for political support in India until after Gandhi returned from the Second Round Table Conference in early 1932 and resumed the temporarily suspended civil disobedience movement. The official initiative in seeking cooperation from the princes to thwart the activities of the Indian National Congress came first from Bombay, which was particularly vulnerable to hit-and-run attacks by noncooperators operating from bases under princely jurisdiction because it contained so many "islands" of state territories and shared long boundaries with several other states.[27] Once Bombay had raised this issue in December 1931, the Home as well as the Foreign and Political Departments of the Government of India decided to request princely collaboration on three levels.

Initially, all political officers were instructed to ask for assistance in whatever manner was most suited to the local circumstances and at the same time to ensure "that special activities of the Civil Disobedience Movement such as the *boycott* of British goods are not allowed to be *practiced* in their States or their territories and that their States are not used as a base for agitation in British India."[28] Then, Charles Watson, the political secretary, appealed to the residents at Hyderabad and Mysore and the AGGs in Rajputana and Central India to ascertain if any of the rulers with whom they were in contact would be willing to issue pronouncements against the civil disobedience movement. He added that any such statement must appear to be spontaneous and should avoid giving the impression of being prompted by the government if it was to have any propaganda value.[29]

Finally, a special message was sent to the AGG in Rajputana drawing to his attention the fact that in the past considerable contributions had been made to the Congress by subjects of Jaipur, Jodhpur, and Bikaner who, while residing and doing business in British India, retained ties to their birthplaces. Since finance would be a problem for the Congress in the forthcoming struggle, these states were to be requested to bring pressure to bear upon their subjects not to make further donations to the Congress treasury.[30] All major Rajputana Durbars responded positively to this governmental request for assistance, and the Jaipur and Jodhpur governments specifically promised to take suitable action against any of their state subjects who contributed to the civil disobedience movement.[31]

During the month of January 1932, many princes responded quickly to the suggestions of their local political officers, and by 29 January Lord Willingdon could publicly announce that nineteen princes had approved of governmental policies to deal with disorder and had offered to cooperate to the fullest extent with the government. The more important princes in this group were the maharajas of Patiala, Indore, Kishangarh, Kapurthala, and Jind.[32] In the following months other prominent princes like the nizam of Hyderabad, the maharajas of Bikaner, Bundi, and Kashmir, and the Council of Regency in Gwalior issued their endorsements of governmental policies.[33] Not content with words, some princes, such as the maharajas of Patiala and Jodhpur, imitated the Government of India in the issuances of ordinances severely regulating all public meetings and presses and rigorously punishing any who abetted sedition.[34]

Unfortunately for harassed British officials, not all states were as quick or as ready to control civil disobedience programs within their borders as the above. The three areas of greatest concern to local officials were central India, Kathiawar, and Mysore, the latter two regions directly affecting the charged political atmosphere of the sprawling Bombay Presidency.

In central India the primary truant was the troublesome maharaja of Rewa, the leading ruler in Baghelkhand, who pursued a conciliatory policy toward Congress activities in his possessions. While commenting that Rewa was setting a bad example that made it difficult to solicit support from other states in the region, the local political agent attributed the prince's permissiveness to his lack of efficient and organized troops capable of dealing with the situation.[35] In May 1932, undoubtedly under British pressure and after a reorganization of his forces, the maharaja issued restrictive ordinances, had 150 agitators arrested, and had his police make *lathi* charges to disperse assemblies, now declared illegal by the new ordinances.[36]

Kathiawar presented a different problem, since here the states were divided in their attitude toward the civil disobedience movement. Because of the interlocking pattern of their territories, this division made it difficult to contain antigovernment agitations. Loyalist states pursuing a strong policy of suppression of Congress activities included Limbdi, Morvi, and Nawanagar; recalcitrant states who more or less permitted the Congress to implement its program of boycott of foreign cloth and defiance of the salt laws were Bhavnagar, Junagadh, Porbandar, Wadhwan, and Gondal.[37] Although the attitudes of some of the latter states wavered, Kathiawar remained a thorn in the British side, since it was never free from Congress agitation or agitators.[38]

The case of Mysore lends insight into the varying attitudes within British officialdom as to just how far a state was obligated to cooperate with the government in the suppression of Congress activities. The Bombay government contended that Mysore was failing to take adequate measures to cut off contributions from Mysoreans to the Congress coffers and to curb agitators, who would cross from Bombay districts into adjoining Mysore territory to escape arrest.[39] After receiving what it considered insufficient cooperation from the Mysore Durbar and the Mysore resident, Bombay appealed to the Home Department of the Government of India for the redress of its grievances against Mysore. Additional complaints raised against Mysore were that its diwan, Sir Mirza Ismail, had spoken publicly about Gandhi and his work with enthusiasm, and that the Congress was permitted to maintain an office in Bangalore.[40] When the government of India eventually instructed the Mysore resident to admonish the Mysore Durbar to take stronger measures, the resident then advised Delhi that he thought the Bombay accusations were unfounded and consequently nothing further need be said to the Mysore government.[41] The Mysore resident and the more distant Government of India in New Delhi were more flexible than the hard-pressed Bombay government, who had to deal with the problems of control created by the Mysore sympathy for the Congress. These ties between the Mysore administration and the Congress also illustrate that a ruler could be willing to risk some British displeasure for the gains in other political spheres. Maharaja Krishnaraja Wadiyar and Sir Mirza were genuinely supportive of the social programs of the Congress, but were also using their image as progressive administrators to advantage within the state of Mysore.[42] Once again, the dual position of an Indian prince would influence his political choices.

Princely Initiative in British Indian Politics

In certain prominent cases princes, concerned about their own interests as they perceived them, did not require any prodding from outside agencies to become active in British Indian politics. The two most outstanding examples in this category were the nizam of Hyderabad and the maharaja of Patiala.

Noted throughout his long life for his miserliness despite his vast personal fortune, the nizam of Hyderabad displayed an uncharacteristic largesse in 1930. In the early part of the year he had contributed generously to the treasury of the Chamber of Princes, but in September he offered to give privately, with no strings attached, about twenty lakhs of rupees to the Government of India to finance programs to counteract the civil disobedience movement.[43]

This unusual proposition put the British bureaucracy into a quandary, since some levels, particularly hard-pressed local governments in Bengal, Bihar and Orissa, Punjab, and the United Provinces could think of many ways to spend such a windfall. Lower-echelon officers in the Foreign and Political and the Home Departments of the Government of India considered the nizam's offer different from previous assistance but still in the tradition of the client supporting his patron when the latter was in need.[44] Harold Wilberforce-Bell, the officiating political secretary of the Government of India, however, deemed it wisest to decline this offer for two reasons. First, the acceptance of such a gift would make the states more directly the object of British Indian political interest, and that should be avoided wherever possible. Second, it would be difficult for the government to make an adequate acknowledgment of such an extraordinary gesture, and the political secretary was especially worried that the nizam might be bargaining for a relaxation of governmental pressure to effect certain political reforms in Hyderabad.[45] Lord Irwin agreed with Wilberforce-Bell's position, and the offer was gratefully declined.[46]

Princely involvement in British Indian politics sometimes had unforeseen results that were more distressing to the imperial patron than to the clients. One such venture was the investment by the rulers of Nawanagar, Bhopal, and Patiala in the *Bombay Chronicle*, a newspaper founded by Pherozeshah Mehta. In early 1927 Chimanlal Setalvad and Lalji Naranji, two prominent Moderate political figures in Bombay, asked Nawanagar to extend financial support to the faltering newspaper so that it might once again become a moderate organ.[47] After agreeing to do so himself, the jam saheb then approached the maharaja of Patiala, and they were later joined by the nawab of Bhopal in a scheme to secure financial control.[48] It is difficult to divine all the factors motivating these princes to join this undertaking. Since the editor, S. A. Brelvi, was one of the two vice-chairmen of the reception committee for the All India States' People's Conference held in Bombay during December 1927 and the *Bombay Chronicle* press printed publications for the conference,[49] it might be speculated that their support was yet another example of the princely preference for buying off opposition rather than accommodating it by negotiations and reforms.

In the political turmoil that followed the appointment of the Simon Commission, the *Bombay Chronicle* maintained a strong antigovernment tone. When informed by Naoroji Dumasia of the *Times of India* about the princely financial support of the *Chronicle*, Charles Watson, the political secretary, eventually warned Nawanager and Patiala orally about the undesirable consequences of their patronage.[50] A year later, in May 1930, Irwin directly suggested to all three princes that they call up their debentures.[51] After much discussion the three princes finally dissociated themselves from this opponent of their overlord.

His continuing interest in the *Bombay Chronicle* did not prevent Patiala from taking a strong progovernment stand on controversial issues arising within British Indian politics. After the Lahore session of the Congress in December 1929 had passed the resolution calling for complete independence,[52] Patiala seized the occasion of the Basant Panchami Durbar in February 1930 at his capital to deliver a strong condemnation of this action. Although he argued that he and his brother princes did not oppose legitimate political progress in British India, Bhupinder Singh declared that they would cooperate fully with the government in the maintenance of law and order in the face of any mass movement calculated to disturb the peace of the country as a whole. In an interesting effort to justify himself and his order, he reasoned that

> the new attitude towards us is that the States are interpolated pages, apocryphal additions, in this history of India. I need not point out to you how wrong this view is, how fundamentally opposed to the evolution of our history. To forget the persistent regionalism of our people which finds expression in the Indian States is an error which as from time to time spelt disaster for India in the past. If the nationalist movement in its desire for a symmetric pattern of Indian political life decides to act as if the States did not exist, the prospects before the whole country are gloomy indeed. . . .[53]

To make sure that he received due credit for his efforts, Patiala forwarded a copy of his speech to the political secretary, who acknowledged it with appreciation.[54]

Two months later, Patiala again intervened in British Indian political affairs, this time in his capacity as a Sikh leader. On 6 May 1930 there had been a disturbance near the Sisganj Gurdwara in old Delhi, and the police had opened fire on the *gurdwara* in an attempt to reestablish order in the area. This aggression at a holy place inflamed the Sikh community against the government at a period when the latter was coping with the second civil disobedience movement inaugurated by Gandhi a few weeks earlier with his walk to the sea. At this crucial juncture Patiala served as a mediator between Lord Irwin and elements within the Sikh community willing to seek a peaceful redress of Sikh grievances in this matter.

After a meeting with moderate leaders, the maharaja forwarded to Irwin a list of Sikh demands that would be presented to the government in an attempt to seek a settlement of grievances. The viceroy rejected these demands as unacceptable but encouraged Patiala to continue in his negotiations to seek a reconciliation between the Sikh community and the government.[55] Persistent as ever, Patiala again wrote to Irwin, arguing that certain demands considered objectionable such as compensation to injured persons, repairs to the Gurdwara buildings, and assurances that the viceroy strongly deprecated the recurrence of such incidents were entirely reasonable and must be conceded to maintain peace. Two other more controversial stipulations—the punishment of officers at fault and a promise to refrain from any action against any inmates of the Gurdwara—might be answered in a noncommittal manner so that satisfaction could be granted without binding the government to a specific course of action.[56] Patiala concluded that he was persevering in his attempt to put together a representative Sikh deputation to meet Irwin to evolve a peaceful settlement.[57]

While the government debated its next move, Patiala negotiated with various Sikh leaders to join his deputation.[58] Two problems confronted the Sikh ruler in his efforts to play mediator. In order to procure a group representative of all sections of the aggrieved Sikh community, members of the SGPC had to be recruited. Patiala's agents had difficulties in obtaining a firm commitment from prominent SGPC figures, but eventually they secured the services of some less-known members.[59] Coupled with this issue was the necessity to act quickly before the extremists within the SGPC could pass a resolution calling for direct confrontation with the government in the form of a *jatha* being dispatched to Delhi. Here Patiala's people on the Executive Committee of the SGPC were able to buy time with various delaying tactics.[60]

When the government finally decided to receive the deputation, Irwin advised the maharaja that it would not be appropriate for him to act as the leader of the group since it was dealing with events that had transpired largely in British India.[61] Although willing to utilize Patiala's contacts within the general Sikh community, the viceroy was aware that Indian politicians were increasingly opposed to princely interference in British Indian politics. Patiala readily agreed, and on 30 June he merely introduced the members of the delegation to the viceroy, and Sundar Singh Majithia, acting as leader, read its address.[62] Both sides benefited from this joint operation. A troublesome affair ended peacefully for the government, and Patiala's position as a Sikh leader was reinforced at a time when he was under growing attack from the Punjab Riyasti Praja Mandal, the regional states' people's body, whose most active members were from the extremist faction of the Akali Dal.[63]

Penetration of British Indian Groups into Princely India

When, in early 1930, Patiala denounced the Lahore independence resolution of the Congress and various princes publicly praised the government's handling of the civil disobedience movement, the nationalist press had warned them that they could expect reciprocal attention from British Indian politicians. This threat was realized faster than anyone thought possible in the guise of engulfing communalism.

The first major instance of British Indian, politically oriented, religious groups moving directly into the internal affairs of princely states occurred in the strategic state of Jammu and Kashmir, situated on the northern frontier of the British Empire in India. In June 1931, at a meeting held in Srinagar to select Muslims to present the grievances of their community to Maharaja Hari Singh, Abdul Qadir, a servant of a European vacationing in Kashmir, made a violent speech and was promptly arrested. On 13 July, the date of his trial at the Central Jail in Srinagar, a protesting crowd gathered outside, rushed the guards, and invaded the outer compound of the jail. Once the leaders of the crowd were arrested, the throng renewed its attack and attempted to set fire to nearby police quarters. At this point the police were ordered to fire on the gathering, which then dispersed and spread the disturbance throughout the city of Srinagar.[64]

Because it was the first major occasion on which Kashmiris *en masse* openly challenged the maharaja and his government, 13 July 1931 is considered the opening date of the freedom struggle in Kashmir by many Indian historians.[65] Unfortunately for the future of the state and of the Indian subcontinent, this political upsurge was tragically complicated by the fact that the agitators were Muslim and the ruler and most of his officials were Hindu. This situation meant that the disturbance could readily assume a communal tone, as Muslims first verbally and later physically attacked Hindu officials and then turned their vengeance on Hindu shopowners and landlords.

Another ominous factor was the common boundary between the Jammu area of the state and the British province of Punjab, which had a Muslim majority split into various groups contending with each other and Hindu communal bodies for political position and power.[66] Punjabi Muslim interest in Kashmir had begun to manifest itself from the early 1900s when the more extreme section of the Punjabi Muslim press had begun a vociferous campaign against the Kashmir durbar and its Hindu officials, and an All-India Muslim Kashmiri Conference was formed at Lahore to secure the interests of Muslim subjects against their Hindu ruler.[67]

After the riots of mid-July in Srinagar, a revitalized All-India Kashmir Committee was formed with Bashir al-Din Mahmud Ahmad as president, Muhammad Iqbal as vice-president, and A. R. Dard as general secretary.[68] It is of particular significance to note that the president was also the khalifa of the Ahmadiyahs, an unorthodox Muslim reform sect based at Qadiyan, Punjab, and the general secretary was the foreign secretary of the latter group. Although castigated by most orthodox Muslims, the Ahmadiyahs maintained an extensive missionary and educational network in Kashmir as well as in Punjab, and were a small but vocal corps.[69] It was also widely believed at the time that Sheikh Abdullah, the young Aligarh graduate who was quickly emerging as the leading Muslim political figure in Srinagar, was either an Ahmadiyah or at least strongly under their influence.[70]

This situation was further complicated by the activities of another Lahore-based group, the recently formed Majlis-i-Ahrar-i-Islam party (hereafter referred to as the Ahrars). Composed largely of nationalist Muslims who supported the Congress objective of complete independence and its program of civil disobedience, the Ahrars had split from the Indian National Congress over alleged discrimination against Muslims within the Congress organization.[71] After extended negotiations between the maharaja and various Muslim representatives, among whom Sheikh Abdullah and leaders of the All-India Kashmir Committee were most prominent, seemed to begin producing results, the Ahrars started to send *jathas* across the Punjab border into Jammu from 4 October. These bands were dispatched ostensibly to direct the agitation of Jammu Muslims against their durbar while preserving Hindu-Muslim unity but actually to counteract the growing Ahmadiyah influence.[72] Although the *Tribune*, the most important

English-language nationalist newspaper in Punjab, might strongly deplore the entrance of the Ahrars into Kashmir politics and the growing communalization of political life in Kashmir, the state had become part of a larger battlefield where Muslims and Hindus clashed with each other for political power.[73]

When Mazhar Ali, the dictator of the Ahrar campaign in Kashmir, intensified pressure in late October by sending larger *jathas*, the Kashmir Durbar lost control over large tracts of Jammu, especially in the Mirpur area.[74] Hari Singh, consequently, requested assistance from the viceroy; British troops arrived on 3 November and began to reestablish order in the disaffected areas. At the same time the Government of India issued an ordinance prohibiting *jathas* from leaving British territory to enter Jammu if they were judged to be likely to create disturbances across the border even though they might be peaceful while they remained on British soil.[75] In return for this timely support, the maharaja was constrained to appoint a commission of inquiry headed by a British official to investigate Muslim grievances and a constitutional conference to discuss measures to associate all state subjects with their state government.[76] Despite these measures, which fostered the reestablishment of governmental control in Jammu, the Ahrars remained strong enough to support a civil disobedience campaign at Mirpur that called for nonpayment of land revenue until Muslim grievances would be alleviated. By the end of January 1932, Hari Singh once again felt compelled to request British military assistance and then to agree to appoint a British officer as prime minister with an executive council of two Hindus and two Muslim members.[77]

Since this study is not concerned with the internal history of Kashmir, it is sufficient to state that the 1931 disturbances were just the beginning of political agitations and of deepening communal divisions that would affect drastically the future political development of that area.[78] For the future of princely India, it is significant to notice two trends. First, a ruler, when challenged by his subjects and outside groups, chose to rely upon internal repression and the military resources of his patron. The latter responded with celerity, accompanied by pressure to remedy legitimate grievances by constitutional means. This failure by the ruler to seize the initiative to deal with the threat in a positive manner was a bad omen for the future of Kashmir in particular and of princely states in general. Second, the incursions of communal groups from British India into a state where there were communal differences between the ruler and large numbers of his subjects had only begun with Kashmir and were to recur with frequency in other vulnerable states.

The second manifestation of this phenomenon appeared in November 1931 when the All-India Hindu Mahasabha appointed a committee to investigate the grievances of Hindus in Bhopal and Hyderabad.[79] Both Muslim rulers faced similar complaints that, though Hindus formed a majority in their states, they held few ministerial posts and insufficient places in government service. A second charge was that the rights of Hindus to freedom of worship and to the maintenance of religious institutions were unduly restricted, whereas disproportionately large amounts of state revenues were spent on Muslim religious institutions that benefited only a small minority of the population in both states.[80]

While it was conducting its inquiry into the situation of Hindus in both states during the first quarter of 1932, the Hindu Mahasabha kept up a steady attack on the administrations of Bhopal and Hyderabad in the press and through public meetings.[81] To meet and thwart this campaign, the Bhopal government on 1 April 1932 issued its version of the 1930 Bengal Ordinances severely restricting political activity within the state.[82] Twelve days later the Hindu Mahasabha Committee issued its report, which imputed that the Hindus of Bhopal were in fact deprived of some of their basic rights of citizenship in the areas of representation in their government and of religious activity.[83] After this incident the Hindu Mahasabha campaign temporarily lagged because it had encountered difficulties in enlisting sufficient support from local Hindus. It continued, nevertheless, to launch sporadic forays[84] that eventually contributed to the strength of the Hindu Mahasabha and the Bharatiya Jana Sangh, a right-wing Hindu political party, in the old Bhopal districts of Madhya Pradesh after 1947.

Fig. 2. Maharaja Ganga Singh of Bikaner. (Courtesy of the India Office Library and Records.)

Fig. 3. Maharaja Bhupinder Singh of Patiala. (Courtesy of the India Office Library and Records.)

Fig. 4. The Punjab Agency Staff, 1938. (Courtesy of the India Office Library and Records.)

Fig. 5. The Chamber of Princes, 1929. (Courtesy of the India Office Library and Records.)

During the second half of 1932, a distant parallel to the Kashmir episode occurred in Alwar, a northern Rajput state that bordered the Gurgaon district in the southeastern section of Punjab. Although Maharaja Jey Singh of Alwar shared his Hindu religion with the majority of his subjects, his possessions contained a Muslim minority. This included part of the Meo tribe, which professed Islam while retaining several tribal customs incompatible with orthodox Islam.[85] During 1931 the Muslim subjects of Alwar began a protest movement over their alleged ill treatment by the durbar, particularly in the matter of educational facilities. Some Muslims active in this campaign fled to Delhi and the surrounding areas of Punjab and Jaipur, and aroused communal groups in those places by their tales of oppression.[86] By November 1932 the Meos in the northernmost districts of Alwar had begun to refuse to pay the land revenue due the state in protest against policies toward them.[87]

On 3 and 4 December an All-India Alwar Conference was held at Firozpur-Jhirka in Gurgaon district a few miles from the Alwar border. Called to review the situation in Alwar, the conference, through the exertions of British officers, the inclination of its organizers, and the apparent readiness of the maharaja to negotiate with Meo representatives, remained moderate in tone and rejected a program of direct action.[88] Meanwhile, the communal press in British India, particularly in Punjab and Delhi, continued to exploit the Meo grievances, and the Ahrars sought funds that would enable them to enter the affray.[89] As Jey Singh procrastinated in his efforts to satisfy the Meo grievances, the agitation continued to grow until it suddenly exploded when state troops fired on Meos at Govindgarh and inflicted several casualties.[90]

After the firing the situation deteriorated so seriously that the maharaja was forced to ask the British for help. They gave it at a price. British troops were sent to reestablish order, and a British officer was deputed to inquire into the grievances of the Muslims, especially those of the Meos.[91] Since Jey Singh refused to cooperate fully with their recommendations, the British government compelled him to make certain changes in his administration. They also demanded that he sever his connection with that administration for at least two years, during which period the state would be governed by a council headed by a British officer.[92] Alwar left his state in May 1933 never to return as its ruling monarch; he died in exile in Paris in 1937.

The Alwar affair followed the Kashmir pattern in two basic aspects. A group of Muslim subjects, protesting against the repressive policies of a Hindu ruler, received support from coreligionists in nearby British Indian districts. In Alwar it was the Meos who lived in adjacent Punjab districts who were the most active interventionists, but the Ahrars also managed to send a few *jathas* to the disturbed areas.[93] Once conditions worsened, state authorities in both cases had to rely upon the British government for troops and legal sanctions to disarm the agitators. Help was rendered, but at a price that included British supervision of their administrations and the inauguration of certain reforms. Beyond these similarities the Alwar incident had a more severe resolution since Jey Singh was eventually deposed, but Hari Singh in Kashmir remained on the throne until the accession crisis in 1947.

These four episodes in Kashmir, Bhopal, Hyderabad, and Alwar were symptoms of both the growing communalization of political life throughout the Indian subcontinent and the quickly vanishing political isolation of princely India from political events in British India. A further indication of the infiltration of British Indian groups into the internal affairs of the states was the rise of the All-India States' People's Conference and the evolution of a more activist Congress policy toward the states.

After its initial meetings in Bombay in 1927, the conference slowly began to organize bases of support and to extend its range of activities. Although the regional groups continued to exist, the central association attempted to coordinate their programs and to utilize them in the execution of all-India policies. Deputations were sent to Britain both during the Butler Committee hearings and the Round Table Conferences to publicize the grievances of state subjects while propaganda campaigns were launched in the Indian press. Committees were appointed to investigate particularly vile complaints against various state administrations. Local repression might temporarily throw a regional group into disarray, but the all-India organization provided staying power to the movement.[94]

After many years of an official posture firmly opposed to intervention in princely India out of respect for the sovereignty of the princes, the Indian National Congress moved to a more ambiguous policy during the late 1920s. The prime indication of this policy shift was a resolution passed at the Calcutta session of the Congress in 1928 that stated:

> This Congress urges on the ruling Princes of the Indian States to introduce responsible government based on representative institutions in the States, and to issue immediately proclamations or enact laws guaranteeing elementary and fundamental rights of citizenship, such as rights of association, free speech, free press and security of person and property.
>
> This Congress further assures the people of the Indian States of its sympathy with and support in their legitimate and peaceful struggle for the attainment of full responsible government in the States.[95]

This changed orientation seems to have been precipitated by two factors. Longtime advocates of a more activist stance in state politics, leftist Congressmen under the shrewd leadership of Jawaharlal Nehru were increasingly able to exert their influence on Congress programs. Their ideas were reinforced among Congress leadership by the dawning realization of the necessity for a firm union between the states and British provinces in order to achieve a viable Indian nation. Many Congressmen, therefore, considered it imperative to promote political, social, and economic reforms within the states to bring them to a level of development parallel to that in British India.[96]

At its Haripura session during February 1938, the Congress passed a more permissive resolution outlining its policy toward the Indian states.[97] Although its organizational backing was not to be extended, popular agitations to secure desired reforms within the states were encouraged. Congressmen, moreover, were free to render assistance in their personal capacities to such campaigns. There was to be a dual policy of moral support and individual participation under the ultimate direction of the Congress leadership. During 1938 and 1939

Congressmen launched agitations in Mysore, Jaipur, Rajkot,[98] Travancore, Kashmir, and Hyderabad. Congress goals were partially reached in the first three states, but their actions in the latter three were overshadowed by incidents of communal violence. Alarmed by these developments, Gandhi terminated Congress-directed operations within these states and even apologized for his role in the Rajkot episode.[99] Though this phase of a political and social reform movement was temporarily suspended due to the coming of World War II, the over-all threat to the authority of Indian princes within their territories was only beginning.

Reactions of the Princes to Changing Political Conditions

An analysis of the varying responses made by the most active princes to shifts within the power structure of the British Indian Empire will lead to no clearly defined pattern but rather will yield several significant generalizations about the princes as politicians.

When the newly emerging political elites of British India began to effectively challenge the imperial authority, those princes who became involved in British Indian politics viewed their interests as being closely linked to those of their imperial patron. In most of their operations as all-Indian politicians, these rulers supported British objectives both overtly, as in their endorsements of governmental policies in 1931, and covertly, as in the 1930 monetary offer from Hyderabad. Aside from the defiant attitude of Baroda and the recalcitrance of some Kathiawar rajas, most of the princes cooperated with imperial directives asking for suppression of noncooperation programs within their borders. During the 1920s and 1930s growing numbers of politically aware Indians had come to reject, or at least to criticize severely, British policies in India. The princes, however, were one of the few groups within the empire who continued to identify their goals with those of the British.

There were a few instances when the princes participating in British Indian politics did pursue aims that were not dictated by their patron. Patiala aided an antigovernment newspaper, and Mysore viewed Congress excursions into its territory with a benevolent eye. Neither one attempted to build up a popular power base but rather tried to buy off potential opposition with monetary or political favors. In the sphere of politically oriented religious groups, certain princes sought a position of leadership based on their special status within a particular community. This weapon of communal leadership was a double-edged sword that could cut its user as well as his enemies. Although Patiala could use his standing as a Sikh leader to defend himself from attacks by Sikhs active in the local states' people's movement, others such as Hyderabad, Bhopal, and Kashmir found their internal position rendered more precarious by their communal activities in British India. Even in this area, moreover, the princes frequently used their influence within communal associations to further British objectives.

In their political operations beyond their borders, the princes did not attempt to open channels of communications with a wide variety of power groups. Unaccustomed by decades of dependence on British protection in the art of conciliating opposition forces, they tried to ignore the burgeoning strength of the Indian nationalists. When the political equilibrium within their own territories was menaced by the ferment spreading throughout the subcontinent, these autocrats either turned directly to the paramount power for armed assistance or imitated imperial repressive measures for dealing with these threats. The ease with which such steps quelled the opposition lulled the princes into a false sense of security and a deepening reliance on their British patron. One example of this excessive dependence was their appeal to the British for a more comprehensive Indian States Protection Act in an effort to immunize their territories from the virus of political turbulence. The Government of India granted this concession in 1934 when it could maintain order within its own provinces only with the sufferance of various Indian elites. Their failure to evaluate accurately the rising power of the Indian nationalists and the declining vigor of their British overlord tragically undermined the efforts of Indian princes to obtain security by acting as politicians on the all-India scene.

Concurrently with their efforts to establish themselves individually as effective political figures on the all-Indian scene, the princes also sought to secure their future along constitutional lines. Lord Irwin's proposal in October 1929 that the princes should join with Indian nationalists and British party leaders in constitutional discussions seemed to be a major concession to the harried autocrats. Although Montagu and Chelmsford as well as the Simon Commission had consulted with the princes, they had restricted the scope of their inquiries to matters that directly affected the states. Under the Irwin scheme the princes were to be allowed to participate in debate about the future constitutional arrangements for the entire subcontinent. With a longstanding attraction to the idea of legal guarantee, the princes eagerly agreed to attend joint talks in London. Through a collective venture, they thought that they might still be able to obtain a defined status within the changing power structure of India.

chapter seven

The Constitutional Quest Reaches a Dead End

The Round Table Conference signaled a major shift in British procedures for formulating constitutional changes for India. Lord Irwin and Wedgwood Benn, who had initiated this mechanism, hoped to proceed by reaching agreement on reforms among all Indian and British parties rather than by following the usual course of the British party in power consulting with Indian leaders. That the princes were invited to participate was recognition both that something should be done about their position and that they might be a useful support group in a political situation that was becoming radicalized. They were Indians still willing to talk with the British, since they only conceived of their future within an imperial structure.

Although the Round Table Conference was far broader in its scope than the Montagu-Chelmsford tour was, many princes viewed it as just one more stage in their effort to achieve a defined constitutional status that would protect their internal sovereignty from encroachment by the paramount power and popular political groups. The federation that was proposed had far more fateful implications for the princes than did the Chamber of Princes, but the activities of the princes in lobbying for, and establishing, the Chamber were a forecast of how they would function and what their goals would be during the constitutional discussions of the 1930s. The elements of continuity, however, should not overshadow those of change. Much had occurred since 1918 that would alter the relationships among the British, the princes, and the Indian politicians. In 1930 the political atmosphere was much tenser, and more groups in Indian society, including the princes, had been politicized; and so new factors would interact with the familiar ones.

Looking backward toward the campaign for the Chamber, the lack of unanimity among the princes stands out. Although others might think of the princes as one order of Indian society, the princes themselves emphasized their individuality and hence their differences rather than their similarities. These internal divisions became more apparent whenever the princes were pulled together and expected to act as a group on the all-Indian scene. Several factors provided the bases for groupings, but the size of their states was the most noticeable one. Rulers of the largest states sought adequate recognition of their preeminence, and were headed by Hyderabad and Mysore, who generally worked on the all-Indian scene through their ministers. The energetic rulers of middle-sized states attempted to dominate by their personal contacts and accomplishments, since they lacked the resources of the largest populations and revenues. The overseers of the smaller states were apprehensive of their future under any scheme, and would form satellite bodies revolving around more prominent princes. The princes also made alliances based on geographical origins, linguistic and ethnic bonds, and religious affiliations. Because of the growing reference to communal identity in all-Indian politics during the 1920s, the princes were approached more frequently as communal leaders in the 1930s and responded to overtures in that sphere. Finally, personal rivalries among these ambitious men could override other bonds to influence their actions and allegiances.

As autocratic rulers the princes employed political techniques that emphasized personal contacts, the maintenance of *izzat*, arbitrary decisions, and covert negotiations. In the late 1910s they entertained moderate British Indian leaders, relied upon a corps of ministers who could deliberate at length without having to commit their employers, lobbied with British officials in India and in England, and had recourse to expensive legal counsel. In 1930 they would follow these well-trod paths.

The princes had seen the Chamber as an institution that would give them direct access to the viceroy and the political secretary, and as a forum for evolving policies through mutual agreement. Since the Chamber, and later the Butler Report, had not fulfilled these expectations, the princes persisted in pursuing these goals. In more specific terms they wanted a definition of paramountcy, a further removal of the Political Department from interference in their states, and a clear statement on their relationship with the British crown. To many British and Indian politicians, these were peripheral issues, but for the princes they were central to their vision of the past, present, and future. The emerging strength of the states' people's groups and the renewed interest of Congressmen in state affairs had only served to reinforce the princes' desire for a reaffirmation of the concern and interest of the British crown in their continued existence.

In 1918 most British officials agreed that something should be done about the princes but disagreed over what to do and how to do it. Even so, no one had the time and energy necessary to address this problem directly. In the 1930s the Congress was much more powerful and Muslim demands were more strident, so the British were even more inclined to pursue a policy of drift toward their more expendable allies. The absence of a clear-cut policy and consensus within the British official hierarchy is reflected in the debate over who was most responsible for the failure to achieve federation. This controversy began in the 1930s in private correspondence between officials, surfaced in the memoirs of these men in the 1950s, and has now bubbled up in the scholarly writing of the 1970s. Most higher officials concurred in criticizing the Political Department and its agents for a lack of support, though there was less unity of opinion and direction of efforts on federation among the political officers than there was between London and New Delhi. There had been similar negative judgments in earlier decades. The key difference in the 1930s, however, was that a coalition government was in power in England in the midst of an unprecedented economic depression, and so a wide range of opinions had to be accommodated.

Although the Round Table Conferences and the subsequent pursuit of federation may be seen as one more stage along a continuum, they also represented major possibilities for significant changes in the position of the princes. Whether they would be willing or able to take advantage of this opportunity reveals much about their past and decides their future.

An Entente between Princes and Politicians

Although certain princes had consulted with prominent Indian nationalists during the debate on the Montagu-Chelmsford reforms, these two groups had not maintained any continuing discussions over matters of common concern. The February 1929 session of the Chamber seemed to mark the beginning of an effort on both sides to reopen old, and to cultivate new, channels of communication. To disarm critics who had labeled the Chamber a part of a government conspiracy to retard the constitutional progress of British India, the maharaja of Patiala moved a resolution to open the proceedings of the Chamber to the public.[1] Agreeing with the chancellor about the need to divest their enemies of ammunition, the maharaja of Bikaner added that the rulers owed it to their subjects to let them know what was happening in the Chamber.[2] Although Lord Irwin, acting as the presiding officer, pointed out the likely increase in criticism if the press was freely admitted to the Chamber, he allowed a vote on the resolution, which was passed unanimously.[3]

At this same session the princes made it clear that they would remain staunch allies of the British crown while seeking closer contacts with British Indian political leaders. To counter the Congress resolution, passed in 1928 at Calcutta, calling for complete independence if dominion status was not granted within one year, the Chamber passed a resolution rejecting any adjustment of relations between their states and British India that was not based on continued ties with Britain.[4] This action was taken at the suggestion of Lord Irwin, who shrewdly emphasized its positive value in England for the princes.[5] Even while supporting their imperial patron, the Chamber members were careful to assuage their moderate British Indian allies by reiterating their support for political advance in British India. As Ganga Singh of Bikaner eloquently stated:

> We the Princes and people of the Indian States are ourselves Indians; and we do most sincerely wish our Motherland and fellow countrymen well; and we do equally sincerely look forward—as proudly as any British Indian—to the day when our united Country would attain to the full height of its political stature, as in every way an equal, and fully trusted, member of the comity of Nations within the British Empire, and as much respected as any other self-governing British Dominion.[6]

These conciliatory gestures evoked appropriate response from older Congress leaders seeking support in their maneuvers to weaken the growing power and appeal of the young Turks within their organization. Shortly after the formal Chamber sessions were concluded, Vithalbhai Patel, brother of Vallabhbhai and himself the president of the Legislative Assembly, invited the maharaja of Bikaner, the nawab of Bhopal, and the maharaja of Kashmir to a tea party on 19 February. He had also invited representatives from various groups in the Assembly along with Gandhi; M. A. Ansari, the Congress president; Lord Irwin; James Crerar, the Home member of the Government of India; and General William Birdwood, the commander-in-chief.[7] There were high expectations that such a prestigious gathering, however informal, would have beneficial political consequences. They were unjustified, for, as the *Tribune* lamented, "not even the fringe of any of the burning topics was touched."[8] The fact that the rulers were invited to such a gathering, however, is evidence that they were considered to be of some political consequence.

The next encounter between the princes and Indian politicians occurred at the end of March, at the request, according to Chamber sources, of Motilal Nehru and M. M. Malaviya. Accepting their overture, the Standing Committee of the Chamber invited the elder Nehru, Malaviya, Ansari, and Vithalbhai Patel to dinner on 22 March.[9] It is noteworthy that Bikaner, Bhopal, and Kashmir, all members of the Standing Committee, had been in contact with these same leaders a month earlier at Patel's tea party.

At this March meeting the discussions remained on a general level, possibly to avoid the controversies sure to arise if more specific questions were considered. As an opening gesture toward unanimity, the maharaja of Bikaner and Motilal Nehru both elaborated on the sympathy and support each part of India felt for the other part. The only major topic raised by the princes was a request that British Indian leaders exert closer control over the increasingly frequent press attacks of a malicious nature made on the princes and their families in the columns of nationalist papers. Motilal ably handled this delicate problem by pointing out that these attacks came from a small, extremist section of the British Indian press over which responsible leaders had little influence. At the end of the evening, Malaviya called for further discussions on topics of mutual interest, and Patel volunteered to hold another meeting at his house on 27 March.[10] The princes agreed to come, but so far it has not been possible to locate any records indicating that this reunion occurred.

In June 1929 Malaviya telegraphed Patiala to request another gathering between the princes and British Indian politicians before the former submitted their views on the recommendations of the Butler Report to the viceroy.[11] Nothing, however, could be arranged before the Chamber members held a series of meetings in Bombay at the end of June and then presented their opinions to Lord Irwin just before he left for England on his midterm leave.

During these intermittent contacts on a private basis, some leading Indian political figures sought to involve the princes in a public project to formulate a constitution acceptable to all major political groups in India. In early 1928 nationalists of varying political affiliations had formed the All-Parties Conference to produce such a document in response to Secretary of State Birkenhead's challenge to do so. M. A. Ansari, the Congress president, became the president of the conference, and Motilal Nehru became chairman of the committee appointed by the conference to draft the basic principles that would underlie such a constitution. The report of this committee was presented in August 1928 and was commonly referred to as the Nehru Report. Its insistence on the abolition of separate electorates came to be the issue that predictably divided the conference into communal groupings.

Although there had been no princes or their representatives on the committee, the Nehru Report did include a chapter on the Indian states, largely written by Tej Bahadur Sapru.[12] The Report viewed a federation as the most desirable form of relations between British India and princely India, but it contained no specific proposals for the formation of a federation at that time. Rather it made two general recommendations. The proposed Commonwealth of British India was to have the same rights and obligations toward the states arising out of the treaties as were exercised and discharged by the Government of India. Any dispute between the Commonwealth and the states arising out of treaty provisions was to be referred by the governor-general-in-council, with the permission of the state concerned, to a supreme court for settlement.[13] Even though the former statement was an intended refutation of the princely contention that their treaties were with the British crown and nontransferable to a third party, the latter proposal was a goal long sought by the princes themselves in the form of arbitration tribunals. The princes, nevertheless, viewed the Nehru Report as a premeditated attack on their constitutional position since it denied their privileged relationship with the crown.

In January 1929 Manilal Kothari, the stormy petrel of Kathiawar politics[14] and a leader in the states' people's movement, suggested at a conference meeting in Calcutta that selected princes be invited to meet with certain members of the conference to discuss further the future status of the states.[15] It was not until 10 August 1929 that Motilal Nehru acted upon this recommendation and invited the maharaja of Patiala, as chancellor of the Chamber, the nizam of Hyderabad, the maharaja of Mysore, and the maharani regent of Travancore to confer with a committee of the All-Parties Conference.[16] The reaction of the Chamber and of the Political Department to this overture prefigures the attitudes and policies of both of these parties during the Round Table Conferences.

Upon receiving his invitation, Patiala immediately wrote to

Charles Watson, the political secretary, as well as to the other members of the Standing Committee of the Chamber for their opinions.[17] With amazing dispatch the Political Department produced two notes in three days on the issues raised. Both opinions, for many of the same reasons, regarded as unwise any participation by the princes in the deliberations of the All-Parties Conference. There was a general fear that the rulers would be at a disadvantage in any debate with the more astute British Indian politicians, and that, in the heat of controversy, they might adopt untenable positions or be unable to answer effectively their opponents' criticism. Then, too, the conference had also invited representatives from states' people's groups, and their presence on a basis of equality at the conference table would inevitably produce friction with the princes, who refused to recognize the legitimacy of such organizations.[18] Finally, Harold Wilberforce-Bell, the undersecretary in the Political Department, argued that

> as regards the first consideration, our unexpressed ideas are so far in favour of the federal ideal. Anything, therefore, which would assist in the attainment of this ideal should normally be supported. On the other hand, any federalisation is bound to take time. It cannot be a matter of months, it can at best be a matter of years, and it may indeed be a matter of decades. There is, therefore, no necessity for the taking of immediate steps to induce federalisation. . . .[19]

His conclusion was that there was little need for theoretical discussions before the practical details had been settled. This attitude that federation was a far distant goal and an unwillingness to foster contact between the princes and the politicians was especially prevalent in the Political Department, and would be a factor of importance during the Round Table Conference period.[20]

All the members of the Standing Committee had asked that Nehru's request be discussed first at their October meeting and then referred to the full Chamber at its next session scheduled for February 1930.[21] On 1 October Patiala finally informed Nehru that his proposition was being considered. Even though the Standing Committee had a "friendly political dinner" with President Patel during their October meeting,[22] they continued to defer any decision on Nehru's overture until the next Chamber session. Although the princes were willing to participate in informal, private gatherings, they remained apprehensive of any public confrontations with major British Indian politicians, and the reluctance of British political officers to allow such contacts reinforced their fears and hesitations.

Preparations for the Round Table Conferences

Much of the excitement among the princes over the opportunities offered by the proposed Round Table Conference was concentrated in the Chamber and particularly in its inner core, the Standing Committee. For the first and only time during its existence, the Chamber became an active institution. Attendance increased; pertinent resolutions were debated; elections were contested. One instance of unprecedented interest in the Chamber was a substantial donation by the nizam of Hyderabad to its coffers.

His benefaction represented the partial success of Patiala's efforts to interest the nizam in the activities of the Chamber. Although the nizam had categorically refused, largely because of personal inclinations and the advice of his ministers, to attend the Chamber sessions, he did decide to send three of his ministers to observe its informal and formal deliberations in February 1930. They were instructed to determine if any monetary aid to the Chamber could be granted with advantage to Hyderabad as well as to the Chamber. Once the delegation recommended that such a contribution would be desirable, the nizam acquiesced.[23] Unfortunately for the cause of unity among the princes, the nizam's support for the Chamber was to be short-lived. By mid-April Terence Keyes, the resident at Hyderabad, was reporting that the Muslim ruler, who was known for his miserliness, was again becoming apprehensive over the Brahmin and Maratha elements and the extravagance within the inner circle of the Chamber.[24]

During the Chamber sessions held in February 1930, the princes debated the deficiencies of the Butler Report from their point of view and acted to improve their image at home and abroad. A propaganda office that had been instituted in

London in 1928 to promote princely interests during the Butler Committee hearings was revived with a fresh infusion of funds.[25] In order to lend substance to the characterization of the princes as men able to move with the times, the maharaja of Bikaner pressed for the passage of a resolution reiterating their commitment to internal reform. Most members present were not sympathetic to debate, let alone promises, in this area, so Bikaner's suggestion was quickly dropped.[26] Despite increasingly acrimonious attacks from a widening circle of opponents, few princes were willing to take the positive but painful steps necessary to modernize their administrations and to establish meaningful contacts with the political forces rising within their territories. Despite repeated warnings from sympathetic patrons such as Irwin and powerful politicians such as Motilal Nehru and M. M. Malaviya, the princes blindly persisted in their refusal to institute moderate reforms from the top until it would be too late for such measures to be effective.

The struggling states' people's groups, meanwhile, were becoming more vocal in their attacks on maladministration in individual states and personal corruption among the princes and in their demands for democratic political and social reforms. The All-India States' People's Conference chose the opening day of the 1930 Chamber session to issue a highly adverse collection of charges against Patiala personally and his administration.[27] Although an official inquiry headed by James A. O. Fitzpatrick, the agent to the governor-general for the Punjab states, would exonerate Bhupinder Singh personally of the charges,[28] the accusations did cause considerable consternation in the British official hierarchy and did reduce Patiala's reputation among certain groups.[29] At the same time threatening letters were sent to other Chamber members such as Rajpipla, who was admonished: "Your huge wastages in England are well-known to us. Your State is going to the dogs by the doings of those who are not of your belief and faith."[30]

In the so-called gutter press, a group of short-lived, inflammatory newspapers, there were numerous, vicious denunciations of princely rule that were difficult to stop or to punish under the provisions of the 1922 Press Protection Act. This hostile publicity campaign received further ammunition during 1929 when Popotlal Chudgar, a pioneer in the states' people's movement, published a scathing, polemical book alleging general maladministration throughout princely India.[31] In an informal gathering held concurrently with the February 1930 Chamber session, some princes talked over various repressive measures designed to curb such criticism. The princes' lack of concern for changing conditions that spawned such adverse comment and their preference for arbitrary controls was an ominous sign of their political orientation as they prepared to enter deliberations about constitutional reforms.[32]

During their 1930 session in Delhi, Chamber members also endeavored to renew their informal contacts with British Indian politicians. On 26 February 1930 the Standing Committee held a large dinner party for political leaders, most of whom did not belong to the Congress. Two days later a smaller affair took place with Tej Bahadur Sapru and Chimanlal Setalvad, a Liberal from Bombay, conferring with the Standing Committee and their ministerial advisers. At this latter gathering it was decided to depute Kailas Haksar to go to various political centers such as Allahabad, Madras, and Bombay and to exchange views informally with local but prominent political figures such as C. P. Ramaswami Aiyer in Madras and M. R. Jayakar and M. A. Jinnah in Bombay.[33] After the Standing Committee had assimilated Haksar's report on political currents in these areas, it would meet again with selected politicians.

The next round of discussions between the Standing Committee and British Indian politicians took place a month later. Although men like Motilal Nehru and Vithalbhai Patel would no longer attend such conferences, there were others like Setalvad who would go to Delhi in the heat of late March because "conversations with the Princes are very important."[34] Among those who came to Delhi on 29 March 1930, were Purshotamdas Thakurdas, an Indian industrialist; M. R. Jayakar, B. S. Moonje, and M. M. Malaviya, Hindu Mahasabha leaders; M. A. Jinnah and Muhammad Ali, spokesmen for the Muslim community; Hari Singh Gour from the Central Provinces; Setalvad from Bombay; C. P. Ramaswami Aiyar from Madras; Muhammad Shafi from Punjab; Ganesh S. Khaparde from Berar; and Hugh Cocke, W. Arthur Moore, and D'Arcy Lindsay, nonofficial European members of the Legislative Assembly.[35]

The maharaja of Patiala opened the proceedings by asking what would be the attitude of a dominion status government toward the states. Most of the British Indian leaders present were prompt to assure the princes that there would be a greater degree of cooperation between a dominion government in British India and the states than existed under the current arrangement.[36] Malaviya promised the establishment of such institutions as a supreme court and machinery for cooperation in common affairs such as defense, further declaring that the princes would not be forced to adopt any prescribed form of government. To work out the details for a United India, D'Arcy Lindsay, the leader of the European members in the Assembly, suggested the appointment of an appropriate committee. Ramaswami Aiyar, Muhammad Ali, Gour, Shafi, Haksar, and Manubhai Mehta were designated to form such a body. As frequently happened, the committee never met, since Muhammad Ali became fatally ill, Ramaswami Aiyar undertook some legal work for Patiala, and Shafi left shortly thereafter for Europe.[37]

Although this series of informal conversations between certain princes and Indian politicians did not produce any tangible results, they are indicative of the relationship existing between these two groups on the eve of the Round Table Conference. It is noteworthy that there were British Indian political leaders still interested in talking with the princes, but it is equally important to realize that those who thought the princes to be of some consequence on the all-India political scene were representative of an increasingly circumscribed group within the Indian political sphere. As their contacts were gradually reduced to a limited number of loyalist politicians, the princes were reinforced in their thinking about British permanence and were led to underestimate the challenge of the noncooperators. Another point to be noted is that among the politicians who maintained contacts with the princes, a prominent majority had ties to communal political organizations such as the Muslim League and the Hindu Mahasabha.

Along with the princes and British Indian politicians, the highest levels of the British government in London and in Delhi were working behind the scenes to solve the problems raised by their unprecedented invitations to Indian princes to participate in constitutional debates.

On the thorny matter of the composition of the Indian states delegation, the viceroy faced two prickly issues. Various spokesmen for the states' people's groups had petitioned Irwin as well as Indian politicians pleading for representation at the conference. On the same day that he had made his announcement on dominion status, Irwin had advised Vithalbhai Patel that representatives of states' people's groups would have no *locus standi* at the conference. Discussions would focus on the relationship between British India and the Indian states, and only the accredited governments of the states, as represented by the princes, could speak with authority in this area.[38]

Supporting Delhi's position on this question, Wedgwood Benn, the Labour secretary of state for India, reasoned that "our prime objective is to make the Conference a success. Merely on the grounds of tactics, therefore, . . . it would be fatal to alienate the princes."[39] Notwithstanding this attitude, the secretary of state also advocated that some conciliatory gesture be made to the states' people's movement. His suggestion was that a leading prince, through the prompting of the Political Department, should announce some major advance in the direction of progressive political reform. He argued that it would be better for the viceroy to pursue a policy of general encouragement of representative institutions in the states rather than to confine himself to the issuance of paternal warnings in individual cases of maladministration.[40]

After officers in the political secretariat spent a couple of weeks researching previous viceregal efforts to encourage positive reforms, Irwin vetoed the proposal from London. His argument was that such a step would accomplish little among the states' people's groups and might unduly frighten the princes at a crucial juncture.[41] It was to be tragic for the princes that the British officials most directly charged with their future preferred to obscure the need for drastic political reform and accommodation with the newly rising political elites within their states. At this point the government needed allies at the Round Table Conference and so even Lord Irwin, who began his term as a strong advocate of reform, declined to take any action that might antagonize longstanding clients.

The position of the government on the representation of states' people's groups was reinforced by opinions of those Indian politicians most anxious for the triumph of constitutional methods. In a private letter to Sapru, B. L. Mitter, the Law member of Irwin's Executive Council, supported the viceroy's position.[42] Setalvad independently argued, as did Wedgwood Benn, that

> it would be most unwise and a great tactical blunder for us to call in representatives of the States subjects. The moment we do that we destroy all chances of the Princes entering into any negotiations with us for the settlement of the All India Constitution, and unless they are prepared to negotiate we will come to a standstill.[43]

Although the above question was quickly settled to the satisfaction of the princes, they were not yet content. There was still the troublesome issue of who would be included in the states delegation. Throughout February and March of 1930, the Standing Committee lobbied with Irwin and the Political Department to ensure that their slate of delegates was chosen.[44] The most disgruntled ruler on this point was the nizam of Hyderabad, who felt that the Chamber had neglected to consult him at all stages and to give him adequate representation on their slate, despite his recent largesse to the Chamber and his position as the premier prince of India. The nizam's plea for separate representation was energetically supported by Terence Keyes, the resident at Hyderabad, who was a staunch opponent of Butler's concept of two Indias, one British India and the other Indian India ruled by the princes, and a firm champion of federation as the best means to preserve the British creation of an Indian nation.[45] Keyes, who had assumed his duties in February 1930, had been able to persuade the nizam and Sir Akbar Hydari, who would represent the nizam in London, that federation was also a mechanism by which Hyderabad could be protected from erosion by popular regional and religious movements.[46]

The Indian States delegation eventually contained sixteen members. They included the Standing Committee of the Chamber (whom Keyes said had been labeled a phalanx of Rolls Royce rajas in the Deccan) and two ministers nominated by the Committee, Manubhai Mehta and Kailas Haksar.[47] The five twenty-one-gun states who had the largest territories and populations were represented by a combination of princes and ministers: Kashmir by Maharaja Hari Singh, since he was also a member of the Standing Committee; Baroda by Maharaja Sayaji Rao; Hyderabad by Hydari and four official advisers; Mysore by Mirza Ismail, its chief minister; and Gwalior by Sahibzada Ahmed Khan.[48] Because of his experience in Bhavnagar, Prabhashankar Pattani, whom Harcourt Butler had once declared to be the uncrowned king of Kathiawar, was designated to represent those states under minority administration.[49] The maharaja of Rewa was selected to guard the interests of the so-called conservative princes, and the chief of Sangli was chosen to represent the smaller states having a nine-gun salute or less.[50] Haksar was appointed the secretary-general of the delegation.

To ensure further the success of the conference, Irwin wanted to forestall the princes from raising all their grievances in London. In July 1930 the viceroy, consequently, held some meetings with the members of the states delegation. After listening to their views on the Simon Report and their complaints about the gutter press, he got them to agree that they would not bring up the issues of paramountcy, intervention, or related disputes in London if efforts would be made in Delhi to reach some agreement on these matters.[51] The princes were willing to separate negotiations on their two goals of a definition of paramountcy and a rationalization of their constitutional position, but they never considered one aspect less important than the other.[52] For them their ties to the British were perpetual, and therefore their relations with the British crown were just as important as those with their fellow Indians in British India.

The Princes at the First Round Table Conference

Invitations to the Conference had been sent in early August, and immediately thereafter the delegates began to leave for England. Among the first to go was Bhupinder Singh of Patiala, who was forced to make a hurried departure. In order to avoid a hostile demonstration that had been arranged at Ballard Pier, from which the mail boat sailed, the chancellor of the Chamber had to take a launch and board the boat in midstream.[53] Other delegates such as the Muslims were able to organize counterdemonstrations by their followers and could thereby depart in a more dignified manner.[54] The leisurely days at sea permitted shipboard encounters between princes and Indian politicians that provided a major channel of communication between the two groups.[55] It must be noted, however, that these conversations were a logical followup of the informal gatherings that had been taking place for the past two years whenever the members of the Standing Committee assembled in Delhi. What is significant is that the circle of politicians still talking with the autocrats was gradually contracting.

By the end of October most members of the states delegation had arrived in London and had begun to hold informal preparatory meetings. At the beginning of November a committee of ministers was appointed to consider what should be the princely attitude if a federal scheme of government for all of India was proposed by the British Indian delegation. If the committee favored the proposal, it was also to suggest what safeguards the princes should demand before acceding to such a federal scheme.[56] The committee strongly advocated acceptance of a federal proposal, and its recommendations were endorsed by a larger committee under the chairmanship of the nawab of Bhopal. This latter group argued that the Simon Report was inadequate because it contained no provision for a princely voice in the settlement of matters of common concern. Therefore, unless the states joined with British India in a federation to share in any further devolution of power, they would be placed at an increasing disadvantage as British India alone gained in power.[57]

Many factors influenced the princes and their ministers to

reach this decision. As early as 1918, the more politically astute among them had begun to ask for some form of joint cooperation with British India.[58] By the time of their 1927 Round Table Conference with Irwin, they were talking about some type of federation. Although wary of a full political union, they were attracted to an economic confederation with a political link to facilitate discussion on pressing political matters. At the time of the Butler Committee Inquiry, Sir Leslie Scott, the chief counsel for the Chamber's Special Organization, had formulated proposals for the establishment of certain joint institutions as a supreme court. These propositions were never formally presented to the government, since the terms of reference of the Butler Committee precluded discussions of future developments. Although there had been little concrete thinking about the structure and implications of a possible federation, the word itself, by 1930, was current in the princely vocabulary. Many rulers viewed acceptance of a federation as one more stage in the progression of their vague aspirations for joint institutions with British India.

Then, too, after the refusal of the Butler Committee to define paramountcy and thereby provide the basis for some restrictions on British intervention, a sizable number of princes were increasingly anxious to limit the prerogatives of political officers. To many of them, federation seemed to be a device that would drastically reduce the power of the Political Department in states that were federal units and consequently were enjoying direct access to the central executive and legislature. As Malcolm Hailey, who attended the First Round Table Conference as a representative of the Government of India, later remarked, "They, the princes, seem to be out for the extinction of the Political department, rather than the creation of a Federal constitution."[59]

The princes were also under constant and persuasive pressure from Tej Bahadur Sapru, a leading proponent of federation, and his close political and personal friend, Kailas Haksar. During the months preceding the Round Table Conference, Sapru and other Indian politicians devoted to constitutional processes were in a quandary. The Congress was now demanding complete independence, but neither the Simon Report nor the Government of India's recommendations on the report conceded any major devolution of power within the central government. It appeared to Sapru that responsible government at the center was the minimum advance necessary to keep India within the British Empire.[60] Federation between British India and princely India with the latter acting as a conservative counterweight to radical elements in the former section was the device by which Parliament might be persuaded to grant central responsibility.[61] In his position as secretary-general of the Indian States delegation, Haksar, who shared Sapru's views, was able to ensure that federation proposals would be displayed in the most flattering light possible at meetings of the delegation.

After months of intense preparations, which ranged from efforts by Sapru to establish rapport between Gandhi and the Nehrus with the government to the construction by the Ministry of Works of a special oval table capable of accommodating all the delegates, the king-emperor inaugurated the Round Table Conference on 12 November 1930. Although the opening ceremony seemed lacking in the pageantry associated with an imperial durbar, George V uttered his words of welcome into a silver and gold microphone that then relayed the imperial message throughout the world.[62] It was a gesture appropriately symbolic of a new era in imperial relations. The remainder of the session took less than forty-five minutes, and the conference adjourned for a few days in order to study the dispatch of the Government of India on the Simon Report. The temper of the constitutional debate, however, had moved far beyond the cautious recommendations of the Simon Report. When the first plenary session of the conference opened on 17 November, the proponents of federation quickly moved forward. When Sapru asked the princes to join an all-Indian federation, he was certain of their response, which was to be delivered in an almost too eloquent manner by the maharaja of Bikaner.[63] Bikaner's acceptance of this offer is widely portrayed as a dramatic, unprecedented departure in the political strategy of the princes.[64] In fact, their support for an all-Indian federation can be viewed as just one more stage in their continuing campaign to stabilize their constitutional relationship with British India. In the euphoria that followed Bikaner's speech, few British politicians and officials or Indian princes bothered to consider what the practical impact of federation would be on the internal autonomy of the princes within their states or on the administrative unity of British India.

After three days of lengthy opening statements by representatives of each group or party participating in the talks, the conference broke up into a number of subcommittees to work out provisions for the structure and operation of a federal system.[65] The most important subcommittees were the Federal Structure Committee headed by Lord Sankey, the lord chancellor, and the Minorities Committee chaired by Ramsay MacDonald. The report of the Federal Structure Committee (the Sankey Report) provided for a bicameral legislature; a council of responsible ministers to advise the governor general, who would continue to control defense and foreign relations; and the retention of various financial safeguards to protect the credit of India on the world market.[66] Unfortunately for the future of a united India, the Minorities Committee could only agree that the rights of minorities should be protected.[67] On 16 and 19 January 1931 the work of the First Round Table Conference was reviewed in a series of thirty-five speeches that were generally enthusiastic and optimistic.

Reactions to Federation

Once the conference had adjourned, various groups began to work for or against the establishment of a federation and its concomitant: responsible government at the center. In England all political leaders emphasized the difficulties to be overcome before a viable federal constitution could be inaugurated. Labour party leaders, nevertheless, wanted to evolve an acceptable constitution; and Liberal party leaders, particularly Lord Reading, were ready to support the Labour government on this issue.[68] Within the Conservative party reactions were mixed. One faction centering around Stanley Baldwin, the former prime minister, and Samuel Hoare, who was to become secretary of state for India in August 1931, was willing to see what could be done. As Irwin commented to his secretary of state:

> I read a day or two ago the report of the debate on the Conference in the House of Commons, and was much struck with the remarkable measure of sympathetic treatment that it showed. . . . Sam Hoare's contribution seemed exactly like himself, precise, prudent, logical, without a redeeming streak of warmth of sympathy and imagination. . . . However on the whole, the debate, as you say, was encouraging—not the least for Stanley Baldwin's contribution.[69]

A so-called diehard faction under the able leadership of Winston Churchill and Lord Salisbury launched an energetic campaign to obstruct federation because they opposed any devolution of power at the center.[70]

In India there were equally varied reactions to the conference proposals. Immediately after reaching India, Sapru met with Gandhi and Jawaharlal Nehru and other Congressmen to ascertain their views. Still engaged in an active civil disobedience movement against the government, Congress leaders were critical of the efforts of the conference. Nehru voiced three main objections: the lack of control by Indians over the army and the salaries of the services; the inclusion of the princes and the landlords, whom he viewed as reactionary forces, in the federation; and the concession made in the area of financial safeguards.[71] Although Gandhi had been noncommittal at his first talks with Sapru, he later raised similar criticisms.[72] The Mahatma, however, was eventually reconciled to Congress participation at the next Round Table Conference through personal persuasion by Lord Irwin shortly before the latter left India in April 1931.[73]

Despite the temporary cessation of the civil disobedience movement, dissensions within as well as among the major communities of India threatened to stymie constitutional advance. Among the Hindus the depressed classes, the so-called untouchables, under the leadership of Dr. B. R. Ambedkar, were agitating for recognition as a separate group distinct from the Hindu community and entitled to separate electorates. The Sikhs were unable to present a united front because of factional splits based on personality differences and disputes left over from the days of the *gurdwara* reform campaign. Within the Muslim community there was a split between proponents of joint electorates, who were labeled Nationalist Muslims, and the champions of separate electorates, who usually belonged to the All-Parties Muslim Conference.

The one prince to become publicly involved in communal politics in an effort to smooth the path for federation was the nawab of Bhopal. With the blessing of Gandhi, Bhopal attempted to seek unity among Muslim leaders so that they might be able to speak with one voice when they were bargaining with Hindu leaders.[74] In early May the nawab convened a meeting of Muslim representatives from the Congress who would accept joint electorates and of members of the All-Parties Muslim Conference that remained staunchly committed to separate electorates.[75] The Muslim leaders assembled in Bhopal, discussed several different proposals for two days, and then dispersed to report back to their respective groups. Another set of meetings was scheduled for early June when, hopefully, a definite settlement would be reached.

Fazl-i-Husain, the Punjabi Muslim who served on the Viceroy's Executive Council, had revived the Muslim Conference in 1930 and had been able to secure substantial funding from the Aga Khan and the nizam of Hyderabad.[76] Thus the two leading Muslim princes favored different strategies for the Muslims of British India, but both had to remain concerned about two spheres of political power, the situation within their states and the broader Muslim community of all-India. Actions within one area would have varied consequences within the other.

In the interval between meetings in Bhopal, the supporters of separate electorates for Muslims gained the upper hand. Fazl-i-Husain was able to persuade the new viceroy, Lord Willingdon, who had previously served as governor in both Bombay and Madras, to appoint advocates of separate electorates to the British Indian delegation to the next Round Table Conference.[77] Informal conversations to resolve differences within the Muslim community were held again at Bhopal in early June, but they ended inconclusively.[78] Although it was proposed to hold a formal conference at a later date in Simla, no further meeting was called, and Muslim separatists were on their way to becoming the most strongly organized political force within the Muslim community.

While the communal problem was the major obstacle to the agreement necessary to the inauguration of a federation in British India, bitter divisions among states and acrimonious rivalries among the rulers were the chief hurdles in Indian India. At first, however, there was a deceptive show of unity before the underlying disunity came to the surface.

In March 1931 the Chamber met, and fifty-two members attended, the largest number present since the inaugural session in February 1921. Patiala, as chancellor, reported on the work of the Indian States delegation in London. Careful emphasis was placed on the tentative nature of the acceptance of the federal scheme and the far-reaching safeguards conceded to the princes. The Sankey Report acknowledged the right of the princes to decide the method by which their representatives to both houses of the federal legislature were to be chosen. State representatives were to be associated with the formation of the federal executive. Each state would enter federation through a separate convention in which its special rights and vested interests would be protected. Dynastic and personal matters involving the princes would continue to be decided by the viceroy as the representative of the crown.[79] The Chamber passed four resolutions endorsing the work of the delegation and expressing gratitude for the efforts of all the personnel connected with the conference.

A noteworthy contrast to this apparent unity occurred during the elections for Chamber offices. Bhopal defeated Patiala in a close race for the chancellorship, and Cutch defeated Alwar for the pro-chancellorship in another contested election. Patiala even had a difficult time securing election to the Standing Committee.[80] After the close of the Chamber sessions, Lord Irwin sagaciously commented that he would "never feel quite certain that the future would not see Patiala putting spokes in the Federation wheel that Bhopal would be pushing round."[81]

Hamidullah Khan of Bhopal and Ganga Singh of Bikaner were quickly emerging as the leading princely lobbyists for federation. The activities of the former among his fellow Muslims have already been cited above. The latter, upon his return to India in February 1931, held an informal conference with leading businessmen in Bombay to explain the decisions reached in London and the future program of the supporters of federation.[82] Bikaner, whose state included the home bases of appreciable numbers of Marwari businessmen, continued to maintain informal contacts with the commercial elements in Bombay but with few apparent results.[83]

In an even more audacious move, the Chamber princes, with Bikaner and Bhopal leading the way, attempted to reopen communications with a wide range of British Indian politicians over the issue of federation. In the social sphere always so dear to their hearts, they invited a diverse group including Ansari and Malaviya as representatives of the Working Committee of the Congress to their farewell banquet for Irwin. After this overture, Bikaner and Bhopal met privately with Gandhi to discuss federation in greater detail.[84] It may be argued that though Gandhi and Congressmen like Ansari and Malaviya might still harbor some sympathy for the princes, the Congress faction, dominated by Jawaharlal Nehru, would not accept a federation with the princes unless the representatives from the states to the federal legislature would be chosen through democratic elections. This condition would remain a major stumbling block throughout the tedious negotiations between the British and the Congress over the latter's acceptance of a federal structure for all of India.

Moving in another direction, Bhopal and Bikaner became actively associated with Tej Bahadur Sapru and Kailas Haksar in their project to organize the various groups supporting federation into a full-scale political party. The proposed organization, which was to be called the Centre party, was to be endowed with its own press syndicate and to include landlords, industrialists, and moderate politicians from British India as well as key princes. Sapru's principal coworkers in British India were Raja Sir Rampal Singh of Kurri Sidhauli, a leading *talukdar* of Oudh and an elected member of the Council of State, and Jwala Prasad Srivastava, the education minister in the United Provinces government and a well-known Kanpur industrialist with contacts to the maharaja of Darbhanga and the nawab of Chhatari, as well as other businessmen.[85] At this time Srivastava began his moves to purchase the *Pioneer* of Allahabad, which Sapru thought would make an excellent first paper in the proposed press syndicate.[86]

Haksar was responsible for drawing up the manifesto that laid out the methods and objectives of the new party. Stress was placed on the need for effective organization at the local and provincial levels, as well as at the center, the noncommunal orientation of the party, and the role of the press syndicate, which would explain and popularize the views of the party.[87] Unwilling to assume the sole initiative in this project so as to avoid any impression of a desire to dominate, Sapru suggested that certain princes help interest others in this venture. His strategy was that Bikaner should contact Ali Imam, Bhopal should speak with Muslim leaders, and joint invitations should be sent to such non-Congress politicians as Jayakar, Setalvad, Ramaswami Aiyer, A. P. Patro, Peroze Sethna, Cowasjee Jahangir, Sachchidanada Sinha, J. Rangachari, Dr. Ranjit Singh of the Zamindars' Association, and representative figures from princely India.[88] It proved impossible, however, to convene any meeting before the delegates had to leave India for the Second Round Table Conference.

Growing Opposition to Federation

Meanwhile, opposition to federation gathered strength as the initial waves of enthusiasm subsided. Moderate Indian politicians who were usually labeled Liberal began to organize against the federal proposals. Located mainly in Bombay or in Poona at the Servants of India Society headquarters, this group protested that the federal scheme allowed the states to enter a permanent constitutional union without any democratization of their governments or adequate provision for the representation of their subjects through popular elections.[89] In their opposition to federation, they were strongly endorsed by the states' people's groups, who demanded that the legislative representatives from the states be elected and that a guarantee of fundamental rights for all citizens of the federation be included in the constitution.[90]

Reminiscent of the resistance by certain provincial governors to the Montagu-Chelmsford proposals in 1919, various British officials now displayed negative attitudes toward federation and its associated goal of responsible government at the center. After a visit to Simla the profederation Keyes complained that he was thoroughly "disgusted with the spirit of defeatism that was rampant in the various Departments of Government and at the ill-concealed hostility of the white babus to the Federal idea. . . ."[91] Official demurral usually took the form of emphasizing the difficulties that would result from federation rather than launching open attacks. One example occurred when Sir George Schuster, the Finance member of the Viceroy's Executive Council, took it upon himself to explain in an unfavorable light the financial burdens that would befall the princes if they entered a federation.[92]

Even without official denigration, there was a growing deflection of support for federation among the states. Smaller entities became afraid that they would not receive sufficient representation in a federal legislature or that they might be grouped and thereby lose their individual identities.[93] Larger units felt that they would not obtain seats in proportion to their size and status. Although he had spoken in favor of federation in London, Akbar Hydari questioned the advisability of a federal arrangement when he returned to India.[94] As the chief representative of the premier state in India, his views carried considerable weight both within and without Hyderabad. The commitment of Hyderabad to federation was further subordinated to the nizam's desire to have his sovereignty over Berar acknowledged by having this long-disputed piece of territory designated as a separate unit distinct from the Central Provinces in any federation.[95] This demand by the premier ruler of princely India had a dampening effect even upon the optimism of his resident.

A major addition to the antifederation forces came on 16 June 1931 when Bhupinder Singh of Patiala officially released an attack on the Sankey Report and issued a counter-scheme labeled confederation. Claiming that the federal structure outlined in that document did not offer sufficient protection to the princes, especially the smaller ones, Patiala recommended a two-step plan ostensibly designed to remedy this defect. Under a reorganized Chamber, a union of states would be created with each present member of the Chamber having equal representation on a union council. This union of states eventually would join British India in a more limited constitutional arrangement known as confederation.[96]

More significant than the contents of Patiala's scheme was the apparent motivation behind its genesis. Although it was frequently alleged in the nationalist press that the Government of India had supplied the initiative in setting up this roadblock to federation, this charge was only partly true. The underlying situation was a complex one in which varying British attitudes toward federation were mingled with long-term rivalries among the princes. The highest levels of the British official hierarchy in India were unaware of Patiala's machinations, and when they learned of the confederation scheme, they were disturbed by its negative implications.[97] The situation was different among some members of the Political Department. Many political officers considered federation to be a threat to their status, and among them was James Fitzpatrick, the AGG for the Punjab states, who was known to have openly denounced federation. Bhupinder Singh was on friendly terms with Fitzpatrick, who had conducted the official inquiry that exonerated the Sikh prince of the charges of maladministration made in the report by the All India States' People's Conference. Although it is probable that the Punjab AGG had a hand in the formulation of the confederation plan, his action was taken without the approval or knowledge of Delhi or London.[98]

Although Patiala was actively encouraged to an undetermined extent in his opposition to federation by his local political officer, he was primarily motivated to take this stance because of his overweening jealousy of Bikaner and Bhopal. These two rivals, particularly Ganga Singh, had played prominent roles at the First Round Table Conference and then were conspicuous promoters of the profederation Centre party. As shown earlier, signs of the jealousy between Bikaner and Patiala had appeared as early as 1918 when the former refused to attend a banquet honoring the latter. Although these two had worked together in the first decade of the Chamber, an undercurrent of tension continued to exist, and it rose to the surface in the turbulent days surrounding the Round Table Conferences.

Because he had stopped in Paris to obtain medical treatment, Patiala had been almost the last prince to arrive in London in November 1930. As soon as he began to attend the meetings of the Indian States delegation to the Round Table Conference, he started to plague Wedgwood Benn, the secretary of state for India, with whining complaints that as chancellor of the Chamber he was not receiving due recognition from the members of the delegation. The role as leader that he had envisioned for himself was being usurped by the maharaja of Bikaner.[99] When he was questioned about these allegations, Ganga Singh claimed that the other princes had informally made him chairman during the absence of Patiala and continued to seek his views even after the arrival of the chancellor.[100] Lord Irwin, when asked for his opinion, advised London that Patiala as chancellor could lay claim only to the leadership of the eight members of the delegation who had been appointed by the Chamber. The remaining personnel who had been selected directly by the viceroy were free to extend or withhold recognition of Patiala as their head as they liked.[101] After the secretary of state communicated these views to Bikaner and Patiala in separate interviews, the nawab of Bhopal was able to effect a formal reconciliation between the two maharajas.[102]

During the first Chamber session after the princes returned to India, Hamidullah Khan of Bhopal proceeded to contest the election for the chancellorship and beat Patiala by a close margin. Besides associating himself with Bikaner in the Centre party project, the Muslim prince captured public attention by his efforts to promote unity within the Muslim community. Pushed into the background by these two rivals, Bhupinder Singh hoped to build up a base of power among the hundreds of smaller princes with his confederation scheme and thereby challenge the stature of the federation proponents in the world of princely politics.

Press comment on Patiala's confederation plan was highly critical, since the general consensus was that such a withdrawal of support would wreck the chances for advances being made at the Second Round Table Conference.[103] Among the profederation British Indian politicians, there was great apprehension about the potential uses that would be made of Patiala's assault on federation. Jayakar feared that dissentient elements such as the diehard Conservatives, states' people's groups, certain Muslims, and some Liberals would endorse Patiala's position to achieve their objective of preventing federation rather than because they thought confederation had any positive values.[104]

Among his fellow rulers, Patiala was having mixed results in his campaign to attract adherents. An early associate, Maharaja Udaibhan Singh of Dholpur, who was also related to Patiala, saw confederation as a vehicle by which he might reach greater prominence than he had attained by his earlier activities on the Standing Committee of the Chamber. An unexpected ally was Maharaja Gulab Singh of Rewa, who was influenced by his advisers—former political officers who were hostile to federation. Some rulers of smaller states such as Palanpur and Jhalawar were lured by the promise of greater representation than was possible under the Sankey scheme.[105] Most of the bantam autocrats upon whom Patiala counted for support retained their usual lethargic attitude toward political events occurring beyond the circumscribed borders of their possessions.

Whatever his hopes might have been, Bhupinder Singh soon learned how little his fellow rulers cared about his or any other constitutional scheme linking them more closely to British India. When the Indian States delegation met at Bombay in June 1931 to plan their strategy at the next Round Table Conference, Patiala lobbied feverishly but unsuccessfully.[106] After repeated canvassing by correspondence, he convened an early August meeting in Bombay in order to explain his scheme; but only three princes—Morvi, Orchha and Cambay—and twenty-six ministers bothered to attend.[107] His campaign received another setback when Lord Willingdon refused to add any supporters of confederation to the Federal Structure Committee, claiming that it was too late to make any changes.[108] Reacting blindly, Patiala deepened the split between himself and Bhopal by accusing the chancellor of being biased against the supporters of confederation who had been nominated for the Federal Structure Committee.[109]

Princes at the Second Round Table Conference

Although there was an outward display of enthusiasm and optimism, the Indian States delegation going to London in late 1931 lacked the luster of its predecessor. The most striking change was that Bhupinder Singh stayed at home. Besides his political problems, he was in serious financial difficulties and had been unable to obtain loans large enough to satisfy his many creditors, who included the Government of India.[110] Stating that he wished to remain in India to work for confederation, Patiala requested that Nawab Liaqat Hayat Khan, his prime minister, be permitted to attend the Second Round Table Conference in his place. Since sending a prime minister was considerably less of a strain on state revenues than sending a prince, the viceroy was glad to accede to this request.[111]

Once again, the main action at the conference, held from September to December 1931, took place in the meetings of the Federal Structure Committee and the Minorities Committee. Despite Gandhi's efforts to act as a mediator between the conflicting communities, the latter committee reached no agreement. The former committee continued to fill out the form of the proposed federal government, but there was little advance with regard to provisions concerning the states. As Samuel Hoare, the Conservative who had replaced Wedgwood Benn as secretary of state for India in August 1931, commented:

> The Round Table Conference has been dragging on most wearily. Everyone has been making the same speeches as he made last year at twice the length, and with nothing new in them. It does, however, appear that the differences upon matters of detail have become greater and that the Princes are more reluctant than ever to show their hand.[112]

One major detail was the composition of the federal legislature. Here British Indian leaders were not willing to concede more than 40 percent in the upper house and 33 1/3 percent in the lower house, whereas the princes demanded 50 percent of the seats in the upper house and substantial weightage in the lower house.[113]

Unlike the previous conference, the princes were now badly split into competing factions, so that in their bargaining with other groups they lacked the strength that comes from unity. Behind the scenes, Liaqat Hayat Khan was trying busily to rally support for his master's program of confederation. When he and the maharaja of Dholpur attempted to defend their cause against the criticisms of Sapru and Bikaner, they were forced to admit to a paucity of support, since few princes cared to commit themselves firmly to any side.[114] The last opportunity to gain support would be the Chamber session to be held in March 1932.

Shortly after the end of the Second Round Table Conference, antifederationists began to promote the immediate introduction of provincial autonomy and the deferment of federation and therefore central responsibility for three or four years until full agreement could be reached on the various points in dispute. The prime supporters of this schedule were the Muslims, the bureaucracy, and various Liberals.[115]

Last Efforts to Rally Support for Federation

With the appearance of this threat, Sapru, Jayakar, and Haksar felt compelled to muster their forces, and they began to lobby with sympathetic British officials and wavering princes.

In August 1931 Samuel Hoare, a Conservative, succeeded Wedgwood Benn, a Labourite, as secretary of state for India. Although the former was a most cautious supporter of federation at the First Round Table Conference, he gradually became a vigorous, indefatigable spokesman for federation in the House of Commons, at subsequent Round Table Conferences, and in his weekly letters to Lord Willingdon. Sapru was confident that London would remain faithful to the federal scheme, but it was a different story in India, where Willingdon was a doubtful supporter of federation. In later conversations with Sapru, the viceroy admitted that he had considered it a mistake for the princes to have first agreed to join a federation but now thought that it would be a greater blunder for them to go back on their original offer.[116] Seeing federation as the lesser of two evils, he could not be expected to push for it with any great zeal or determination. Willingdon's indifference was negatively reinforced by the generally recognized lack of sympathy among the Government of India bureaucracy, especially in the Political Department, for federation. Sapru and Hoare as well as Keyes all remarked on the inimical attitude of the officials in India.[117]

Sapru and Jayakar were more successful in their efforts with Lord Lothian, the chairman of the Franchise Committee, which was touring India in early 1932.[118] A pivotal figure because of his contacts in England and in India, Lothian actively worked for federation and made the prophetic assessment that

> they [the princes] should join the Federation and that if they did not, they would expose themselves to the criticism that they had stood in the way of British India and that ultimately after a few years they would find themselves compelled to join the Federation—perhaps on worse terms.[119]

Because of their vacillation and rivalries, the princes were a troublesome ally who refused to take seriously any painful advice about their own interests. In mid-March of 1932, however, the inner core of the Chamber and their ministers met and resolved their differences. Bikaner agreed to support a demand for separate and equal representation in the federal legislature for all members of the Chamber, and Patiala declared that his scheme, intended only to correct certain defects in the original federal proposals, was not meant to condemn the basic idea of federation.[120] At the March 1932 Chamber session, therefore, Bhopal moved, and Patiala seconded, a resolution declaring that the states would join an All-Indian Federation as long as the British crown provided safeguards, among which were the inviolability of the treaty rights of the princes and the preservation of their internal sovereignty.

The princes seemingly secure, Sapru and Haksar revived their program to form a Centre party and to secure the *Pioneer* as a party mouthpiece. As an initial step, a committee, consisting of V. T. Krishnamachari from Baroda, Manubhai Mehta from Bikaner, Liaqat Hayat Khan from Patiala, and Haksar, was formed to cooperate with British Indian supporters of the proposed party.[121] Haksar and Srivastava, meanwhile, had been able to interest Malcolm Hailey, the governor of the United Provinces, in this undertaking regarding the *Pioneer*; and Hailey, in turn, disposed the viceroy to influence the princes to favor the project.[122] Under pressure from Lord Willingdon, Hamidullah Khan, and Haksar, the princes pledged to contribute two lakhs of rupees to the venture, and by 1935 fifteen princes had paid 108,000 rupees.[123]

Princely enthusiasm for this type of political activity, however, soon evaporated. There was a variety of reasons. Haksar once remarked that "the Princes are not merely the creatures of moods—they are the victims of moments—and one who hopes to persuade them to a particular course of action, has to watch for such a moment."[124] These fickle leaders might be convinced to back some project during a favorable moment, but their commitment to their decision usually proved to be equally transitory. Besides, the general economic depression in the early 1930s dried up financial resources; and many princely patrons thought that the *Pioneer* did no more for them in the area of publicity than the *Statesman*, a British nonofficial newspaper of Calcutta and Delhi, did for free.[125] Finally, some ministerial advisers argued strongly against any alliance with the so-called Liberals. It was claimed that the Liberals were unrepresentative of the masses and that at times of crisis their party would either disintegrate or be ignored in favor of more dynamic and representative political groups. The basic dedication of the Liberals to popular rights and democratic government, moreover, made them an unacceptable ally for autocratic rulers who did not wish to be pressured into far-reaching political and social reforms.[126]

Growing Disunity among the Princes

Just as the open breach between Patiala and Bikaner was being closed, other rifts within the ranks of the princely order were appearing. In February 1932 Prabhashankar Pattani, administrator of Bhavnagar and a major figure in Kathiawar politics, where small states were concentrated, began to circulate two constitutional alternatives to the Sankey proposals for federation. They enabled smaller states to have representation in a federation of states that would eventually join British India in a loose arrangement.[127] The content of these schemes is less important than the fact that they caused confusion among the rulers and allowed their support to be dissipated on trivial differences.

A second dissenter now emerged in the inner circles of the Chamber in the person of Jam Saheb Ranjit Sinhji of Nawanagar, who had been recently elected as a compromise candidate to the chancellorship of the Chamber. According to Haksar, the jam saheb, under the influence of Rushbrook Williams, openly opposed the formation of the Centre party and the acquisition of the *Pioneer*.[128]

The new chancellor further weakened the federation position by calling a conference in Bombay, ostensibly to define the mandate to be given to the states delegation to the third and last Round Table Conference. While even such an obstructionist as Patiala opposed this gathering, reasoning that the resolutions passed at the last Chamber session offered adequate guidelines,[129] Sapru became worried about Nawanagar's intentions and was critical of the inability of the princes to stick to any decision.[130]

Maqbool Mahmud, a minister in Jhalawar and formerly in the Chamber Secretariat, aptly characterized the Bombay meetings as "excursions for dewans and outlets for ministerial gasbags."[131] Although the Delhi resolutions favoring federation were affirmed and support for a bicameral legislature was strengthened, the Bombay assembly passed a resolution that 51 percent of the states must agree to join before a federation could be established. Sapru was now concerned that this stipulation might constitute a stumbling block to a quick inauguration of federation.[132] Moreover, the diehard Conservatives, under the leadership of Churchill, were able to interpret the princely debates at Bombay as a basic questioning of federation, and they then proceeded to launch a formidable attack in Parliament on the government's support of such a program.[133]

Not deterred by the results of the Bombay caucus, Nawanagar continued to point out the difficulties rather than the advantages of, or the necessity for, federation. While in England for his summer holiday, he engaged Sir Leslie Scott to draft alternate proposals to federation; but this project was repudiated by the rest of the Standing Committee, who were disillusioned with Scott's legalistic solutions.[134]

Among the giants who had remained aloof from the Chamber but were initially attracted to the federal idea, there was a parallel, growing coolness toward federation as negotiations dragged on. Hydari continued to claim that it was detrimental to the interests of Muslims in general and to those of Hyderabad in particular.[135] The nizam himself was rumored to be increasingly apprehensive that in an all-India federation the states' representatives would ally with the Hindus from British India to the detriment of Hyderabad and his position as the premier Muslim ruler in India.[136] The other major spokesman for federation from a southern state, Mirza Ismail of Mysore, began to argue that federation had hopelessly receded into the distant future because of opposition from various states, C. Y. Chintamani and the states' people's groups, and some Liberals, as well as the rising tide of communalism.[137]

In September 1932, Willingdon made one final effort to effect some agreement with the princes about the federal provisions that most concerned them. Discussions with the Standing Committee of the Chamber and other members of the states delegation were initiated on four overarching topics: relations between the paramount power and the states in federal matters, relations between the two parties in nonfederal matters, financial aspects of the proposed federation, and the allocation of seats in the federal legislature.[138]

Regarding the relation between themselves and the paramount power, the princes, on the one hand, reiterated their demand for a definition of paramountcy. Following the text of the Butler Report, Lord Willingdon, on the other hand, admonished the rulers not to fetter the personal discretion of the viceroy since his powers were their greatest safeguard. Despite this ominous warning, they reasserted that they would not join a federation unless the paramountcy dispute was settled to their satisfaction.[139]

After the above stalemate a slight advance was made on the issue of the handling of justiciable matters. In federal areas justiciable disputes were to be decided by the Federal Supreme Court, and in nonfederal areas such disagreements were to be obligatorily referred to *ad hoc* tribunals, whose findings were to be recommendations but not mandates to the viceroy.[140]

On the two other issues, difficult decisions were once again postponed. The Second Round Table Conference had appointed a committee, usually referred to as the Davidson Committee, to examine the existing financial organization between the two parts of India and to advise on future financial adjustments necessary in a federation. Although this committee had submitted its report, the government had yet to draw up its recommendations. Because of their longstanding attitude that they were being victimized in such areas as custom duties and subsidies, the princes were particularly concerned that future financial arrangements should be more equitable to their interests. Akbar Hydari and the maharaja of Rewa both stated that they wanted to see the financial working of the federation before they made any commitments.[141] To avoid controversy, the meeting decided to delay further discussion until the government's position on the Davidson Report was made known.

The second perplexing decision deferred was on the allocation of seats in the federal legislature. At the First Round Table Conference, it had been agreed that the states would be free to allot among themselves the seats to be given to them. Two conflicting opinions quickly arose over this matter. One faction reasoned that there should be proportional representation, with the largest states having multiple votes and the smallest states joined together to form constituencies each having one vote. The other side advocated separate, equal representation for, at least, all members of the Chamber.[142] Using the excuse that the total number of seats to be allotted to them was still unknown, this latter group was able to delay any decisions.[143] What neither party fully realized was that the longer they procrastinated, the more difficult any decision satisfactory to all princes became and the more ammunition that was supplied to the opponents of federation.

Third Round Table Conference

Federation was sinking fast, and the deliberations of the Third Round Table Conference offered little encouragement to its tired advocates. At this critical juncture there was a major change in the composition of the Indian States delegation. Because of his continuing financial problems, the Political Department vetoed the idea of Patiala going to London. To preserve his *izzat*, Bhupinder Singh pleaded with Bikaner and Bhopal not to attend the conference. When these two agreed to stay in India, it was decided that the princes should be represented by their ministers. Princes already in London or otherwise planning to go there were free to advise the ministers but were not to take an active role in the deliberations of the conference.[144] Although many of the ministers appointed were extremely capable and experienced men and often more sympathetic than their masters to federation, they, according to Hoare, had "explicit instructions not to commit their rulers too far."[145] Another notable change in personnel was the elimination of K. N. Haksar from the states delegation. Haksar was Sapru's closest collaborator and a firm advocate of federation, but he was thoroughly disliked by Terence Keyes and Akbar Hydari, who led a coalition of larger and smaller states who supported federation but wanted different procedures and structures than those proposed by the Standing Committee and Sapru.[146] Haksar attributed his deletion to the displeasure that he had provoked among official circles opposed to federation,[147] and Sapru and the Standing Committee of the Chamber lost an astute proponent in the states delegation.

Although the Third Round Table Conference further elaborated the structure of a federal Government of India, it failed to bring federation closer to reality because it avoided painful decisions on thorny problems. A major example of this tendency was the question of the size of the two houses of the federal legislature and the proportion of seats, particularly in the upper house, to be allotted to the states. The British Indian delegates offered 40 percent of the places in the upper house, but the states' agents held out for 50 percent. Some princes and ministers privately said that they were favorably disposed to the British Indian offer, but they lacked the political courage necessary to state their views publicly.[148] Sapru repeatedly bemoaned the double-speaking of the princes, who said one thing to the British Indian delegates and another to the government delegates. His conclusion was that such actions would result in further estrangement between British India and the states in the future.[149]

The conferees also were unsuccessful in their efforts to frame the specific procedures by which the states would join the federation and to set a definite date by which they must enter. Although anxious to arrange a constitutional solution to the predicament of the princes, Sapru did not want to sacrifice his goal of central responsibility to placate their apprehensions. At this juncture he urged the immediate inauguration of responsible government at the center with only the British Indian provinces as the federating units. The princes might later join such a federation on whatever terms they could then negotiate.[150]

The British government now drafted its scheme for an Indian constitution and issued it as a White Paper on 19 March 1933.[151] A Joint Select Committee from both houses of Parliament was then appointed to examine and to hold hearings on the provisions of this constitution. Chaired by Lord Linlithgow, who would go to India as viceroy in 1936, this committee received evidence from a lengthy parade of Indian and British witnesses. Their testimony revealed a wide variety of attitudes toward federation. During a marathon performance that extended over nineteen days and included almost six thousand questions, Hoare emerged as a firm advocate of federation. Malcolm Hailey, once again in London as a representative of the Government of India before the Joint Select Committee, remarked that Hoare

> has completely identified himself with the White Paper proposals. Indeed he has changed greatly from the very cautious and conservative attitude which I saw him taking in 1930 and . . . has attracted to his own head the brickbats which a short time ago used to be directed at Lord Irwin. It is indeed curious that we should now find a small band of Conservative politicians who are pleading the Indian cause with all the fervour (though, no doubt, with far more discretion and with far more statesmanship) which was once displayed by Mr. Montagu and who seem willing to run the dangers which fell to his lot.[152]

On behalf of the states' representatives, Akbar Hydari and Liaqat Hayat Khan made unequivocal announcements that the princes were firm in their support of federation.[153] Still some British Indian delegates attempted to deter the princes by statements that federation would only be acceptable if states' representatives were elected and were barred from voting in the federal legislature on British Indian subjects.[154] The princes were courted from the other end of the political spectrum by the diehard conservatives led by Churchill in Commons and Salisbury in Lords who were opposed to any changes at the Centre and anxious to use the reluctance of many princes to join a federation to support their opposition to the White Paper proposals.[155] In the end the Report of the Joint Select Committee endorsed most recommendations of the White Paper, but it laid particular emphasis on the voluntary character of the accession of the states to federation.[156]

Demise of Federation

Inexorably and unmistakably profederation elements among the princes were disappearing as the fragile unity they had achieved in the deliberations of the First Round Table Conference crumbled. Federation would have been a viable political reality only if a majority of the princes chose to join and then, once a part of such an arrangement, chose to act as a bloc on crucial issues. Throughout the discussions in and surrounding the Round Table Conferences, most princes seemed unaware of these considerations and preoccupied by petty rivalries and short-term interests.

In a desperate attempt to keep the path to federation open, the maharaja of Bikaner, in January 1933, pleaded for unity and argued against any hasty commitment to any one constitutional scheme until the next session of the Chamber in March 1933.[157] Further support for an early federation with British India came from Manubhai Mehta and Liaqat Hayat Khan, two leading members of the Indian States delegation at the Third Round Table Conference. They accurately predicted that

> later on, the States would be at the mercy of the predominant partner and would have to agree to come in on terms then offered by the "dictator" and without any bargaining power in the hands of the States. The States would by that time have grown considerably weaker in influence and they would not then be able to secure the same guarantees whether from the Paramount Power or from the self-India [*sic*] of the day, that they can secure without difficulty at the present day.[158]

Despite this shrewd warning, the princes became increasingly engrossed in vain rivalries and debates over issues irrelevant to existing political conditions. At the March 1933 Chamber session, it was Bhopal's turn to feel slighted by Patiala and Bikaner, and the nawab refused to run for any Chamber office.[159] When Patiala was elected to the chancellorship at this time, he was given a Standing Committee composed of Bikaner, Bahawalpur, Dungarpur, Jhalawar, Panna, Rampur, Sangli, and Wankaner.[160] Hearing of these results, Haksar became despondent about the future of federation since these men, except for Bikaner, carried little influence in either British or princely India and tended to be political reactionaries, likely to parrot the line propagated by the Political Department.[161]

The strength of the Chamber as a unifying force and an advocate of federation was further shattered as many of its most active members began to resign. Such giants as Hyderabad and Baroda had withdrawn from it as soon as the initial flurry over federation had subsided. Now the maharajas of Kashmir and Kapurthala, the former a longtime member of the Standing Committee, resigned, declaring that they felt the Chamber had failed to protect adequately their legitimate interests.[162] When the Political Department announced a scheme to enlarge the Chamber by admitting more smaller princes, medium-sized princes including the stalwart Bikaner protested against this supposed flooding of the Chamber and threatened to resign.[163] Eventually even Patiala as chancellor questioned the value of an institution so depleted in its ranks and divided in its counsels.[164]

A final illustration of the bankruptcy of the princes in political acumen and foresight occurred during a meeting between Willingdon and some Chamber members held concurrently with the 1933 Chamber session. The viceroy wished to ascertain their views on the recently released White Paper and to learn what agreement had been reached on the crucial point of the allocation of seats in a federal legislature. Nawanagar, on behalf of the Chamber, had to answer that they were still working on the matter and that no agreement had yet been reached.[165] Throughout the conference the princes refused to commit themselves on any aspect of the White Paper, and the viceroy, when terminating the proceedings, remarked that he regretted calling them together since the meeting had been a total waste of time.[166]

The Chamber was not to meet again until 1935 when coincidentally the Government of India Act was passed, eight years after the Simon Commission had first taken up the problem of the next installment of constitutional reform. Although the Act's provisions concerning fully responsible government in the provinces came into effect, its federal sections were stillborn.

Once the British had provided a constitutional focus for political expectations and activity in British Indian provinces, they turned under new leadership to other concerns of which the princes were only one. In June 1935 the marquess of Zetland, who as Lord Ronaldshay had served as governor of Bengal from 1917 to 1922, replaced Samuel Hoare as secretary of state for India. In April 1936 Lord Linlithgow sailed for India to succeed Lord Willingdon as viceroy. Both men wanted to bring the princes into a federation, but they differed over procedures and timing. Linlithgow quickly appointed three political officers, Courtenay Latimer, Arthur C. Lothian, and Francis Wylie, as special emissaries to the princes on the provisions of the 1935 Government of India Act, wanting them to be both friendly advisers and ministers plenipotentiary. Zetland urged caution and a two-stage process that defined their task as "exploratory and elucidatory" and deferred actual negotiations to another round. He claimed:

> It does, however, occur to me that there may be a point in the negotiations with the Princes beyond which the application of more haste might result in the achievement of less speed. My experience of the Princes, such as it is, leads me to the conclusion that they are shy birds and that they might easily take fright if they got it into their heads that we were trying to rush them into decisions before they were quite ready to take them. . . . Let me add that I shall have to keep a sharp eye on Parliament in all matters connected with the establishment of the Federation. I have been warned more than once by Salisbury and his friends that their acquiescence in the passage of the various Orders in Council dealing with the establishment of Provincial Autonomy must not be taken as an indication of their attitude towards feder-

> ation, which they regard as the much more dangerous part of the scheme of self-government embodied in the Act of 1935.[167]

The viceroy acceded, and ultimately the collective peregrinations of his trio produced little formal accord.[168]

Meanwhile, the Indian National Congress came to power in the majority of the provinces, passed the Haripura Resolution, and supported popular political agitations in states ranging from Rajkot to Jaipur to Mysore. The princes became frightened and retired to their treaties and the soothing advice of highly paid legal counsel.[169] The London-inspired policy of leisurely negotiations did not produce positive results, since in April 1939 the princes rejected categorically the revised Instruments of Accession that the viceroy had recently distributed to them, even though they continued to discuss federation as a goal. During the summer of 1939 C. P. Skrine, the resident for the Punjab States, thought that

> the anti-Federation influences among the Punjab States are weakening. An extension has been given them up to Sept. 1st to make up their minds, and I think a satisfactory "formula" will be found which will enable them to accede without loss of face. We in Simla can do little more—the various points at issue are under consideration by the Home Govt. in consultation with the Viceroy, and a good deal will depend on the conclusions reached in those exalted quarters.[170]

The date of 1 September 1939 was to be, unfortunately, far more than a deadline for the princes, for Germany chose to invade Poland on that day. Linlithgow postponed further steps toward federation for the duration of the war, and many princes uttered a short-lived sigh of relief.

Conclusion

The attitudes and reactions of the three major groups involved in negotiations over federation ensured that it would never be implemented. Among sympathetic British Indian politicians, epitomized by Tej Bahadur Sapru and M. R. Jayakar, federation was a device that would obtain central responsibility. It was not their primary goal, and, consequently, even their generous support had its limits. For more radically oriented political figures, as characterized by Jawaharlal Nehru, federation meant the inclusion of reactionary elements in an all-Indian constitution without providing the adequate means to counter their negative attitudes toward political and social reform. By the early 1930s Nehru and his cohorts, who were in the ascendancy within the nationalist power structure of India, were no longer willing to permit the Indian states to maintain their autocratic existence. Muslim politicians had been divided in their attitudes toward federation but had become increasingly apprehensive of its consequences after the Congress ministries came to power in 1937. They in turn communicated their anxiety to Muslim princes who had also become less committed to federation as the years passed.

In Britain itself the diversity of opinion toward federation and central responsibility was mirrored in a split within the Conservative party between those willing to accept these two objectives as long as they were tied together and those opposed to any change in the structure of the Government of India. Although the latter group never became dominant, its leaders acted vigorously to stymie negotiations over accession to federation. They constantly appealed to the fears of the princes that federation precluded any meaningful existence as rulers, and they utilized the Joint Select Committee's promise that accession must be voluntary to make it difficult for the Government of India to exert overt pressure upon the princes to move them toward federation. Since the head of the India Office was a member of Parliament, he and his subordinates were more subject, and more responsive, to threats from Parliamentary opponents of federation.

The British official hierarchy directly concerned with Indian affairs also exhibited its characteristic assortment of outlooks on any given issue—in this instance, federation. Personnel changes in London and in Delhi during the Round Table Conference period, though not involving any dramatic reversals of policy, meant a lack of consistent direction from the top. British officials in India had varied reactions to federation and the claims of the princes upon the British for protection. Willingdon, who had been born in 1866 and had extensive dealings with the princes while serving as governor in Bombay, was willing to promote their cause; but Linlithgow, who was twenty-one years younger and of a different generation, was disposed to fulfill obligations but not to take extraordinary measures on their behalf. His formal and distant personal manner, in contrast to the greater ease of Willingdon, inhibited the close personal ties that several of his predecessors had maintained with the princes and had used to advantage. The members of the ICS had mixed opinions on federation, as they did on most other issues. Most of them serving in British India evinced little interest in federation or were protective of their own prerogatives, as was the case in the Finance Department. Some political officers such as Terence Keyes and C. P. Skrine were strongly in favor of it, and others such as J. A. O. Fitzpatrick were opposed. The key factor is that the lack of a clear-cut policy coupled with the stresses within the imperial relationships and the established bureaucratic procedures led to dilatory negotiations that allowed external events, particularly the outbreak of World War II, to remove what little initiative the British still possessed.

The princes themselves, however, were the principal party precluding the establishment of a federation. At this crucial juncture in the early 1930s, the British government and Indian politicians were courting the princes as they had not been courted since the early nineteenth century. For divergent and not always compatible reasons, officials and politicians were willing to offer a constitutional guarantee of continued existence to the autocratic rulers. After an initial interest in federation, the princes came to reject the opportunities so generously extended to them. Although there had been much rhetoric about the need for joint cooperation with British India for many years preceding the Round Table Conferences, there had been no disciplined thinking in princely circles about what would be demanded of them in any cooperative arrangement. Closer relations with British India were seen as a one-way street bringing benefits to the princes and asking nothing in return. After the blow to their illusions delivered in the Butler Report, many princes, reacting wildly, were willing to enter into a pact with anyone—the devil not excluded—in order to reduce British interference in their affairs. Most of the princes in London who agreed on the desirability of federation had little understanding of the demands likely to be made on federating units or of the techniques needed by anyone aspiring to political power within such a constitutional system. Not realizing the always narrowing range of political options open to them, the princes were not ready to compromise when this last opportunity to do so was presented to them.

chapter eight

The Princes in India in 1939

By 1939 the Indian princes had been unable to gain any constitutional guarantees for their continued existence that they had not already enjoyed in 1914. After two decades of dedicated effort by a small group of activists to prove their enduring value as military and political allies, these clients were rewarded by growing indifference from their British patron. At the same time Indian nationalists, after holding a wide variety of opinions about them, had come to entertain a common disdain for these political vestiges. The basic reason for the unenviable position of the princes in 1939 was their inability, because of a variety of factors, to respond realistically to the unprecedented changes that had occurred in the relationships among themselves, the British government, and the Indian nationalists during the years from 1914 to 1939.

Indian Society and Politics in 1939

Drastic, if not revolutionary, changes had taken place within Indian society during the short era between the outbreaks of the two World Wars. The overarching feature of Indian politics in 1939 was the involvement for the first time of large segments of Indian society in the political process. Mahatma Gandhi was clearly the foremost figure engaging sizable numbers of Indians in the nationalist movement; but other Indian politicians, particularly those who were regionally or communally oriented, also gathered widespread popular support for their programs. Gandhi's techniques of nonviolent noncooperation with governmental institutions and civil disobedience of laws judged to be immoral enabled the political elites of India to convert illiterate, unarmed adherents into a powerful, coercive weapon. The members of these elites could no longer be accused of being leaders without followers; the civil disobedience campaigns of 1920 and 1930 proved otherwise.

The progressive politicization of new strata such as the peasantry, the untouchables, and women as well as the princes was mirrored in the gradual but meaningful incorporation of larger numbers of Indians into policy-making and policy-executing levels of the Government of India. From a single place in 1914 on the Viceroy's Executive Council, a minority position in the Central and Provincial Legislative Councils, and a miniscule representation in the ICS, Indians by 1939 had come to form responsible cabinet governments in the provinces, to constitute an elected majority in all legislative assemblies, and to penetrate the ICS and other all-Indian services. Indian politicians could no longer be told that they lacked the ability or the experience to govern themselves; the records of the Indian provincial ministries from 1937 to 1939 proved otherwise.

The enlargement of the franchise in 1919 and 1935 brought millions of Indians into the process, thereby providing an added channel of political participation for previously mute groups. In order to attract the votes necessary to obtain positions of power, Indian politicians were pushed to formulate new programs and to utilize different techniques than those effective during an era of elite politics.[1] The formidable success of the Indian National Congress in the 1937 provincial elections emphasized the value of an appealing economic as well as a vigorous political platform, a tightly controlled, comprehensive organization, and energetic campaigning. These elections also revealed the effectiveness of appeals to special interests, either economic, communal, or political.

Concurrent with these advances to responsible, democratic government, there was a deepening division of political forces on the basis of religious affiliations. Religious revivalism had made individual Indians increasingly conscious of their distinctive religious heritages just as Indians were being asked to form a common nationality. This personal awareness of religious differences was institutionalized by the formation of politically oriented religious and cultural bodies concerned mainly with protecting the interests of their memberships. The period from 1914 to 1939 witnessed the emergence of the Shiromani Gurdwara Parbandhak Committee, the Rashtriya Swayamsevak Sangh, the Central Khilafat Committee, the reactivation of the Muslim League under the astute direction of Muhammad Ali Jinnah, the flourishing of the Hindu Mahasabha, and the organization of the "untouchables" by Dr. B. R. Ambedkar. Gandhi's use of religious terminology such as *Ram raj* to describe political goals and the actions of many Congress provincial governments heightened the Hindu overtones of even the avowedly secular Indian National Congress. The 1920s were years of tragic communal strife that temporarily abated during the 1930s but rose again to horrendous proportions during the 1940s. Indian politicians in responsible government and party leadership positions were becoming alarmed over their inability to control communal outbursts.

Besides these political developments, there was a new consciousness of the need for thoroughgoing economic as well as social reform if a free India was to be a strong India. The position of the landlord class came under heavy attack, and the Congress Socialist party founded in 1934 sought to secure equality of economic opportunities for all. Programs of social reform took up complex issues focusing on such millennium-old problems as the status of the scheduled castes within Indian society.

The Government of India in 1939

On the eve of World War II, the British still possessed a highly integrated bureaucratic structure in India with the governor general at the apex. Together with the provincial governors he possessed the power to pass ordinances and to veto any legislation passed by the Indian-controlled legislatures if such action was deemed necessary for the maintenance of internal law and order or to protect the external security of India. Despite this ultimate control the power of the British within the Government of India had sharply declined. Legislative reforms had produced elected Indian majorities in all legislative assemblies and responsible ministries on the provincial level. Difficulties in obtaining British recruits and gradual Indianization had enlarged the number of Indians in the ICS.[2] Congress campaigns to win popular support had erased the passivity of Indian multitudes that had allowed a small group of British officials to govern India with relatively little force for so many years. Most importantly, British leaders at home had decided that dominion status was the goal of constitutional development in India and were willing to proceed in this direction despite determined opposition from the so-called diehard faction of the Conservative party and the dire predictions of retired ICS officers.

The differences between 1914 and 1939 were dramatically revealed in what happened upon the outbreak of war in September 1939. When Britain declared war on Germany and her allies, Lord Linlithgow, who had become viceroy in 1936, immediately added India to that declaration. His failure to consult any Indian representatives so enraged the key Working Committee of the Congress that it ordered all of its members to resign their ministerial posts. Despite repeated efforts to negotiate for their wartime support, the British never obtained the cooperation of the Congress during the war, and even had to cope with obstreperous opposition that culminated in the Quit India movement of 1942.[3]

The Indian Princes in 1939

With the beginning of war in 1939, in striking contrast to the response of the Congress, the Indian princes once again were quick to volunteer their personal services and the resources of their states in support of the British cause. Imbued with nineteenth-century ideas about their obligations and privileges as British clients, they dreamed that their loyal assistance would be generously rewarded upon the eventual cessation of hostilities. Forgetting that similar hopes had been only partially fulfilled in 1918, when the British had some power to grant meaningful concessions, these imperial dependents seemed oblivious to the fact that their overlord was no longer able to compensate faithful service. In 1946 the British Cabinet Mission seemed hardly aware of the existence of the princes, and the last British viceroy, Lord Mountbatten, had little time to consider the princes. He relied more upon the advice and views of Jawaharlal Nehru about them than on that of Sir Conrad Corfield, his political adviser on the princes.[4]

What had happened to bring most princes, including those active in all-Indian politics, to such a forlorn impasse? Many have attributed their demise to the lack of political and social reform in their states. These critics argue that reform might have produced stronger ties between ruler and subject and transformed these physically isolated and scattered states into viable political entities. They usually ascribe the absence of reform both to British lack of initiative and princely preferences. Recent research on individual states, such as that of James Manor, indicates that even in such a progressive state as Mysore reform would not have produced the conditions necessary for the continued existence of the state as an autonomous unit. This thesis supplies only partial answers, since reform alone would not be enough. It also overlooks the diversity of policies and attitudes within the British hierarchy.

Although it is alleged that Minto's commitment at Udaipur precluded British pressure to effect internal reforms within the states, it must be realized that earlier British interference had been in the sphere of administrative rather than political reforms. Curzon had advocated efficient governance and not representative or popular government. Thus Minto did not deflect a British thrust toward more democratic arrangements in the states. The British continued to intervene in instances of maladministration throughout the twentieth century, as demonstrated most dramatically in Nabha, Jammu and Kashmir, and Alwar and more covertly in Patiala and Udaipur. These actions aimed not only at correcting existing abuses but also at establishing new institutions such as a legislative assembly in Jammu and Kashmir. The British did not aggressively promote reform, but they did not totally disregard the internal governance of the states.

It is too simple to think that one man alone could determine policy, such as that of noninterference, for forty years unless subsequent circumstances and officials favored it. Many political officers after Minto's departure saw the princes as the last survivals of the traditional India that they claimed to govern in trusteeship in order to raise it to Western standards of civilized life. The corruption and inefficient administration prevalent in princely India only served as further justification for the presence of the British as guardians of the best interests of India. The pomp and ceremony decorating the princely durbars were pleasant reminders of a bygone era when the British had all the answers. Some political officers were interested in promoting reform by the 1930s, but others were not. Some like Edward Wakefield had entered the Political Service partly to escape the conditions in British India created by the popularization and Indianization of government. At the viceregal level there was some support for reform but greater consideration of imperial objectives. Lord Irwin arrived as an apostle of good government, but when he produced a note on the essentials of good government, he directed that it was to be circulated only to those requesting a copy. By 1930 even he had become reluctant to press for reforms if such activity would jeopardize broader imperial concerns, which at that point meant a successful Round Table Conference.

Still, it must be remembered that although nineteenth-century British critics and twentieth-century Indian antagonists frequently portrayed the states as cesspools of corruption and maladministration, state governments were not so much more autocratic than the nineteenth-century British Indian administration could be. From the beginning of the twentieth century, however, the Indian states assumed an increasingly anachronistic aura as major advances leading to more representative and then to responsible government and a more open society were made in British India. The introduction and the gradual widening of the franchise, the opening of high-level posts first by nomination and then by election, the readiness to consult popular opinion, the repeal of press censorship, all were measures barely comprehensible to the princes. During the period of greatest change from 1919 to 1939, these autocrats were hardly willing to debate the need for political reform, let alone implement it. Basic institutions of good administration such as an independent judiciary and a privy purse were the exception rather than the rule in Indian states as late as 1930. Among those princes active in British Indian politics, such as Bikaner, Bhopal, Kashmir, and Patiala, there was no major effort to move beyond token reforms in fundamental areas such as the franchise and a responsible executive. The princes had fallen slightly behind in the process of political modernization by 1900. They had become hopelessly outdistanced by 1939 because of their own preferences for autocracy and British unwillingness to risk the support of these collaborators by prodding them into unwanted political reforms.

The path of internal reform failed because it had not been tried in most cases, but why did the princely strategy of relying upon the British and expanding their activities in the all-Indian political arena also miscarry? Some have contended, as was done in an earlier version of this study, that the princes were victims of a colossal self-delusion as to their importance and permanence within the Indian political structure. Illusions did exist among the princes. It is, however, necessary to understand that the princes developed perceptions of their positions and decided to act in particular ways for a wide variety of factors. They were responding partly to personal propensities evolved during their socialization and partly to external conditions over which they had limited control. Rearing patterns, education, and autocratic governmental structures influenced the princes to form definite ideas about their superiority to most other individuals. At court and in school princes were the centers of attention and were indoctrinated with pronounced notions of *izzat*. They were generally indulged and denied few requests. One promising area for further research would be a comparison of the administrations of princes who were designated heirs at birth and those adopted closer to maturity. It has been argued that Maharaja Sayaji Rao of Baroda developed his interest in social reform because he had lived close to ordinary people prior to his adoption. Once princes ascended their *gadis*, they became the central target for both supporters and opponents. It was inevitable that they should develop a strong sense of self-importance when even states' people's groups proclaimed that they were all-powerful and could effect change if only they wanted to do so. Autocracy provided a framework that reinforced illusions of grandeur. One analysis of Rajput aristocrats after 1947 emphasizes that fellow feeling among them spread only with growing equality and access to, and use of, political power.[5] Democracy leads one to view opponents as individuals, whereas autocracy lumps them together as an illegitimate resistance.

External conditions were at least equally important in sustaining princely visions of an autonomous future and in ensuring that it would not materialize. The British made conflicting demands on the princes as they attempted to juggle the pleas of their collaborators with the demands of their challengers. At the same time they increasingly revealed a willingness to sacrifice the interests of the former in favor of the latter, who had become the most powerful force. The imperial overlord, furthermore, had actually changed little of the phraseology and ceremony from the late nineteenth century that governed their relationships with the princes. These symbols were an inexpensive concession for the British, and masked the widening gap between the reality and the myth of the British commitment to the princes. The Political Service, which still provided the princes with their most immediate contact with their British patron, also tended to exalt the position of the princes once they acknowledged the ultimate paramountcy of the British and their representatives. Indian groups were partly responsible for the princely dreams as well as for their lack of realization. Many Indians had been attracted to the princes during the nineteenth century, but during the subsequent decades there was a growing divergence of opinion and attitude. Socially and politically radical leaders became critical and even hostile, and moderate and conservative ones continued to seek the princes as allies and financial supporters. Expanding communal mobilization helped to reinforce, and in some cases to create, myths about the historical importance of certain princes and to offer the princes new opportunities for leadership along with new threats to their internal stability.

As in many other areas, the British never formulated a consistent policy that was carefully implemented at all levels of their official hierarchy with regard to the princes. To look for or to reconstruct such a policy is to distort reality. Chelmsford might proclaim the need for a new policy toward the princes, but neither he, his successors, nor his superiors in London felt compelled to devote much attention to the matter. They continued to operate as if the upheavals of World War I had little impact in what Butler labeled Indian India. Although the Political Department continued to act and speak as if the treaties were a basis for decisions, the Home Department bluntly declared them to be irrelevant to prevailing conditions. During the twentieth century the princes had the capacity only to annoy and not to threaten. The imperial patron knew that the range of choices left to the princes was narrowing though not absolutely closed. The British, therefore, responded to enough princely requests in order to reaffirm the appearance of their commitment to them but did not plan to devote any major resources such as military forces to these expendable allies. They were willing to discuss constitutional arrangements but not to exert pressure on the princes to agree to them. Here as in the matter of internal reform the British were unwilling to lose whatever support they might receive from their collaborators.

The princes compounded their difficulties by their readiness to place full confidence in the ability of the British to overcome challenges from any quarter to the existence of the empire. Some of them were aware of changing political conditions on the Indian subcontinent, but their response was to obtain a firm promise from their patron as to their position as an integral part of the Indian political system and in return to prove their value as political allies in the unprecedented circumstances. To achieve their first objective, the princes sought a definition of paramountcy, a constitutional assembly of princes, arbitration tribunals, courts of inquiry, and some form of joint consultations with British Indian legislators. Throughout their meetings with political officers, their interviews with viceroys and secretaries of state, their sessions with committees of inquiry, these men were unable to comprehend that constitutional arrangements remain viable only so long as they adequately reflect the political relationships existing among the component units. Despite great expenditures of time, money, and personal energies, these politicians were unable to attain even the basic minimum of their aims. The ultimate irony is that even if they had been successful in obtaining the desired concessions from a patron in decline, they would have been found wanting in the final confrontation between princes and nationalists. The various reorganizations of state boundaries and changes in governmental structures in both India and Pakistan after 1947 and the Princely Derecognition Act of 1971 in India reveal the impermanence of such provisions.

Conscious that their overlord was facing exceptional political opposition in the post-1918 era, many of the same princes who worked so earnestly to secure legal assurances from the British were also anxious to demonstrate their versatility as allies. Ambitious men, they wanted to achieve status as all-India figures in politics and to utilize their influence to stifle new forms of opposition to British policies and their own rule. Although they did not always act according to British desires, since their own goals were wide-ranging, they did so often enough that they became identified as British lackeys. Their activities also lacked a certain consistency since there was disagreement within the British hierarchy about how overtly and how frequently the princes should intervene in all-Indian politics. Some provincial governors who were particularly threatened, such as Sir Frederick Sykes of Bombay during the civil disobedience movement of the 1930s, welcomed such support, and others tried to discourage it. Even within the Political Service itself, there was not unanimity of opinion about what should be done with the princes and what roles they should play.

The Political Service presented problems for both the princes and the British despite the presence in it of several able men. Although E. M. Forster's comments on the local political officers in *Hill of Devi* may appear to be a caricature, they may be substantiated in many different sources including some written by former political officers. A prime example of the latter category is the autobiography of Sir Edward Wakefield, a member of the Political Service from 1927 to 1947. In his characterization of Sir Harold Wilberforce-Bell, under whom he had served when Sir Harold was resident for the Punjab states in the late 1930s, Wakefield reveals the extraordinary concern for rank and correct form that prevailed within the Political Service. Sensitive about the fact that the governor of Punjab outranked him, the resident avoided attending receptions in Lahore where the governor would be present. In Simla, the summer headquarters of the Punjab government, he was careful to arrange that his *dhobi*, or washerman, occupied a washing stone above that of his immediate subordinate in rank, the commissioner of Lahore. Equally zealous in his efforts to preserve the dignity of the British crown, Wilberforce-Bell engaged in frequent arguments with his princely charges over their unauthorized usage of the adjective royal and the symbol of an arched crown. He averred that the presence of an arched crown in a princely coat of arms almost amounted to high treason since it impinged upon the prerogatives of the British crown.[6]

The Political Service was recruited from the ICS and from the Indian army, and its officers oversaw British relations with frontier tribes as well as the princely states. In the days of Elphinstone, Malcolm, and Metcalfe, the Political Service attracted able, adventurous young men who preferred to conduct negotiations with sovereign princes rather than to collect revenue and distribute justice within the territories of the Company. By the 1920s, however, the ICS had begun to experience difficulty in recruiting British graduates, and the Political Service had special problems in attracting able applicants. The opportunities for advancement were limited in the Political Service to seven first-class residencies after the reforms of 1919. Within the revenue and judicial branches of the ICS, talented officers could aim for high secretariat posts, positions on provincial and viceregal executive councils, and the governorships in all provinces except for the original three presidencies, which were party patronage appointments. There were, theoretically, possibilities to move between the two divisions of the ICS, but the last person to do so at a high level was Sir Michael O'Dwyer. Coupled with these restricted occasions for promotion and gains in prestige and monetary returns, there was the feeling that the challenges were in the British Indian districts and not in the residency at some princely court. As a consequence of these factors, the Political Service was a hybrid, frequently understaffed and usually more conservative in its political orientation than the remainder of the ICS. Largely because of opposition from the princes, the Political Service also had a much lower proportion of Indian members than did the revenue and judicial branches of the ICS. It was a service increasingly demoralized and isolated from the mainstreams of political development in the British Indian Empire. It would not provide a large number of astute political advisers for the princes.

Soothing memories of praise and offers of alliance from Indian nationalists also fortified the hopes of the princes as to their permanence and importance on the all-Indian political scene. Although nationalists had displayed a wide variety of attitudes toward them, the princes tended to remember only the favorable comments and the deferential treatment. In the late nineteenth and early twentieth centuries, many British Indian reformers had glorified the states as examples of how well Indians were able to govern themselves in order to refute arguments about the necessity for British trusteeship. Every instance of political and social reform in the Indian states was magnified, partly to inflate the image of Indian rulership and partly to obliquely criticize British policies. In the 1880s certain organizers of the Indian National Congress had appealed for personal and financial backing from a few princes and had achieved some success until the British Government intervened. Although princes never became engaged in the internal dynamics of the Congress, their support continued to be solicited by Congress leaders. Until 1930 dominant figures such as Vithalbhai Patel, Motilal Nehru, and Muhammad Ali Jinnah thought it desirable to maintain contacts and hold consultations with the princes. Once the Congress adopted its resolution at Lahore calling for total independence, the ties between the Congress and the princes were abruptly broken. The latter could not conceive of any existence without British protection and did little to prepare themselves for such an eventuality. The former became disgusted by the intransigence of the princes and consequently more vehement in their attacks upon them.

Even after Congressmen had severed contacts with the princes, moderate politicians of all-India stature like Tej Bahadur Sapru and M. R. Jayakar persisted in their efforts to draw the princes into constitutional and political alliances. Despite their persuasive talents and their willingness to make generous concessions, the princes spurned their proposals to join a federation or the Centre party. Faced with such a display of unperceptive obduracy, even these sympathetic politicians could only leave the princes to their inevitable demise.

One group of British Indian politicians who carried on active relationships with the princes beyond the 1930s were the leaders of politically oriented religious and cultural groups. There was a long heritage of princely interest and participation in the ceremonial, educational, and cultural affairs of their respective religious communities that provided a firm foundation for this coalition. Princes became patrons of the Muhammadan Anglo-Oriental College at Aligarh, the Khalsa College at Amritsar, and the Hindu University at Benares. They contributed to charitable institutions and underwrote works of scholarship glorifying the illustrious past of their communities. It was a short step further to support with funds and personal influence the ambitions and programs of assorted communal associations.

Finally the princes were unable to achieve their goals because their ideas about their distinctive status precluded the unity necessary for political strength. Much of the princely opposition to the Chamber and to federation was based on fears that such constitutional devices would reduce everyone to the same level. Able to conceive of themselves only as sovereigns, many princes, whether ruling large or small states, spurned relations with anyone, including other princes, on the basis of equality. Besides this desire to maintain their uniqueness, there were bitter rivalries among the princes based on historical feuds and personal ambitions. As a result the princely order was lacerated by internal divisions: between larger and smaller, Maratha and Rajput, northern and southern, a Patiala and a Bikaner. When the inner core of the

Chamber attempted to achieve some status within all-Indian politics by claiming to speak for one-third of the territory and one-fifth of the population of the Indian subcontinent, their right to do so was hotly contested by their brethren. Few rulers, even minor ones, were ready to delegate the authority to a brother prince to act as their representative.

The need for a united front in order to obtain bargaining power was particularly important because neither the British nor the nationalists were primarily concerned about the future of the princes. The two main protagonists in the power struggle being waged on the Indian subcontinent were willing to grant concessions to the princes only when it suited their own purposes. The British were concerned to save their stake in India, and the nationalist politicians tried to keep their list of allies as short as possible to reduce the need of awkward repayments in the future. Both sides were ready to negotiate with the princes over a federation only to find a way out of a dangerous stalemate. Even if the princes had entered a federation, they would have lacked the unity necessary to exert pressure on the majority elements.

Although partially inhibited by their lack of unity and organization and their private image of Indian politics, the effort of certain princes to act as all-Indian politicians was circumscribed by the sparse opportunities available to them. On the one hand, their patron was inclined to allow them to become involved beyond their borders only when their activities would sustain the imperial strategy. On the other hand, members of British Indian elites were not disposed to allow positions of leadership to fall to the princes once the British had been displaced. Most efforts of the princes to act as conservative spokesmen appear ineffective except for the area of politically oriented religious affairs. Here they were able to achieve some stature since neither the British nor the nationalists could question their credentials or deny them entry into this sphere.

Sheltered until too late by the British policy of isolation, placing too much reliance on constitutional guarantees, and riven by internal dissensions, the princes were woefully unprepared to accommodate themselves to the rising tides of nationalism, democracy, and socialism. The larger as well as the smaller princes refused to cooperate with the British and the moderates in forming a federation or to appease the radicals with a thoroughgoing program of internal reform. By 1939 no one of political significance on the Indian scene bothered to worry about the future of these stubborn autocrats. The last to realize that their imperial patron was capable of unilaterally abrogating their relationship, they had few options but to accept integration into India and Pakistan.

The Legacy of the Interwar Years

In 1947 the princes as all-Indian politicians carried assets as well as liabilities into the era of independence. They continued to rely upon constitutional provisions and legal maneuvers to retain whatever extraordinary status and privileges they kept after the integration of their states into India and Pakistan. When those guarantees were threatened in the late 1960s, the princes once again organized and resorted to legal counsel and remedies. In India some princes formed the Consultation of Rulers of Indian States, which was divided into the Concord, a registered, public-purpose society, and the Comity, a private lobby for princely interests. The Comity was particularly active in the unsuccessful struggle to maintain privy purses for Indian princes. Although there were several significant differences, the Consultation inherited many of the traditions, procedures, and problems of the Chamber.[7]

As the Chamber and constitutional debates were not the sole focus of princely activity during the interwar years, so after 1947 some princes remained prominent in other political spheres. The most noticeable was as governors and deputy governors of their erstwhile state territories in both India (where they were called rajpramukhs and uprajpramukhs) and Pakistan. In this capacity they once again provided a link between traditional authority and new forms of governance embodied in centralized, popularly controlled governments. In areas where regional identities were strong and vestiges of isolation persisted, the new governments hoped that the princes would function as transitional figures in helping to redirect the primary focus of political loyalty from locality and religious community to central governments that appointed these men as governors and later would abolish their positions.

Since we began with Bhupinder Singh as a typical prince in 1914, we will conclude with some references to the career of his son after 1947, supplemented with other random examples, to highlight what continuity there was in the options for the princes. Sikh proponents of an independent Sikh state and central ministers wanting to avoid balkanization considered Yadavindar Singh of Patiala an important symbolic ally. The last maharaja of Patiala was one of the first princes to accede to the Indian Union and was rewarded with the governorship of the Patiala and East Punjab States Union (PEPSU). Most other princely governors and deputy governors were the likely candidates for the position, such as the nizam of Hyderabad and the maharaja of Mysore, who became the rajpramukhs of their former states. In Pakistan the khan of Kalat was appointed governor of Baluchistan, and as late as mid-1975 the amir of Bahawalpur was named governor of Punjab. Some princes still possessed remnants of political authority that hard-pressed national politicians desired.

The princes were well-prepared for participation in another ceremony-rich and status-conscious world, that of diplomacy. The independent Indian government appointed former princes as ambassadors both to international organizations and to individual countries. In some instances these individuals were following in the footsteps of their fathers. Jam Sahib Ranjit Sinhji of Nawanagar went to the League of Nations in 1920 and 1922, and his son eventually served at the United Nations after being the rajpramukh of Saurashtra. Maharaja Bhupinder Singh of Patiala attended the League, and his son represented India both at the United Nations and as ambassador to Italy and to the Netherlands, where he died in 1974. Younger princes also have entered the Indian Foreign Service and have progressed upward through the ranks.

The princes maintained their religious affiliations after 1947 and their ties with communal organizations. They still patronized educational institutions, charitable foundations, and cultural associations that assisted their coreligionists. They retained some potential as mediators between various segments of Indian society. Yadavindar Singh occasionally acted as an intermediary between the central and state governments and the Akali Dal in the agitation for a Punjabi-speaking state, or Punjabi Suba. When he was governor and later an elected legislator, he supported the movement for an institution of higher education in which Punjabi would be the medium of instruction. Eventually Punjabi University was founded in Patiala City, and a Guru Gobind Singh Bhavan was established as a unit of it. Although princes should not be branded as communalist, it is worthy of further study why communally oriented political parties have been prominent in some of the territories of the former princely states: the Akali Dal in PEPSU, the Hindu Mahasabha in Gwalior, the Bharatiya Jana Sangh in Bhopal and Gwalior, and the Ram Rajya Parishad in Rajasthan and Madhya Pradesh.

In a democracy electoral politics hold the most potential for wielding power, and some princes have ventured into this sphere. In post-1947 India 284 princely families had received privy purses, and more than one-third of them have offered candidates for the state legislative assemblies and the central Parliament. Here the most active were from "upper-middle-level families: those from states which had 17 gun salutes, 5,000 to 10,000 square miles of territory, and population (in the 1931 census) of from half a million to a million."[8] This category is the same one that was most prominent in the Chamber and all-Indian politics prior to 1947, and there are some princely families who are active in both eras. In 1967 both Yadavindar Singh of Patiala and Rajmata Vijaya Raje of Gwalior were elected to state legislative assemblies, and could have formed ministries in Punjab and in Madhya Pradesh but declined to do so. Yadavindar was apparently put off by the squabbling among his fellow legislators, did not seek reelection in the 1969 mid-term election, and retreated to the quieter world of diplomacy. The rajmata preferred to be the power behind the throne and backed a defector from Congress for the chief ministership. There is a continuity of political style as well as of familial background. Maharaja Rajindar Narayan Singh Deo of Patna-Bolangir in Orissa, the founder of the Ganatantra Parishad, did become chief minister of Orissa in 1967, but he may be counted as the exception proving the rule that princes and their relatives were more inclined to covert political activity rather than risking public failure through overt leadership.

Not all princes who entered electoral politics had been active in the Chamber, but there is a startling similarity in patterns of political participation in the all-Indian sphere before and after 1947 among the princely families from twenty-one- and nineteen-gun salute states. In the first category the rulers of Hyderabad and Mysore continued to concentrate their attention on their own territories, and the nizam served only as the rajpramukh of Hyderabad; Chamaraja Wadiyar of Mysore served first as rajpramukh of his former state and then as governor of neighboring Madras. The princes of Baroda, Gwalior, and Jammu and Kashmir were either governors or the equivalent and prominent themselves or through close relatives in electoral politics on both the state and national levels. Princes from these three states had been active in both the Chamber and all-Indian politics, and their descendents carried on these interests. In the nineteen-gun group the post-1947 leaders of the princely families from Kalat, Travancore, and Udaipur became governors, and the scions of Bhopal, Indore, and Kolhapur were inactive. Bhopal and Kolhapur are exceptions, since the rulers from these states had been prominent in the Chamber. Bhopal's passivity might be partially attributed to the problems arising when a Muslim ruler is left in a stronghold of right-wing Hindu parties.

These similarities should not obscure the fact that some princes who were not active prior to 1947 became ambassadors and entered electoral politics after 1947 (the most notable examples are a cluster of former rulers in Orissa). Rather these parallels should be seen as indicating that princely political activity during the interwar period revealed areas of aptitude and potential success as well as failure. It also left a tradition of all-Indian political exposure in some princely families that willing heirs and relatives could exploit in changed circumstances.

Abbreviations

AGG	Agent to the Governor General
Ch	Chief
Ch Sec	Chief Secretary
CID	Criminal Investigation Department
Cmd	Command
CP-NNR	Central Provinces, Native Newspaper Reports
CR	Crown Representative Records
CS	Chamber Section
Dep Sec	Deputy Secretary
Est-A	Establishment-A; a category of government records
For Sec	Foreign Secretary
F&P	Foreign and Political Department
GOI	Government of India
Govr	Governor
Govt	Government
Home Dept	Home Department
Home Pol	Home Political
Home Pol Dep	Home Political Deposit
Home Sec	Home Secretary
I	Internal
I-A	Internal-A; a category of government records
I-B	Internal-B; a category of government records

I-D	Internal-Deposit; a category of government records
ICS	Indian Civil Service
IK	Ijlas-i-Khas at Patiala
IOR	India Office Records
Leg Dept	Legislative Department
Lt Govr	Lieutenant Governor
MAO	Muhammadan Anglo-Oriental College at Aligarh
MP	Member of Parliament in Great Britain
NAI	National Archives of India, New Delhi
Off	Officiating
Off Add Sec	Officiating Additional Secretary
Off AGG	Officiating Agent to the Governor General
Off Pol Sec	Officiating Political Secretary
Pol	Political
Pol-A	Political-A
Pol Ag	Political Agent
Pol Dep	Political Deposit
Pol Sec	Political Secretary
Pro. Nos.	Proceeding Numbers
P&S	Political and Secret
PGCS	Punjab Government Civil Secretariat
PPA	Punjab Press Abstracts
PSAP	Punjab State Archives at Patiala
PSR	Patiala State Records
Pvt Sec	Private Secretary
S of S	Secretary of State
Sec Pol Dept	Secretary of the Political Department
SGPC	Shiromani Gurdwara Parbandhak Committee
S-I	Secret-Internal
S-R	Secret-Reform
UP	United Provinces of Agra and Oudh

Glossary

AHMADIYAHS. A heterodox Muslim sect founded in the 1890s by Mirza Ghulam Ahmad, who proclaimed that he was a shadow-prophet who had come to clear away the corruption within Islam.

AHRARS. Literally, "the free." A Punjab-based Muslim political party that began in the early 1930s when a group of Muslims who had attended the 1929 Lahore Congress organized separately because of their disagreement with the Nehru Report, which advocated joint electorates.

ARYA SAMAJ. A reformist Hindu sect founded in the late nineteenth century by Dayananda Saraswati; it was particularly active in Punjab and the United Provinces.

ATTAR. Perfume; scent.

BASANT PANCHAMI. A festival considered sacred to Saraswati, the Hindu goddess of literature and the fine arts; however, the festival has few religious connections and is celebrated mainly as the harbinger of spring.

CRORE. 10,000,000.

DHOBI. Washerman.

DIWAN. The prime minister.

DIWAN-I-AM. Public audience chamber.

DURBAR. Basically, the court of a ruler. By extension it has come to be the administration of a state as well as the ceremonies held by a ruler to mark important events such as his installation, the birth of an heir, or various religious holidays.

DUSSEHRA. A Hindu festival in the autumn that celebrates Rama's defeat of Ravana, a demon king thought to be from Ceylon (now called Sri Lanka).

FIRMAN. A royal order or decree.

GADI (or GADDI). Literally, "cushion." The usual term for the throne in princely states.

GHADR. Revolt; revolutionary. The name given to conspiratorial movements against the British principally among Muslims and Sikhs in Punjab and the United States.

GHATS. Literally, "steps." It is also the name of step-like mountains on the west and east coasts of peninsula India.

GURDWARA. A Sikh temple.

GURU. A holy man; spiritual guide; religious leader.

GURMUKHI. Script of the Punjabi language evolved by Guru Nanak, first guru of the Sikhs. Used for Sikh religious writings and later among Sikhs for secular purposes.

HARTAL. A traditional form of strike usually undertaken for moral reasons.

HIDAYAT. Order or decree.

'ID. A Muslim holy day.

IZZAT. Honor; prestige; reputation.

JAGIRDAR. The individual holding a jagir, a tract of land granted by a government to an individual in return for, or in recognition of, service to the government.

JATHA. Band or group of people.

JIHAD. A war waged by Muslims for a religious cause: a holy war.

KAISER-I-HIND. Title of British sovereign meaning "Emperor of India." It was first assumed by Queen Victoria in 1877.

KAR SEWA. Ritual service. Among Sikhs it usually refers to a periodic cleaning of the sacred tank that surrounds the Golden Temple at Amritsar.

KHARITA. Document; decree.

LAKH. 100,000.

LAMBARDAR. A representative selected from a local property-holding group who is responsible for the payment of the land revenue. He also functions informally as an agent of the police and is found most frequently in the United Provinces and Punjab.

LATHI. A bamboo staff, sometimes tipped with metal, used as a weapon.

MANDIR. Market.

MANSABDAR. A noble in a structured hierarchy under the Mughal emperor.

MISL. An egalitarian confederation of Sikh military leaders and followers. Twelve *misls* became the dominant political authority in Punjab during the second half of the eighteenth century.

MULKI. Native; someone from the country or rural area.

PAN. A snack of betel nut and assorted spices wrapped in a green leaf; usually eaten to aid digestion.

PANTH. Sikh community.

PEPSU. Patiala and East Punjab States Union, which existed from 1948 to 1956 when it was integrated into Punjab State.

PURANAS. Compendia of Hindu legends and doctrines which assumed their present form from the fourth to sixth centuries A.D.

RAJ. A rule; sovereignty. When used with the definite article in the British period, British rule is implied.

RAJPRAMUKH. Governor of a former princely state or union of such states in India between 1947 and 1956.

RAM RAJ. Literally, the rule of Rama, the hero of the great Hindu epic *The Ramayana*. It signifies the rule of goodness when order prevails.

SARDAR. A landed aristocrat.

SHAMIANA. A large tent, frequently open on all sides.

TALUKDAR. A revenue-collecting intermediary in the Mughal period; generally applied to a special class of landlords in United Provinces during the British period.

TEHSIL A revenue subdivision of the British district.

ULAMA. Muslim learned men who function as religious leaders.

UPRAJPRAMUKH. A deputy governor of a former princely state or union of such states in India between 1947 and 1956.

VAKIL. An agent.

VEDAS. Ancient collections of Aryan religious hymns and ancillary literature.

VEDOKTA. A particular type of religious rites performed only for certain castes.

ZAILDAR. A local revenue official in Punjab.

ZAMINDAR. In the Mughal and Sikh periods, an individual or group with hereditary rights to collect revenue from a number of villages; in the British period a village landowner and cultivator.

List of Persons

Ali, Muhammad (1878–1931), Aligarh graduate, UP Muslim journalist and politician, brother of Shaukat Ali.

Ali, Shaukat (1873–1938), Aligarh graduate, UP Muslim journalist and politician.

Alwar, Maharaja Jey Singh of (1882–1937), succeeded 1892, ruled 1903–33.

Ansari, Mukhtar Ahmad (1880–1936), physician, Delhi Muslim politician.

Bahawalpur, Nawab Sadiq Muhammad Khan Abbasi of (1904–66), succeeded 1907, ruled 1924–55.

Baroda, Maharaja Sayaji Rao, Gaekwar of (1863–1939), succeeded 1875, ruled 1881–1939.

Benn, W. Wedgwood, first Viscount Stansgate (1877–1960), Liberal MP, 1906–27, joined Labour Party in 1927, Labour MP, 1928–31, S of S for India, 1929–31.

Bhopal, Nawab Hamidullah of (1894–1960), ruled 1926–48.

Bhopal, Nawab Sultan Jahan Begum of (1858–1930), ruled 1901–26.

Bikaner, Maharaja Ganga Singh of (1880–1943), succeeded 1887, ruled 1898–1943.

Birkenhead, first Earl of, Frederick Edwin Smith (1872–1930), Conservative MP, 1906–19, S of S for India, 1924–28.

Bundi, Maharao Raghubir Singh of (1869–1927), ruled 1889–1927.

Butler, Sir Spencer Harcourt (1869–1938), ICS, 1888–1928, For Sec, GOI, 1907–10, chaired Indian States Commission, 1928.

Chamberlain, Sir (Joseph) Austen (1863–1937), Liberal Unionist, S of S for India, 1915–17, S of S for Foreign Affairs, 1924–29.

Chelmsford, third Baron and first Viscount of, Frederick John Napier Thesiger (1868–1933), Govr of Queensland, 1905–9, Govr of New South Wales, 1909–13, Viceroy of India, 1916–21.

Chintamani, Chirravoori Yajneswara (1880–1941), born in Andhra Pradesh but political career in UP as editor, Liberal politician, and legislator.

Crump, Sir Leslie M. (1875–1929), ICS, 1897–1929, Pol Ag, Phulkian States, 1916–21, Resident at Gwalior, 1924–28, Resident at Mysore, 1928–29.

Curzon, first Marquess of, George Nathaniel (1859–1925), Conservative MP, Under S of S for India, 1891–92, Viceroy of India, 1899–1905, S of S for Foreign Affairs, 1919–24.

Cutch, Maharao Kengarji of (1866–1942), succeeded 1876, ruled 1885–1942.

Dholpur, Maharaja Udaibhan Singh of (1893–1954), succeeded 1911, ruled 1913–48.

Dutt, Romesh Chunder (1848–1909), Bengali, ICS, 1871–97, lawyer, writer, president of Indian National Congress, 1899.

Fitzpatrick, Sir James A. O. (1879–1937), ICS, 1902–35, AGG, Punjab States, 1927–35.

Gandhi, Mohandas Karamchand, Mahatma (1869–1948), Gujarati, father was diwan of Rajkot, 1875–81, creator of satyagraha, dominant figure of Indian nationalism.

Ghose, Aurobindo (1872–1950), Bengali, professor, politician, and then religious teacher in Pondicherry, 1910–50.

Gokhale, Gopal Krishna (1866–1915), Maharashtrian, Bombay moderate Congress politician, member of Imperial Legislative Council, 1905–15.

Gwalior, Maharaja Madho Rao, Scindia of (1876–1925), succeeded 1886, ruled 1894–1925.

Hailey, Malcolm, Baron (1872–1969), ICS 1894–1934, Govr of Punjab, 1924–28, Govr of UP, 1928–34.

Haksar, Sir Kailas Narain (1878–1953), Kashmiri Brahmin, Gwalior state service, 1903–38, Prime Minister of Kashmir, 1943–44.

Hardinge, Charles, Baron (1858–1944), diplomat, Viceroy of India, 1910–16.

Hoare, Sir Samuel, later Lord Templewood (1880–1959), Conservative MP, 1910–44, S of S for Air, four times, S of S for India, 1931–35.

Hydari, Sir Akbar (1869–1942), Bombay Muslim, member of Tyabji family, Hyderabad state service, chiefly in finance, 1905–42.

Hyderabad, Nizam Mir Osman Ali Khan of (1886–1967), ruled 1911–48.

Imam, Sir Ali (1869–1932), Bihari, Muslim politician, lawyer,

Prime Minister of Hyderabad, 1919–22, later advisor to Nizam of Hyderabad.

Indore, Maharaja Tukoji Rao, Holkar of (1890–?), succeeded 1903, abdicated 1926.

Irwin, later first Earl of Halifax, Edward Frederick Lindley Wood (1881–1959), Conservative, Viceroy of India, 1926–31, later Ambassador to USA during World War II.

Ismail, Sir Mirza (1883–1959), related to Tyabji family, Mysore state service, 1905–41, diwan from 1926–41, Prime Minister of Jaipur, 1942–44.

Jaipur, Maharaja Madho Singh of (1862–1922), ruled 1880–1922.

Jammu and Kashmir, Maharaja Hari Singh of (1895–1949), ruled 1925–49.

Jammu and Kashmir, Maharaja Pratap Singh of (1850–1925), ruled 1885–1925.

Keyes, Brigadier General Terence H. (1877–1939), Indian Army, 1897–1903, ICS, 1903–33, Resident at Hyderabad, 1930–33.

Jayakar, Mukund Ramrao (1873–1959), lawyer, Bombay moderate politician, member, Indian Legislative Assembly, 1926–30.

Jhalawar, Maharaja Bhawani Singh of (1874–1929), ruled 1899–1929.

Jhalawar, Maharaja Rajendra Singh of (1900–1943), ruled 1929–43.

Jinnah, Muhammad Ali (1876–1948), lawyer, Bombay Muslim politician, leader of the movement for Pakistan, Governor General of Pakistan, 1947–8.

Jodhpur, Maharaja Umaid Singh of (1903–47), succeeded 1918, ruled 1923–47.

Kolhapur, Maharaja Shahu Chhatrapati (1874–1922), succeeded 1884, ruled 1894–1922.

Liaqat Hayat Khan (1887–1952), son of Muhammad Hayat Khan of Wah, early Muslim member of Indian Police Service, Patiala state service, 1923–38, Prime Minister, 1930–38.

Linlithgow, second Marquess of, Victor Alexander John Hope (1887–1952), Conservative, Chairman, Joint Select Committee on Indian Reforms, 1933–34, Viceroy of India, 1936–43.

Lloyd, Sir George (1879–1941), Conservative MP, 1910–18, Govr of Bombay, 1918–23.

Lytton, first Earl of, Edward Robert Bulwer (1831–91), son of Bulwer Lytton, diplomat, poet, Conservative, Viceroy of India, 1876–80.

Majithia, Sir Sunder Singh (1872–1941), Aitchison graduate, moderate Sikh politician and legislator.

Malaviya, Madan Mohan (1861–1946), UP lawyer, politician, legislator, and founder of Benares Hindu University, 1916.

Mehta, Sir Manubhai (1868–1946), Gujarati, lawyer, professor, administrator, Prime Minister of Baroda, 1916–27, Prime Minister of Bikaner, 1927–37, Gwalior state service, 1937–46.

Minto, fourth Earl of, Gilbert John Murray Kynynmond Elliot (1845–1914), British Army, 1867–82, Conservative, Govr General of Canada, 1898–1904, Viceroy of India, 1905–10.

Montagu, Edwin Samuel (1879–1924), Liberal MP, 1906–22, Under S of S for India, 1910–14, S of S for India, June 1917–March 1922.

Mysore, Maharaja Chamaraja Wadiyar of (1919–75), ruled 1940–48.

Mysore, Maharaja Krishnaraja Wadiyar of (1884–1940), succeeded 1895, ruled 1902–40.

Nabha, Maharaja Ripudaman Singh of (1883–1942), ruled 1912–23.

Nawanagar, Maharaja Digvijay Sinhji, Jam Saheb of (1895–1966), ruled 1933–48.

Nawanagar, Maharaja Ranjit Sinhji, Jam Saheb of (1872–1933), ruled 1907–33.

Nehru, Jawaharlal (1889–1964), Kashmiri Brahmin, UP lawyer, president, Indian National Congress, 1929, 1936–37, 1946, 1951–54, Prime Minister of India, 1947–64.

Nehru, Motilal (1861–1931), father of Jawaharlal Nehru, UP lawyer and politician, Congress leader.

O'Dwyer, Sir Michael (1864–1940), ICS, 1882–1920, Resident of Hyderabad, 1908–10, Resident at Indore, 1910–13, Lt Govr of Punjab, 1913–19.

Pertab Singh, Maharaja of Idar (?–1922), abdicated from Idar *gadi* to serve as regent in Jodhpur, first for Sumer Singh (1911–18) and then for his younger brother, Umaid Singh (1918–22).

Palanpur, Nawab Taley Muhammad Khan of (1883–1957), ruled 1918–47.

Patel, Vallabhbhai (c.1875–1950), Gujarati, lawyer, follower of Gandhi, organizer for Indian National Congress, Deputy Prime Minister of India and Minister for States, 1947–50.

Patel, Vithalbhai (1870–1933), brother of Vallabhbhai Patel, Gujarati, lawyer, President of Indian Legislative Assembly, 1925–30.

Patiala, Maharaja Bhupinder Singh of (1891–1938), succeeded 1900, ruled 1909–38.

Patiala, Maharaja Yadavindar Singh of (1913–74), ruled 1938–48.

Peel, first Earl of, William Robert Wellesley (1867–1937), Conservative, S of S for India, 1922–24, 1928–29, member, Joint Select Committee on Indian Reforms, 1933–34.

Ramaswami Aiyer, Sir C. P. (1879–1966), Madras Liberal politician, lawyer, legislator, Diwan of Travancore, 1936–47.

Rampur, Nawab Muhammad Hamid of (1875–1930), succeeded 1889, ruled c. 1895–1930.

Reading, first Marquess of, Rufus Issacs (1860–1935), Liberal MP, 1904–13, Lord Chief Justice of England, 1913–21, Viceroy of India, 1921–26.

Rewa, Maharaja Gulab Singh of (1903–46), succeeded 1918, ruled 1922–42.

Sangli, Raja Chintamanrao Dhundriao of (1890–1965), succeeded 1903, ruled 1910–47.

Sapru, Sir Tej Bahadur (1875–1949), Kashmiri Brahmin, daughter married to son of K. N. Haksar, UP lawyer, Liberal politician, Law Member, Viceroy's Executive Council, 1920–23.

Scott, Sir Leslie (1869–1950), lawyer, Conservative MP, 1910–29, Lord Justice of Appeal, 1935–48.

Setalvad, Chimanlal (1866–1947), Bombay lawyer, Liberal politician.

Simon, Sir John (1873–1954), lawyer, Liberal politician, chaired Indian Statutory Commission, 1927–30, S of S for Foreign Affairs, 1931–35.

Tilak, Bal Gangadhar, Lokamanya (1856–1920), Maharashtrian, journalist, radical Congress leader.

Thompson, Sir John P. (1873–1935), ICS, 1896–1932, Ch Sec, Punjab Govt, 1916–21, Pol Sec, GOI, 1922–28, Chief Commissioner of Delhi, 1928–32.

Wakefield, Sir Edward B. (1903–69), married Lalage Thompson, daughter of John P. Thompson, ICS, 1927–47, Sec to Resident for Punjab States, 1937–39, President, Council of Regency, Nabha, 1939–41.

Watson, Sir Charles C. (1874–1934), ICS, 1897–1933, AGG, States of Western India, 1924–27, Pol Sec, GOI, 1927–33.

Wilberforce-Bell, Sir Harold (1885–1956), Indian Army, 1908–9, ICS, 1909–40, Resident for Punjab States, 1934–39.

Williams, Lawrence Frederic Rushbrook (1891–), professor of history, publicist, Sec to Patiala as Chancellor of Chamber of Princes, 1926–30.

Willingdon, Baron, Freeman Freeman-Thomas (1866–1941), Liberal MP, 1900–10, Govr of Bombay, 1913–18, Govr of Madras, 1919–24, Viceroy of India, 1931–36.

Wood, Sir John (1870–1933), ICS, 1893–1928, Pol Sec, GOI, 1914–22, Resident for Jammu and Kashmir, 1923–27.

Zetland, second Marquess of, formerly Lord Ronaldshay, Lawrence John Lumley Dundas (1876–1961), Conservative MP, 1907–17, author, Govr of Bengal, 1917–22, S of S for India, 1935–40.

Notes

INTRODUCTION

1. The realm of lurid polemical works ranges from Kanhayalal Gauba, *H. H.: Or, the Pathology of Princes*, which is currently available as Khalid Latif Gauba, *His Highness: Or the Pathology of Princes*, rev. 10th ed., with notes upon certain events and privy purses (Ludhiana: Kalyani Publishers, 1971) to Diwan Jarmani Dass, *Maharaja: Lives and Loves and Intrigues of Indian Princes*. Recent popular accounts are John Lord, *The Maharajahs*, and Larry Collins and Dominique Lapierre, *Freedom at Midnight*. The best of the novels are Manohar Malgonkar, *The Princes*, and Ruth Prawer Jhabvala, *Heat and Dust*.

2. The good raja cooperates with the British and is seen in such films as *Lives of a Bengal Lancer* (Paramount, 1935) and *The Rains Came* (20th Century-Fox, 1939), whereas the treacherous raja supports border tribes or foreign powers who are conspiring to overrun India as in *Charge of the Light Brigade* (Warner Brothers, 1936) and *The Bengal Brigade* (Universal-International, 1954). Dorothy B. Jones, *The Portrayal of China and India on the American Screen, 1896-1955: The Evolution of Chinese and Indian Themes, Locales, and Characters as Portrayed on the American Screen*, pp. 62-64. James Ivory has conveyed more subtle images of Indian princes and their palaces in three more recent films: *Shakespeare Wallah* (1964), *The Guru* (1968), and *Autobiography of a Princess* (1974). His evocative reminiscences of traveling and working in some erstwhile Indian states and their palaces and the script of the last film are in *Autobiography of a Princess: Also Being the Adventures of an American Film Director in the Land of the Maharajas*. This book is also noteworthy for an extensive and haunting collection of photographs of past and present princes, their palaces, and their British overlords.

3. The classics are George B. Malleson, *An Historical Sketch of the Native States of India in Subsidiary Alliance with the British Government*; William Lee-Warner, *The Native States of India*; Kadayam R. R. Sastry, *Treaties, Engagements, and Sanads of the Indian States*; and Edward J. Thompson, *The Making of the Indian Princes*.

4. The most reliable works are Vapal P. Menon, *The Story of the Integration of the Indian States*; and Wayne A. Wilcox, *Pakistan: The Consolidation of a Nation*.

5. A good sample of this work is in Robin Jeffrey (ed.), *People, Princes, and Paramount Power: Society and Politics in the Indian Princely States.* Much of the work on individual states has concentrated on those in Rajasthan and south India. On the former area key examples are Susanne Hoeber Rudolph, "The Princely States of Rajputana: Ethics, Authority and Structure"; Lloyd I. Rudolph and Susanne Hoeber Rudolph, "The Modernization of an Indian Feudal Order: An Analysis of Rajput Adaptation in Rajasthan"; Susanne Hoeber Rudolph and Lloyd I. Rudolph, with Mohan Singh, "A Bureaucratic Lineage in Princely India: Elite Formation and Conflict in a Patrimonial System"; Laxman Singh, *Political and Constitutional Development in the Princely States of Rajasthan (1920-1949)*; R. S. Darda, *From Feudalism to Democracy: A Study in the Growth of Representative Institutions in Rajasthan, 1908-1948.* On south India there is the work of James Manor on Mysore and Karen Leonard on Hyderabad cited below and Robin Jeffrey's *The Decline of Nayar Dominance: Society and Politics in Travancore, 1847-1908.*

6. The basic works here are Urmila Phadnis, *Towards the Integration of Indian States, 1919–1947*; and Robin J. Moore, *The Crisis of Indian Unity, 1917–1940.*

7. I am grateful to Michael Pearson for pointing out to me the definition of Anton Blok of patronage as "a structural principle which underlies asymmetric, personal transactions involving protection and loyalty between two persons or groups of persons. By definition, transactions refer to those sequences of interaction which are governed by reciprocity." "Variations in Patronage," *Sociologische,* GIDA, 16th year, No. 6 (November-December 1969), p. 365, quoted in M. N. Pearson, *Merchants and Rulers in Gujarat: The Response to the Portuguese in the Sixteenth Century*, p. 133, n. 1.

CHAPTER ONE

1. There is no history of Patiala State or biography of Maharaja Bhupinder Singh generally available. There is a brief sketch in Barbara N. Ramusack, "The Sikh States," *Encyclopaedia of Sikhism*, edited by Harbans Singh; and a survey of sources for such studies in Barbara N. Ramusack, "The Princely States of the Punjab: A Bibliographic Essay," pp. 374–449, in *Sources on Punjab History*, edited by W. Eric Gustafson and Kenneth W. Jones. The above description is based on data from assorted administrative reports and official publications such as the Census of India. Statistics on the territories of Patiala state and an excellent map highlighting the scattered arrangement of state territories are in *Report on the Administration of the Punjab and Its Dependencies for 1914–15*, Part 2, p. 1. Full details on the physical characteristics of the state are in Punjab State Gazetteers, *Phulkian States: Patiala, Jind & Nabha,* XVII–A, 1904.

2. There is further information on Phul and Ala Singh in Lepel H. Griffin, *The Rajas of the Punjab: Being the History of the Principal States in the Punjab and Their Political Relations with the British Government*, especially, pp. 2–30; and Kirpal Singh, *Life of Maharaja Ala Singh of Patiala and His Times.*

3. Specific figures for the major communities are 563,940 Hindus, 532,292 Sikhs, and 307,384 Muslims. *Census of India, 1911, Punjab*, Vol. 14, Part 2, Tables, compiled by Harikishan Kaul (Lahore: Punjab Government Publication, 1912), p. 129 for over-all figures of the major breakdown of those totals among the various sects within each community. It must be pointed out that the distinction between Hindu and Sikh was not as sharply defined in 1911 as it was to be by the 1920s and 1930s.

4. There is a solid general description of the rights and obligations of each side under this subsidiary alliance system in Thompson, *The Making of Indian Princes*, pp. 21–22. Specific details on events surrounding Patiala's entry into this system are in Imperial Gazetteer of India: Provincial Series, *Punjab*, Vol. 2 (Calcutta: Superin-

tendent of Government Printing, 1908), pp. 282–83; Khushwant Singh, *A History of the Sikhs*, Vol. I, *1469–1839*, pp. 219–31; and K. N. Panikkar, *British Diplomacy in North India: A Study of the Delhi Residency, 1803–1857*, pp. 99–109.

5. Bhupinder Singh of Patiala to A. C. Elliott, Pol Ag for the Phulkian States and Bahawalpur, 4 July 1913, NAI, GOI, F&P, S-I, Aug. 1913, Pro. Nos. 18–19.

6. C. A. Barron, Ch Sec, Govt of Punjab, to A. C. Elliott, 26 July 1913, and H. Wilkinson, Dep Sec, F&P, GOI, to C. A. Barron, 12 Aug. 1913, ibid.

7. J. B. Wood, Offg Sec, F&P, GOI, to C. A. Barron, 25 Nov. 1913, IOR, CR, R/1/3/12. The Crown Representative Records are files of the Foreign and Political Department of the Government of India that were transported from India to London in 1947 and, therefore, are the original files and not printed copies sent home in the normal procedure. Although they also carry a designation according to their place in the F&P sequence, they will be cited by the CR designation, since that one is required to requisition them at the India Office Records.

8. Annual Report on Native States in Punjab for the year 1913–14, NAI, PGCS, B-P, July 1914, No. 163.

9. A general survey of the evolution of the Patiala state government is in PSAP, PSR, IK, Basta No. 173, File No. 2075. Specific comments on the judiciary in the early 1910s are in the Annual Reports on the Native States in Punjab, 1910–11, 1911–12, and 1913–14, NAI, PGCS, B-P, July 1911, No. 142, July 1912, No. 162, and July 1914, No. 163 respectively.

10. Each political officer annually had to submit a report on the number of serviceable and unserviceable guns within every state under his jurisdiction. *Manual of Instruction to Officers of Political Department*, pp. 87, 130–31. Any unexplained or unauthorized change in the number of either type of gun was questioned punctiliously by the political secretary in Delhi. Such reports and questions for 1915 are in NAI, GOI, F&P, S-I, Jan. 1917, Pro. Nos. 4–13.

11. Armament Return for Patiala State for 1915, ibid.

12. Ibid.

13. The origins and uses of the Imperial Service Troops are outlined in George F. MacMunn, *The Indian States and Princes*, pp. 182–84. There are specific comments on the efficiency of the Imperial Service Troop contingents maintained by Patiala in the Annual Reports on the Native States in the Punjab, 1912–13 and 1913–14, NAI, PGCS, B-P, July 1913, No. 105, 112, and July 1914, No. 163 respectively.

14. A lakh equals 100,000, and a crore is 10,000,000. Receipts were estimated at 89,97,506 rupees against an estimated expenditure of 94,90,800. Annual Report on the Native States in the Punjab, 1913–14, NAI, PGCS, B-P, July 1914, No. 163.

15. A partial listing of expenditures is given in ibid.

16. Based on an average of the years 1926–30; see John Hurd II, "Some Economic Characteristics of the Princely States of India, 1901–1931," pp. 123–25, 248. These later figures give some approximation of the situation in 1914 since there was little subsequent increase in the cultivated area, irrigation facilities or revenue rate.

17. For irrigation figures, see Annual Report on the Native States in the Punjab, 1913–14, NAI, PGCS, B-P, July 1914, No. 163.

18. Ibid.

19. Ibid.

20. Census of India, 1911, *Punjab*, Vol. 14, Part 2, Tables, p. 129.

21. The proposal to construct additional feeder lines was raised as early as 1910, see *Report on the . . . Punjab . . . 1910–11*, Part 2, p. 2. These feeder schemes raised numerous objections from existing railway lines: see R. E. Holland, Dep Pol Sec, GOI, to J. P. Thompson, Ch Sec, Punjab Govt., 22 June 1916, and Thompson to J. B. Wood, Pol Sec, GOI, 11 June 1917, NAI, GOI, F&P, I-A, Oct. 1917, Pro. Nos. 49–57.

22. For a penetrating discussion of the need of a colonizer to justify his rule and some methods employed in an African setting, see Albert Memmi, *The Colonizer and the Colonized*, pp. 51–73.

23. The best general description of this process in the Indian setting is in Thompson, *The Making of the Indian Princes.*

24. The number of 113 princes with salutes excludes eight Burmese princes with 9-gun salutes. *India Office List*, 1920, pp. 202–3.

25. Minutes of 30 Aug. 1848, Great Britain, Parliamentary Papers, 1849, Vol. 39, 227.

26. Muhammad Abdur Rahim, *Lord Dalhousie's Administration of the Conquered and Annexed States.*

27. Philip Woodruff, *The Men Who Ruled India*, Vol. 1: *The Founders*, pp. 349–50.

28. Bhupen Qanungo, "A Study of British Relations with the Native States of India, 1858–62," and Thomas P. Metcalf, *The Aftermath of Revolt: India, 1857–1870*, pp. 219–27.

29. *Manual of Instructions to Officers of Political Department*, p. ix.

30. *Memoranda on the Indian States, 1939*, pp. 64–65 and pp. 153–60, for data on Banka Pahari and Hyderabad respectively.

31. There is a description of the Maratha-Rajput conflicts from their origins up to World War I in Michael F. O'Dwyer, *India As I Knew It, 1855–1925*, pp. 150–57.

32. A most succinct statement on the incongruities of the salute table, the rivalries among princes it engendered, and the need for rationalization is in E. S. Montagu, Secretary of State for India, to Lord Reading, Viceroy, 17 Nov. 1921, IOR, MSS Eur D 523/13.

33. E. D. Maclagan, Ch Sec, Punjab Govt, to Wood, 5 Oct. 1915, NAI, GOI, F&P, S-I, Nov. 1918, Pro. Nos. 1–39.

34. Karen Leonard, "The Hyderabad Political System and its Participants." This system was subject to serious strain in the late nineteenth century as Western-educated Indians from outside the state were recruited to fill high-level administrative positions. The controversy between the local subjects, or *mulki*, and the outsiders, or non-*mulki*, is the most pronounced example of a situation that arose in many states and persists to the last quarter of the twentieth century in the old Hyderabad territory. Karen Leonard, "The Mulki/Non-Mulki Conflict in Hyderabad State," in *People, Princes, and Paramount Power*, and "Cultural Change and Bureaucratic Modernization in 19th Century Hyderabad: Mulkis, non-Mulkis and the English," in *Studies in the Foreign Relations of India: Prof. H. K. Sherwani Felicitation Volume*, ed. by P. M. Joshi, pp. 443–54.

There is an evocative account of Hyderabad and in particular it is ruler, Nizam Mahbub Ali Khan, on the eve of the twentieth century in Harriet Ronken Lynton and Mohini Rajan, *The Days of the Beloved.*

35. A balanaced analysis of this controversial figure and his career is in Bawa Satinder Singh, *The Jammu Fox: A Biography of Maharaja Gulab Singh of Kashmir, 1792–1857.*

36. According to the 1911 census, Jammu province had a total population of 1,597,865 of whom 626,439 were Hindu and 953,293 were Muslim, or 59% and Kashmir province had a total population of 1,295,211 of whom 62,414 were Hindu and 1,217,786 were Muslim, or 94%: Census of India, 1911, *Kashmir*, Vol. 20, Part 2, Tables, compiled by Matin-uz-zaman Khan (Lucknow: Newul Kishore Press, 1912), pp. 18–19.

37. For a detailed account of the numerous reorganizations of the Foreign Department, see D. Anthony Low, J. C. Iltis, and M. D. Wainwright (eds.), *Govern-*

ment Archives in South Asia: A Guide to National and State Archives in Ceylon, India and Pakistan, pp. 39–46, 131–36.

38. *Manual of Instructions to Officers of Political Department*, p. xii.

39. The most comprehensive study of the Political Department by a former member is Terence Creagh Coen, *The Indian Political Service.* More limited in scope is a more insightful analysis of the Political Service and its deficiencies by I. F. S. Copland, "The Other Guardians: Ideology and Performance in the Indian Political Service," in *People, Princes and Paramount Power.* Memoirs of political officers convey a strong sense of their personal commitment, attitudes, and goals. Some notable examples of this genre by men active in the twentieth century are Walter R. Lawrence, *The India We Served*; Arthur C. Lothian, *Kingdoms of Yesterday*; Kenneth Fitze, *Twilight of the Maharajas*; and Conrad Corfield, *The Princely India I Knew: From Reading to Mountbatten.*

40. There is a helpful discussion of the role and functions of *jagirdars* within the states in Hurd, "Some Economic Characteristics of the Princely States of India, 1901–1931," pp. 103–9. A careful analysis of how *jagirdars* lose their rights to political participation in Alwar with the introduction of a Westernized bureaucracy is in Edward S. Haynes, "Jagirdars and Government: The Political Role of the Kinship Elite in Alwar (Rajputana, India), 1858–1910."

41. Based on replies received by the political secretary from March to November 1901 to a circular letter issued by Lord Curzon on 14 Feb. 1901 requesting information on how many princes had set limits on their personal expenditures. On 20 Sept. 1902 the viceroy then sent a second circular letter to all provincial governments and political officers advising them that they should lose no opportunity to encourage the introduction of a budget and of a privy purse system. As will be seen later, his directive had little positive effect. IOR, CR, R/1/19/282.

42. John Hurd has made a pioneering effort to determine the degree of progressiveness of a state and its ruler in terms of the percentage of revenue spent on social overhead capital between 1901-31. There is a lack of data on many states included in the sample, so it is still difficult to make broad generalizations. Those states for whom statistics were available who spent more than 35% of their revenue on social overhead capital were Mysore 37%, Travancore 38%, Sikkim 39%, Bikaner 44%, and Cochin 47% (Hurd, "Some Economic Characteristics of the Princely States of India, 1901–1931," pp. 117–20, pp. 203–5 for categories included in social overhead capital, and pp. 239–42).

43. This concept is developed in Francis G. Hutchins, *The Illusion of Permanence: British Imperialism in India.*

44. The key sources on the princes are in footnote 28 above and on the *talukdars* are Metcalf, *Aftermath of Revolt*, pp. 134–62, and the work of the Cambridge school of South Asian historians.

45. Edward Maclagan, '*Clemency*' *Canning*, pp. 271–72.

46. Briton Martin, Jr., *New India, 1885: British Official Policy and the Emergence of the Indian National Congress*, pp. 8–10.

47. Elizabeth E. Balfour, *The History of Lord Lytton's Indian Administration, 1876 to 1880*, pp. 110–11.

48. Ibid. and notes by Lytton dated 18 May 1876 and 27 May 1876, IOR, CR, R/1/19/81.

49. Balfour, *The History of Lord Lytton's Indian Administration*, p. 111.

50. Romesh Dutt, *The Economic History of India in the Victorian Age: From the Accession of Queen Victoria in 1837 to the Commencement of the Twentieth Century*, p. 32.

51. Leonard A. Gordon, *Bengal: The Nationalist Movement, 1876–1940*, pp. 43–59, has an excellent analysis of Dutt's written work, which ranged from novels to

histories to polemical political tracts, and was produced in either English or Bengali. Dutt was a member of the ICS from 1871 to 1897 and served in the Baroda administration as revenue minister from 1904 to 1908.

52. In ibid. there is a full description of Ghose's years in Baroda from 1892 to 1906 on pp. 107–15.

53. The Patiala administrators came largely from Government College, Forman Christian College, and Aitchison College. Punjab States Agency, *List of Ruling Princes, Notables and Principal Officials*, available at IOR, L/P&S/20, F. 157.

54. Richard I. Cashman, *The Myth of the Lokamanya: Tilak and Mass Politics in Maharashtra*, pp. 27–28 on the Sabha, and p. 62 for the role of the princes.

55. A. O. Hume to Nawab Sidi Ahmad Khan of Janjira, 1 Oct. 1888, and Hume to Pandit Hetram, Diwan of Rewa, inviting the maharaja to attend the 1888 Congress, 16 Dec. 1888, IOR, CR, R/1/19/89. Open Letter from Sayyid Ahmad Khan, dated 25 Aug. 1888, published in the *Indian Mirror* of 20 Sept. 1888, ibid.

56. Martin, *New India, 1885*, pp. 324–26.

57. D. Mackenzie Wallace, Pvt Sec to Viceroy Dufferin, to W. J. Cunningham, Undersec, Foreign Dept, GOI, 26 Jan. 1888, IOR, CR, R/1/19/69; and G. S. Forbes, Acting First Asst to Resident, Hyderabad, to Nawab Asman Jah, Minister of Hyderabad, 28 Nov. 1888, IOR, CR, R/1/19/89.

58. Earl of Ronaldshay, *The Life of Lord Curzon*, Vol. 2, *Viceroy of India*, p. 89.

59. Mary Minto, *India, Minto, and Morley, 1905–1910*, p. 344. For the rationale behind this speech, see Martin Gilbert, *Servant of India: A Study of Imperial Rule from 1905 to 1910 as Told through the Correspondence and Diaries of Sir James Dunlop Smith*, pp. 196–200.

60. Even more immediately Edwin Montagu, while touring India as undersecretary of state for India, claimed that Minto had gone too far in the direction of noninterference; see Montagu Diary, 11 Jan. 1913, IOR, MSS Eur D 523/39.

61. Minto, *India, Minto, and Morley*, p. 29, and Urmila Phadnis, *Towards the Integration of Indian States, 1919–1947*, p. 19.

62. Ibid., and B. L. Grover, *A Documentary Study of British Policy towards Indian Nationalism, 1885–1909*, pp. 239, 278–80.

CHAPTER TWO

1. Patiala to Lord Chelmsford, Viceroy of India, 31 Dec. 1916, IOR, Chelmsford Papers, MSS Eur E 264/16. Patiala quoted a report published by the *Pioneer* of Allahabad that two Indian representatives would be appointed to the 1917 Imperial War Conference.

2. J. Maffey, Pvt Sec to the Viceroy, to J. B. Wood, Pol Sec, GOI, 31 Dec. 1916, ibid.

3. Nawanagar to Chelmsford, 30 Dec. 1916, ibid.

4. Patiala to Chelmsford, 31 Dec. 1916, ibid.

5. L. M. Crump, Pol Ag for Phulkian states, to Maffey, 19 Jan. 1917, IOR, MSS Eur E 264/18. Some indication of the extent of the aid rendered by this state is in *Patiala and the Great War*.

6. Maffey to Crump, 22 Jan. 1917, ibid.

7. *Tribune*, 23 Jan. 1917, p. 1. Founded by a Sikh landlord, Sardar Dyal Singh of Majithia, in 1889, the *Tribune* was known for its pro-Congress and anti-Government tone. For further information on the *Tribune*, see N. Gerald Barrier and Paul Wallace, *The Punjab Press, 1880–1905*, p. 149.

8. *Khalsa Advocate*, 3 Feb. 1917, p. 3. The *Tribune* had a series of Bengali editors who were frequently the focus for attacks by educated Punjabis.

9. Wood to Maffey, 31 Dec. 1916, IOR, MSS Eur E 264/16.

10. H. M. Bull and K. N. Haksar, *Madhav Rao Scindia of Gwalior, 1876–1925*, pp. 109–11, 142.

11. Ibid., pp. 66–68, 100–101, 245–70.

12. Reading to Lord Birkenhead, 19 Feb. 1925, Reading Papers, MSS Eur E 238/8. Reading expressed similar sentiments to Birkenhead's predecessor Lord Peel on 9 Nov. 1922, IOR, MSS Eur E 238/5.

13. Bikaner to Chelmsford, 17 Feb. 1918 and 15 Apr. 1918; Resident at Gwalior to Maffey, 18 Apr. 1918; Chelmsford to Patiala, 22 Apr. 1918; IOR, MSS Eur E 264/20.

14. Here both the *Tribune*, 26 Apr. 1918, p. 1, and the *Khalsa Advocate*, 4 May 1918, p. 1, agreed.

15. Edwin S. Montagu, *An Indian Diary*, p. 375.

16. Extract from Diary of Crump, Pol Ag for Phulkian States, 20–31 May 1918, NAI, GOI, F&P, I-B, June 1918, Pro. Nos. 38–43.

17. Montagu to Chelmsford, 26 July 1918, IOR, MSS Eur D 523/7.

18. Chelmsford to Montagu, 28 Oct. 1919, IOR, MSS Eur D 523/9.

19. *Tribune*, 24 Oct. 1918, p. 1.

20. A succinct survey of the 1907 disturbances is in Norman G. Barrier, *The Punjab Alienation of Land Bill of 1900*, pp. 90–92. The viewpoint of a principal participant is in V. C. Joshi (ed.), *Lajpat Rai Autobiographical Writings*, 1:115–94.

21. F. Younghusband to L. Dane, For Sec, GOI, 13 May 1907, Pro. No. 18, IOR, CR, R/1/19/352.

22. Telegram from Younghusband to Home Dept, GOI, 12 May 1907, NAI, GOI, Home-Public-A, June 1907, Pro. Nos. 114–16.

23. Note by L. Dane dated 11 May 1907, IOR, CR, R/1/19/352.

24. J. Thompson, Ch Sec to Punjab Govt, to Members of the Council of Regency of Patiala, 21 Aug. 1909, PSAP, PSR, IK, Basta No. 155, File No. 256.

25. *Tribune*, 22 Dec. 1909, p. 5.

26. Petition dated 17 Jan. 1910, PSAP, PSR, IK, Basta No. 155, File No. 256.

27. Maclagan, Ch Sec, Punjab Govt, to S. H. Butler, For Sec, GOI, 11 May 1910, NAI, GOI, Home Pol-Part B, Sept. 1910, Pro. No. 6.

28. See above letter and its reply from Butler to Maclagan, 13 June 1910, ibid.

29. Minto to Residents, AGGs, and Local Govts, 6 Aug. 1909, IOR, CR, R/1/19/400.

30. See princely replies in both IOR, CR, R/1/19/400 and R/1/19/415.

31. Sant Nihal Singh, *The King's Indian Allies: The Rajas and Their India*, p. 16.

32. Ibid., p. 18.

33. B. C. Allen, Ch Sec to Ch Commissioner of Assam, to Wood, 5 Aug. 1916, NAI, GOI, F&P, I-B, Apr. 1917, Pro. No. 180.

34. *Memoranda on the Indian States, 1939*, p. 159.

35. List of princely subscribers dated 18 Sept. 1916, NAI, GOI, F&P, I-B, Feb. 1917, Pro. Nos. 32–42.

36. Note by Wood dated 28 Jan. 1916, ibid. Jaipur was a Kachhwaha Rajput, Kishangarh a Rathor Rajput, and Kotah a Chauhan Hara Rajput.

37. The usual plea followed this example: "At this critical time it is the bounden duty of British India, the Native States, especially my State (which had special and

old relations with the British Government) to render complete assistance to the British forces and to enlist as many recruits for the army so that the number of our forces may increase enormously and the enemy may be forced to surrender in spite of his desperate efforts." Speech by Patiala on 15 Feb. 1918, NAI, PGCS, Mar. 1918, Part B, Political-Native States, No. 37.

38. *Khalsa Advocate*, 28 Oct. 1916, p. 4.

39. Minute by William Meyer, President, Central Recruiting Board of India, dated 5 June 1917, NAI, GOI, F&P, I-B, Oct. 1918, Pro. Nos. 285–307.

40. Wood to Major General A. H. Bingley, Army Sec, GOI, 8 June 1917, ibid.

41. G. Lowndes, President of the Indian Soldiers Board, to O'Dwyer, 28 Mar. 1919; O'Dwyer to Lowndes, 31 Mar. 1919; Holland to Patiala, 21 Apr. 1919; Patiala to Holland, 2 May 1919; NAI, GOI, F&P, I-B, June 1919, Pro. No. 260.

42. Circular letter from Chelmsford, 18 Apr. 1918, IOR, MSS Eur E 264/20.

43. Those invited to attend were the rulers of Hyderabad, Baroda, Mysore, Gwalior, Kolhapur, Kashmir, Bhopal, Jaipur, Patiala, Nawanagar, Travancore, Alwar, Udaipur, Cooch Behar, and Cutch. Ibid.

44. Judith M. Brown, *Gandhi's Rise to Power: Indian Politics 1915–1922*, p. 146.

45. O'Dwyer to Chelmsford, 14 May 1918, IOR, MSS Eur E 264/20.

46. For a perceptive analysis of how these characteristics handicapped the *talukdars*, see P. D. Reeves, "Landlords and Party Politics in the United Provinces, 1934–7," in *Soundings in Modern South Asian History*, ed. D. A. Low, pp. 268–79.

47. For a survey of the earlier years of the Ghadr movement, see Khushwant Singh and Satindra Singh, *Ghadar 1915: India's First Armed Revolution.*

48. Annual Report on Patiala, 1915–16, NAI, PGCS, B-Pro, Dec. 1916, File No. 262, No. 215.

49. O'Dwyer, *India As I Knew It*, p. 295. Also see Thompson to Wood, 21 Sept. 1918, NAI, GOI, F&P, S-I, Aug. 1921, Pro. No. 3.

50. Draft telegram prepared by the India Office for transmission to the Governor-General of Canada, 9 Jan. 1917, NAI, GOI, Home Pol-A, May 1917, Pro. Nos. 124–28.

51. Austen Chamberlain, Sec of State for India, to Colonial Office, 9 Jan. 1917, ibid.

52. Speech by the maharaja of Bikaner on 7 Feb. 1917, in Panikkar, *His Highness the Maharaja of Bikaner,* p. 174.

53. Chelmsford to Chamberlain, 15 Feb. 1917, IOR, MSS Eur E 264/18.

54. Speech by the maharaja of Bikaner on 4 Nov. 1917, PSAP, CS, Case No. II (b) 1 of 1917.

55. Memorandum by the maharaja of Bikaner dated 17 Apr. 1917, IOR, MSS Eur E 264/13.

56. Chamberlain to Chelmsford, 8 May 1917, IOR, MSS Eur E 264/3.

57. Gwalior to Chelmsford, 14 Mar. 1918, IOR, MSS Eur E 264/20, and Bull and Haksar, *Madhav Rao Scindia of Gwalior*, p. 264.

58. This agitation was a reflection of orthodox Hindu resentment against the passage of the United Provinces Municipalities Bill in 1916. This act introduced separate representation for Muslims on local bodies, and orthodox Hindu leaders saw this provision as a reduction in the opportunities for their support groups. C. A. Bayly, *The Local Roots of Indian Politics: Allahabad, 1880–1920*, pp. 205–6.

59. J. Meston, Lt Govr of the United Provinces, to Chelmsford, 10 Jan. 1917, IOR, MSS Eur E 264/3.

60. Bayly has pointed out that "independent political leaderships could be held in check within formal institutions whether by direct or indirect official influence. But religious and communal organizations were always more volatile." *The Local*

Roots of Indian Politics, p. 169. Thus the British were more likely to experiment with diverse agents of control such as the princes which were not necessary in other situations.

61. *Khalsa Advocate*, 25 Jan. 1913, p. 2, has high praise for princes such as Rampur, Kashmir, Dewas, who are active in helping communal causes. It then proceeds to upbraid the Sikh princes for not taking greater initiative in Sikh affairs.

62. *Khalsa Advocate*, 12 Feb. 1913, p. 4, 1 Mar. 1913, p. 4, 27 Mar. 1915, p. 5. Speech delivered by Maharaja Scindia Madho Rao of Gwalior at Benares Hindu University in April 1918, cited in *Speeches of Indian Princes on Politics*, p. 116.

63. These princes contributed 203,140 rupees out of a total of 356,236. The most generous were the Brahmin chiefs of Jamkhandi, Inchalkaranji, and Maraj Senior; the Maratha rulers of Baroda, Kolhapur, and Mudhol; and the Rajput prince of Gondal. Cashman, *Myth of the Lokamanya*, pp. 100–102.

64. Note by D. Petrie, Assistant Director of the CID, GOI, dated 11 Aug. 1911, reprinted in *Gurdwara Gazette*, Apr. 1969, and [Ganda Singh,] *A History of the Khalsa College Amritsar*, pp. 29, 57, 66, 85.

65. [Singh,] *A History of the Khalsa College Amritsar*.

66. Gerald Rufus Isaacs Reading, *Rufus Isaacs: First Marquess of Reading*, Vol. 2, *1914–1935*, pp. 179–80.

67. For samples of Alwar's rhetoric see the *Proceedings of the Chamber of Princes*. The *Vedas* are ancient collections of religious hymns and ancillary literature; the *Puranas* are compendia of Hindu legend and doctrine.

68. Cashman, *Myth of the Lokamanya*, pp. 76, 98–120, and Gordon Johnson, "Chitpavan Brahmins and Politics in Western India in the Late Nineteenth and Early Twentieth Centuries," in *Elites in South Asia*, ed. Edmund Leach and S. N. Mukherjee, pp. 113–14.

A general history of the Kolhapur ruling family is in Manohar Malgonkar, *Chhatrapatis of Kolhapur*, which has only short sketches of Shahu and his successors. The basic work on Shahu is still A. B. Latthe, *Memoirs of His Highness Shri Shahu Chhatrapati, Maharaja of Kolhapur*.

69. One issue was the refusal of Brahmin priests to perform certain religious rites known as the *vedokta* ceremony unless the maharaja did penance for a lapse of Vedic ritual in his family. Kolhapur resisted this demand since it called into question the Kshatriya and twice-born status of his family and other Marathas. Cashman, *Myth of the Lokamanya*, pp. 116–19, and Ian Copland, "The Maharaja of Kolhapur and the Non-Brahmin Movement 1902–1910."

70. In his essay "The Temple-Entry Movement in Travancore, 1860–1940: Radicalizing the Politics of a Princely State," in *People, Princes and Paramount Power*, Robin Jeffrey emphasizes how the maharaja and his mother (she is important since inheritance passed through the female line in Travancore) could open the government-run temples in what was essentially a theocratic state in a direct way which was denied to the British.

71. Memorandum by the Nizam of Hyderabad dated 20 July 1918, IOR, MSS Eur E 264/21.

72. Ibid.

73. Chelmsford to Hyderabad, 26 July 1918, ibid.

74. *Memoranda on the Indian States, 1939*, pp. 49–52.

75. *Speeches of Indian Princes on Politics*, pp. 41–49.

76. O. V. Bosanquet, AGG, Central India, to J. B. Wood, 9 Dec. 1914, IOR, CR, R/1/22/97.

77. R. Burn, Sec, Govt of the United Provinces, to H. Wheeler, Sec, GOI, Home Dept, 14 Nov. 1914, ibid.

78. O. V. Bosanquet to Wood, 9 Dec. 1914, ibid.

79. Extract from Diary of AGG, Central India, for first half of May 1919, IOR, CR, R/1/19/667.

80. Rampur had an area of 892.54 square miles and a population of 539,212 with 291,133 Hindus; 241,163 Muslims; and 916 others according to the 1901 census. United Provinces of Agra and Oudh, *Gazetteer of the Rampur State*, pp. 41–43.

81. There were only 683 Shias in Rampur; ibid., pp. 47–49.

82. *Khalsa Advocate*, 25 Jan. 1913, p. 2, and 11 Oct. 1913, p. 4.

83. Reading to Montagu, 8 Nov. 1921, IOR, MSS Eur E 238/10, and Barbara N. Ramusack, "Incident at Nabha: Interaction between Indian State and British Indian Politics." This particular relationship between Bhupinder Singh and Yadavindar Singh, his son, and the Sikh community is explored in greater depth in Barbara N. Ramusack, "Maharajas and Gurdwaras: Patiala and the Sikh Community," in *People, Princes, and Paramount Power.*

84. Revised Rules of Khalsa College dated 22 June 1908, private library of Dr. Ganda Singh, Patiala, Punjab, India.

85. C. R. Cleveland, Director, CID, GOI, to A. Henry McMahon, Sec, For Dept, GOI, 18 Mar. 1912, IOR, CR, R/1/22/78, that Patiala should be discouraged. On 25 January 1913, the *Khalsa Advocate* expressed regret that Patiala had been forced by indisposition to decline that invitation. It was also rumored that Patiala had been asked to preside over the fourth session at Rawalpindi but declined on the advice of his nobles. See Petrie note, *Gurwara Gazette*, April 1969.

86. The full text of this address is in the *Tribune*, 3 Jan. 1911, p. 5. Also see comments in *Khalsa Advocate*, 6 Jan. 1911, pp. 3 and 5.

87. *Tribune*, 5 Aug. 1916, p. 4.

88. Ibid., 17 Aug. 1916, p. 2.

89. Ibid.

90. A full list of the prominent Sikhs present is in ibid.

91. Ibid., 8 Aug. 1916, p. 4.

92. Ibid., 17 Oct. 1916, p. 5. Although the *Khalsa Advocate* applauded this venture, it called for revision of Gyani Gyan Singh's work before republication in order to eliminate the myths and superstitions included in the original edition. 8 July 1916, p. 3.

CHAPTER THREE

1. Chelmsford to Chamberlain, 1 Mar. 1917, IOR, MSS Eur E 264/3.

2. Coen, *The Indian Political Service*, pp. 49–53.

3. Copland, "The Other Guardians," argues that technology and the policy of noninterference initiated by Lord Minto but implemented by Sir Harcourt Butler as foreign secretary reduced drastically the initiative of political officers after 1909.

4. Both of these men ignored the implications for democratic government which resulted from their paternalistically motivated administrations. James Manor, "Princely Mysore before the Storm: The State-level Political System of India's Model State, 1920–1936," and Cashman, *The Myth of the Lokamanya*, pp. 110–11.

5. The minuteness of the majority of administrative units termed princely states is reflected in the following data from evidence presented to the Indian States Committee of 1928. The population figures cited represent some increase over comparable figures of 1916, but the area figures would be the same for both periods.

Classification	No.	Total area in square miles	Population	Revenue in crores of rupees
Princes in Chamber in own right	108	514,886	59,847,186	42.16
Princes represented in Chamber by 12 elected members	127	76,846	8,004,114	2.89
All other princes	327	6,406	801,674	.74

SOURCE: Indian States Committee, 1928, *Oral Evidence Recorded Before the Committee* (n.n., n.p., 1929), p. 6.

6. Speech of Shaukat Ali at Rajputana Political Conference at Ajmer on 15 Mar. 1921, IOR, CR, R/1/19/676.

7. A good discussion of the foundation of Rajkumar College in Rajkot and the arguments presented for and against attendance at it is in Sant Nihal Singh, *Shree Bhagvat Sinhjee: The Maker of Modern Gondal*, pp. 22–31. Proposals for combining the best of both traditions were later made by Khasherao Jadhava in *Wake Up Princes*, pp. 105–14.

8. The Higher Chiefs' College would roughly correspond to the educational level of an American college. The Chiefs' Colleges were the equivalent of American preparatory schools or English public schools.

9. Charles Hardinge, *My Indian Years, 1910–1916*, p. 84.

10. Note by R. E. Holland, Dep Sec, F&P, GOI, dated 23 May 1916, and note by Wood dated 24 May 1916, NAI, GOI, F&P, I-D, Aug. 1917, Pro. No. 8.

11. Kavalam M. Panikkar, *His Highness the Maharaja of Bikaner: A Biography*, p. 143.

12. Note by J. Wood, dated 27 May 1916, IOR, CR, R/1/19/560.

13. Chelmsford to Chamberlain, 30 June 1916, IOR, MSS Eur E 264/2.

14. Chamberlain to Chelmsford, 25 July 1916, 8 Aug. 1916, and 29 Aug. 1916, ibid.

15. Chelmsford to Chamberlain, 8 Sept. 1916, ibid.

16. Circular Letter from Bikaner, 25 Sept. 1916, PSAP, CS, Case No. II (a) 1 of 1916.

17. I was unable to locate a copy of the proceedings of the 1916 informal meetings of the princes, but a complete copy of the agenda and proceedings of the November 1917 informal meetings and of subsequent meetings give an adequate outline of the general pattern which prevailed. See PSAP, CS, Case No. II (b) 1 of 1917.

18. *Proceedings of the Conference of Ruling Princes and Chiefs: Held at Delhi on the 30th October 1916 and Following Days* (Delhi: Superintendent of Government Printing, 1916), pp. 15–18.

19. Ibid., p. 16.

20. Ibid., pp. 18–19.

21. Ibid., pp. 22–36 and 80–86.

22. Ibid., p. 84.

23. Ibid., p. 7.

24. The princes eventually passed a resolution that excluded any mention of whether approval by the government was or was not necessary for a valid succession. Ibid., pp. 62–80 and pp. 97–98.

25. Hardinge, *My Indian Years*, pp. 51–52.

26. E. M. Forster, *The Hill of Devi: Letters and Journals While Secretary to the Maharaja of Devi*, pp. 94–95.

27. Chelmsford to Chamberlain, 2 Nov. 1916, IOR, MSS Eur E 264/2.

28. Chelmsford to Chamberlain, 10 Nov. 1916, ibid.

29. Report on the 1916 Conference of Ruling Princes and Chiefs, signed J. B. Wood, 7 Nov. 1916, ibid.

30. Chamberlain to Chelmsford, 3 Jan. 1917 and 7 Feb. 1917, IOR, MSS Eur E 264/3.

31. In his note dated 27 May 1916 Wood stated that Morley "was impressed by the practical difficulties, such as expense, precedence, housing. . . . He thought moreover that, unless the Council were definitely constituted with a view to assemble, it would possess little or no reality and doubted whether the project commanded the approval of those Chiefs whose presence in the Council would be essential to its success." Wood countered that Morley's criticism on the basis of princely attitudes might be disregarded since absence of old-fashioned princes like Udaipur and Hyderabad would not seriously affect the value of deliberations and their successors might realize disadvantages of isolation. The practical difficulties should also disappear in time with the move to Delhi and the fact that rarely more than half of eleven guns princes would attend. IOR, CR, R/1/19/560.

32. Chelmsford to Chamberlain, 25 Mar. 1917, IOR, MSS Eur E 264/3.

33. Chamberlain to Chelmsford, 8 May 1917, ibid.

34. *Conference Proceedings*, 1917, p. 5.

35. Montagu, *An Indian Diary*, p. 20.

36. Chelmsford to Patiala, 18 Oct. 1917, PSAP, CS, Case No. II (a) 4 of 1917.

37. Bikaner to Patiala, 26 Sept. 1917, PSAP, CS, Case No. II (a) 3 of 1917.

38. Bikaner to Patiala, 5 Oct. 1917, ibid.

39. Patiala to Bikaner, 10 Oct. 1917, ibid.

40. Patiala to Bikaner, 21 Oct. 1917, ibid.

41. Digest of Proceedings of Informal Meetings of Princes held in Delhi in November 1917, PSAP, CS, Case No. II (b) 1 of 1917.

42. Reading to Peel, Secretary of State for India, 23 Nov. 1922, IOR, Reading Papers, MSS Eur E 238/5.

43. *Conference Proceedings*, 1917, pp. 33–36.

44. Minutes of 10 Nov. 1917 meeting of princes in Delhi, PSAP, CS, Case No. II (b) 1 of 1917.

45. Montagu, *An Indian Diary*, p. 17.

46. Ibid., pp. 20–23, 29, 245, 290–94.

47. Ibid., pp. 138, 212.

48. Ibid., p. 25 and p. 103.

49. Diary entry for 11 Jan. 1913, IOR, MSS Eur D 523/39, pp. 158–62.

50. Draft Scheme, PSAP, CS, Case No. III (c) 2 of 1917.

51. Patiala to Samrath et al., 20 Dec. 1917, ibid. The invited British Indian political leaders were Tej Bahadur Sapru, a prominent High Court lawyer; C. Y. Chintamani, the editor of the *Leader* and a member of the United Provinces Legislative Council; M. M. Malaviya, the Congress and Hindu leader from Allahabad; N. M. Samrath, Sir Narayan Chandavarkar, and Sir Ibrahim Rahimatoolah from Bombay; Srinivasa Shastri of the Servants of India Society; Sir S. P. Sinha, a member of the Governor of Bengal's Council; Sir Ali Imam, a member of the Viceroy's Executive Council; and Sir Rash Behari Ghose from Calcutta. Both Sapru and Malaviya also were then serving on the Governor General's Legislative Council as nonofficial members from United Provinces.

52. J. P. Thompson, Ch Sec, Punjab Govt, to Wood, 28 Dec. 1917, Pro. No. 28, NAI, GOI, F&P, S-I, Feb. 1918, Pro. Nos. 28–34.

53. Ibid. Coen argues that V. P. Menon and other authors have incorrectly stated that political officers were against interstate cooperation. O'Dwyer is a prime

example of those who clung to the doctrine of isolation long into the twentieth century. *The Indian Political Service*, p. 64.

54. Wood to Thompson, 6 Jan. 1918, NAI, GOI, F&P, S-I, Feb. 1918, Pro. No. 33.

55. Minutes of meetings from 4–10 Jan. 1918 at Patiala, PSAP, CS, Case No. III (c) 2 of 1917. It must be noted that these minutes are obviously not complete and some discussions were not recorded.

56. Extract from Diary of L. M. Crump, Pol Ag for the Phulkian states, 1–15 Jan. 1918, NAI, GOI, F&P, S-I, Feb. 1918, Pro. Nos. 28–34.

57. Montagu, *An Indian Diary*, p. 188.

58. Minutes of meetings from 4–10 Jan. 1918 at Patiala, PSAP, CS, Case No. III (c) 2 of 1917.

59. Ibid.

60. The lengthy record of Nabha's dispute with the Punjab and central governments is in IOR, CR, R/1/19/513. The Nabha-Patiala rivalry is explored in Ramusack, "Incident at Nabha," p. 654, and "Maharajas and Gurdwaras."

61. Malerkotla to Patiala, 24 Jan. 1918; Bikaner to Patiala, 24 Jan. 1918; Patiala to Bikaner, 25 Jan. 1918 and 26 Jan. 1918; Dewas Junior to Patiala, 29 Jan. 1918, when Bikaner forwarded Wood's reply; PSAP, CS, Case No. II (b) 2 of 1918.

62. Montagu, *An Indian Diary*, pp. 232–33.

63. In attendance were the maharajas of Alwar, Bikaner, Cutch, Gwalior, Jaipur, Jodhpur, Kolhapur, Nawanagar, and Patiala, the begum of Bhopal, Wood, William Morris of the Reforms Office, and Robert E. Holland, then deputy secretary in the Political Department. It is important to note that no princes from south India were there. Minutes of meetings on 4–5 Feb. 1918 in Delhi NAI, GOI, F&P, S-I, May 1918, Pro. No. 1.

64. Ibid.

65. Montagu to Chelmsford, 3 Mar. 1918, IOR, MSS Eur E 264/4.

66. Wood to Bikaner, 20 Mar. 1918, PSAP, CS, Case No. II (a) 8 of 1919.

67. Nizam Mir Osman Ali Khan of Hyderabad to Lord Willingdon, Viceroy, 27 June 1935, IOR, CR, R/1/20/142.

68. Alwar to Bikaner, 31 Mar. 1918; Bikaner to Patiala, 8 Apr. 1918; Bikaner to Alwar, 8 Apr. 1918; PSAP, CS, Case No. II (b) 2 of 1918.

69. *Report on Indian Constitutional Reforms, 1918*, chap. 10, par. 310, pp. 196–97. *Local Governments* is the designation used by the Government of India to refer to provincial governments.

70. Chelmsford to Montagu, 20 Jan. 1919, IOR, MSS Eur D 523/8.

71. Ibid., and Chelmsford to Montagu, 31 Mar. 1920, IOR, MSS Eur D 523/10. Sir Conrad Corfield has said that he later discovered that Lloyd also greatly enjoyed visiting the states under his charge because of the unique hunting they offered. *The Princely India I Knew*, pp. 25–26.

The Bombay government had a long tradition of opposition to efforts by the central government of India to achieve a greater centralization of control over relations between the British and the native states. A detailed analysis of the conflict between the Government of India and the Bombay government over the transfer of Baroda is in I. F. S. Copland, "The Baroda Crisis of 1873–77: A Study in Governmental Rivalry."

72. Chelmsford in Council to Montagu, 20 Jan. 1921, IOR, CR, R/1/19/660.

73. Reading to Peel, 3 June 1922, IOR, MSS Eur E 238/16; Lloyd to Reading, 19 June 1923, ibid., E 238/25; Reading to Peel, 16 Aug. 1923; Reading to Peel, 27 Sept. 1923; ibid., E 238/6.

74. Wood's notes of his discussion with O'Dwyer on 4 July 1918, NAI, GOI, F&P,

S-I, Aug. 1918, Pro. Nos. 35–40; and Thompson to Wood, 23 July 1918 and 21 Sept. 1918, NAI, GOI, F&P, S-I, Aug. 1921, Pro. Nos. 1–21.

75. Thompson to Wood, 21 Sept. 1918, Pro. No. 3, NAI, GOI, F&P, S-I, Aug. 1921, Pro. Nos. 1–21.

76. R. E. Holland, Off Pol Sec, GOI, to Thompson, 2 Oct. 1918, Pro. No. 4, ibid.

77. Thompson to Holland, 12 Oct. 1918, Pro No. 5, ibid. In 1921 Thompson confided in his diary that official gossip said that the Punjab government became pugnacious and inclined to dispute Government of India rulings when he was chief secretary and that he was disliked by some for his close identification with O'Dwyer. Entry for 6 June 1921, IOR, J. P. Thompson Papers, MSS Eur F 137/14.

78. Chelmsford to Montagu, 31 Mar. 1920, IOR, MSS Eur D 523/10.

79. Minutes of meetings on 4–5 Feb. 1918 in Delhi, NAI, GOI, F&P, S-I, May 1918, Pro. No. 1.

80. Minutes of cabinet meeting at Patiala, 26–27 Nov. 1919, PSAP, CS, Case No. IV (d) of 1919. Some of the ministers at Patiala considered direct relations to be a mixed blessing, but the Maharaja declared himself to be in favor of the policy and asked only for suggestions on the best means of implementation. The Punjab princes and ministers met at Patiala on 13 Dec. 1919; minutes are in PSAP, PSR, IK, Basta No. 64, File No. 982.

81. Minutes of conference on 18 Dec. 1919 at Lahore, PSAP, CS, Case No. IV (d) 3 of 1919.

82. L. French, Off Ch Sec, Punjab Govt, to Wood, 2 Jan. 1920, NAI, GOI, F&P, S-I, Aug. 1921, Pro. Nos. 1–21.

83. For a concise outline of the final composition and powers of the Chamber, see Phadnis, *Towards the Integration of Indian States*, pp. 24–34.

84. *Conference Proceedings, November 1919*, pp. 25–26.

85. Meeting on 24 Dec. 1917 in Bombay, PSAP, CS, Case No. III (c) 1 of 1917.

86. Bikaner at informal meeting of princes in Delhi on 6 Feb. 1921, PSAP, CS, Case No. II (b) 3 of 1921.

87. Montagu to Chelmsford, 7 Nov. 1918, IOR, MSS Eur D 523/2.

88. C. L. S. Russell, Resident at Hyderabad, to Wood, 12 Feb. 1920, NAI, GOI, F&P, Reforms-A, Sept. 1920, Pro. Nos. 45–51.

89. Chelmsford to Montagu, 3 June 1920, IOR, MSS Eur D 523/10. Also see R. A. E. Benn, Off AGG in Rajputana, to Wood, 23 June 1920, NAI, GOI, F&P, Reforms-A, Sept. 1920, Pro. Nos. 45–51.

90. *Conference Proceedings, November 1919*, p. 48 and p. 52. Also see Chelmsford to Montagu, 22 Jan. 1919, IOR, MSS Eur E 264/5.

91. Chelmsford to Montagu, 5 Nov. 1919, IOR, MSS Eur D 523/9.

92. Montagu to Chelmsford, 4 Mar. 1919, IOR, MSS Eur D 523/3.

93. Chelmsford to Montagu, 1 Apr. 1919, IOR, MSS Eur D 523/8.

94. Wood to Russell, 29 Jan. 1920, NAI, GOI, F&P, Reforms-A, Sept. 1920, Pro. Nos. 45–51. Sir Stuart M. Fraser was resident in Hyderabad from 1916 to 1919.

95. *Conference Proceedings, November 1919*, pp. 49–50.

96. Wood to Benn, 29 June 1920, NAI, GOI, F&P, Reforms-A, Sept. 1920, Pro. Nos. 45–51.

97. In 1920 Khasherao Jadhava of Baroda, a minister who had been present at the committee meetings in 1918 where the princes drew up their proposals for reform, published a most acute analysis of why the Chamber would not be successful for all the reasons given above. See Jadhava, *Wake Up Princes*, pp. 144–71.

98. Sir James Roberts, Physician to Hardinge, to Hardinge, 4 Apr 1920, IOR, MSS Eur D 523/4. There is listed in the Index to the Foreign & Political Records of

the Government of India a file on the fear of Rajput domination of the Chamber, but this file is not available.

99. *Conference Proceedings, November 1919*, p. 24.

100. Ibid., pp. 28–29, and Chelmsford to Montagu, 13 Nov. 1919, IOR, MSS Eur D 523/9.

101. The members of the Codification Committee were the maharajas of Gwalior, Patiala, Bikaner, and Alwar, the jam saheb of Nawanagar, the maharao of Cutch, Sir George Lowndes, the Law Member of Chelmsford's Council, and Sir John Wood, the political secretary. Chelmsford-in-Council to Montagu, 7 May 1919, NAI, GOI, F&P, S-R, Feb. 1920, Pro. No. 1.

102. Chelmsford to Montagu, 9 Feb. 1921, IOR, MSS Eur D 523/5.

103. Bikaner was a Rathor Rajput, Cutch and Nawanagar were Jadeja Rajputs, Jhalawar was a Jhala Rajput, and Patiala claimed a Bhatti Rajput origin. Their salutes ranged from 21 guns for Gwalior, to 17 for Bikaner, Cutch and Patiala, to 13 for Nawanagar, and 11 for Jhalawar and Palanpur. Palanpur was the only Muslim, and he was a Lohani Pathan.

104. In a recent comprehensive study of the 1919 Indian Councils Act and related changes in policies of the Government of India, Peter Robb argues that "in none of these measures is there much evidence of serious thinking about the princes." *The Government of India and Reform: Policies towards Politics and the Constitution, 1916–1921*, p. 267.

CHAPTER FOUR

1. Punjab Govt to Home Dept, GOI, 16 Apr. 1919, Pro. No. 163, NAI, GOI, Home Pol-B, May 1919, Pro. Nos. 148–73.

2. Rupert Furneaux, *Massacre at Amritsar*, p. 24.

3. For a penetrating analysis of the varied reactions, see Jawaharlal Nehru, *Toward Freedom: An Autobiography*, pp. 49–53.

4. Report of T. Millar, Pol Ag in the Phulkian states, on the April 1919 disturbances in the Phulkian states, dated 23 June 1919, NAI, GOI, Home Pol Dep, July 1919, Pro. No. 71. See also Patiala's account to Montagu related later by Montagu to Reading, 12 Apr. 1921, IOR, MSS Eur E 264/22.

5. Chelmsford to Patiala, 17 Apr. 1919; Chelmsford to Nabha, 17 Apr. 1919; Chelmsford to Jind, 17 Apr. 1919; Chelmsford to Malerkotla, 17 Apr. 1919; Chelmsford to Baroda, 17 Apr. 1919; Nabha to Chelmsford, 19 Apr. 1919; Jind to Chelmsford, 23 Apr. 1919; Baroda to Chelmsford, 28 Apr. 1919; IOR, MSS Eur E 264/22.

6. Bundi made the following observation: "I have seen with utmost concern in newspapers very regrettable news of riots and disturbance in some localities in British India *engineered by insensate people of anarchical ideas* which are very condemnable and *un-Aryan* in their nature which deserve prompt remedy." [Italics are mine.] Bundi to Chelmsford, 24 Apr. 1919, IOR, MSS, Eur E 264/22.

7. Brown, *Gandhi's Rise to Power*, is the best general work on this period; and R. Kumar (ed.), *Essays on Gandhian Politics: The Rowlatt Satyagraha of 1919*, covers some specific aspects in greater depth.

8. The key role of the Hindu Mahasabha both before and after the first noncooperation movement is carefully explored in Richard Gordon, "The Hindu Mahasabha and the Indian National Congress, 1915 to 1926."

9. Chelmsford to All Princes, 9 May 1919, Pro. No. 4, NAI, GOI, F&P, S-I, Oct. 1920, Pro. Nos. 3–36.

10. The maharajas of Patiala, Dholpur, Ratlam, Baria, and two sons of the nawab of Loharu actually served at the front; and troops from Alwar, Bahawalpur,

Bharatpur, Bhopal, Faridkot, Gwalior, Indore, Jaipur, Kashmir, Khairpur, Malerkotla, Patiala, Rampur, Sirmur, and Tehri were selected for active service or garrison duty on the frontier. Chelmsford to Montagu, 4 June 1919, Pro. No. 155, NAI, GOI, F&P, I-A, Jan. 1921, Pro. Nos. 1–230.

11. Nizam's Manifesto on Afghan War, published 11 May 1919, Translation Forwarded by S. M. Fraser, Resident at Hyderabad to Wood, 14 May 1919, Pro. No. 14, NAI, GOI, F&P, S-I, Oct. 1920, Pro. Nos. 3–36.

12. H. Butler, Lt Govr of United Provinces, to Chelmsford, 10 May 1919, IOR, MSS Eur E 264/22.

13. F&P, GOI, to All Residents and AGGs, 16 Dec. 1919, NAI, GOI, F&P, S-I, Aug. 1920, Pro. Nos. 8–26.

14. Dholpur to Holland, AGG in Rajputana, 16 Feb. 1920, ibid.

15. It was alleged that Dholpur not only ordered the Arya *mandir* pulled down but also ordered a latrine to be built on the site. For a running account of the Dholpur-Arya conflict, see the following selections from the Punjab Press Abstracts, Vol. 31: *Arya Patrika*, 4 May 1918, p. 167; *Urdu Bulletin*, 20 July 1918, p. 397; *Darshananand*, 4 Aug. 1918, and *Desh*, 4 Aug. 1918; and *Urdu Bulletin*, 4 Dec. 1918. In 1919 the Arya Samajists ended their agitation by apologizing to the maharana of Dholpur and promising not to allow outsiders to interfere in their affairs nor to attack any non-Vedic religion. See PPA, Vol. 32, *Sanatan Dharam Patrika*, 22 June 1919, p. 217.

16. Dholpur to Holland, AGG in Rajputana, 16 Feb. 1920, NAI, GOI, F&P, S-I, Aug. 1920, Pro. Nos. 8–26.

17. Bikaner to Holland, 25 Feb. 1920, ibid.

18. Alwar to Holland, 28 Apr. 1920, ibid.

19. *Report of the Indian Statutory Commission*, Vol. 4, Part 1, pp. 8–26.

20. Bikaner to W. Vincent, Home Member of the Viceroy's Executive Council, 16 Oct. 1919, IOR, MSS Eur E 264/23.

21. Bikaner to Chelmsford, 10 Nov. 1919, ibid.

22. Patiala to Maffey, Pvt Sec to the Viceroy, 13 Dec. 1919, IOR, MSS Eur E 264/13.

23. Gwalior to Chelmsford, 13 Dec. 1919, and Malaviya to Gwalior, 6 Dec. 1919, IOR, MSS Eur E 264/23.

24. Three survey accounts of the Khilafat movement are: Ahmad Aziz, *Islamic Modernism in India and Pakistan, 1857–1964*, pp. 123–40, which concentrates on the intellectual origins; Ram Gopal, *Indian Muslims: A Political History, 1858–1947*, pp. 136–51; and P. Hardy, *The Muslims of British India*, pp. 185–97. A more detailed analysis is in Gail Minault Graham, "The Khilafat Movement: A Study of Indian Muslim Leadership, 1919–1924"; and Gail Minault, "Islam and Mass Politics: The Indian Ulama and the Khilafat Movement," in Donald E. Smith (ed.), *Religion and Political Modernization*, pp. 168–82.

25. Report by the Pol Ag, Bhopal, 24 May 1919; S. M. Fraser, Resident at Hyderabad, to R. E. Holland, Off Pol Sec, GOI, 13 May 1919, Pro. No. 27; Chelmsford to Montagu, 30 Mar. 1920, Pro. No. 37; IOR, CR, R/1/19/667.

26. Fraser to Holland, 13 May 1919, ibid.

27. Note by Chelmsford dated 18 May 1919, ibid.

28. Weekly report of the Director of the CID, GOI, dated 19 Apr. 1920, NAI, GOI, Home Pol, Apr. 1920, Pro. No. 103.

29. Extract from Diary of the AGG, Central India, for the first half of May 1919, IOR, CR, R/1/19/667.

30. Weekly Report of the Director of the CID, GOI, dated 19 Apr 1920, NAI, GOI, Home Pol, Apr. 1920, Pro. No. 103.

31. Bundi to Chelmsford, 19 Apr. 1920, IOR, MSS Eur E 264/24.

32. Fortnightly Report from Hyderabad for period from 15–31 May 1920, NAI, GOI, Home Pol Dep, July 1920, Pro. No. 95. Copies of the firmans were forwarded by Fraser, the resident in Hyderabad, on 20 and 22 May 1920, IOR, CR, R/1/19/667.

33. The *Siyasat* of Lahore was a strong critic of Rampur. See PPA, Vol. 33, 10 Apr. 1920, p. 160, and 17 Apr. 1920, pp. 168–69. It should be remembered that Rampur was a Shi'a, and would not have the usual ties to the Khilafat as would the orthodox Sunni.

34. The *Vakil* of Amritsar and the *Siyasat* and *Zamindar* of Lahore were particularly critical of Hyderabad. See PPA, Vol. 33, 26 June 1920, p. 257; 10 July 1920, p. 277; 17 July 1920, p. 286; 4 Sept. 1920, p. 363. Ali Imam was also a Shi'a, and had few reasons to be concerned about the extinction of the Khilafat.

35. Note by J. B. Wood dated 16 Sept. 1921 of interview on 14 Sept. 1921 with Ali Imam, IOR, CR, R/1/19/678.

36. Hyderabad to Chelmsford, 8 July 1920, IOR, MSS Eur E 264/25. In this letter Hyderabad cited the *Zamindar, Siyasat*, and *Zamana* as prime examples of the irresponsible Urdu press. After the Punjab government had taken two thousand rupees from the *Zamindar*, its editor, Zafar Ali Khan, wrote to the nizam in early August declaring that the Muslims of India regarded Hyderabad as a patrimony handed down to them by the Mughal Empire and that they looked to the nizam to influence Lloyd George on the Turkish issue. Hyderabad to Chelmsford, 12 Aug. 1920, IOR, CR, R/1/19/666.

37. Hyderabad to Chelmsford, 8 July 1920, IOR, MSS Eur E 264/25.

38. The Vernacular Press Act provided that "Magistrates of districts and commissioners of police in presidency towns were authorized, with the previous sanction of the local government, to demand bonds from printers and publishers and either a deposit of such sum as the local government might think fit or the submission of proofs for inspection. If the government found any matter they regarded as objectionable, they would publish a notice of contravention in the *Gazette*. If this warning were disregarded, the deposit, the machinery and copies of the paper could be confiscated." S. Gopal, *British Policy in India, 1858–1905*, pp. 118–19. Also Martin, *New India*, pp. 9–10.

39. When the Government of India pleaded with the Punjab and Madras governments to give effective protection to their staunch ally, the former responded more positively than the latter. H. McPherson, Off Sec, Home Dept, GOI, to all local governments and administrations, 23 Aug. 1920; J. P. Thompson, Ch Sec, Punjab Govt, to McPherson, 28 Sept. 1920; Ch Sec, Govt of Madras to J. B. Wood, 19 Jan. 1921 and 3 Feb. 1921; IOR, CR, R/1/19/66.

40. Hyderabad to Reading, 7 July 1921, IOR, MSS Eur E 238/23.

41. Ibid.

42. Reading to Hyderabad, 8 Aug. 1921, ibid.

43. Hyderabad to Reading, 1 Sept. 1921, ibid.

44. Wood to Russell, 26 Oct. 1920, Wood to AGG in Central India, 26 Oct. 1920, Wood to Ch Sec, Punjab Govt, 26 Oct. 1920, NAI, GOI, F&P, S-I, Mar. 1921, Pro. Nos. 18–27.

45. Bhopal to AGG in Central India, 20 Oct. 1920, ibid.

46. Russell to Wood, 27 Oct. 1920, ibid.

47. Bhopal to AGG in Central India, 20 Oct. 1920, ibid.

48. The Shivaji Memorial in Poona was an outgrowth of Tilak's long-term effort to revive Shivaji as an activist political symbol. This movement had languished in the 1910s, and Tilak's death in 1920 eliminated its major impetus. See above, Chapter 2, pp. 00-00, and Cashman, *The Myth of the Lokamanya*, Chapter 5, "The Development of the Shivaji Tradition," pp. 98–122.

49. George Lloyd to Reading, 19 Aug. 1921, IOR, MSS Eur E 238/23.

50. Kolhapur to Reading, 1 Sept. 1921, ibid.

51. Gwalior to Reading, 14 Sept. 1921, ibid., and Bull and Haksar, *Madhav Rao Scindia of Gwalior*, p. 210.

52. L. F. Rushbrook Williams, *The History of the Indian Tour of H. R. H. the Prince Wales, 1921–1922*, pp. 10–16.

53. Kolhapur to G. DeMontmorency, Pvt Sec to Reading, 4 Dec. 1924, IOR, MSS Eur E 238/26.

54. Reading to Lord Birkenhead, Secretary of State for India, 4 Dec. 1925, IOR, MSS Eur E 238/14. Reading proposed an inquiry into the complicity of Indore in the murder of the lover, Mr. Bawla, and the abduction of the girl, Mumtaz Begum. Indore eventually abdicated rather than face such an inquiry.

55. Irwin to Birkenhead, 18 Apr. 1928, IOR, Irwin-Halifax Papers, MSS Eur C 152/9.

56. *Khalsa Advocate*, 30 June 1917, p. 3; 7 Sept. 1917, p. 1; 8 Dec. 1917, p. 1; 23 Feb. 1918, p. 1.

57. *Khalsa Advocate*, 22 Sept. 1917, p. 1.

58. Fortnightly Report from the Punjab Government for first half of Aug. 1918, NAI, GOI, Home Pol Dep, Sept. 1918, Pro. No. 40.

59. *Khalsa Advocate*, 23 Dec. 1919, p. 1.

60. Contemporary accounts of these momentous events and Patiala's role in them are in *Khalsa Advocate*, 16 Nov. 1920, pp. 2, 6; 23 Nov. 1920, p. 2; 30 Nov. 1920, p. 3; a strongly biased note prepared by Daya Kishan Kaul, minister of Patiala, and forwarded to H. B. St. John, Off AGG, Punjab States, Aug. 1925, in Ganda Singh, ed. *Some Confidential Papers of the Akali Movement*, pp. 175–94; and a note by V. W. Smith, Asst Supt of Police, Punjab, 22 Feb. 1922, NAI, GOI, Home Pol, July 1921–Dec. 1922, File No. 459-II. A broader overview is in Ramusack, "Maharajas and Gurdwaras."

61. H. D. Craik, Off Add Sec Home, GOI, to E. Joseph, Ch Sec, Punjab Govt, 27 Jan. 1922, IOR, CR, R/1/29/53, and fortnightly report from Punjab States for first half of Jan. 1922, NAI, GOI, Home-Pol, July 1921–Dec. 1922, File No. 459-II. For a running account of Patiala's effort to organize a base among the Akalis, the paramilitary branch of the SGPC, see the entire run of fortnightly reports from the Punjab States for 1922, IOR, CR, R/1/18/53.

62. In September 1925 Hailey commented: "The real fact is, however, that Patiala has always occupied a somewhat curious position in regard to the Sikh agitation. Where it seemed to threaten him in any way, he has been keen on all manner of repression; but the existence of a strong Sikh agitation in the Punjab has given him an importance he would not otherwise possess. Nabha was the Akali and the enemy of the Government, he was the friend, and he was always anxious to come in with solutions of our difficulties based on the assumption that he alone could control the situation. He certainly had no real power of doing so, for in spite of his occasional appearances at Amritsar and concessions to the Akalis, he is much mistrusted and a good deal disliked by Sikhs generally." Hailey to Arthur Hirtzel, India Office, 23 Sept. 1925, Hailey Papers, IOR, MSS Eur E 220/8. While his assessment seems correct in many conclusions, it overlooks the repeated appeals to Patiala for support by both ends of the spectrum in Sikh politics.

63. Fortnightly Report from Punjab for the period from 1–15 Nov. 1920, NAI, GOI, Home Pol Dep, Dec. 1920, Pro. No. 74.

64. *Tribune*, 11 Jan. 1921, p. 6.

65. The Maratha Educational Conference, founded in 1907 by B. V. Jadhav, met annually and sought to secure the social uplift of the Maratha community by promoting education and social reform. Marathas from British India as well as such

Maratha princes as the maharaja of Dhar, who served as president in 1921, the raja of Satara, and the chiefs of Jath and Phaltan attended. There were similar bodies in other communities, such as the Sikh Educational Conference, and they were a favorite arena for princes. Fortnightly Report from Gwalior for the period from 15–30 Apr. 1921, NAI, GOI, Home Pol Dep, June 1921, Pro. No. 13. Bull and Haksar, *Madhav Rao Scindia of Gwalior*, p. 211.

66. Ibid. The British resident at Gwalior considered the proscription an injudicious step but could do nothing to stop it. A typical criticism by the nationalist press is in the *Tribune*, 6 May 1921, p. 1.

67. Kolhapur to Chelmsford, 19 Jan. 1920, IOR, MSS Eur E 264/24.

68. Reading to Montagu, 16 Apr. 1921, NAI, GOI, Home Pol Dep, Apr. 1921, Pro. No. 55.

69. Within his state Shahu reserved places in educational institutions and posts in the state service for non-Brahmins. Externally he supported B. V. Jadhav, his revenue minister, in the revival of the Satya Shodhak Samaj, a non-Brahmin organization founded by Jotirao Phule in 1873, and the promotion of the Maratha Educational Conference. Maureen L. P. Patterson, "A Preliminary Study of the Brahman versus Non-Brahman Conflict in Maharastra," pp. 98–102, is the pioneering analysis of Kolhapur's role. There is additional material in Cashman, *The Myth of the Lokamanya*; Copland, "The Maharaja of Kolhapur"; Latthe, *Memoirs of His Highness Shri Shahu Chhatrapati*; and Malgonkar, *Chhatrapatis of Kolhapur*.

70. This correspondence was widely reprinted; see the *Tribune*, 18 Mar. 1921, p. 7.

71. Chelmsford to Montagu, 3 June 1920, IOR, MSS Eur D 523/10.

72. Gwalior to Chelmsford, 2 July 1920, IOR, MSS Eur D 523/11.

73. Patiala to Montagu, 16 Apr. 1921, IOR, MSS Eur D 523/12.

74. Montagu to Reading, 20 Apr. 1921, ibid.

75. A flowery description of the royal progress is in Williams, *The History of the Indian Tour of H. R. H. the Prince of Wales*, passim.

76. Minutes of the informal meeting of the princes on 13 Feb. 1921 at Delhi, PSAP, CS, Case No. II (b) 3 of 1921.

77. Edward Haynes has argued that the British introduced a Westernized bureaucratic structure into Alwar that emasculated Maharaja Jey Singh, so that he was prevented "from fulfilling either the modern ruler's rule which his education had defined or that of the traditional Rajput lineage head. . . . He came, as a result, to generally ignore the administration of his state, to press his influence on the bureaucracy only when it touched matters of his personal privilege or comfort, and to content himself with activity on the all-India political scene. . . ." "Administrative Rationality versus the Alwar Jagirdars, 1892–1910," in *People, Princes, and Paramount Power*.

78. A particularly vivid account of their circumscribed world is given by E. M. Forster when he describes the maharaja of Chhatarpur: see *Hill of Devi*, pp. 126–27; and Joe R. Ackerley, *Hindoo Holiday: An Indian Journal*.

79. A. Montgomerie, Sec Pol Dept, Bombay Govt, to Pol Sec, GOI, 4 May 1921, NAI, GOI, F&P, Internal, 1922, File No. 323-Part I, Serial Nos. 1–6.

80. Codification Committee Meeting, 13 Dec. 1920, NAI, GOI, F&P, Reforms, 1928, File No. 54-R/28.

81. Holland to Thompson, 18 June 1921, NAI, GOI, Home Pol, July 1921 to Dec. 1922, File No. 199.

82. Bikaner to Benn, 14 June 1920; and Thompson to Wood, 10 Sept. 1920, NAI, GOI, F&P, Est-A, Nov. 1921, Pro. Nos. 1–29.

CHAPTER FIVE

1. See the *Karmavir*, 19 Feb. 1921, and *Hitavada*, 12 Nov. 1921, Central Provinces Native Newspaper Reports, Jan. to Dec. 1921, p. 87 and p. 540.

2. See the *Rajasthan Kesari*, 19 June 1921, ibid., p. 261; also the *Tribune*, 2 Dec. 1924, p. 5.

3. N. N. Mitra, *Indian Annual Register, 1922–23*, p. 733. Also the *Tribune*, 2 Dec. 1923, p. 5.

4. For example, see the *Rajasthan Kesari*, 20 Feb. 1921, CP-NNR, Jan. to Dec. 1921, p. 87.

5. Maharaja Rameshwara Singh of Darbhanga to Hignell, Pvt Sec to Chelmsford, 19 Feb. 1921, NAI, GOI, Home Pol Dep, Mar. 1921, Pro. No. 18.

6. Hignell to Darbhanga, 4 Mar. 1921, ibid.

7. *Chamber Proceedings, November 1921*, p. 135.

8. Montagu to Chelmsford, 1 Sept. 1919, NAI, GOI, Home Pol-A, July 1920, Pro. Nos. 265–78; and Montagu to Chelmsford, 28 Nov. 1919, NAI, GOI, Home Pol Dep, Mar. 1920, Pro. No. 10. The changing attitudes within the British official hierarchy toward restrictive press laws and the lengthy consultations between London and New Delhi are thoroughly delineated and documented in N. Gerald Barrier, *Banned: Controversial Literature and Political Control in British India, 1907–1947*, especially pp. 76–91 on the maneuvers involved in the repeal of the 1910 Press Act.

9. Montagu to Chelmsford, 15 Jan. 1920, NAI, GOI, Home Pol-1921, File No. 4, Part I, Serial Nos. 1–31 and 1–33; and Montagu to Chelmsford, 4 Nov. 1920, IOR, MSS Eur D 523/4. Lord Ronaldshay of Bengal was the leader of the provincial opposition: Barrier, *Banned*, pp, 83–84.

10. Chelmsford to Montagu, 16 Dec. 1920, Telegram, NAI, GOI, Home Pol Dep, Dec. 1920, No. 63.

11. Resolution by Home Department, GOI, dated 21 Mar. 1921, NAI, GOI, Home Pol-1921, File No. 4, Part I, Serial Nos. 1–31 and 1–33. The nonofficial members of the Committee were Jamnadas Dwarkadas, Seshagari Ayyar, Sachchidananda Sinha, Bakhshi Sohan Lal, Munshi Iswar Saran, Jogendra Nath Mukherjee, and Mir Asad Ali.

12. Reading to Peel, 26 Apr. 1922, IOR, MSS Eur E 238/6.

13. This quotation as well as the preceding summary of the Press Act are in the Report of the Press Act Committee dated 14 July 1921, NAI, GOI, Home Pol-1922, File No. 4/IX.

14. Montagu to Chelmsford, Telegram, 4 Aug. 1921, ibid.

15. Chelmsford to Montagu, Telegram, 28 Aug. 1921, ibid.

16. Wood to Bikaner, 10 Oct. 1921, NAI, GOI, Home Pol-1923, File No. 258.

17. *Chamber Proceedings, November 1921*, p. 141.

18. Ibid., pp. 139–40.

19. Ibid., pp. 145–48.

20. D. B. Shukla, President of Kathiawar Hitvardhak Sabha, to Wood, 28 Nov. 1921; and K. J. Bakshi, President of Praja Mandal of Rajkot, to Wood, 12 Dec. 1921; GOI, NAI, Home Pol-1923, File No. 258.

21. *Tribune*, 10 Nov. 1921, p. 1.

22. "Editorial Notes" in *Feudatory and Zemindari India*, Oct. and Nov. 1921, pp. 158–59.

23. Wood to Local Governments, Residents and Agents to the Governor General, 28 Feb. 1922, NAI, GOI, Home Pol-1923, File No. 258.

24. For the difficulties involved in finding a suitable post for Thompson, see Reading to Montagu, 28 Dec. 1921 and 2 Mar. 1922, IOR, MSS Eur D 523/14; and Montagu to Reading, 18 Jan. 1922, IOR, MSS Eur D 523/13.

25. In an interview on 14 May 1921 with William Vincent in which Thompson made these remarks, he also said that he thought Montagu wanted to take revenge on O'Dwyer by an attack on his chief secretary. Thompson Diary, 14 May 1921, IOR, MSS Eur F 137/14.

26. Geoffrey DeMontmorency, then an additional deputy secretary in the Foreign and Political Department, and John Wood both made this suggestion to Thompson: Thompson Diary, 23 May 1921 and 29 Sep. 1921, ibid.

27. Peel to Reading, Telegram, 25 Mar. 1922, NAI, GOI, Home Pol-1922, File No. 4, Part I-B, Serial Nos. 1–15. Also see the public letter from Peel to Reading dated 25 May 1922, in which Peel advised Delhi that he was withholding his final assent to the Repeal Act until he received definite assurances that the princes would be protected. Ibid.

28. Reading to Peel, 7 July 1922, ibid.

29. Note by Thompson dated 25 July 1922, NAI, GOI, Home Pol-1923, File No. 258.

30. Note by Vincent dated 1 Aug. 1922, ibid.

31. Note by Gwynne dated 17 June 1922, NAI, GOI, Home Pol-1922, File No. 4 of 1922, Part I-B, Serial Nos. 1–15.

32. Note by Sapru dated 2 Aug. 1922, ibid.

33. In 1909 Sapru began an intensive legal practice among the princes, counting such prominent ones as Bikaner, Bhopal, Gwalior, Hyderabad, and Kolhapur among his clients. For a full résumé of his contacts to 1921, see Sapru to Hignell, Sapru Manuscripts, File R, Series III.

34. An Order-in-Council [Sapru dissenting] dated 11 Aug. 1922 directed that legislation to protect the princes should be drawn up, NAI, GOI, Home Pol-1923, File No. 258.

35. Mitra, *Indian Annual Register*, 1922–1923, p. 720. Vincent was sensitive about his position as one of the signers of the Report of the Press Act Committee and, according to Thompson, was particularly discourteous to Thompson during the debate over the Princes Protection bill, attacking his position, misquoting him, and even talking during his speech! Reading had to serve as peacemaker with Thompson. Thompson Diary, 25–29 Sept. 1922, IOR, MSS Eur F 137/14.

36. See the PPA from October 1922 to February 1923 for a sampling of adverse press criticism. Reading to Peel, 22 Mar. 1923, IOR, MSS Eur E 238/6.

37. Gerald Rufus Isaacs Reading, *Rufus Isaacs: First Marquess of Reading*, 2:262.

38. Speech by Alwar on 18 Jan. 1924, PSAP, CS, Case No. III (a) of 1924.

39. Speech by Bikaner on 18 Jan. 1924, ibid.

40. Speech by Patiala on 18 Jan. 1924, ibid.

41. Speech by Thompson on 18 Jan. 1924, ibid.

42. S. Gopal, *British Policy in India*, pp. 254–55; and *Imperial Gazetteer of India*, Provincial Series, *Berar* (Calcutta: Superintendent of Government Printing, 1909), pp. 12–16.

43. The nizam's minister, Ali Iman, had informally raised the Berar issue with Reading in 1921, and had then proceeded to London to launch a supportive propaganda campaign in England. Since Ali Iman claimed that Curzon had browbeaten Mahbub Ali Khan into the 1902 settlement, Curzon started a vigorous counterattack that neutralized much of the Hyderabadi minister's efforts. Reading to Peel, 5 Apr. 1922, IOR, MSS Eur E 238/5; Reading to Peel, 10 May 1923, ibid., E 238/6;

Reading to Olivier, 12 Mar. 1924, ibid., E 238/13; Olivier to Reading, 10 Apr. 1924, ibid., E 238/7. The newspaper propaganda appears to have been concentrated in the Muslim press of Punjab. See the PPA for almost weekly references to the Berar question from 1919 to 1924. The *Paisa Akhbar* was a staunch advocate of the return of Berar to the nizam, and it was alleged that the nizam gave 225 rupees monthly to the *Paisa Akhbar: Kashmiri Magazine*, PPA, Vol. 31, p. 151.

44. After the Political Department prepared a lengthy study of the entire history of the Hyderabad Contingent and British control over Berar, Reading decided in September 1924 that Curzon had not exerted undue pressure and that the nizam had no case on any other point. Reading to Olivier, 19 Sept, 1924, IOR, MSS Eur E 238/18, and 9 Oct. 1924, ibid., E 238/7.

45. Hyderabad to Reading, 20 Sept. 1925. Great Britain, Parliamentary Papers, Vol. 22 (Accounts and Papers, Vol. 7), Cmd. 2621, 1926, "East India-Hyderabad," pp. 443–62.

46. Reading, *Rufus Isaacs*, 2:319. Reading to Birkenhead, Telegram, 6 Oct. 1925, IOR, MSS Eur E 238/14, and 14 Jan. 1926, ibid., E 238/8.

47. Reading to Hyderabad, 27 Mar. 1926, Great Britain, Parliamentary Papers, Vol. 22 (Accounts and Papers, Vol. 7), Cmd. 2621, 1926, "East India-Hyderabad," pp. 460–62.

48. Thompson to Patiala, 1 July 1926, PSAP, CS, Case No. III (a) of 1926.

49. Undated note by Thompson enclosed in above letter, ibid.

50. *Chamber Proceedings, January 1926*, p. 69. The committee was to be composed of the maharajas of Alwar, Bikaner, Kashmir, Nawanagar, and Patiala and the following ministers: Manubhai Mehta of Baroda, who was soon to become prime minister at Bikaner; Prabha Pattani of Bhavnagar, Kailas Haksar of Gwalior, L. F. Rushbrook Williams of Patiala, and an undesignated representative from Mysore. Ibid., p. 73.

51. At the height of debate over whether special protection against press attacks should be given to the princes, Maharaja Shahu Chhatrapati of Kolhapur wrote a note asking for such protection because the princes were as important an asset to the government as the army, navy, or police. See note dated 9 Feb. 1922, NAI, GOI, Home Pol-1923, File No. 258.

52. For a typical action by the political secretary rejecting many suggested items for the Chamber agenda, see Thompson to Patiala, 1 July 1926, PSAP, CS, Case No. III (a) 22 of 1926. The government seemed to reject more proposed agenda items as time went on. See Patiala's résumé and plea for princes to stand up for their rights over agenda, PSAP, CS, Case No. II (a) 24 of 1927.

53. *Chamber Proceedings, November 1924*, pp. 88–91.

54. Ibid., pp. 92–94.

55. *Chamber Proceedings, February 1929*, pp. 33–46.

56. For a description of this procedure, see C. C. Watson, Pol Sec, GOI, to Patiala, 23 May 1930, PSAP, CS, Case No. III (c) 27 of 1930; and Panikkar, *His Highness the Maharaja of Bikaner*, pp. 245–46.

57. *Chamber Proceedings, February 1923*, pp. 75–83.

58. Bikaner to Reading, 18 May 1922, IOR, MSS Eur E 238/24. Bikaner had suggested the following princes as participants: Bombay-Cutch and Nawanagar, Rajputana-Alwar and Kotah, Central India-Gwalior and Bhopal, Punjab-Patiala and Kapurthala, Bengal-Cooch Behar, United Provinces-Rampur or Benares and Baroda, Mysore and Cochin, as well as himself as chancellor of the Chamber.

59. Reading to Bikaner, 30 July 1922, ibid.

60. Despite the reputation of being a man with personal charm, Reading was remembered as having poor personal relations with many of the princes. See Forster, *Hill of Devi*, and Frederick W. F. Smith, Second Earl of Birkenhead, *Halifax: The Life of Lord Halifax*, p. 186.

61. Smith, *Halifax*, pp. 184–86 and pp. 229–30.

62. Panikkar, *His Highness the Maharaja of Bikaner*, p. 248, and *Chamber Proceedings, January 1926*, pp. 91–94.

63. Reading to Birkenhead, 28 Jan. 1926, IOR, MSS Eur E 238/8.

64. Ibid.

65. For a highly laudatory characterization, see H. M. Bull and K. N. Haksar, *Madhav Rao Scindia of Gwalior, 1876–1925*. A balancing, more critical view is given in Forster, *Hill of Devi*, pp. 82–85.

66. This position had been a cause of fierce debates before it was finally adopted. Those in favor of it wanted to preserve the exclusive character of the Chamber and to bar ministers from states under minority rule from sitting in their princely assembly. Those who opposed it argued that states should have firsthand information on the Chamber proceedings through their own representatives. *Chamber Proceedings, February 1921*, pp. 60–66, *November 1921*, pp. 128–33, and *February 1923*, pp. 52–79.

67. Maud Diver, *Royal India: A Descriptive and Historical Study of India's Fifteen Principal States and Their Rulers*, pp. 285–87, and Smith, *Halifax*, p. 185.

68. Irwin to Birkenhead, 5 May 1927 and also 3 and 11 Apr. 1927, IOR, MSS Eur C 152/3.

69. Reading, *Rufus Isaacs*, 2:321–23. This complex issue along with the Berar question occupied most of the energy of the Political Department from 1924 to 1926. In this instance Reading reversed the negative decision of his Political Department on the basis of early nineteenth-century precedents of Muslim succession. Reading to Birkenhead, 14 Jan. 1926, 30 Mar. 1926, IOR, MSS Eur E 238/8.

70. S. P. O'Donnell, Acting Governor of the United Provinces, to Irwin, 14 Oct. 1926, IOR, MSS Eur C 152/20, and Irwin to Birkenhead, 7 Sept. 1927, ibid., C 152/3.

71. See Patiala's circular letters to all members of the Chamber dated 23 July 1926 and 28 Oct. 1926, PSAP, CS, Case No. II (b) 5 of 1926.

72. Patiala to Mysore, 7–8 Nov. 1926; Patiala to Hyderabad, 12 Nov. 1926; PSAP, CS, Case No. II (b) 5 of 1926, Vol. 1. Mysore to Patiala, 17 Nov. 1926, PSAP, CS, Case No. II (a) 19 of 1926. Mysore had replied that he was unable to leave his state to make the long journey to Delhi.

73. Patiala to Bikaner, 23 July 1926, PSAP, CS, Case No. II (a) of 1926.

74. Irwin to Birkenhead, 30 June 1926, IOR, MSS Eur C 152/2.

75. Birkenhead to Irwin, 22 July 1926, ibid., and *Chamber Proceedings, November 1926*, p. 14.

76. Ibid., pp. 68–70.

77. Irwin to Birkenhead, 24 Nov. 1926, IOR, MSS Eur C 152/2.

78. Ibid.

79. Among the ministers present were P. S. Pattani from Bhavnagar, M. Mehta from Bikaner, K. N. Haksar from Gwalior, L. F. Rushbrook Williams from Patiala, Abdus Samad Khan from Rampur, Raja Oudh Narayan and Qazi Ali Hyder Abbasi from Bhopal, M. V. Kibe from Indore, and P. K. Wattal from Kashmir. See PSAP, CS, Case No. II (b) 9, 10, and 11 of 1927 for details of these meetings.

80. Patiala to Kashmir, Bhopal, Nawanagar, and Cutch, 26 Feb. 1927, PSAP, CS, Supplementary Index, Case No. 1, File No. 5 of 1927, Vol. 1.

81. Despite repeated checking of various archives, I was unable to locate a copy of this letter. However, its contents may be reconstructed from replies, which quoted it extensively.

82. Irwin to Birkenhead, 20 Oct. 1926, IOR, MSS Eur C 152/2.

83. Patiala to Bhopal, 19 Apr. 1927, PSAP, CS, Supplementary Index, Case No. V, File No. 5 of 1927, Vol. 2.

84. Rewa to all members of the Chamber of Princes, 25 Mar. 1927, ibid. Rewa had first protested to Patiala on 19 Mar. 1927.

85. Patiala to Rewa, 26 Mar. 1927, ibid.

86. Cutch to Patiala, 21 Mar. 1927, plus a copy of Cutch's telegram to Rewa, ibid.

87. Patiala to Bikaner et al, 8 Apr. 1927, PSAP, CS, Supplementary Index, File No. 9 of 1927.

88. The rulers of Alwar, Bhopal, Bikaner, Kashmir, Nawanagar, and Patiala as well as the following ministers: Ismail from Mysore, Haksar from Gwalior, Mehta from Bikaner, Pattani from Bhavnagar, and Rushbrook Williams from Patiala.

89. Minutes of Conferences at Simla on 6 May 1927, NAI, GOI, F&P, 1928, Pol, File No. 201-R.

90. Ibid.

91. Note by Lord Irwin dated 14 June 1927, NAI, GOI, F&P, 1927, Pol, File No. 727.

92. Irwin to Birkenhead, 5 May 1927, IOR, MSS Eur C 152/3.

93. Irwin to Birkenhead, 11 May 1927, ibid.

94. Birkenhead to Irwin, 16 June 1927, 15 Dec. 1927, ibid.

95. Malcolm Hailey, then the governor of Punjab, remarked that he thought "that Mr. Thompson has undoubtedly great capacity, but he is rigid in mind, unaccommodating in temperament, and suffers in consequence both in European and Indian opinion." Hailey to Reading, 1 Dec. 1925, IOR, MSS Eur E 220/8B. The Standing Committee, particularly at the urging of Alwar, purposely delayed its 1927 meeting until after the departure of Thompson. Alwar to Patiala on 19 July 1927 and 29 Aug. 1927, PSAP, CS, Case No. III (a) 29 of 1927.

96. Minutes of meeting on 12 Dec. 1927, PSAP, CS, Case No. III (a) 29 of 1927.

97. Birkenhead to Irwin, 15 Dec. 1927, IOR, MSS Eur C 152/3.

98. Irwin to Butler, 19 Feb 1928, NAI, GOI, F&P, Reforms Branch, 1928, File No. 91-R.

99. Ibid.

100. Proceedings of an Informal Conference of Political Officers at Simla on 4 July 1927, IOR, CR, R/1/29/322.

101. Notes by E. H. Kealy, AGG, Central India for the Political Officers Conference on 4-5 July 1927, IOR, CR, R/1/29/299.

102. Birkenhead had experienced great difficulty in obtaining personnel willing to serve on this Committee. For the chairmanship he approached both Lord Robert Cecil and Lord Ronaldshay, who refused, before he asked Butler, about whom Irwin had some reservations. Birkenhead to Irwin, Telegram, 4 Nov. 1927, IOR, MSS Eur C 152/8. It is striking that an *aide-mémoire* prepared by the Chamber mentioned Cecil and Ronaldshay as the type of chairman desired. PSAP, CS, Supplementary Index, Case No. V, 8 of 1927. Sydney Chapman, Laurence Guillemand, and Layton all refused the economist's position before Sidney Peel was approached and agreed to serve. Birkenhead to Irwin, Telegrams, 10 Nov. 1927, 16 Nov. 1927, 29 Nov. 1927, 12 Dec. 1927, IOR, MSS Eur C 152/7.

103. Birkenhead to Irwin, 9 Feb. 1928, ibid.

104. The committee went to Alwar, Baroda, Bhopal, Bikaner, Gwalior, Hyderabad, Jaipur, Jodhpur, Kashmir, Mysore, Nawanagar, Palanpur, Patiala, Rampur, and Udaipur. Butler kept a diary of his impressions of the states and princes visited and the comments of his princely hosts on the Indian political situation. Although much of the narrative is of the travelogue variety, Butler does give insight into the differences among the princes and the controversy over the retention of Sir Leslie Scott as counsel. Harcourt Butler Papers, IOR, MSS Eur F 116/108.

105. Speech of Patiala on 2 Feb. 1928, Maharaja Bhupinder Singh Patiala, *Public Pronouncements*, p. 14.

106. *Chamber Proceedings, February 1928*, p. 72.

107. Ibid., pp. 86–97.

108. There are no minutes available of the February 1928 informal meetings, but Patiala summarized the conclusions reached in a circular letter to all members of the Chamber dated 27 Feb. 1928, PSAP, CS, Case No. III (c) 12 of 1928.

109. For attendance lists, see ibid.

110. Butler to Irwin, 22 Mar. 1928, and Butler to Geoffrey Dawson, editor of the *Times*, 18 May 1928, IOR, MSS Eur F 116/85. Entry in Butler's Diary for 13 Mar. 1928 of conversations with the gaekwar of Baroda, IOR, MSS Eur F 116/108. Scott's fee was rumored to be a million and a half rupees.

111. Speech by Scott on 19 Apr. 1928, PSAP, CS, Case No. II (b) 28 of 1930.

112. Note by Watson, Pol Sec, GOI, dated 10 May 1928 on a conversation with Patiala in which Patiala expressed these sentiments. NAI, GOI, F&P, Reforms Branch, 1928, File No. 16-R.

113. Irwin to Birkenhead, 11 May 1927, IOR, MSS Eur C 152/3.

114. A good summary of Scott's scheme appeared in the *Tribune*, 24 May 1928, p. 8.

115. Speech by Patiala on 23 July 1923 before the East India Association in London. Patiala, *Public Pronouncements*, pp. 21–40. For critical remarks on this speech and on the comments contributed by the audience, see the *Tribune*, 19 Aug. 1928, p. 4.

116. For a record of Patiala's statements, see Patiala, *Public Pronouncements*. His articles and statements appeared in such places as the *Sunday Express* and the *Contemporary Review*, and his speeches were given at meetings like those held by the Royal Institute of International Affairs.

117. For background on the early years of the All India States' People's Conference, see R. L. Handa, *History of Freedom Struggle in Princely States*, pp. 122–45, and below.

118. Great Britain, Parliamentary Papers, Vol. 6 (Reports, Vol. 2), Cmd. 3302, 1928-29, "Report of the Indian States Committee, 1928–1929," p. 31.

119. *Work in the England of the Deputation of the Indian States' People's Conference* (Bombay: G. R. Abhyankar under the auspices of the Indian States' Conference, 1929), pp. 1–4.

120. Ibid., passim.

121. Ibid., pp. 17–18, 23–32.

122. Great Britain, Indian States Committee, 1928. *Oral Evidence Recorded before Committee.*

123. For further assessment of the reactions, see Phadnis, *Towards the Integration of Indian States*, pp. 49–52.

124. Great Britain, Parliamentary Papers, "Report of the Indian States Committee, 1928–1929," p. 31.

125. Ibid.

126. Patiala to all members of the Chamber of Princes, 29 Apr. 1929, PSAP, CS, Case No. III (c) 18 of 1929.

127. Great Britain, Parliamentary Papers, "Report of the Indian States Committee, 1928–1929," p. 32.

128. Irwin in Council to Birkenhead, 15 Sept. 1927, IOR, MSS Eur F 116/85 and remarks by Irwin at the Informal Conference of Political Officers in July 1927, Conference Proceedings, IOR, CR, R/1/29/322.

129. Copland in "The Other Guardians" and Manor in "The Demise of the

Princely Order: A Reassessment," in *People, Princes and Paramount Power*, argue that Minto's statement and Butler's efforts forestalled British pressure for political reform in the states. Their basic thesis is valid, but one should give more weight to the attitudes of individual political officers who were not sympathetic to reform. Men such as Edward Wakefield said that one of the blessings of joining the Political Service in 1929 was that it meant that he "would be out of range of irresponsible criticism from a hostile Legislative Assembly." *Past Imperative: My Life in India, 1927–1947*, p. 81.

130. Sarvepalli Gopal, *The Viceroyalty of Lord Irwin, 1926–1931*, pp. 19–28.

131. The evolution of this proposal and the suspenseful story of how Irwin, Wedgwood Benn, then the secretary of state for India, and Ramsey MacDonald, the prime minister, had to overcome powerful opposition to it is ably presented in Moore, *The Crisis of Indian Unity*, pp. 41–94.

132. Simon to MacDonald, 16 Oct. 1929, and MacDonald to Simon, 25 Oct. 1929, Great Britain, Parliamentary Papers, Vol. 11 (Reports, Vol. 4), Cmd. 3568, May 1930, "Report of the Indian Statutory Commission," Vol. 1, pp. xxii–xxiv.

CHAPTER SIX

1. Members of the Standing Committee of the Chamber were usually chosen as representatives to the League of Nations: the maharao of Cutch in 1921, the jam saheb of Nawanagar in 1920 and 1922, the maharajas of Alwar in 1923, of Bikaner in 1924 and 1930, and of Patiala in 1925. The one exception to this rule was the maharaja of Kapurthala, who was not a member of the Standing Committee and who served at the League in 1926, 1927, and 1929. See the Chamber Proceedings for their reports. After Bikaner led the Indian delegation to the League in 1930, the princes began to be represented by their ministers so as to avoid the situations when a prince would be subordinate to a British Indian who was functioning as leader of the delegation.

2. For an analysis of this period that gained widespread adherence within the Government of India, see L. F. Rushbrook Williams, *India in 1925–26*, p. 293.

3. O'Dwyer, *India As I Knew It*, p. 141.

4. Mitra, *Indian Quarterly Register*, 1 (Jan.-June 1925): 26–27.

5. In 1917 during the dispute over the construction of a canal headworks at Hardwar, Sir James Meston, the lieutenant governor of the United Provinces, commented on the close relationship between Alwar and Malaviya: Meston to Chelmsford, 19 Jan. 1917, IOR, MSS Eur E 264/3.

6. Fortnightly Report from Punjab for the first half of Jan. 1927, NAI, GOI, Home Pol-1927, File No. 32. The Sanatan Dharm was an orthodox Hindu reform movement founded in opposition to the Arya Samaj. Alwar had a continuing relationship with the Sanatan Dharm. In November 1922 he had presided at the opening of a Sanatan Dharm College hostel in Lahore. Alwar to Reading, 11 Nov. 1922, IOR, MSS Eur E 238/24.

7. *Tribune*, 22 Nov. 1924, p. 3.

8. Ibid.

9. Others who attended were Abul Kalam Azad, Hakim Ajmal Khan, Dr. M. A. Ansari, Muhammad Ali, Dr. S. Kitchlew, M. M. Malaviya, Lala Lajpat Rai, M. A. Jinnah, N. C. Kelkar, M. R. Jayakar, R. S. Kedernath, and Ujjal Singh. Mitra, *Indian Quarterly Register* 2 (July-Dec. 1927): 39–50.

10. *Tribune*, 27 Sept. 1927, p. 5.

11. Samuel Hoare, Secretary of State for India, to Lord Willingdon, Viceroy, 22 Dec. 1932, Templewood Papers, IOR, MSS Eur E 240/2. Hoare also reported

that Bikaner and Bhopal had sent messages of support, which the Aga Khan and his Muslim friends viewed with resentment.

12. *Tribune*, 21 June 1923, p. 8.

13. The Sikh states were allotted a total of twelve seats, and the others received one or two apiece. The rationalization for the miniscule representation was that *gurdwaras* in the princely states did not come under the control of the SGPC. Malcolm Hailey, Govr of Punjab, to J. P. Thompson, Pol Sec, GOI, 12 July 1926 and 14 July 1926, NAI, GOI, F&P, 1925, File No. 423-P.

14. Patiala received deputations from the SGPC on 16 Feb. 1926, 5–6 Apr. 1926, 1 Apr. 1927, and in May 1927. Documentation on the items discussed in these exchanges is as follows: 16 Feb. 1926: *Tribune*, 27 Feb. 1926, p. 4, and report of Mehtab Singh, Kartar Singh, and Bawa Harkishan Singh dated 26 Mar. 1926 in Singh, *Some Confidential Papers of the Akali Movement*, pp. 215–18; 5–6 Apr. 1926, *Tribune*, 11 Apr. 1926, p. 9; notes by Dhian Singh and Bhagwan Das, Superintendent, Intelligence Bureau, Home-GOI, dated 5 Apr. 1927 and 8 Apr. 1927 respectively, IOR, CR, R/1/29/332; May 1927, note by J. P. Thompson of conversation with Bhupinder Singh on 7 May 1927, ibid.

15. *Tribune*, 23 Jan. 1929, p. 1.

16. For the Patiala version of the campaign, see the secret note dated 1 Mar. 1929, PSAP, PSR, Prime Minister's Office, Basta No. 20, Serial No. 588, File No. 241 of 1929. For Sikh protests against the Akali-directed agitation, see *Khalsa Advocate*, 16 Feb. 1929, p. 1, and 2 Mar. 1929, p. 1, and *Tribune*, 7 Feb. 1929, p. 3, 9 Feb. 1929, p. 7, 22 Feb. 1929, p. 4, and 27 Feb. 1929, p. 7.

17. For Patiala's motives in hosting this conference, see a note by Arjan Shah Singh dated 8 Jan. 1924 and Daya Kishan Kaul to Patiala, 10 Jan. 1924, PSAP, PSR, IK, Basta No. 24, File No. 355.

18. *Tribune*, 25 June 1927, p. 4.

19. A major statement of this position was made by M. K. Gandhi in his presidential address at the Third Kathiawad Political Conference held at Bhavnagar on 8 Jan. 1925: Mohandas K. Gandhi, *Indian States' Problem*, pp. 7–28.

20. There is an introductory survey in Handa, *History of Freedom Struggle in Princely States*, pp. 122–33. An excellent study on the movement in one particular area is Ramesh Walia, *Praja Mandal Movement in East Punjab States*.

21. See the report on the Deccan Indian States Conference in the *Tribune*, 1 June 1922, p. 1; the presidential address of N. C. Kelkar to the Indian States' Subjects' Conference on 30 Dec. 1924, Mitra, *Indian Quarterly Register* 2 (July-Dec. 1924): 494–98; the presidential address of Shankerlal Kaul to the Indian States' Subjects' Conference on 29 Dec. 1925, *Indian Quarterly Register* 2 (July-Dec. 1925): 374–75.

22. See Kelkar's speech on 30 Dec. 1924, Mitra, *Indian Quarterly Register* 2 (July-Dec. 1924): 495–96.

23. Indian States' People's Conference, *Report of the Bombay Session: 17th, 18th December 1927*. Also see V. S. S. Sastri's speech in 1926 in Cochin, P. Kodanda Rao, *The Right Honourable V. S. Srinivasa Sastri: A Political Biography*, pp. 201–5.

24. Irwin to Wedgwood Benn, 24 May 1930, IOR, MSS Eur C 152/11. The initial impetus for such a statement came from T. H. Keyes, the resident in Hyderabad, who said that the nizam was anxious to justify his position as "Premier Ruler and Faithful Ally": Keyes to Irwin, 4 May 1930, IOR, CR, R/1/29/576.

25. Here Irwin was acting at the request of Malcolm Hailey, now governor of the United Provinces, where Deoband was located: Hailey to C. C. Watson, 2 July 1930, IOR, CR, R/1/29/631. For further information on Madani and his political philosophy, see Aziz Ahmad, *Islamic Modernism in India and Pakistan, 1857–1964*, pp. 189–93.

26. T. H. Keyes, Resident at Hyderabad, to Watson, 28 Feb. 1931, and Watson to G. B. Lambert, Govr of United Provinces, 11 Mar. 1931, IOR, CR, R/1/29/631.

27. Bombay Govt to GOI, Home Dept, 3 Dec. 1931, NAI, GOI, Home Pol-1932, File No. 5/4/32.

28. Watson to all Residents and AGGs, 7 Jan. 1932, ibid.

29. Watson to Residents at Hyderabad and Mysore, and AGGs in Rajputana and Central India, 7 Jan. 1932, ibid.

30. Watson to AGG in Rajputana, 7 Jan. 1932, ibid. The government was obviously referring to the Marwari contributors to the Congress treasury.

31. L. Reynolds, AGG in Rajputana, to Watson, 10 Feb. 1932, IOR, CR, R/1/29/838.

32. *Tribune*, 31 Jan. 1932, p. 7.

33. *Tribune*, 8 June 1932, p. 15; Fortnightly Report from Hyderabad for the first half of Feb. 1932, NAI, GOI, Home Pol-1932, File No. 18/IV, and the Fortnightly Report from Gwalior for the second half of Mar. 1932, NAI, GOI, Home Pol-1932, File No. 18/V. Copies of princely replies to the governmental request for assistance are in IOR, CR, R/1/29/837 and R/1/29/838.

34. For Patiala's ordinances see the *Tribune*, 6 Jan. 1932, p. 7. For Jodhpur see the Fortnightly Report from Rajputana for the first half of Mar. 1932, NAI, GOI, Home Pol-1932, File No. 18/V.

35. Fortnightly Report from Central India for the first half of Sept. 1931, NAI, GOI, Home Pol-1931, File No. 18/IX.

36. Fortnightly Reports from Central India for the first and second half of May 1932, NAI, GOI, Home Pol-1932, File No. 18/VIII, and for the first half of June 1932, NAI, GOI, Home Pol-1932, File No. 18/IX.

37. E. H. Kealy, AGG in the States of Western India, to Watson, 31 Jan. 1931, NAI, GOI, F&P, 1930, Reforms, File No. 186-R/30.

38. See the Fortnightly Reports from the States of Western India for the first half of May 1931, NAI, GOI, Home Pol-1931, File No. 18/V; for the first half of Jan. 1932, NAI, GOI, Home Pol-1932, File No. 18/I; for the first half of June 1932, NAI, GOI, Home Pol-1932, File No. 18/IX.

39. C. B. Clee, Sec to Bombay Govt, Home Dept, to M. G. Hallett, Home Sec of GOI, 5 Aug. 1932, NAI, GOI, Home Pol-1933, File No. 3/4.

40. Hallett to B. J. Glancy, Pol Sec of GOI, 4 Oct. 1933, Glancy to Mirza Ismail, 16 Oct. 1933, Mirza Ismail to Glancy, 24 Oct. 1933, IOR, CR, R/1/29/1150; and C. G. Prior, Off Dep Sec, F&P, GOI, to C. T. Plowden, Resident in Mysore, 8 Jan. 1934, NAI, GOI, Home Pol-1934, File No. 58.

41. Plowden to B. J. Glancy, 4 Apr. 1934, NAI, GOI, Home Pol-1934, File No. 4/6/34. Since the matter had been dragged out for two years because of bureaucratic procedures, the Government of India could conveniently drop it after Plowden's letter.

42. An excellent analysis of the Mysore situation is in Manor, "Princely Mysore before the Storm," pp. 31–38.

43. Keyes to G. Cunningham, Pvt Sec to the Viceroy, 1 Sept. 1930, NAI, GOI, Home Pol-1930, File No. 364.

44. Note by D. Gladding in Home Dept, GOI, dated 6 Sept. 1930, and one by C. P. Hancock, F&P, GOI, dated 12 Sept. 1930, ibid.

45. Note by H. Wilberforce-Bell dated 12 Sept. 1930, ibid.

46. Note by G. Cunningham dated 13 Sept. 1930, and one by E. H. Emerson, Home Sec, GOI, dated 24 Sept. 1930, ibid.

47. Nawanagar to Irwin, 12 May 1930, IOR, CR, R/1/29/638.

48. Patiala to Irwin, 9 May 1930, and Bhopal to Irwin, 7 May 1930, ibid.

49. Indian States' People's Conference, *Report of the Bombay Session: 17th, 18th December 1927*, Part 1, p. 6, Part 2, p. 18, Part 3, p. 23. It should be remembered that the *Bombay Chronicle* was also the first English-language newspaper to publish the correspondence between the maharaja of Kolhapur and British officials about the need to take stronger action against the noncooperation movement in 1921.

50. M. Hailey, Govr of Punjab, to J. Crerar, Home Member, GOI, 7 June 1928, NAI, GOI, Home Pol-1929, File No. 141. Dumasia had written to Hailey, who forwarded the information to Crerar. Note by C. C. Watson dated 9 May 1929, ibid.

51. Irwin to Bhopal, Patiala, and Nawanagar, 2 May 1930, IOR, CR, R/1/29/638.

52. A comprehensive and balanced analysis of the Lahore session and the 1930 civil disobedience movement is in Judith M. Brown, *Gandhi and Civil Disobedience: The Mahatma in Indian Politics, 1928–34.*

53. Speech delivered by the Maharaja of Patiala on 3 Feb. 1930, PSAP, CS, Case No. II (a) 34 of 1930, Vol. 2. It should be noted that this statement by Patiala appeared before the princes as a group condemned the Lahore Independence resolution at the Chamber session later in February 1930.

54. Patiala to Watson, 1 Feb. 1930, and Watson to Patiala, 3 Feb. 1930, NAI, GOI, F&P, 1930, Special, File No. 20-Spl.

55. Irwin to Patiala, 29 May 1930, PSAP, PSR, IK, Basta No. 65, File No. 994.

56. Patiala to Irwin, 4 June 1930, ibid.

57. Ibid. It is interesting to note that both James A. O. Fitzpatrick, the AGG in the Punjab States, and moderate Sikh leaders kept urging Patiala to continue his efforts. See Fitzpatrick to Patiala, 30 May 1930 and 19 June 1930, and a telegram from certain Sikh leaders to Patiala, 16 May 1930, ibid.

58. Liaqat Hayat Khan to Sir Sundar Singh Majithia, 18 June 1930, and Arjan Shah Singh to Patiala, 16 June 1930, ibid.

59. Liaqat Hayat Khan to Sir Sundar Singh Majithia, 18 June 1930, ibid.

60. Patiala to Irwin, 24 June 1930, ibid.

61. Irwin to Patiala, 19 June 1930, ibid.

62. Address presented to the Viceroy by Representatives of the Sikh Community of Punjab on the Sisganj Gurdwara Affair on 30 June 1930, ibid.

63. For the connection between the Akali Dal and the Punjab Riyasti Praja Mandal, see Khushwant Singh, *A History of the Sikhs*, Vol. 2: 1839–1964, pp. 215–16. The Mandal attack on Patiala is well-documented in the *Tribune* from 1929 onward and in Walia, *Praja Mandal Movement in East Punjab States*, pp. 76–102.

64. Fortnightly Report from Kashmir for first half of July 1931, IOR, CR, R/1/29/689. A major published source on twentieth-century political developments in Kashmir is Prem Nath Bazaz's *The History of the Struggle for Freedom in Kashmir: From the Earliest Times to the Present Day* (see particularly pp. 151–71 for commentary on the early 1930s). Since Bazaz, a secularist Kashmiri pandit, was active in politics from the late 1920s and was acknowledged, at one point, by Sheikh Abdullah as his political guru, his account is colored by personal opinions that must be carefully evaluated; but it provides an important statement from an active participant. A helpful, detailed secondary source is Prithivi Nath Kaul Bamzai, *A History of Kashmir*, pp. 648–64.

65. Bazaz, *The History of the Struggle for Freedom in Kashmir*, pp. 154–55, and Bamzai, *A History of Kashmir*, p. 657.

66. Because of British concern about the repercussion of events in Kashmir on the communal situation in British India as well as within the state itself, Willingdon extended "authoritative advice" to the maharaja that he should take immediate steps to remedy the more obvious grievances of his Muslim subjects and then for-

mally ask the British for the loan of a British officer to conduct a full inquiry into Muslim grievances and to make suitable recommendations. Watson to C. Latimer, Resident in Kashmir, 25 Sept. 1931, IOR, CR, R/1/29/780.

67. Bamzai, *A History of Kasmir*, pp. 655–56; Bazaz, *The History of the Struggle for Freedom in Kashmir*, p. 151; and Spencer Lavan, "The Ahmadiyah Movement: Its Nature and Its Role in Nineteenth and Early Twentieth Century India," p. 316.

68. Punjab Government, *Report of the Court of Enquiry Constituted under the Punjab Act II of 1954 to Enquire into the Punjab Disturbances of 1953* [President: M. Munir], p. 11.

69. A detailed analysis of the Ahmadiyah involvement in Kashmir from 1931 to 1934 is in Spencer Lavan, *The Ahmadiyah Movement: A History and Perspective*, p. 145–64.

70. Latimer to Watson, 27 Sept. 1931; Memorandum by Latimer dated 28 Sept. 1931. But later the resident denied that Sheikh Abdullah was an actual member of the sect: Fortnightly Report for the second half of Oct. 1931. IOR, CR, R/1/29/780 for the first two documents; R/1/29/689 for the third.

71. For further information on the Ahrars, see Wilfred C. Smith, *Modern Islam in India: A Social Analysis*, pp. 252–57. An inside source on the Ahrars is Aziz-ur-Rahman, *Raisul-ul-Ahrar, Maulana Habib-ur-Rahman, Ludhiani*, a biography in Urdu of the founder of the Ahrars by his son. I am indebted to Spencer Lavan for sharing his English translation of sections of this work with me.

72. Watson to Latimer, 6 Oct. 1931; Latimer to Watson, 7 Oct. 1931; Telephone Message from E. A. R. Eustace, Dep Commissioner, Sialkot, 9 Oct. 1931; IOR, CR, R/1/29/78, Aziz-ur-Rahman, *Raisul-ul-Ahrar*, pp. 156–58.

73. *Tribune*, 8 Aug. 1931, p. 8; 7 Oct. 1931, p. 8; 22 Oct. 1931, p. 8.

74. Eustace to F. L. Brayne, Commissioner, Lahore Division, 2 Nov. 1931, IOR, CR, R/1/29/805.

75. *India in 1931–1932*, pp. 31–32. For a copy of Ordinance No. 10 of 1931, see NAI, GOI, Home Pol-1931, File No. 13/26.

76. Telephone Message from G. F. DeMontmorency, Govr of Punjab, to Willingdon, 3 Nov. 1931, IOR, CR, R/1/29/805; Press Communiqué issued by the Govt of India, 4 Nov. 1931, NAI, GOI, Home Pol-1931, File No. 13/26. Bertrand J. Glancy, an officer of the Political Department who had served before in Kashmir on a food relief commission in the early 1920s, was appointed chairman of both commissions.

77. Watson to Latimer, 29 Jan. 1932, IOR, CR, R/1/29/878. At first the Government of India was reputed to be inclined to demand the appointment of a British administrator for the state, but later Willingdon softened the terms, partly because of the lobbying efforts of Nawab Hamidullah of Bhopal, a princely associate of Hari Singh from the Chamber of Princes, and Kailas Haksar, a close friend of Tej Bahadur Sapru who was a major political adviser to the maharaja. Haksar to Sapru, Sapru MSS, I, H 51.

78. For a more detailed analysis of Kashmir politics from July 1931 to October 1934, when a Representative Assembly was inaugurated in Kashmir, see Barbara Ramusack, "Exotic Imports or Home-grown Riots: The Muslim Agitations in Kashmir in the Early 1930's."

79. *Tribune*, 24 Jan. 1932, p. 7.

80. *Tribune*, 17 Dec. 1931, p. 8, and the Fortnightly Report from Hyderabad for the second half of Mar. 1932, NAI, GOI, Home Pol-1932, File No. 18/V.

81. *Tribune*, 10 Mar. 1932, p. 6, 11 Mar 1932, p. 15, 11 Apr. 1932, p. 2, 13 Apr. 1932, p. 2, for attacks on Bhopal; and for Hyderabad see Fortnightly Reports from Hyderabad for the first half of Feb. 1932, NAI, GOI, Home Pol-1932, File No. 18/IV, and for the second half of Mar. 1932, NAI, GOI, Home Pol-1932, File No. 18/V.

82. *Tribune*, 2 Apr. 1932, p. 8.

83. *Tribune*, 11 Apr. 1932, p. 2.

84. Fortnightly Reports from Central India for the second half of Mar. 1932, NAI, GOI, Home Pol-1932, File No. 18-V, and from Hyderabad for the second half of Mar. 1932, ibid., and for the second half of June 1932, NAI, GOI, Home Pol-1932, File No. 18/IX.

85. "They [Meos] are Musalmans in name but their religion is lax and they still worship the Hindu village deities Bhumia or Khera and Hanuman. . . . They seldom erect any mosques in their villages and their religious observances are confined for the most part to attending *Id* prayers once a year. It has been said of them that they are ready to observe the feasts of both the Musalman and Hindu religions, the fasts of neither." *Census of India, 1901*. Vol. 25: *Rajputana*, Part 1—Report, p. 157. This volume contains a full description of Meo customs, occupations, and clans.

86. J. N. Johnson, Chief Commissioner of Delhi, to M. G. Hallett, 11 Aug. 1932, NAI, GOI, Home Pol-1932, File No. 175, and Fortnightly Reports from Punjab and Rajputana for the second half of Nov. 1932, NAI, GOI, Home Pol-1932, File No. 18/XIII.

87. Fortnightly Report from Punjab for the second half of Nov. 1932, NAI, GOI, Home Pol-1932, File No. 18/XII.

88. Fortnightly Report from Punjab for the first half of Dec. 1932, NAI, GOI, Home Pol-1932, File No. 18/XV.

89. Fortnightly Reports from Punjab for the first and second halves of Jan. 1932, NAI, GOI, Home Pol-1933, File No. 18/1/33.

90. *India in 1932–33*, pp. 21–22, Mitra, *Indian Annual Register, 1933*, 1:2.

91. Sir Arthur Lothian was sent on temporary duty to Alwar in February 1933 until Sir Francis Wylie could return from England and take up the post of prime minister. Lothian claimed that "the root cause of all the trouble was, however, the Maharaja's personal extravagance. He took a leading place amongst the Princes by reason of his personality, but he was Ruler of a comparatively small State and could not hope to compete financially with the Rulers of the much larger and wealthier States of Bikanir [*sic*], Gwalior, Kashmir and Patiala, who were his main rivals. His arrogance was such, however, that he could not endure being outclassed in any way by these other Princes, and this led him ever deeper into debt, with the consequence that the condition of his State grew progressively worse, and in the end a crash had to come." Lothian, *Kingdoms of Yesterday*, p. 124. This explanation is too simplistic, but it points up how maneuvers in the all-India sphere could have negative results within a ruler's own territories.

92. *Tribune*, 23 Feb. 1933, p. 8; 21 May 1933, p. 1; 22 May 1933, p. 1.

93. In Alwar the Ahrars were poorly received and much less successful than they had been in Kashmir. Fortnightly Report from Punjab for the second half of Jan. 1932, NAI, GOI, Home Pol-1933, File No. 18/1/33.

94. Handa, *History of Freedom Struggle in Princely States*, pp. 134–57, and Phadnis, *Towards the Integration of Indian States*, pp. 84–97.

95. Gandhi, *Indian States' Problem*, p. 61, and Handa, *History of Freedom Struggle in Princely States*, p. 104.

96. Handa, *History of Freedom Struggle in Princely States*, pp. 106–18, and Phadnis, *Towards the Integration of Indian States*, pp. 113–28.

97. Gandhi, *Indian States' Problem*, pp. 401–3, has a full copy of the Haripura resolution and his comments on it, pp. 72–75. Background on the role of the younger leftists and Subhas Chandra Bose, who presided at the Haripura Congress, is in Gordon, *Bengal*, pp. 265–67.

98. A penetrating analysis of the Rajkot campaign is in John R. Wood, "Indian Nationalism in the Princely Context: The Rajkot Satyagraha of 1938–39," in *People, Princes, and Paramount Power*.

99. Reginald Coupland, *The Indian Problem*, 2:167–68, and Vapal P. Menon, *The Story of the Integration of the Indian States*, pp. 42–44.

CHAPTER SEVEN

1. *Chamber Proceedings, February 1929*, pp. 34–36.

2. Ibid., pp. 36–38.

3. Ibid., pp. 43–45.

4. Ibid., pp. 71–82.

5. Irwin to Peel, 21 Feb. 1929, IOR, MSS Eur C 152/5.

6. *Chamber Proceedings, February 1929*, p. 75.

7. *Tribune*, 20 Feb. 1929, p. 1. Patel was active even earlier in maintaining contacts between Chamber princes and Indian nationalists. In March 1928 he arranged a dinner party that included Patiala, Motilal Nehru, Sarojini Naidu, Lajpat Rai, and Muhammad Ali Jinnah. According to Patiala's account, he was warned that the states would be eliminated if they attempted to block British Indian political development. Irwin to Birkenhead, 8 Mar. 1928, IOR, MSS Eur C 152/4.

8. *Tribune*, 21 Feb. 1929, p. 2. This meeting and the subsequent ones discussed below should modify the statement of Robin Moore that "in the interval between the appearance of the Butler Report [February 1929] and the Simla meeting [14 July 1930] the princes showed no serious inclination to gather together for discussions with British Indian politicians." Moore, *Crisis of Indian Unity*, p. 129. The princes and politicians met, but the lack of positive results indicates how far apart they were and the reluctance on both sides to seek an accommodation.

9. Haksar to Maqbool Mahmud, 3 Mar. 1929, PSAP, CS, Case No. III (c) 20 of 1929.

10. The minutes of this meeting are undated, but from the personnel present and the allusions made, the date most reasonable is 22 Mar. 1929, PSAP, CS, Supplementary Index, Case No. V, File No. 14 of 1930.

11. Malaviya to Patiala, 15 June 1929, PSAP, CS, Case No. III (c) 19 of 1929.

12. In an interview with P. N. Sapru and A. N. Sapru on 14 Nov. 1964, they claimed that their father, T. B. Sapru, wrote much of the chapter on the princes; but Nanda in his biography of the Nehrus quotes Motilal as saying that Sapru only wrote a "few paragraphs on Indian states." B. R. Nanda, *The Nehrus: Motilal and Jawaharlal*, pp. 289–90.

13. All Parties Conference, 1928, *Report of the Committee Appointed by the Conference to Determine the Principles of the Constitution for India*, pp. 83–84.

14. Kothari was a subject of Wadhwan and later would be a leader in the organization of the civil disobedience movement in Kathiawar in the early 1930s. E. H. Kealy, AGG, Western India States, to C. C. Watson, 22 Mar. 1930, IOR, CR, R/1/29/554.

15. Kothari on 1 Jan. 1929 at the All-Parties Conference suggested that Motilal Nehru, Jayakar, Ansari, Malaviya, Satyamurti, Ramachandra Rao, Sapru, Ali Imam, Sardul Singh, and he should meet with the princes. Mitra, *Indian Quarterly Register, 1928*, 1:139–40.

16. Motilal Nehru to Patiala, 10 Aug. 1929, PSAP, CS, Case No. IV (c) 11 of 1929.

17. Patiala to Bikaner, Sangli, Dholpur, Bhopal, Kashmir, and Cutch, 26 Aug. 1929, ibid.; Patiala to Watson, 27 Aug. 1929, NAI, GOI, F&P, 1929, Reforms Branch, File No. 193-R.

18. Note by H. Wilberforce-Bell dated 30 Aug. 1929 and one by B. J. Glancy dated 31 Aug. 1929, ibid.

19. Note by Wilberforce-Bell dated 30 Aug. 1929, ibid.

20. James Crerar, the Home member, agreed that it would be best for the princes not to be involved in any conference in British India unless it was held under government auspices. Crerar also wanted Watson, the political secretary, to inform Patiala orally of their views rather than by letter; apparently Crerar did not want any evidence of government pressure readily available. Note by C. C. Watson, 29 Sept. 1929, ibid.

21. Bhopal to Patiala, 6 Sept. 1929; Bikaner to Patiala, 23 Sept. 1920; Cutch to Patiala, 27 Sept. 1930; Dholpur and Kashmir to Patiala in undated letters; PSAP, CS, Case No. IV (c) 11 of 1929.

22. *Tribune*, 31 Oct. 1929, p. 8.

23. Patiala had made his appeal to the nizam on 2 Feb. 1930. Sadr-ul-Maham, Pol Dept, Nizam's government, to T. H. Keyes, Resident at Hyderabad, 1 Mar. 1930, forwarded by Keyes with comments to GOI on 16 Mar. 1930, NAI, GOI, F&P, 1930, Reforms Branch, File No. 65-R/30. The grant from the nizam was to be made in three parts and included one lakh of rupees for the preparation of the case on economic and fiscal relations between the Indian states and British India; one lakh for the expenses of the Chamber delegation to the Round Table Conference; and an annual contribution of 50,000 rupees to the general budget of the Chamber for the subsequent five years. *Chamber Proceedings, February 1930*, p. 72.

24. Keyes to Watson, 15 Apr. 1930, IOR, Keyes Collection, MSS Eur F 131/28.

25. Minutes of informal meeting of the Standing Committee on 21 Feb. 1930, PSAP, CS, Case No. II (b) 22 of 1929.

26. Nawanagar was against a resolution on reform, arguing that such action implied that the princes had deprived their subjects of fundamental rights in the past, ibid.

27. All-India States' People's Conference Patiala Enquiry Committee, *Indictment of Patiala.* For press comment see *Tribune*, 27 Feb. 1930, p. 9.

28. Report of Enquiry by J. A. O. Fitzpatrick, dated 17 July 1930, IOR, CR, R/1/29/545 (O).

29. Irwin as well as Wedgwood Benn were apprehensive about whether Patiala should be allowed to attend the Round Table Conference when the indictment first appeared. Irwin to Wedgwood Benn, 2 Apr. 1930, IOR, MSS Eur C 152/11, and Wedgwood Benn to Irwin, 4 July 1930 and Irwin to Wedgwood Benn, 18 July 1930, ibid., C 152/6. Keyes to George Cunningham, Pvt Sec to Irwin, 5 July 1930, IOR, MSS Eur F 131/28.

30. *Tribune*, 27 Feb. 1930, p. 1.

31. Popotlal L. Chudgar, *Indian Princes under British Protection.*

32. Minutes of meeting on 23 Feb. 1930, PSAP, CS, Case No. II (b) 22 of 1929.

33. Forty-five politicians plus ministers and members of the Standing Committee were invited to the dinner on 26 Feb., PSAP, CS, Case No. II (a) 33 of 1929. Only six politicians were invited to the second meeting on 28 Feb., PSAP, CS, Supplementary Index, Case No. V, File No. 14 of 1930.

34. Setalvad to Sapru, 10 Mar. 1930, Sapru MSS, I, 24, S 124.

35. Meeting of 29 Mar. 1930, PSAP, CS, Supplementary Index, Case No. V, File No. 14 of 1930. Most of these leaders were members of the Legislative Assembly except for Khaparde, who was a member of the Council of State, Ramaswami Aiyar, Muhammad Ali, Setalvad, and Shafi.

36. Ibid.

37. Note by K. S. Fitze of his conversation with Haksar on 1 Aug. 1930, NAI,

GOI, F&P, 1930, Special, File No. 23-Spl. The results accurately fulfilled an earlier prediction by Irwin that he did not expect the committee to produce anything very precise. Irwin to Wedgwood Benn, 3 Apr. 1930, IOR, MSS Eur C 152/6.

38. Irwin to Wedgwood Benn, 5 Nov. 1929, NAI, GOI, F&P, 1929, Reforms Branch, File No. 193-R.

39. Wedgwood Benn to Irwin, 13 Nov. 1929, ibid.

40. Wedgwood Benn to Irwin, 12 Dec. 1929, ibid.

41. Irwin to Wedgwood Benn, 12 Jan. 1930, ibid. Manor in "The Demise of the Princely Order" and Copland in "The Other Guardians" in *People, Princes, and Paramount Power* argue that the British declined to put pressure on the princes in the area of reform because of the Minto declaration. Their general conclusion is well-founded, but it fails to take into account individual efforts such as those initiated by Irwin that were eventually abandoned.

42. Mitter to Sapru, 20 Nov. 1929, Sapru MSS, I, 15, M 121.

43. Setalvad to Sapru, 13 Feb. 1930, Sapru MSS, I, 24, S 120.

44. A note by R. R. Das of the Chamber Secretariat outlined the whole series of negotiations and was dated 11 June 1930, PSAP, CS, Case No. III (c) 27 of 1930.

45. Keyes to Watson, 15 Apr. 1930, for this support of the nizam; and Keyes to Denis Bray, Member of India Council, 21 July 1930, IOR, MSS Eur F 131/28, for his criticism of Butler and support for federation.

46. An excellent account of Keyes's role in Hyderabad and the position of the nizam and his ministers on federation is in Moore, *Crisis of Indian Unity*, pp. 132–43.

47. Keyes to Bray, 21 July 1930, IOR, MSS Eur F 131/28. The Standing Committee then included Alwar, Bhopal, Bikaner, Dholpur, Nawanagar, Kashmir, the pro-chancellor, and Patiala, the chancellor.

48. The nizam tried to obtain special privileges for the advisers since he thought that his state was entitled to multiple representation. Note by P. J. Patrick, Pol Sec at the India Office, dated 31 Oct. 1930, NAI, GOI, F&P, 1930, Special, File No. 24 (3).

49. Diary entry of Harcourt Butler for 10 Mar. 1928, IOR, MSS Eur F 116/108.

50. Irwin to Wedgwood Benn, 16 July 1930, IOR, MSS Eur C 152/11.

51. Meeting at Simla on 14 and 15 July, PSAP, CS, Supplementary Index, Case No. V, File No. 16 of 1930.

52. The nawab of Bhopal was named chairman of the princely committee that was to continue the negotiations in India on the issue of paramountcy. Ibid.

53. *Times*, 25 Aug. 1930, p. 10.

54. *Times*, 6 Oct. 1930, p. 13.

55. D. A. Low, "Sir Tej Bahadur Sapru and the First Round-Table Conference," *Soundings in Modern South Asian History*, p. 315, and the *Times*, 20 Oct. 1930, p. 13. Sapru was the most active British Indian politician canvassing the princes, but others included the unpredictable Jinnah, who was a frequent companion of Jey Singh of Alwar. M. R. Jayakar to Sapru, 4 Apr. 1934, Sapru MSS, III, J.

56. The committee was made up of Haksar, Hydari, Krishnamachari, Mehta, K. C. Neogy, the adviser to the Orissa states, Pattani, and N. S. Subba Rao, a member of the states' secretariat at the Round Table Conference, PSAP, CS, Case No. IV (c) 19 of 1931.

57. Ibid.

58. K. M. Panikkar in *His Highness the Maharaja of Bikaner* points out that as early as 1914 Bikaner had been advocating federation as the solution to the problems of two Indias, p. 335. However, it was only during Montagu's tour of India that the princes as a group began to ask for joint institutions.

59. Hailey to Irwin, 19 Nov. 1930, IOR, MSS Eur E 220/34.

60. Low, "Sir Tej Bahadur Sapru and the First Round-Table Conference," in *Soundings in Modern South Asian History*, pp. 302–18.

61. T. B. Sapru to P. N. Sapru, 19 Nov. 1930, Sapru MSS, I, 23, S 17; Sapru to Palanpur, 28 Nov. 1930, Sapru MSS, III, File P.

62. *Times*, 13 Nov. 1930, p. 12.

63. As Samuel Hoare later recounted, "The keynote of the Conference was at once struck by the Princes who, one after another, declared their newly-found belief in All-India Federation. Amongst them were several remarkable personalities. The most notable was Bikaner. When he spoke in vigorous and almost too fluent English, his fine figure and resonant voice dominated the Federal Structure Committee." Viscount Templewood, *Nine Troubled Years*, p. 50. (Viscount Templewood was Sir Samuel Hoare.)

64. Even so astute an observer as Malcolm Hailey expressed surprise at the princely support for federation. Hailey to Irwin, 14 Nov. 1930, IOR, MSS Eur E 220/34. His shock was echoed by Wedgwood Benn and Lord Irwin. Wedgwood Benn to Irwin, 17 Nov. 1930, IOR, MSS Eur C 152/6; and Irwin to Wedgwood Benn, 24 Nov. 1930, ibid. Keyes, in Hyderabad, dramatically commented: ". . . Things seemed at their worst when the miracle happened and the Princes rose to a great occasion. Whether they will keep on the heights or not I cant say; but Inshallah!" Keyes to F. S. Oliver, 24 Nov. 1930, IOR, MSS Eur F 131/28.

65. Wedgwood Benn supplied an insightful running commentary on the princes at the First Round Table Conference for Irwin in letters of 4 Nov. 1930, 8 Nov. 1930, 15 Nov. 1930, 4 Jan. 1931, 12 Jan. 1931, 15 Jan. 1931, IOR, MSS, Eur C 152/6. The best general account of the Round Table Conferences is in Moore, *Crisis of Indian Unity*.

66. Great Britain, Parliamentary Papers, Vol. 12 (Reports, Vol. 3), Cmd 3778, Jan. 1931, "Indian Round Table Conference, 12 Nov. 1930 to 19 Jan. 1931," pp. 208–23.

67. Ibid., pp. 331–35.

68. Reading, *Rufus Isaacs*, 2:354–57.

69. Irwin to Wedgwood Benn, 16 Feb. 1931, IOR, MSS Eur C 152/6.

70. Templewood, *Nine Troubled Years*, p. 48.

71. Sapru to Bikaner, 11 Feb. 1931, Sapru MSS, I, 24, S 174.

72. Sapru to Bikaner, 10 Mar. 1931, Sapru MSS, I, 24, S 175.

73. Sarvepalli Gopal, *The Viceroyalty of Lord Irwin*, pp. 97–122. Also see F. W. F. Smith, *Halifax*, pp. 291–312, Moore, *Crisis of Indian Unity*, pp. 181–207, and Brown, *Gandhi and Civil Disobedience*, pp. 153–191.

74. Haksar to Sapru, 27 Apr. 1931, Sapru MSS, I, 7, H 29.

75. In London before the First Round Table Conference, Bhopal had hosted an earlier series of talks initiated by Sapru, Sastri, and Setalvad to which the Aga Khan, Muhammad Ali Jinnah, and Muhammad Shafi were invited. Sapru to Nawab of Palanpur, 28 Nov. 1930, Sapru MSS, III, P. These talks produced a compromise allowing for joint electorates with some restrictions, but that accord evaporated when telegrams from supporters of separate electorates inundated the Muslim delegation. Moore, *Crisis of Indian Unity*, pp. 126–27, 144, 158–63. There is a discrepancy between the *Tribune*, 15 May 1931, p. 8, and Azim Husain, *Fazl-i-Husain, A Political Biography*, p. 258, in reporting on who attended. The *Tribune* cites Muhammad Shafi, Muhammad Iqbal, Shaukat Ali, and Ismail Khan as the Conference representatives and M. A. Ansari and T. A. K. Sherwani as the Congressmen. Husain adds Maulana Shafi Daudi and eliminates Ismail Khan from the Conference slate and adds Chaudhri Khaliquzzaman to the Congress contingent. Azim was the son of Fazl.

76. Husain, *Fazl-i-Husain*, p. 247.

77. Haksar to Sapru, 1 June 1931, Sapru MSS, I, 7, H 36, and Husain, *Fazl-i-Husain*, pp. 256–61.

78. Haksar to Sapru, 11 June 1931, Sapru MSS, I, 7, H 40; *Tribune*, 11 June 1931, p. 3, and 12 June 1931, p. 8.

79. *Chamber Proceedings, March 1931*, pp. 21–23.

80. Ibid., pp. 67–70. Bhopal defeated Patiala 28 to 23, and Cutch defeated Alwar 32 to 16.

81. Irwin to Wedgwood Benn, 23 Mar. 1931, IOR, MSS Eur C 152/6.

82. Prominent leaders in attendance included Tej Bahadur Sapru, Purshotamdas Thakurdas, Lalji Narainji, and Chunilal Mehta. *Tribune*, 8 Feb. 1931, p. 10.

83. Irwin to Stamfordham, Pvt Sec to George V, 11 June 1930, IOR, MSS Eur C 152/1.

84. Irwin to Wedgwood Benn, 23 Mar. 1931, IOR, MSS Eur C 152/6.

85. Sapru to Bhopal, 20 Apr. 1931, Sapru MSS, I, 8, H 165, and Sapru to Bhopal, 25 May 1931, Sapru MSS, I, 8, H 167. For further insight on the place of the Centre party in the politics of the United Provinces, see P. D. Reeves, "Landlords and Party Politics in the United Provinces, 1934–7," in *Soundings in Modern South Asian History*, pp. 264–67.

86. Sapru to Bhopal, 25 May 1931, Sapru MSS, I, 8, H 167.

87. Haksar to Sapru, 27 Apr. 1931, Sapru MSS, I, 7, H 29, and the scheme as amended by Sapru was forwarded to Haksar on 9 June 1931, Sapru MSS, I, 7, H 39.

88. Sapru to Haksar, 9 June 1931, ibid.

89. H. L. S. Polak to Sapru, 31 Mar. 1931, Sapru MSS, I, 17, P 85, and Sapru to M. R. Jayakar, 5 Feb. 1932, Sapru MSS, III, J.

90. Govindlal, Chairman of Indian States' People's Conference Convention Committee, to Srinivasa Sastri, 21 Feb. 1931, and Govindlal to Sapru, 22 Feb. 1931, Sapru MSS, II, bundle of unnumbered telegrams. Sapru to Lord Sankey, 14 Mar. 1931, Sapru MSS, I, 23, S 6/1.

91. Keyes to Lord Lothian, 30 Aug. 1931, IOR, MSS Eur F 131/29.

92. B. L. Mitter to Sapru, 7 Apr. 1931, Sapru MSS, I, 15, M 127.

93. E. H. Kealy to Watson, 12 Jan. 1932, NAI, GOI, F&P, 1931, Reforms, File No. 237-R/31.

94. Sapru to Bhopal and Bikaner, 12 Jan. 1932, Sapru MSS, II, H 36, and Sapru to Haksar, 12 Jan. 1932, Sapru MSS, II, H 35.

95. Keyes to Lothian, 30 Aug. 1931, IOR, MSS Eur F 131/29.

96. *Tribune*, 18 June 1931, p. 1, and Maharaja of Patiala, "Federation and the Indian States," PSAP, CS, File No. III (c) 36 of 1931.

97. Samuel Hoare, Secretary of State for India, to Lord Willingdon, 11 June 1931, Willingdon to Hoare, 12 June 1931, NAI, GOI, F&P, 1931, Special, File No. 31-Spl.

98. Haksar to Sapru, 13 June 1931, Sapru MSS, I, 7, H 42.

99. Wedgwood Benn to Irwin, 15 Nov. 1930, NAI, GOI, F&P, 1930, Special, File No. 24 (3)-Spl.

100. Ibid.

101. Irwin to Wedgwood Benn, 18 Nov. 1930, ibid.

102. Bikaner to Irwin, 27 Nov. 1930, ibid. Although Bikaner thought that Patiala was particularly nervous and irritable now because of his recent ill health and sense of grievance about the Fitzpatrick Inquiry, he also claimed that Patiala's jealousy was one reason why he had not gone to England at the time of the Butler Committee Inquiry.

103. Fortnightly Reports for the second half of June 1931 from Bombay, Madras, and the Central Provinces, NAI, GOI, Home Pol-1931, File No. 18/VI.

104. Jayakar to Sapru, 17 June 1931, Sapru MSS, I, 10, J 26.

105. Sapru to Polak, 12 July 1931, Sapru MSS, I, 17, P 96. For another source on the fear among the smaller states, see Kealy to Watson, 15 Jan. 1932, NAI, GOI, F&P, 1931, Reforms, File No. 237-R/31.

106. Minutes of June meetings at Bombay, PSAP, CS, Case No. IV (c) 18 of 1931. Also *Tribune*, 3 July 1931, p. 1.

107. Minutes of meetings on 9–10 Aug. 1931, PSAP, CS, Case No. III (c) 32 of 1931.

108. Watson to Patiala, 11 Aug. 1931, PSAP, CS, Case No. IV (c) 25 of 1931.

109. Patiala to Bhopal, 8 Aug. 1931, ibid.

110. Patiala's financial problems were not resolved until March 1934 when he finally secured a loan for a crore of rupees from the Bank of India, NAI, GOI, F&P, 1933, Political, File No. 584-P.

111. Patiala to Willingdon, 14 Aug. 1931, and Willingdon to Hoare, 23 Aug. 1931, NAI, GOI, F&P, 1931, Reforms, File No. 15 (3)-Spl/31.

112. Hoare to Willingdon, 17 Sept. 1931, IOR, MSS Eur E 240/1.

113. Great Britain. Parliamentary Papers, Cmd. 3997, Jan. 1932, "Indian Round Table Conference, 7 Sept. 1931 to 1 Dec. 1931," pp. 15–20.

114. Minutes of meetings on 23 Sept. and 30 Sept. 1931 with accompanying notes, PSAP, CS, Case No. IV (c) 30 of 1931.

115. Sapru to Jayakar, 5 Feb. 1932, Sapru MSS, III, File J.

116. Sapru to Jayakar, 4 Apr. 1932, ibid.

117. ". . . The attitude of the Government here [London] is distinctly helpful and hopeful, certainly more helpful than that of the Officials in India." T. B. Sapru to P. N. Sapru, 23 Dec. 1932, Sapru MSS, II, S 52. Hoare to Willingdon, 18 Mar. 1932, IOR, MSS Eur E 240/1.

118. Jayakar to Sapru, 17 Mar. 1932, Sapru MSS, III, File J.

119. Sapru to Jayakar, 4 Apr. 1932, ibid. Lothian was the former Philip Kerr and had had extensive experience in South Africa, had edited the *Round Table* during 1910–16, had served as secretary to Lloyd George, 1916–21, and had served as secretary of the Rhodes Trust since 1925. He was a cousin of the tenth marquis of Lothian and his heir.

120. *Chamber Proceedings, March 1932*, pp. 60–62.

121. Haksar to Sapru, 3 Apr. 1932, Sapru MSS, I, 7, H 57.

122. Ibid.

123. Desmond Young of the *Pioneer* to Ian M. Stephens, Director of Public Information, GOI, 24 Dec. 1934, NAI, GOI, Home Pol-1935, File No. 33/4/35.

124. Haksar to Sapru, 3 Apr. 1932, Sapru MSS, I, 7, H 57.

125. According to Desmond Young, the failure to give better coverage to the princes was due to a lack of funds necessary to maintain correspondents in the major states. Young to Stephens, 24 Dec. 1934, NAI, GOI, Home Pol-1935, File No. 33/4/35.

126. These views were forcefully argued in an undated and unsigned memorandum in PSAP, PSR, IK, Basta No. 66, File No. 1008. From a reference in this memorandum to the recent acquisition of the *Pioneer* by some princes and a syndicate, it may be inferred that the note was written in late 1932 or early 1933.

127. One plan proposed a "Council of United India" that would be a preparatory step to the distant federation of the two parts of India. The other advocated a federation of states prior to their joining a confederation with British India. There was to be a large federal legislature, with an upper house of 300 and half of the seats held by the states and a lower house of 450 with a third of the seats allotted to the states. Fortnightly Report from states of Western India for the first half of Mar. 1932, NAI, GOI, Home Pol-1932, File No. 18/V.

128. Haksar to Sapru, 26 Apr. 1932, Sapru MSS, I, 7, H 59.

129. Patiala to Nawanagar, 1 May 1932, PSAP, CS, Case No. IV (c) 33 of 1932.

130. Sapru to Haksar, 30 Apr. 1932, Sapru MSS, I, 7, H 60.

131. Maqbool to Patiala, 7 May 1932, PSAP, CS, Case No. IV (c) 33 of 1932.

132. Sapru to Haksar, 20 May 1932, Sapru MSS, I, 7, H 65.

133. According to Hoare, the king was greatly angered by this apparent disaffection of the princes toward federation. Templewood, *Nine Troubled Years*, pp. 86–87, and Hoare to Willingdon, 31 Mar. 1933, IOR, MSS Eur E 240/3.

134. Nawanagar to Patiala, 29 Sept. 1932, PSAP, CS, Case No. IV (c) 34 of 1932, Vol. 1. Also, Haksar to Sapru, 4 Sept. 1932, Sapru MSS, I, 7, H 95. Hoare was most anxious for Willingdon to unite the larger states against Nawanagar, but Willingdon had to do little to stimulate their opposition. Hoare to Willingdon, 9 Sept. 1932, IOR, MSS Eur E 240/3.

135. Sapru to S. Mushran, Assistant Solicitor, Leg Dept, GOI, 3 Sept. 1932, Sapru MSS, I, 15, M 201, and Haksar to Sapru, 4 Sept. 1932, Sapru MSS, I, 7, H 95.

136. Keyes also claimed that the nizam was disturbed by the opinion of Sir Stafford Cripps that insufficient protection was afforded to the states under the proposed federation. Keyes to B. J. Glancy, 16 Sept. 1932, IOR, MSS Eur F 131/30. There is a detailed analysis of Cripps's advice in Moore, *Crisis of Indian Unity*, pp. 275–76.

137. Ismail to Sapru, 3 Aug. 1932, Sapru MSS, I, 9, I 86.

138. Meeting at Viceregal Lodge in Simla, 20–21 Sept. 1932, PSAP, CS, Case No. III (c) 34 of 1932.

139. Ibid.

140. Ibid.

141. Ibid.

142. Haksar to Sapru, 5 Oct. 1932, Sapru MSS, I, 7, H 99.

143. Ibid.

144. Minutes of the meeting of the Standing Committee of the Chamber, 17 Sept. 1932, PSAP, CS, Case No. III (b) 9 of 1932.

145. Hoare to Willingdon, 18 Nov. 1932, IOR, MSS Eur E 240/2. The Indian States delegation included the raja of Sarila speaking for the smaller states, Raja Oudh Narain Bisarya from Bhopal, V. T. Krishnamachari from Baroda, Liaqat Hayat Khan from Patiala, Wajahat Hussain from Kashmir, Akbar Hydari representing Hyderabad and Rewa, Mirza Ismail from Mysore, Manubhai Mehta from Bikaner, Sukhdeo Prasad representing Udaipur, Jaipur, and Jodhpur, D. A. Surve from Kolhapur, and Rushbrook Williams from Nawanagar.

146. Keyes had said that Haksar was of very ordinary intelligence and a bitter Brahmin who sought the revival of Maratha Brahmin dominance. Keyes to Bray, 21 July 1930, IOR, MSS Eur F 131/28. This judgment is curious. Haksar was a loyal servant of Gwalior, the leading Maratha state, and the Maratha revival clearly threatened the territorial integrity of Hyderabad. Still, Haksar was a Kashmiri Brahmin and not a Chitpavan Brahmin, who were usually most active in the Maratha revival. Although Chitpavan Brahmins are Marathi-speakers, it is not usual to refer to them as Maratha Brahmins.

147. Haksar to Sapru, 21 Oct. 1932, Sapru MSS, I, 7, H 102.

148. Sapru to Haksar, 9 Dec. 1932, Sapru MSS, I, 7, H 105.

149. Ibid.

150. Ibid. and Sapru on 23 Dec. 1932 in Great Britain, Parliamentary Papers, Vol. 11 (Reports, Vol. 2), Cmd 4238, Jan. 1933, "Indian Round Table Conference, 17 Nov 1932-24 Dec 1932," pp. 77–78.

151. For a succinct discussion of the major provisions of the White Paper and

the princely reactions to them, see Phadnis, *Towards the Integration of Indian States*, pp. 70–72.

152. Hailey to Willingdon, 26 Apr. 1933, IOR, MSS Eur E 220/34.

153. Hailey to Willingdon, 27 May 1933, ibid.

154. Ibid.

155. Hoare to Willingdon, 31 Mar. 1933, IOR, MSS Eur E 240/3, Hailey to Willingdon, 26 Apr. 1933, IOR, MSS Eur E 220/34, and John Glendevon, *The Viceroy at Bay: Lord Linlithgow in India, 1936–1943*, pp. 19–20.

156. Great Britain, *Report of the Joint Committee on Indian Constitutional Reform* (Session 1933–34), Volume 1, Part 1, p. 86. For the differences between the White Paper and this report that were of concern to the princes, see Phadnis, *Towards the Integration of Indian States*, pp. 73–75.

157. Bikaner in Letter dated 11 Jan. 1933, PSAP, CS, Case No. IV (c) 39 of 1933.

158. Report by Mehta and Liaqat dated 5 Mar. 1933, PSAP, PSR, Basta No. B-67, File No. 1018.

159. Bhopal to Patiala and Bikaner, 14 Mar. 1933, PSAP, CS, Case No. II (a) 44 of 1932.

160. Listed in Minutes of meeting on 25 Mar. 1933, PSAP, CS, Case No. II (b) 21 of 1933.

161. Haksar to Sapru, 26 Mar. 1933, Sapru MSS, I, 8, H 112.

162. Kashmir to Chancellor of Chamber, 23 Mar. 1933, NAI, GOI, F&P, 1933, Reforms, File No. 127-R.

163. *Tribune*, 17 Mar. 1933, p. 1.

164. Patiala to Glancy, 2 Feb. 1934, NAI, GOI, F&P, 1933, Reforms, File No. 127-R.

165. Minutes of meeting on 24 Mar. 1933, NAI, GOI, F&P, 1933, Reforms, File No. 69-R.

166. Ibid.

167. Zetland, Secretary of State for India, to Linlithgow, Viceroy, 25 Sept. 1936, IOR, Linlithgow Collection, MSS Eur F 125/3.

168. The recollections and views of two members are available in Lothian, *Kingdoms of Yesterday*, pp. 146–50, and "Sidelight on Indian Federation," *Quarterly Review* 605 (July 1955), seen in IOR, Lothian Collection, MSS Eur F 144/1; and Francis Wylie, "Federal Negotiations in India 1935–9, and After," in *The Partition of India: Policies and Perspectives, 1935–1947*, ed. C. H. Philips and Mary Doreen Wainwright, pp. 517–22.

169. Wylie, "Federal Negotiations in India," pp. 520–21, and "Some Thoughts on British Policy and the Indian States, 1935–47, in Reply to Some Questions put to Sir Conrad Corfield," in Philips and Wainwright, *The Partition of India*, p. 527.

170. C. P. Skrine to Helen Lucy Stewart Skrine, his mother, 23 July 1939, IOR, Skrine Collection, MSS Eur F 154/24.

CHAPTER EIGHT

1. P. D. Reeves skillfully delineates the inability of the landlords in the United Provinces to make the transition from elite to popular politics. P. D. Reeves, "Landlords and Party Politics in the United Provinces, 1934–7," *Soundings in Modern South Asian History*, pp. 261–93.

2. A thought-provoking analysis of the extent of these personnel changes within the ICS and their impact on the timing of the British withdrawal from India is in David C. Potter, "Manpower Shortage and the End of Colonialism: The Case of the Indian Civil Service."

3. A view from the viceregal perspective filtered through the prose of a son is in Glendevon, *The Viceroy at Bay*, passim.

4. A strongly biased but important view of this period is in Corfield, *The Princely India I Knew*, pp. 151–60. A more balanced view is in H. V. Hodson, *The Great Divide: Britain—India—Pakistan*, pp. 356–85.

5. Lloyd I. Rudolph and Susanne Hoeber Rudolph, *The Modernity of Tradition: Political Development in India*, pp. 104–6.

6. Wakefield, *Past Imperative*, pp. 156–59.

7. A comparative analysis of these two organizations is in William L. Richter and Barbara Ramusack, "The Chamber and the Consultation: Changing Forms of Princely Political Association in India."

8. William L. Richter, "Traditional Rulers in Post-Traditional Societies: The Princes of India and Pakistan," in *People, Princes, and Paramount Power*. This study is the basis for many of my conclusions on princes and electoral politics.

Bibliography

UNPUBLISHED SOURCES: PRIMARY

Government

Chamber of Princes Records, Punjab State Archives, Patiala, Punjab
- Proceedings of Formal and Informal Meetings of the Chamber
- Proceedings of Formal and Informal Meetings of the Standing Committee
- Proceedings of Miscellaneous Meetings
- Records on the Federation and Confederation Proposals
- Records on the Punjab States Conference
- Records Relating to the Round Table Conference

Government of India Records, India Office Records, London
- Crown Representative Collection, 1870–1939

Government of India Records, National Archives of India, New Delhi
- Foreign and Political Department Proceedings, 1910–1937
- Home Department-Political Section Proceedings, 1910–1937
- Reform Office Records, 1919–1932

Patiala State Records, Punjab State Archives, Patiala, Punjab
- Proceedings of the Foreign and Political Department
- Proceedings of the Ijlas-i-Khas
- Proceedings of the Prime Minister's Office

Punjab Government Civil Secretariat Records, National Archives of India, New Delhi

Private Papers

India Office Records, London
Harcourt Butler Collection, MSS Eur F 116
Lord Chelmsford Collection, MSS Eur E 264
Lord Hailey Collection, MSS Eur E 220
Lord Halifax [Irwin] Collection, MSS Eur C 152
Terence H. Keyes Collection, MSS Eur F 131
Lord Linlithgow Collection, MSS Eur F 125
Arthur C. Lothian Collection, MSS Eur F 144
Edwin S. Montagu Collection, MSS Eur D 523
Lord Reading Collection, MSS Eur E 238
Clarmont Percival Skrine Collection, MSS Eur F 154
Lord Templewood [Samuel Hoare] Collection, MSS Eur E 240
John P. Thompson Collection, MSS Eur F 137
Indian National Library, Calcutta
Tej Bahadur Sapru Collection, Series I-III

UNPUBLISHED SOURCES: SECONDARY

Graham, Gail Minault. "The Khilafat Movement: A Study of Indian Muslim Leadership, 1919–1924." Ph.D.Diss. University of Pennsylvania, 1972.

Haynes, Edward S. "Jagirdars and Government: The Political Role of the Kinship Elite in Alwar (Rajputana, India), 1858–1910." Ph.D. Diss. Duke University, 1975.

Hurd, John, II. "Some Economic Characteristics of the Princely States of India." Ph.D. Diss. University of Pennsylvania, 1969.

Lavan, Spencer. "The Ahmadiyah Movement: Its Nature and Its Role in Nineteenth and Early Twentieth Century India." Ph.D. Diss. McGill University, 1970.

Patterson, Maureen L. P. "A Preliminary Study of the Brahman versus Non-Brahman Conflict in Maharastra." Master's Thesis. University of Pennsylvania, 1952.

Ramusack, Barbara N. "Exotic Imports or Home-Grown Riots: The Muslim Agitations in Kashmir in the Early 1930's." Paper read at Third Punjab Studies Conference, University of Pennsylvania, 7 May 1971.

PUBLISHED SOURCES: PRIMARY

Government Records

Great Britain. *India Office List, 1916 to 1938*. London: Harrison & Sons, 1916–38.

———. Indian States Committee, 1928. *Oral Evidence Recorded before the Committee*. N.p., 1929.

———. Parliamentary Papers. House of Commons. Sessional Papers.

———. *Report of the Indian Statutory Commission*. London: His Majesty's Stationery Office, 1930.

———. *Report of the Joint Committee on Indian Constitutional Reform*. Volume 1, Part 1. London: His Majesty's Stationery Office, 1934.

Government of India. *Census of India, 1901 and 1911*.

———. *Imperial Gazetteer of India*.

———. *India in 1921–1922 to 1938–1939*. Formerly entitled *Statement Exhibiting the Moral and Material Progress and Condition of India*.

———. *Manual of Instructions to Officers of Political Department*. 2d ed. Simla: Government of India Press, 1924.

———. *Memoranda on the Indian States, 1939*. Delhi: Manager of Publications, Government of India, 1939.

———. *Proceedings of the Chamber of Princes (Narendra Mahal), 1921–1947*.

———. *Proceedings of the Conference of Ruling Princes and Chiefs, 1916–1919*.

———. *Report on Indian Constitutional Reforms, 1918*. Delhi: Government of India Press, 1918.

Punjab Government. *Punjab Press Abstracts, 1916–1924*.

———. *Report on the Administration of the Punjab and Its Dependencies for 1908–1909 to 1914–1915*.

———. *Report of the Court of Inquiry Constituted under the Punjab Act II of 1954 to Enquire into the Punjab Disturbances of 1953* [President: M. Munir]. Lahore: Printed by the Superintendent, Government Printing, Punjab, 1954.

Punjab States Agency. *List of Ruling Princes, Notables and Principal Officials*. Delhi: Manager of Publications, 1938.

Punjab States Gazetteers. *Phulkian States: Patiala, Jind & Nabha*. Vol. 18-A, 1904. Lahore: Punjab Government Press, 1909.

United Provinces of Agra and Oudh. *Gazetteer of the Rampur State*. Allahabad: Officiating Superintendent, Government, United Provinces, 1911.

Williams, L. F. Rushbrook. *The History of the Indian Tour of H. R. H. The Prince of Wales, 1921–1922*. Calcutta: Superintendent of Government Printing, India, 1922.

Newspapers and Periodicals

Asiatic Review. London.

Feudatory and Zemindari India. Trichinopoly.

Indian Annual Register. Calcutta.

Khalsa Advocate. Lahore.

Modern Review. Allahabad.

Times. London.

Tribune. Lahore.

Articles

Alwar, Maharaja Jey Singh. "The Princes and the Viceroy's Announcement: The Princes and Dominion Status." *Asiatic Review*, n.s. 26 (January 1930): 10–12.

Bikaner, Maharaja Ganga Singh. "The Princes and the Viceroy's Announcement: The Princes and the Conference." *Asiatic Review*, n.s. 26 (January 1930): 5–10.

Cotton, H. E. A. "The Viceroyalty of Lord Chelmsford." *Contemporary Review* 119 (June 1921): 746–70.

Lethbridge, Roper. "The Future Development of the Feudatory States of the Indian Empire." *Asiatic Review*, n.s. 3–4 (January-May 1914): 145–56.

Mills, J. Saxon. "The Butler Report and the Indian Princes." *Asiatic Review*, n.s. 25 (July 1929): 413–20.

Molson, A. H. E. "The Indian States and the Butler Committee's Report." *Asiatic Review*, n.s. 25 (October 1929): 580–87.

O'Dwyer, Michael F. "Relations of the Indian States to British India." *Fortnightly Review* 127 (June 1927): 759–68.

Patiala, Maharaja Bhupinder Singh. "Indian Princes and the British Empire." *Nineteenth Century and After* 105 (February 1929): 179–89.

———. "The Present Situation of the Indian Princes." *Contemporary Review* 134 (November 1928): 561–67.

———. "The Princes and the Viceroy's Announcement: The Indian States and the Future Constitution." *Asiatic Review*, n.s. 36 (January 1930): 1–5.

Petrie, D. "Developments in Sikh Politics, 1900–1911: A Report." (Dated 11 August 1911, Simla.) Reprinted in *Gurdwara Gazette*, April 1969, Amritsar.

Speeches and Letters

Curzon, George. *Lord Curzon in India: Being a Selection from His Speeches as Viceroy and Governor-General of India, 1898–1905*. London: Macmillan, 1906.

Haksar, Kailas N. *Indian States and the Federation.* Address delivered to the European Progressive Group, Bombay, on 11 February 1937. Bombay: D. B. Taraporevala Sons, 1937.

Holland, Robert. *The Speeches of the Hon'ble Sir Robert Holland.* Ajmer: P. V. Ramunni, 1925.

Patiala, Maharaja Bhupinder Singh. *Public Pronouncements in Connection with the Indian States Committee*. London: Spottiswoode & Ballantyne, 1928.

Speeches of Indian Princes on Politics. Allahabad: S. Ranga Iyer at Leader Press, 1919.

Srinivasa Sastri, V. S. *The Future of Indian States.* Two lectures delivered at Maharaja's College, Ernakulam, Cochin, on 2-3 October 1926. Poona: n.p., 1926.

Contemporary Polemics

Abhyankar, G. R. *Native States and Post-War Reforms.* Poona: Anant Vinayak Patwardhan, 1917.

All-India States' People's Conference, Patiala Enquiry Committee. *Indictment of Patiala.* Bombay: General Secretaries, Indian States' People's Conference, 1930.

———. *Work in England of the Deputation of the Indian States' People's Conference.* Bombay: G. R. Abhyankar under the auspices of Indian States' People's Conference, 1929.

All Parties Conference, 1928. *Report of the Committee, Appointed by the Conference to Determine the Principles of the Constitution of India.* Allahabad: n.p. 1928.

Chamber of Princes. *The British Crown and the Indian Princes: An Outline Sketch Drawn up on Behalf of the Standing Committee of the Chamber of Princes by the Directorate of the Chamber's Special Organization.* London: P. S. King & Son, 1929.

Chudgar, Popotlal L. *Indian Princes under British Protection.* London: Williams & Norgate, 1929.

Desai, Akshayakumar R. *Indian Feudal States and National Liberation Struggle.* Bombay: Published by the author, n.d.

"Ferret." *Princes or Puppets?* Bombay: Thacker & Co., 1946.

Gandhi, Mohandas K. *The Indian States' Problem.* Ahmedabad: Navajivan Press, 1941.

Gauba, Kanhayalal. *His Highness: Or, the Pathology of Princes.* Lahore: Times Publishing, 1930.

Gundappa, D. V. *The Problems of Indian Native States.* Madras: Home Rule League, 1917.

Haksar, Kailas N., and K. M. Panikkar. *Federal India.* London: M. Hopkinson, 1930.

India Conciliation Group. *The Indian States: Reform and Federation.* London: Friends Book Centre, 1939.

Indian States' People's Conference. *Report of the Bombay Session: 17th, 18th December 1927.* Bombay: G. R. Abhyankar and Manishanker S. Trivedi, 1928.

Jadhava, Khasherao. *Wake Up Princes.* 2d ed. Bombay: Published by the author, 1920.

Panikkar, Kavalam M. *Indian States and the Government of India.* London: Martin Hopkinson, 1932.

Patiala and the Great War. . . . Compiled from secretariat and other records. Printed for private circulation. London: Medici Society, 1923.

Pattabhisitharamayya, B. *Home Rule and Indian States.* Madras: Sons of India, 1918.

Pattani, P. D. *The Indian States: A Letter on their Relations with British India.* London: Published by the author, 1930.

———. *Indian States' Inquiry Committee: A Memorandum.* London: n.p., 1928.

Wedderburn, David. *Protected Princes in India.* London: British Committee of the Indian National Congress, 1914.

Collected Documents

Aitchison, Charles. *Collection of Treaties, Engagements and Sanads Relating to India.* 11 vols. Calcutta: Office of the Superintendent of Government Printing, India, 1862–92.

Banerjee, Anil Chandra, ed. *Indian Constitutional Documents.* 2 vols. Calcutta: A. Mukherjee, 1945–49.

Grover, B. L. *A Documentary Study of British Policy Towards Indian Nationalism, 1885–1909.* Delhi: National Publications, 1967.

Singh, Ganda, ed. *Some Confidential Papers of the Akali Movement.* Amritsar: Shiromani Gurdwara Parbandhak Committee, Sikh Itihas Research Board, 1965.

Memoirs and Autobiographies

Ackerley, Joe Randolph. *Hindoo Holiday: An Indian Journal.* New York: Viking Press, 1932.

Brinda, Maharani of Kapurthala. *Maharani: The Story of an Indian Princess.* As told to Elaine Williams. New York: Holt, 1954.

Butler, Harcourt. *India Insistent.* London: William Heinemann, 1931.

Corfield, Conrad. *The Princely India I Knew: From Reading to Mountbatten.* Madras: Indo British Historical Society, 1975.

Craik, Henry. *Impressions of India.* London: Macmillan, 1908.

Fitz Roy, Yvonne A. *Courts and Camps in India: Impressions of Vice-Regal Tours, 1921–1924.* London: Methuen, 1926.

Fitze, Kenneth S. *Twilight of the Maharajas.* London: Murray, 1956.

Forster, E. M. *Hill of Devi: Letters and Journal While Secretary to the Maharaja of Devi.* Harmondsworth: Penguin Books, 1965.

Frazer, Andrew. *Among Indian Rajas and Ryots.* London: Seeley, 1911.

Gilbert, Martin. *Servant of India: A Study of Imperial Rule from 1905 to 1910 As Told through the Correspondence and Diaries of Sir James Dunlop Smith.* London: Longmans, Green, 1966.

Gould, Basil J. *The Jewel in the Lotus: Recollections of an Indian Political.* London: Chatto & Windus, 1957.

Hardinge, Charles, Baron. *My Indian Years, 1910–1916.* London: John Murray, 1948.

Joshi, V. C., ed. *Lajpat Rai Autobiographical Writings*. Vol. 1. Delhi: University Publishers, 1965.

Kennion, Roger Lloyd. *Diversions of an Indian Political*. Edinburgh: William Blackwood, 1932.

Latthe, A. B. *Memoirs of His Highness Shri Shahu Chhatrapati Maharaja of Kolhapur*. 2 vols. Bombay: Times Press, 1924.

Lawrence, Walter R. *The India We Served*. London: Cassell, 1929.

Lothian, Arthur C. *Kingdoms of Yesterday*. London: Murray, 1951.

Montagu, Edwin S. *An Indian Diary*. London: William Heinemann, 1930.

Munshi, K. M. *The End of an Era: Hyderabad Memories*. Bombay: Bharatiya Vidya Bhavan, 1957.

Nehru, Jawaharlal. *Toward Freedom: An Autobiography*. Boston: Beacon Hill Press, 1963.

O'Dwyer, Michael F. *India As I Knew It*. 3d ed. London: Constable, 1926.

Ramarau Rama, V. M. G. *Of Men, Matter, and Me*. New York: Asia Publishing House, 1961.

Reed, Stanley. *The India I Knew, 1897–1947*. London: Odhams Press, 1952.

Simon, John A. *Retrospect: The Memoirs of Viscount Simon*. London: Hutchinson, 1952.

Singh, Sant Nihal. *Shree Bhagvat Sinhjee: The Maker of Modern Gondal*. Gondal: Golden Jubilee Committee, 1934.

Sultan Jahan Begam. *An Account of My Life. Gohur-i-Ikbal*. Translated from the Urdu by C. H. Payne. London: John Murray, 1912.

Sultan Muhammad Shah, Agha Khan. *The Memoirs of Aga Khan*. London: Cassell, 1954.

Sykes, Frederick. *From Many Angles: An Autobiography*. London: George G. Harrap, 1942.

Templewood, Viscount, Samuel Hoare. *Nine Troubled Years*. London: Collins, 1954.

Wakefield, Edward. *Past Imperative: My Life in India, 1927–1947*. London: Chatto & Windus, 1966.

Waley, S. D. *Edwin Montagu: A Memoir and an Account of His Visits to India*. New York: Asia Publishing House, 1964.

Wingate, Ronald. *Not in the Limelight*. London: Hutchinson, 1959.

Wrench, John E. *Geoffry Dawson and Our Times*. London: Hutchinson, 1955.

Zetland, Marquess of (Earl of Ronaldshay). *"Essayez": The Memoirs of Lawrence, Second Marquess of Zetland*. London: John Murray, 1956.

PUBLISHED WORKS: SECONDARY

Biographies

Aziz-ur-Rahman. *Raisul-ul-Ahrar, Maulana Habib-ur-Rahman, Ludhini*. Delhi: Talimi Samaji Markaz, 1961.

Balfour, Elizabeth. *The History of Lord Lytton's Indian Administration, 1876 to 1880*. London: Longmans, Green, 1899.

Bull, H. M., and Kailas N. Haksar. *Madhav Rao Scindia of Gwalior, 1876–1925*. Gwalior: Alijah Durbar Press, 1926.

Butler, James R. M. *Lord Lothian (Philip Kerr), 1882–1940*. London: Macmillan, 1960.

Glendevon, John. *The Viceroy at Bay: Lord Linlithgow in India*. London: Collins, 1971.

Gopal, Sarvepalli. *The Viceroyalty of Lord Irwin, 1926–1931*. Oxford: Clarendon Press, 1957.

Gupta, J. N. *Life and Work of Romesh Chunder Dutt*. London: J. M. Dent & Sons, 1911.

Hunter, William W. *Life of the Earl of Mayo*. Oxford: Clarendon Press, 1891.

Husain, Azim. *Fazl-i-Husain, A Political Biography*. Bombay: Longmans, Green & Co., 1946.

Kodanda Rao, P. *The Right Honourable V. S. Srinivasa Sastri: A Political Biography*. Bombay: Asia Publishing House, 1963.

Maclagan, Edward. *"Clemency" Canning*. London: Macmillan, 1962.

Minto, Mary C. *India, Minto, and Morley, 1905–1910*. London: Macmillan, 1934.

Nanda, B. R. *The Nehrus: Motilal and Jawaharlal*. London: George Allen & Unwin, 1962.

Panikkar, Kavalam M. *His Highness the Maharaja of Bikaner: A Biography*. London: Oxford University Press, 1937.

———. *The Indian Princes in Council: A Record of the Chancellorship of His Highness the Maharaja of Patiala, 1926–1931 & 1933–1936*. London: Oxford University Press, 1936.

Reading, Gerald Rufus Isaacs, Second Marquess of. *Rufus Isaacs: First Marquess of Reading*. Vol. 2, *1914–1935*. London: Hutchinson, 1945.

Rice, Stanley. *Life of Sayaji Rao III, Maharaja of Baroda*. 2 vols. London: Oxford University Press, 1931.

Ronaldshay, Earl of (later Marquess of Zetland). *The Life of Lord Curzon*. Vol. 2, *Viceroy of India*. London: E. Benn, 1929.

Singh, Bawa Satinder. *The Jammu Fox: A Biography of Maharaja Gulab Singh of Kashmir, 1792–1857*. Carbondale: Southern Illinois University Press, 1974.

Singh, Kirpal. *Life of Maharaja Ala Singh of Patiala and His Times*. Amritsar: Sikh History Research Department, Khalsa College, 1954.

Smith, Frederick W. F., Second Earl of Birkenhead. *Halifax: The Life of Lord Halifax*. London: Hamish Hamilton, 1965.

Syngal, Munnalal. *The Patriot Prince, or the Life Story of Maharaja Ripudaman Singh of Nabha Who Died as a Martyr*. Ludhiana: Doaba House, 1961.

"Trench, Victor." *Lord Willingdon in India.* Bombay: Samuel A. Ezekiel, 1934.

Wild, Roland. *"Ranji": The Biography of Ranjitsinhji.* London: Rich & Cowan, 1934.

Articles

Copland, I. F. S. "The Baroda Crisis of 1873–77: A Study in Governmental Rivalry." *Modern Asian Studies* 2 (April 1968): 97–123.

Copland, Ian. "The Maharaja of Kolhapur and the Non-Brahmin Movement, 1901–1910." *Modern Asian Studies* 7 (April 1973): 209–25.

Erdman, Howard L. "Conservative Politics in India." *Asian Survey* 6 (June 1966): 338–47.

Gordon, Richard. "The Hindu Mahasabha and the Indian National Congress, 1915 to 1925." *Modern Asian Studies* 9 (April 1975): 145–203.

Leonard, Karen. "Cultural Change and Bureaucratic Modernization in the 19th Century Hyderabad: Mulkis, non-Mulkis, and the English." In *Studies in the Foreign Relations of India: Prof. H. K. Sherwani Felicitation Volume*, pp. 443–54. Ed. P. M. Joshi. Hyderabad: State Archives, Government of Andhra Pradesh, n.d.

———. "The Hyderabad Political System and Its Participants." *Journal of Asian Studies* 30 (May 1971): 569–82.

Manor, James "Princely Mysore before the Storm: The State-level Political System of India's Model State, 1920–1936." *Modern Asian Studies* 9 (February 1975): 31–58.

Minault, Gail. "Islam and Mass Politics: The Indian Ulama and the Khilafat Movement." In *Religion and Political Modernization*, pp. 168–82. Ed. Donald E. Smith. New Haven, Conn.: Yale University Press, 1974.

Potter, David C. "Manpower Shortage and the End of Colonialism: The Case of the Indian Civil Service." *Modern Asian Studies* 7 (February 1973): 47–73.

Qanungo, Bhupen. "A Study of British Relations with the Native States of India, 1858–62." *Journal of Asian Studies* 26 (February 1967): 251–65.

Ramusack, Barbara N. "Incident at Nabha: Interaction between Indian States and British Indian Politics." *Journal of Asian Studies* 28 (1969): 563–77.

Richter, William L., and Barbara N. Ramusack. "The Chamber and the Consultation: Changing Forms of Princely Political Association in India." *Journal of Asian Studies* 34 (May 1975): 755–76.

Rudolph, Lloyd I., and Susanne Hoeber Rudolph. "Rajputana under British Paramountcy: The Failure of Indirect Rule." *Journal of Modern History* 38 (June 1966): 138–60.

Rudolph, Susanne Hoeber. "The Princely States of Rajputana:

Ethic, Authority, and Structure." *Indian Journal of Political Science* 24 (January 1963): 14–32.

———, and Lloyd Rudolph, with Mohan Singh. "A Bureaucratic Lineage in Princely India: Elite Formation and Conflict in a Patrimonial System." *Journal of Asian Studies* 34 (May 1975): 717–53.

General Works

Aberigh-Mackay, George R. *The Native Chiefs and Their States in 1877*. 2d ed. Bombay: Times of India Press, 1878.

Ahmad, Aziz. *Islamic Modernism in India and Pakistan, 1857–1964*. London: Oxford University Press, 1967.

Bamzai, Prithivi Nath Kaul. *A History of Kashmir*. Delhi: Metropolitan Book Co., 1962.

Barrier, N. Gerald. *Banned: Controversial Literature and Political Control in British India, 1907–1947*. Columbia: University of Missouri Press, 1974.

———. *The Punjab Alienation of Land Bill of 1900*. Durham: Duke University Program in Comparative Studies on Southern Asia, 1966.

———, and Paul Wallace. *The Punjab Press, 1880–1905*. East Lansing: Research Committee on the Punjab and Asian Studies Center, Michigan State University, 1970.

Barton, William P. *The Princes of India, with a Chapter on Nepal*. London: Nisbet, 1934.

Bayly, C. A. *The Local Roots of Indian Politics: Allahabad, 1880–1920*. Oxford: Clarendon Press, 1975.

Bazaz, Prem Nath. *The History of the Struggle for Freedom in Kashmir: From the Earliest Times to the Present Day*. New Delhi: Kashmir Publishing Co., 1954.

Brown, Judith M. *Gandhi and Civil Disobedience: The Mahatma in Indian Politics, 1928–1934*. Cambridge: Cambridge University Press, 1977.

———. *Gandhi's Rise to Power: Indian Politics, 1915–1922*. Cambridge: At the University Press, 1972.

Cashman, Richard I. *The Myth of the Lokamanya: Tilak and Mass Politics in Maharashtra*. Berkeley: University of California Press, 1975.

Coen, Terence Creagh. *The Indian Political Service*. London: Chatto & Windus, 1971.

Collins, Larry, and Dominique Lapierre. *Freedom at Midnight*. New York: Simon & Schuster, 1975.

Coupland, Reginald. *The Indian Problem: Report on the Constitutional Problem in India*. 3 vols. in 1. New York: Oxford University Press, 1944.

Darda, R. S. *From Feudalism to Democracy: A Study in the Growth of Representative Institutions in Rajasthan, 1908–1948*. New Delhi: S. Chand. 1971.

Das, Taraknath. *Sovereign Rights of the Indian Princes*. Madras: Ganesh, 1924.

Dass, Diwan Jarmani. *Maharaja: Lives and Loves and Intrigues of Indian Princes*. Delhi: Hind Pocket Book, 1970.

DeMontmorency, Geoffrey F. *The Indian States and Indian Federation*. Cambridge: At the University Press, 1942.

Diver, Maud. *Royal India: A Description and Historical Study of India's Fifteen Principal States and Their Rulers*. New York: Appleton-Century, 1942.

Dutt, Romesh. *The Economic History of India in the Victorian Age: From the Accession of Queen Victoria in 1837 to the Commencement of the Twentieth Century*. 4th ed. London: Kegan Paul, Trench, Trübner & Co., 1916.

Forbes, Rosita. *India of the Princes*. London: The Book Club, 1939.

Furneaux, Rupert. *Massacre at Amritsar*. London: George Allen & Unwin, 1963.

Gangulee, Nagendranath. *The Making of Federal India*. London: J. Nisbet, 1936.

Gopal, Ram. *Indian Muslims: A Political History, 1858–1947*. Bombay: Asia Publishing House, 1959.

Gopal, Sarvepalli. *British Policy in India, 1858–1905*. Cambridge: At the University Press, 1965.

Gordon, Leonard A. *Bengal: The Nationalist Movement, 1876–1940*. New York: Columbia University Press, 1974.

Griffin, Lepel H. *The Rajas of the Punjab: Being the History of the Principal States in the Punjab and Their Political Relations with the British Government*. First published in 1873. Reprint edition, Patiala: Department of Languages, Punjab, 1970.

Gustafson, W. Eric, and Kenneth W. Jones, eds. *Sources on Punjab History*. Delhi: Manohar Book Service, 1975.

Handa, R. L. *History of Freedom Struggle in Princely States*. Delhi: Central News Agency, 1968.

Hardy, Peter. *The Muslims of British India*. Cambridge: At the University Press, 1972.

Hodson, H. V. *The Great Divide: Britain—India—Pakistan*. London: Hutchinson, 1969.

Hutchins, Francis G. *The Illusion of Permanence: British Imperialism in India*. Princeton: Princeton University Press, 1967.

Ivory, James, comp. *Autobiography of a Princess: Also Being the Adventures of an American Film Director in the Land of the Maharajas*. New York: Harper & Row, 1975.

Jeffrey, Robin. *The Decline of Nayar Dominance: Society and Politics in Travancore, 1847–1908*. New York: Holmes & Meier, 1976.

———, ed. *People, Princes, and Paramount Power: Society and Politics in the Indian Princely States*. New Delhi: Oxford University Press, 1978.

Jhabvala, Ruth Prawar. *Heat and Dust*. New York: Harper & Row, 1975.

Jones, Dorothy B. *The Portrayal of China and India on the American Screen, 1896–1955: The Evolution of Chinese and Indian Themes, Locales, and Characters as Portrayed on the American Screen.* Cambridge: Center for International Studies, Massachusetts Institute of Technology, 1955.

Kincaid, Charles A. *The Land of "Ranji" and "Duleep."* Edinburgh: William Blackwood, 1931.

Khan, Shafa'at Ahmad. *The Indian Federation: An Exposition and Critical Review.* London: Macmillan, 1937.

Khosla, Karan R. *His Imperial Majesty King George V and the Princes of India and the Indian Empire, Historical-Biographical.* Lahore: Imperial Publishing, 1937.

Kumar, R., ed. *Essays on Gandhian Politics: The Rowlatt Satyagraha of 1919.* Oxford: Clarendon Press, 1971.

Lavan, Spencer. *The Ahmadiyah Movement: A History and Perspective.* Delhi: Manohar Book Service, 1974.

Leach, Edmund, and S. N. Mukherjee, eds. *Elites in South Asia.* Cambridge: At the University Press, 1970.

Lee-Warner, William. *The Native States of India.* Rev. 2nd ed. London: Macmillan, 1910.

Lord, John. *The Maharajas.* London: Hutchinson, 1972.

Low, D. Anthony, ed. *Soundings in Modern South Asian History.* Berkeley: University of California Press, 1968.

———, J. C. Iltis, and M. D. Wainwright, eds. *Government Archives in South Asia: A Guide to National and States Archives in Ceylon, India, and Pakistan.* Cambridge: At the University Press, 1969.

Low, Sidney J. M. *The Indian States and Ruling Princes.* London: E. Benn, 1929.

Lynton, Harriet Ronken, and Mohini Rajan. *The Days of the Beloved.* Berkeley: University of California Press, 1974.

MacMunn, George F. *The Indian States and Princes.* London: Jarrolds, 1936.

Malgonkar, Manohar. *Chhatrapatis of Kolhapur.* Bombay: Popular Prakashan, 1971.

———. *The Princes.* New York: Viking Press, 1963.

———. *The Puars of Dewas Senior.* Bombay: Orient Longmans, 1963.

Malleson, George B. *An Historical Sketch of the Native States of India in Subsidiary Alliance with the British Government.* London: Longmans, Green, 1875.

Martin, Briton, Jr. *New India, 1885: British Official Policy and the Emergence of the Indian National Congress.* Berkeley: University of California Press, 1969.

Memmi, Albert. *The Colonizer and the Colonized.* Boston: Beacon Press, 1967.

Menon, Vapal P. *The Story of the Integration of the Indian States.* New York: Macmillan, 1956.

Metcalf, Thomas R. *The Aftermath of Revolt: India, 1857–1870.* Princeton: Princeton University Press, 1964.

Moore, R. J. *The Crisis of Indian Unity, 1917–1940.* Oxford: Clarendon Press, 1974.

Mujeeb, Muhammad. *The Indian Muslims.* London: George Allen & Unwin, 1967.

Nicolson, Arthur P. *Scraps of Paper: India's Broken Treaties, Her Princes, and the Problem.* London: E. Benn, 1930.

O'Malley, L. S. S. *The Indian Civil Service, 1601–1930.* London: John Murray, 1931.

Palmer, Julian. *Sovereignty and Paramountcy in India.* London: Stevens, 1930.

Panikkar, K. N. *British Diplomacy in North India: A Study of the Delhi Residency, 1803–1857.* New Delhi: Associated Publishing House, 1968.

Pearson, M. N. *Merchants and Rulers in Gujarat: The Response to the Portuguese in the Sixteenth Century.* Berkeley: University of California Press, 1976.

Phadnis, Urmila. *Towards the Integration of Indian States, 1919–1947.* London: Asia Publishing House, 1968.

Philips, C. H., and Mary Doreen Wainwright, eds. *The Partition of India: Policies and Perspectives, 1937–1947.* Cambridge: M.I.T. Press, 1970.

Rahim, Muhammad Abdur. *Lord Dalhousie's Administration of the Conquered and Annexed States.* Delhi: S. Chand, 1963.

Robb, P. G. *The Government of India and Reform: Policies towards Politics and the Constitution, 1916–1921.* Oxford: Oxford University Press, 1976.

Rudolph, Lloyd I., and Susanne Hoeber Rudolph. *The Modernity of Tradition: Political Development in India.* Chicago: University of Chicago Press, 1967.

Sastry, Kadayam R. R. *Indian States.* Allahabad: Kitabistan, 1941.

———. *Indian States and Responsible Government.* Allahabad: Published by the author, n.d.

———. *Treaties, Engagements, and Sanads of the Indian States.* Allahabad: Published by the author, n.d.

Sen, Dhirendra K. *The Indian States: Their Status, Rights, and Obligations.* London: Sweet & Maxwell, 1930.

Sinh, Raghuber. *Indian States and the New Regime.* Bombay: D. B. Taraporwala, 1938.

[Singh, Ganda.] *A History of the Khalsa College, Amritsar.* Amritsar: n.p., 1949.

Singh, Harbans. *Encyclopedia of Sikhism.* Patiala: Punjabi University Press, forthcoming.

Singh, Khushwant. *A History of the Sikhs.* 2 vols. Princeton: Princeton University Press, 1963–66.

———, and Satindra Singh. *Ghadar, 1915: India's First Armed Revolution.* New Delhi: R & K Publishing House, 1966.

Singh, Laxman. *Political and Constitutional Development in the Princely States of Rajasthan (1920–1949).* New Delhi: Jain Brothers, 1970.

Singh, Sant Nihal. *The King's Indian Allies: The Rajahs and Their India.* London: S. Low, Marston, 1916.

Smith, Donald E., ed. *Religion and Political Modernization.* New Haven: Yale University Press, 1974.

Smith, Wilfred C. *Modern Islam in India: A Social Analysis.* Lahore: Sh. Muhammad Ashraf, 1963.

Stone, Julia A. *Illustrated India: Its Princes and People.* Hartford: American Publishing, 1877.

Thayyur, R. S. *Achievements of the Indian Raj.* New Delhi: New India Publishers, 1936.

Thompson, Edward J. *The Making of the Indian Princes.* London: Oxford University Press, 1943.

Tod, James. *Annals and Antiquities of Rajasthan: Or the Central and Western Rajpoot States of India.* London: George Routledge, 1914.

Varadachariar, Nadadur D. *Indian States in the Federation.* Bombay: Oxford University Press, 1936.

Walia, Ramesh. *Praja Mandal Movement in East Punjab States.* Patiala: Department of Punjab Historical Studies, Punjabi University Press, 1972.

Wilcox, Wayne A. *Pakistan: The Consolidation of a Nation.* New York: Columbia University Press, 1963.

Williams, L. F. Rushbrook. *India in 1925–26.* Calcutta: Government of India, Central Publications Branch, 1925.

Woodruff, Philip. *The Men Who Ruled India.* 2 vols. London: Jonathan Cape, 1953.

Index